Unfocused Kids:

Helping Students to Focus
on Their Education and Career Plans

A Resource for Educators

Suzy Mygatt Wakefield, Editor
Howard Sage, Associate Editor
Doris Rhea Coy, Assistant Editor
Tami Palmer, Assistant Editor

CAPS Press
CAPS PRESS An independent imprint of

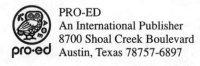

PRO-ED
An International Publisher
8700 Shoal Creek Boulevard
pro·ed Austin, Texas 78757-6897

© 2004 by PRO-ED, Inc.
8700 Shoal Creek Boulevard
Austin, Texas 78757-6897
800/897-3202   Fax 800/397-7633
www.proedinc.com

Library of Congress Cataloging-in-Publication Data

Unfocused kids : helping students to focus on their education and career plans : a
   resource for educators / edited by Suzi Mygatt Wakefield ... [et al.].
     p.   cm.
   "This book was developed and produced by CAPS Press, formerly associated
with ERIC/CASS"—t.p. verso.
   Originally published: Greensboro, NC : CAPS Press, c2004.
   Includes bibliographical references.
   ISBN 1-4164-0041-9 (softcover : alk. paper)
   1. Vocational guidance.   2. Career education.   3. Educational counseling.
I. Wakefield, Suzy Mygatt.

HF5381.U458 2004
373.14'2—dc22

                                                2004043169

This book was developed and produced by CAPS Press, formerly
associated with ERIC/CASS, and creator of many titles for the
counseling, assessment, and educational fields. In 2004, CAPS Press
became an independent imprint of PRO-ED, Inc.

This publication was funded in part by the U.S. Department of Education,
Office of Educational Research and Improvement, Contract No. ED-99-
CO-0014. Opinions expressed in this publication do not necessarily
reflect the positions of the U.S. Department of Education or OERI.

Previously published by CAPS Press under
ISBN 1-56109-105-7

Printed in the United States of America

1   2   3   4   5   6   7   8   9   10   09   08   07   06   05

Dedication

This book is dedicated to parents everywhere, especially my father, Donald Lapham Mygatt (who sadly passed away in the spring of 2003 just as we were finishing this book), who had just the right touch in providing his kids with support and a sense of focus.

This book is also dedicated to my editor (and mentor since graduate school days at the University of Michigan), Dr.Garry R. Walz, Co-Director of ERIC/CASS and Professor Emeritus at the University of Michigan, for his continual support with this book. Dr. Walz has given much to the field of career development over his lifetime and has received the National Career Development Association (NCDA) Eminent Career Award (1997) and has also been awarded the American Counseling Association Gilbert Wrenn Humanitarian Award for his outstanding lifetime contributions.

Finally, this book is also dedicated to Dr. Kenneth B. Hoyt, retired Distinguished Professor at the Kansas State University, who is also an NCDA Eminent Career Award recipient (1981). He cares deeply about kids and about their career education.

Table of Contents

Dedication .... *iii*
Foreword .... *xi*
Acknowledgements .... *xiii*
Preface .... *xvii*
Contributors .... *xix*
About the Authors .... *xxi*
Introduction .... *xxxiii*

PART I—SOCIETAL TRENDS AND WORKPLACE ISSUES

Chapter 1: "Unfocused Kids" Tend to Choose "the Path of Least Resistance"
Suzy Mygatt Wakefield 7

Chapter 2: The Importance of Career Guidance and Employability Skills for *All* Students
Suzy Mygatt Wakefield 29

Chapter 3: Dreams Can Come True—Building a K-12 Career Development System that Inspires Hope
Christine M. Jensen and Mark A. Madison 59

Chapter 4: Aligning Student Planning with the Changing Workplace
Richard W. Feller 97

Chapter 5: Factors that Influence Women and Minorities to Choose High-Tech Careers
Teresa I. Yohon and Laurie A. Carlson 109

PART II—COMPREHENSIVE SCHOOL COUNSELING PROGRAMS

Chapter 6: Building a National Model
Trish Hatch and Judy Bowers 133

Chapter 7: School Counseling Programs: Supporting a Nation of Learners
Carol A. Dahir *143*

Chapter 8: Unfocused Kids/Unfocused Counseling
Keith Anderson *155*

Chapter 9: Career Resource Centers—Programs and Resources for *All* Students
Yvonne Hines and Suzy Mygatt Wakefield *171*

Chapter 10: The Phantom Student
Doris Rhea Coy *189*

Chapter 11: A Model School Counseling Program Brochure: Implications for Helping Students Focus on their Plans after High School
Jim Whitledge *207*

PART III: PROJECT-BASED CAREER GUIDANCE MODELS

Chapter 12: Using Projects to Teach Career Planning Skills and Tools, Incorporating the *ASCA National Standards* as Guidelines
Suzy Mygatt Wakefield *219*

Chapter 13: Policy—The View from on High
Larry Davis *235*

Chapter 14: The False Promise of the Diploma: One District's Approach to Improving the System for all Students
Julie Goldsmith *251*

Chapter 15: Culminating Projects: Providing Real World Relevance and Rigor
Bridgette Belasli *261*

Chapter 16: Authentic Assessment—Bridge to the Workplace
Nancy McCorkle Miller 285

PART IV—INNOVATIVE APPROACHES TO WORKPLACE TRAINING

Chapter 17: Career Preparation Programs in Secondary Education—A Sampler of Current Trends, Exemplary Programs, Model Practices, and the Bottom Line
Willa Smith Davis 299

Chapter 18: Working Connections: Business-Education Partnerships that Work
Carola F. S. Dopps 325

Chapter 19: The Crooked Career Path
Laura Jo Severson 337

PART V—INVOLVING PARENTS IN THEIR TEEN'S CAREER PLANNING

Chapter 20: The Important Role of Parents in their Teen's Career Development
Howard Sage 349

Chapter 21: The Right Tools–Helping High School Students Consider their Postsecondary Options
Kenneth B. Hoyt 361
(reprinted by permission of the American School Counselor Association)

PART VI—INNOVATIVE CAREER DEVELOPMENT ACTIVITIES/GAMES

Chapter 22: *The Real Game*: A Real Hook to Involvement
Nancy S. Perry 371

Chapter 23: Your Best Plans Should Use Your Best Strengths
Jerald R. Forster 383

Chapter 24: *Designing the Dog:* Career Development Activities that Work
Anton Wishik 395

PART VII—INNOVATIVE CAREER DEVELOPMENT PRACTICES FOR SPECIAL POPULATIONS

Chapter 25: Career Guidance in Rural Schools: Special Needs, Concerns and Strategies
Laurie A. Carlson and Teresa I. Yohon 413

Chapter 26: Career Development from a Multicultural Perspective
Doris Rhea Coy, Christopher Simpson and Steve Armstrong 427

Chapter 27: The Dream Board—A Visual Approach for Career Planning with At-Risk 8th and 9th Grade Students
James W. Allen and Jackie M. Allen 445

Chapter 28: Career Education for Special Education Students
Jackie M. Allen 455

Chapter 29: Successful Transitions for High School Special Education Students from School to the Workplace
Diane Fabish *469*

PART VIII—INTERNET DELIVERY SYSTEMS IN CAREER GUIDANCE

Chapter 30: Electronic Portfolios: Convenient Storage for Career and Educational Planning Records
Tami Palmer *483*

Chapter 31:   O*Net in Action—Expanding Youth Career Horizons
Harvey Schmelter-Davis *489*

CONCLUSION—SUMMING UP

Chapter 32: How Do We Put All of This Together? What Needs to Be Done?
Suzy Mygatt Wakefield and Howard Sage *513*

Foreword

Having worked with high school students for 35 years as a high school counselor (and teacher before that), I was concerned that many students do not seem to have much of a grasp of their future plans or even how to think about them, particularly students not doing well in school. Our dropout rate is substantial, and we are turning out many students (both graduates and dropouts) who have little or no idea as to how to rationally plan and prepare for their future, so they tend to gravitate toward the path of least resistance.

As I approached retirement, I considered doing a book that would pull together a lot of ideas and suggestions in one resource document that educators could use in helping students to discuss, plan, and prepare for their future. Thus, this book was begun. I invited school counselors from around the country and colleagues from the Washington State Board of Education, university counselor education programs, the American School Counselor Association leadership, school district administration, regional occupational programs, and others to submit chapters. Then this book began to write itself! As colleagues asked what topic I wanted them to cover, I gave them free rein to write about the topic of *unfocused kids needing help with their plans after high school* as they wished. I thought that collectively, without much specific direction from me other than to encourage my colleagues to use their extensive backgrounds, knowledge, experience and creativity, we would cover a lot of areas. My dreams were far exceeded. The book has eight sections:
- Societal Trends and Workplace Issues
- Comprehensive School Counseling Programs
- Project-Based Career Guidance Models
- Innovative Approaches to Workplace Training
- Involving Parents in their Teen's Career Planning
- Innovative Career Development Activities/Games
- Innovative Career Development Practices for Special Populations
- Internet Career Delivery Systems in Career Guidance

Having been a public educator for 35 years in two different states, I knew that all public school educators have one thing in common: limited time. There are so many demands on school personnel that time is of the essence. Therefore, if a book were available with a lot of ideas, suggestions, resources, and models in one place, educators might find it useful, with references and websites for further perusal as their time permitted.

I have loved serving as a high school counselor for almost 30 years, as high school kids have always interested me—with their issues, deep-felt concerns, views of the world, sense of humor, and appreciation for adults who care about them. Through their educators, I hope that ideas in this book will be of help to them.

I am indebted to my editor, Dr. Garry Walz, Co-Director of ERIC/ CASS and former professor at the University of Michigan, for having confidence in an inexperienced editor. His encouragement over the last two years has been extraordinary, and without his confidence in me and our writers, this book would not have been possible. This book caps a most fulfilling and interesting career in public education.

Suzy Mygatt Wakefield, Ph.D.
April 7, 2003

Acknowledgements

When I took on this book project two years ago just as I was retiring as a public high school counselor, little did I realize what a remarkably complicated but interesting project this was going to be. When Dr. Walz, Co-Director of ERIC/CASS at the University of North Carolina at Greensboro, cautioned me that this book would be "a *lot* of work," he was certainly being honest. As I asked colleagues from around the country to contribute a chapter, the response was invariably very positive, for Dr. Walz is widely respected in the field of school guidance and counseling, and colleagues were glad to be included in a book under his tutelage. So I first want to thank Dr. Garry Walz for offering me this opportunity to make a contribution to the field of school guidance and counseling. Always patient and kind, he has been a supportive and encouraging mentor, with a wonderful sense of humor, just as I remember him from graduate school days.

I would also like to thank my Associate Editor, Dr. Howard Sage, school counselor at Issaquah High School (in Issaquah, Washington), for his support, thoughtful insights, and interesting conversations about the field of school counseling. His insights, particularly around the distinction between the terms *school counseling* and *school guidance*, have given me a better grip on how to approach the ticklish issue of delivery of career guidance services (so central to this book), as that responsibility belongs to all appropriate educators and not just overworked school counselors. Howard has a vast knowledge of many aspects of school counseling. I have learned much from our conversations and am so grateful for having had the chance to share ideas with a colleague.

Dr. Doris Rhea Coy, Associate Professor at the University of North Texas, has served as my Assistant Editor and has brought several colleagues on board: Dr. Steve Armstrong of Texas A&M University, Dr. Christopher Simpson of San Francisco State University, and Harvey Schmelter-Davis, our O*NET guru, at the Heldrich Center for Workforce Development at Rutgers University. Doris has added immensely to this book, not only by bringing her colleagues on board, but also with her support, insights, discussions, and enthusiasm. Further, Harvey Schmelter-Davis initially was to write a two-page overview of the O*NET but chose to do an in-depth chapter, much to my delight, as it will be so valuable to readers of this book to know of the latest developments involved with this national resource.

Tami Palmer, Deputy Director of WOIS/The Career Information System (in Olympia, Washington) and our Assistant Editor, has been our "track tool" editor who has worked tirelessly on countless manuscripts, going over every word with her skills. Tami has the nicest way of making editing suggestions and our writers have seemed to accept her comments well.

Dr. Kenneth B. Hoyt, Distinguished Professor at Kansas State University, has been a mentor, often in his office when I've phone or e-mailed him with a question. He is still an advocate for career education and cares deeply about adolescents and their issues regarding the workplace.

Dr. Rich Feller, Dr. Laurie Carlson, and Dr. Teresa Yohon of Colorado State University have all made excellent contributions to the book, and Dr. Feller has helped me to understand the profound changes in the workplace and the implications for kids.

My Lake Washington School District (Redmond, Washington) colleagues, Julie Goldsmith, (Assistant Superintendent for Curriculum and Instruction) Bridgette Belasli (now Manager of Secondary Curriculum, Edmonds School District, Edmonds, Washington), Nancy Miller (now International Baccalaureate Program teacher in the Bellevue School District, Bellevue, Washington) Yvonne Hines, Career Specialist in the Career Center at Lake Washington High School, and Diane Fabish, Special Education teacher at Eastlake High School in the Lake Washington School District, have all contributed interesting, useful, and insightful chapters in their respective fields.

Dr. Jackie Allen and her husband, Jim Allen, both have contributed interesting chapters, hers on special education programs for special needs kids and his about a hands-on approach to help at-risk youngsters with career planning with a "dream board." Jim has also developed his own career planning website for kids: www.edpathways.com

Larry Davis, Executive Director of the Washington State Board of Education, has written an interesting chapter about Washington state law requiring new graduation requirements, including a *high school + education plan* and a *culminating project*. Larry is a prolific writer and his chapter is most instructive.

Dr. Keith Anderson, Counseling Department Chair at Anacortes High School (Anacortes, Washington) has provided one of the most provocative chapters in the book: *Unfocused Counseling/Unfocused Kids*.

Keith is always one to tell it like it is, and he has, delightfully, done so again, helping school counselors to take a look at their program priorities and discrepancies.

Dr. Christine Jensen and Mark Madison have written a remarkable chapter incorporating a fully developed, hypothetical K-12 comprehensive career guidance program, with the suggestion that teachers must help with its delivery. It is their hope that every student develops a meaningful career plan.

Dr. Trish Hatch, Judy Bowers, and Dr. Carol Dahir have generously provided chapters detailing the ASCA National Standards and the *ASCA*

National Model: A Framework for School Counseling Programs. Kathleen Rakestraw, editor at ASCA, has also been very supportive with sending needed documents.

Dr. Jim Whitledge, Guidance and Counseling Program Consultant for Oakland Schools in Michigan, has provided a useful template for a model school counseling program brochure and an informed consent brochure. Jim, also an editor, has offered clarifying editing suggestions to me.

I met Willa Davis over breakfast at the International Career Development Conference in Irvine in November, 2002 and quickly signed her on, as she is a counselor at a Regional Occupational Program in California. She has written a chapter on many career preparation programs around the country, including models and best practices.

Carola Dopps is a business-education partnership consultant for school districts. She has written a very useful chapter, based on her own extensive experience, on the benefits of partnerships, how to set them up, and how to deal effectively with people in the community.

Laura Jo Severson, former President of the Washington School Counselor Association and strong supporter of the ASCA National Standards and ASCA National Model, has written a most provocative chapter, *The Crooked Career Path,* from her standpoint as a counselor at the Sea-Tac Occupational Skills Center. Laura Jo tells it like it is and reminds us of the important message that students need both academic and technical training while in school, as their future is uncertain.

Nancy Perry, former ASCA President and Executive Director, is deeply concerned about unfocused kids and has contributed an interesting approach: *The Real Games Series TM*, with age-specific curriculum and hands-on activities. She sees this as a "hook" to involvement.

Dr. Jerald Forster, a frequently seen colleague at the University of Washington in Seattle as he chairs the PEAB (Professional Education Advisory Board) for school counselor education, is very interested in the construct of optimism and has contributed an article about the Dependable Strengths Articulation Model, developed by the late Dr. Bernard Haldane. The DSA model is based on the identification of personal strengths and is used as the basis of career planning.

Anton Wishik, who has developed a manual (his own copyright) entitled the *Careers Now Activities Manual*, has shared two of his creations: Designing the Dog, and the 7-Minute Job Interview. Anton is a high school counselor in Port Angeles, Washington.

I am indebted as well to staff members at ERIC/CASS at the University of North Carolina in Greensboro who will be involved in the completion of this book. This book is a dream come true. Long ago, when my father was alive, I told him I would do a book one day, and here it is. I hope that readers find it worth their while.

Suzy Mygatt Wakefield, Ph.D., Editor
April 7, 2003

Preface

We have many pressing priorities in education but certainly a very high priority, if not the highest priority, is that focusing on students dropping out of school "before their time." To that we should add students who graduate, but do so without either a plan for after high school, or even more serious, no concern or prior thinking about what they will do or what options they have. Traditionally, the job of providing career guidance to all students has fallen to school guidance counselors, who tend to be overworked. In this book, the suggestion is made that the issue of providing career guidance for all students is so pervasive and systemic that all appropriate educators and community members need to be enlisted to contribute to the effort. School counselors may be encouraged to help design the overall career guidance programs in schools (and carry out selected portions of it), but all appropriate educators and community members (who can provide field experiences) need to be engaged to help each student develop an education and career plan, a career planning portfolio, and, perhaps, a culminating project about a career interest. Parent involvment is also encouraged.

Both the popular media and professional educational press lament at great length over the serious negative consequences of the premature departure of students from school. Unfortunately, the usual response is to identify the problem and its serious consequences; but, beyond exhortations that "something needs to be done," seldom are meaningful responses provided.

This publication is the rare exception to the usual bland suggestions in that it offers not only an insightful analysis of the roots of the problem, but goes beyond to provide specific ideas and interventions which can be utilized by counselors, other educators, and family members. A particular strength of the monograph is that Dr. Mygatt Wakefield has assembled an exceptional body of supporting editors (Howard Sage, Doris Rhea Coy, and Tami Palmer) and the covey of experienced and knowledgeable writers who know of what they write. The result is a book that offers the reader the penetrating insights of multiple educators as well as over 30 chapter authors who offer specific suggestions as to what an individual counselor or educator can do as well as suggestions pertaining to a broader school and community response. I was especially pleased that counselors who frequently are overlooked in suggested remedies were recognized for the pivotal role they can play.

At a time when the escalation in publishing costs has made obtaining a book more of an investment than a purchase, this book will standout as a judicious choice for the number of educational specialists and parents who will find it useful and highly rewarding reading. Also, because of its encyclopedic coverage, it is a book readers will turn to again and again.

As always, I welcome your comments and suggestions. I like to think that the real learning occurs after you have read a book and share your thoughts and interactions with another interested person. So please do so!

Read, enjoy, and put into practice what you can. Best wishes for what I expect will be a rewarding reading experience.

Garry R. Walz, PhD, NCC
grwalz@aol.com

Contributors

About the Editors

Suzy Mygatt Wakefield, Ph.D., C.D.F., Editor, a retired high school counselor, has worked in two states (Michigan and Washington) in three school districts since 1970, when she earned her Master's Degree in Education from the University of Washington. In 1978, she earned her Ph.D. in Education from the University of Michigan. (Earlier, she had worked as a high school Spanish teacher in Washington State.) She was a part-time program coordinator for the Washington Pre-College Program (1981-85) in Seattle. She served as President of the Washington School Counselor Association (1988-89) and helped to pass the *Fair Start Bill* to fund elementary counseling (1992). She is a certified Career Development Facilitator and has taught in the Career Development Certificate Program at the University of Washington. Suzy enjoys people, tennis, photography, writing, traveling, entertaining with her husband (also an editor) and their little dog, Nanuk. Suzy can be reached at mygattwakefield@attbi.com

Howard Sage, Ed.D., Associate Editor, is a retired high school counselor, formerly with the Issaquah School District, 20 miles east of Seattle. Howard was a full-time high school counselor, and part-time parent educator, teacher, mental health counselor and counselor educator. He has developed School to Career Programs in four different school districts. Howard completed his doctorate from Seattle University in Education and has taught Life Planning and Career Development at City University, Heritage College, Seattle University and the University of Washington. He lives in Bellevue, Washington, with his wife Lynne and has two grown children. Dr. Sage can be reached at h.sages@gte.net

Doris Rhea Coy, Ph.D., LPC, NCC, NCSC, NCCC, CDF, Assistant Editor, an associate professor at the University of North Texas (Denton, Texas), coordinates the school-counseling program. A former middle school teacher, high school counselor, and department chair in the Whitehall School District in Whitehall, Ohio, Doris is a past president of the American Counseling Association, the American School Counselor Association, the Ohio Counseling Association, the Ohio School Counselor Association, the Texas Career Development Association and past editor of the *ASCA Counselor*. She is the current president of the Texas Association for Counselor Education and Supervision, Secretary of the Texas School Counselor Association and chair of the ACA Insurance Trust. Dr. Coy travels extensively internationally and has provided numerous programs and workshops. She has published over 50 articles and chapters; she was Lead Editor of *Toward the Transformation of Secondary School Counseling*; *American Counseling Association — A 50-Year History 1952-2002*, and Co-Author of *Bullying — An Activity and Resource Book for School Counselors, Teachers, and Parents.* Dr. Coy can be reached at coy@unt.edu

Tami Palmer, Assistant Editor, is Deputy Director of WOIS/The Career Information System in Olympia, Washington and Professional Development Manager for the National Training Support Center in Seattle. Tami has worked at WOIS for 23 years. Tami started working at WOIS while a student at The Evergreen State College. After 6 months of exploring career information with WOIS resources, Tami changed her career direction. As Deputy Director, Tami oversees many of the company's daily operations and most special projects. She trains and provides presentations at conferences and workshops. Summers are spent reviewing updates to WOIS information. At the National Training Support Center in Seattle, Tami assists with development and coordination of resources to support the work of America's Career Resource Network, a project of the Department of Education's Office of Vocational and Adult Education. Her favorite project is a web-based parent guide to provide parents tools to help their children succeed in school and in their careers. Tami Palmer can be reached at tami@wois.org

About the Authors

Jackie M. Allen, Ed.D., a past president of the American School Counselor Association, has been a school counselor and bilingual school psychologist for over 30 years. She is a licensed Marriage Family Therapist, Certified Clinical Neuropsychologist, and an adjunct faculty member at La Verne University and National University. Jackie is an accomplished presenter and author. She is editor of the popular book, *School Counseling: New Perspectives & Practices* and editor of the *California School Counselor*, the newsletter of the California Association ofSchool Counselors. The H.B. McDaniel Foundation recently announced Dr. Jackie Allen as the winner of the 2003 H.B. McDaniel Individual Award for Outstanding Leadership. Dr. Allen is known throughout the state and the nation as being an effective school counseling leader and an unwavering supporter of the school counseling profession. Jackie is currently an education programs consultant in the Counseling and Student Support Office of the California Department of Education. Dr. Allen can be reached at JAllen@cde.ca.gov

James W. Allen, M.S., is a retired educator with over 30 years of experience in the public school system. He has been a junior high, senior high, and adult school counselor. In addition, he has taught at both the elementary and junior high school levels. He served the last four years of his career as an at-risk transition counselor with 8th grade junior high school students and with 9th grade senior high school students — developing his Dream Formula approach to counseling at-risk students. He has recently developed a website, specifically for students in California considering postsecondary options, at http://www.edpathways.com. Jim Allen can be reached at jallen491@attbi.com

Keith Anderson, Ed.D., LMHC, a high school counselor, serves as the Counseling Department Chair for Anacortes High School. He earned a Bachelor of Arts and a Master of Education degree from Western Washington University. His doctorate is from Seattle University. He began his counseling career in 1978 for the Neah Bay Schools located on the Makah Indian Reservation in Washington State. In 1985 he moved to Anacortes and helped to begin the comprehensive counseling program process. The Anacortes High School Counseling Center has received recognition as an "exemplary counseling program" from the Washington School Counselor Association as well as an "honorable mention" from the American School Counselor Association (as an exemplary counseling program). Dr. Anderson has served, twice, as president of the Washington School Counselor Association, once as president of the Washington

Counseling Association and as chair of the American Counseling Association Western Region. Dr. Anderson's email address is norsemen@attbi.com or kanderson@asd103.org

Stephen A. Armstrong, Ph.D., LPC-S, is an assistant professor of counselor education at Texas A&M University-Commerce. Stephen was an elementary school counselor for 11 years and has extensive experience working in culturally diverse schools with African American, Hispanic American, and Asian American students. His research interests include play therapy, group counseling, and school counseling. He recently published an article, "Expressive Arts in Family Therapy: Including Young Children in the Process," in the *Texas Counseling Association Journal* (Fall, 2002). He is currently involved in research projects involving play therapy in elementary schools and counselor/principal relationships. He is an active member of the American Counseling Association, American School Counselor Association, Association for Counselor Education and Supervision, Association for Specialists in Group Work, and the Texas Counseling Association. Stephen also serves on the editorial board of the Texas Counseling Association. Dr. Armstrong can be reached at Steve_Armstrong@tamu-commerce.edu

Bridgette Belasli, M.Ed., is currently the Manager of Secondary Curriculum for the Edmonds School District. She was formerly a curriculum specialist in the Lake Washington School District, where she worked as a secondary educator for eleven years. She graduated from the University of Washington with a degree in English literature in 1989 and earned a Master's Degree in Curriculum and Instruction in 2001. Her specialties in education include developing performance-based graduation standards and assessment tools. Bridgette Belasli can be reached at belaslib@edmonds.wednet.edu

Judy Bowers, M.S., supervises the 165 K-12 school counselors who serve 61,000 students in the Tucson Unified School District (TUSD), in Tucson, Arizona. Judy was a teacher for six years, a high school counselor for 16 years and has been the counselor supervisor for eight years. She has worked with the state of Arizona and TUSD since 1990 to restructure school counseling programs. This work led to the TUSD Governing Board adopting the Comprehensive Competency-Based Guidance (CCBG) in 1993. Under her guidance, the TUSD school-counseling department, awarded two federal elementary demonstration grants, has increased from 95 counselors in 1994 to 165 counselors in 2002. Leadership activities include President of the Arizona School Counselor Association, Supervisor/ Post Secondary and Western Region Vice-President for the American School

Counselor Association (ASCA), and she was recently elected to serve as President-Elect for ASCA. She is also a consultant to school districts developing comprehensive school counseling programs. Judy Bowers can be reached at judybowers@cox.net

Laurie A. Carlson, Ph.D., is an assistant professor in the counseling/career development program at Colorado State University. Dr. Carlson holds a Ph.D. in Counselor Education from the University of Arkansas and is both a Nationally Certified Counselor and Nationally Certified School Counselor. Dr. Carlson is a member of many professional associations including the honor societies, Kappa Delta Pi and Chi Sigma Iota International. Dr. Carlson's professional experience includes ten years of experience in public schools, four of those years as a K-12 school counselor in Minnesota. Dr. Carlson can be reached at laurie.carlson@colostate.edu

Carol A. Dahir, Ed.D., Assistant Professor and Coordinator of Counselor Education Programs at New York Institute of Technology, has an extensive background in education as an elementary school teacher, middle and high school counselor, and as a district administrator supervising school counseling programs and student support services. Carol holds graduate degrees in education, school counseling, and educational administration; she earned her doctorate from Hofstra University with a research agenda in school counseling reform. She recently served as the *National Standards* project director for the American School Counselor Association (ASCA) and as project manager for *Planning for Life*, the national recognition program for exemplary career planning programs in partnership with the US Army. Dr. Dahir is an accomplished national presenter, trainer, and program evaluator for school counseling program development, implementation and evaluation. She is also involved with implementing National Standards-based programs, school counselor accountability and career development. Dr. Dahir can be reached at caroldahir@aol.com

Larry Davis, B.A., is in his 23rd year of public service in Washington State, counting over 14 years on Washington State Senate staff, including 11 years as Senior Analyst for the Senate Education (K-12) Committee, and now in his ninth year as Executive Director for the State Board of Education. Almost all of Larry's time as a public servant has been spent participating in the crafting of education policy "on high." His experience working inside and outside the legislative arena has given him a unique perspective from which to comment on public policy formation and implementation. Larry is a native of Washington State and a product of the public K-12 and higher education systems. In his spare time, Larry particularly likes to travel and has combined his love of travel and sports with trips to three Summer Olympics: Montreal (1972), Atlanta (1996), and Sydney (2000). He also enjoys music, movies, and theatre. Larry Davis can be reached at Ldavis@ospi.wednet.edu

Willa Smith Davis, NCCC, Career Development Consultant, is a National Certified Career Counselor with over 20 years experience as a career development professional, and is a certified trainer for "Career Development Facilitators". She has worked for the U. S. Department of Labor in San Francisco, and higher educational institutions in both Colorado and Tennessee before starting an educational and career consulting practice in Colorado Springs. She returned home to Northern California in the year 2000 and currently works for 49er Regional Occupational Program (R.O.P.) as a counselor for adults and serves as 49er R.O.P.'s liaison to the One-Stop Career Centers in Placer and Nevada counties. She has designed and co-facilitated a career development support group for One-Stop Career Center customers based on Barbara Sher's "Success Teams" model. She has also taught career management, counseling, and psychology courses for Regis University, Chapman University and Pikes Peak Community College. Willa may be reached at wsdavis@lycos.com

Carola F. S. Dopps, M. Ed., both a certified school counselor and vocationally certified in diversified occupations, was born and raised in the Netherlands. She has experience in advertising and marketing, as a family therapist, a career specialist, and a community college instructor. She develops partnerships between business and education; she has developed partnerships for the High Tech Learning Centers, a consortium of 25 high schools on the Eastside of Seattle, part of the Northeast Vocational Area Cooperative (NEVAC). She is the Director for the Academy of Information Technology (in the Highline School District, Seattle) and a Faculty Development Representative for the Educator-to-Educator IT Institute for the National Workforce Center for Emerging Technologies. She coordinates the IGNITE (Inspiring Girls Now In Technology Evolution) program for schools on the Eastside and south of Seattle and, several years ago, approached Microsoft Corporation with the idea of a high tech camp for girls, now an annual event named DigiGirlz. Carola Dopps can be reached at doppsc@ix.netcom.com

Diane Fabish, M.Ed., a high school special education teacher in the Lake Washington School District (in Redmond, Washington), graduated Phi Beta Kappa from the University of Washington, then moved to San Jose, California, where she taught reading, writing and job training courses at

Evergreen Valley College for thirteen years. She has a Master's Degree in Education from San Jose State University and was in one of the first groups of teachers in California to receive the Learning Handicaps Resource Specialist credential in the 1970s. She has given numerous presentations on special education issues, served on her district's bargaining team, and participated on a Congressional special education task force. She has served on the Board of Directors for Lutheran Social Services of Northern California and currently serves as Washington State Vice-President for Alpha Delta Kappa, an international honorary sorority for women educators. She has been married for thirty years and has raised three lively sons. Diane can be reached at dfabish@lkwash.wednet.edu

Richard W. Feller, Ph.D., is Professor of Counseling and Career Development at Colorado State University where he directs the Career Development Institute. He is co-author of *Career Transitions in Turbulent Times* and the *CDM Career Video Series: Tour of Your Tomorrow*, and a contributing author of ACT's *DISCOVER* and Riverside Publishing Company's *GIS* computerized career planning systems. He has consulted in 49 states, Thailand, Japan, Sudan, China, Switzerland, and Canada. A nationally recognized speaker, he serves on the Board of the National Career Development Association and is the proud father of son Chris and husband of Barbara. Email: feller@cahs.colostate.edu Website: http:// soe.cahs.colostate.edu/faculty/feller

Jerald R. Forster, Ph.D., has been a Counselor Educator since 1966 when he joined the faculty at the University of Washington's College of Education soon after receiving his Ph.D. at the University of Minnesota. His research and writing has focused on the construction of meaning and the articulation of self-identities. He has devised methods to help individuals articulate their goals and their strengths. In 1987, he collaborated with Bernard Haldane to establish the Dependable Strengths Project, a research and demonstration program at the University of Washington that has helped thousands of people articulate their dependable strengths. He has also been active in professional organizations for counselors, being honored as the Advocate of the Year in 2000 by the Washington School Counselor Association. Dr. Forster can be reached at counsel@u.washington.edu

Julie Goldsmith, M.A., a leader in education reform, creates systems to engage all stakeholders in the design process for changing schools. This process has resulted in substantive change at both the school and district level. Julie is currently the Assistant Superintendent for Curriculum and Instruction for the Lake Washington School District in Redmond,

Washington. Her work has resulted in a nationally acclaimed K-12 standards-based curriculum, performance-based graduation requirements, and a standards-based reporting system. The curriculum, which has evolved over the past eight years, has been purchased by over 300 districts across the nation and is featured in Lynn Erickson's book (April 1998), *Concept-Based Curriculum and Instruction,* Corwin Press. In addition, Julie, a conference organizer, has presented at numerous state and national conferences on topics of standards, assessment, student learning, and school reform. She received her BA from Washington State University and an MA in Educational Leadership from Seattle University. Julie Goldsmith can be reached at JGoldsmith@lkwash.wednet.edu

Patricia Hatch, Ph.D., is co-author of the *ASCA National Model: A Framework for School Counseling Programs* (ASCA, 2003). She serves as the Supervisor/Post-Secondary Level Vice President of the American School Counselor Association (ASCA), and was awarded Administrator of the Year by ASCA in 2001. Dr. Hatch serves on the assessment design team for the National Board for Professional Teaching Standards' (NBPTS) new school counseling certificate, and a national trainer for the Education Trust's Met-Life School Counselor Initiative. Trish has helped author legislation and has testified as an expert in Senate and Assembly Education and Appropriations committees. Trish served as a school counselor for ten years, before moving to administration as the Coordinator of Student Services in Moreno Valley Unified School District. She is part-time faculty in counselor education, is a frequent guest speaker and trainer at state and national school counseling conferences, and serves as a consultant to school districts. Dr. Hatch can be reached at thatch@mvusd.k12.ca.us

Yvonne Hines has been the Career Specialist in Lake Washington High School's Career Center (in Kirkland, Washington) for over twenty years. Her previous background was in business; she worked in business cost accounting for several firms before raising a family. During the child-raising years, she owned her own business in Interior Decorating. Yvonne has attended Bellevue Community College, Seattle Central and the University of Washington. Among her accomplishments are: setting up the first Career Center at Lake Washington High School; coordinating a large Career Fair for eight years; starting a lunch time Cyber Café (outreach program) for parents and students; creating the Career Center web site for parents and students to access scholarships and other information at home; and coordinating a 20-hour Senior Service Learning Internship for all seniors in 2002. Yvonne was awarded the Washington Association Career and Technical Education "Career Specialist of the Year" in 2000. Yvonne can be reached at yhines@lkwash.wednet.edu

Dr. Kenneth B. Hoyt, Ph.D., is a University Distinguished Professor of Education at Kansas State University. Since receiving his Ph.D. degree in Educational Psychology at the University of Minnesota in 1954, Hoyt has devoted most of his career to serving as a Counselor Educator at the: (1) University of Iowa (1954-69), (2) University of Maryland (1969-74), and (3) Kansas State University (1984-present). From 1974-1983, he served as Director, Office of Career Education, U.S. Department of Education. He has published 10 books and 150+ articles/monographs mostly on some aspect of education/work relationships. His major research interest, since 1962, has been career development of persons seeking some form of postsecondary career-oriented education at the sub-baccalaureate level. In this connection, he served as Director, Specialty-Oriented Student Research Program from 1962 until 1974 and as Director, Counseling for High Skills Project, from 1992-2000. Dr. Hoyt has served as President both of the American Counseling Association (1966-67) and National Career Development Association (1992-93). He was the founding Editor of *Counselor Education and Supervision* from 1961 until 1965. The 23 special national honors awarded him include: (1) Distinguished Professional Service Award, American Counseling Association (1994); (2) Outstanding Career Achievement Award, Association for Counselor Education and Supervision (1990); and (3) Eminent Career Award, National Vocational Guidance Association (1981). Dr. Hoyt can be reached at KHoyt@ksu.edu

Christine M. Jensen, Ed.D., experienced in all facets of education and counseling, integrates knowledge and skills that span every educational venue. She has taught, counseled and managed in K-12 schools, has provided district and statewide leadership as a counseling specialist, has developed and delivered executive training for two multinational companies, and has instructed adult learners from basic education and English-as-Second Language to graduate-level courses in education, counseling and leadership. In Alaska, Chris contributed to statewide task forces on Outcomes for Public Education, Tech Prep and School-to-Work. Currently, Dr. Jensen is an associate professor in the Department of Counseling and School Psychology at Seattle University and serves on the School Counseling Committee for the National Board for Professional Teaching Standards. She also provides consulting services to K-16 educational systems and health care organizations, where she specializes in leadership, strategic planning, systemic change, performance improvement, and comprehensive school counseling. Dr. Jensen can be reached at jensenc@seattleu.edu

Mark A. Madison, M.Ed., is an experienced school counselor, career guidance specialist, and counselor educator in the field of career counseling and guidance. He is author of the *Navigator Comprehensive Career Guidance Curriculum* series for middle and high schools, and frequent speaker on such topics as aligning career guidance with education reform, developing education pathways, and building effective K-12 career guidance and counseling models. Presently, Mark is a Career and Technical Education Specialist for the Edmonds School District in Washington State where he manages K-12 career guidance, coordinates alignment of Career and Technical Education programs with new state standards, and facilitates development of education pathways and majors. He also serves as Adjunct Professor for the School of Education's School Counseling program at Seattle Pacific University, and is currently a member of the Superintendent of Public Instruction's advisory committee for career guidance and planning for Washington State. Mark can be reached at madisonm@edmonds.wednet.edu

Nancy McCorkle Miller, M.A., a National Board Certified teacher, currently teaches in the International Baccalaureate program at Interlake High School in Bellevue, Washington. She also serves as a candidate mentor for Washington Initiative at the University of Washington, a Washington State initiative to support NBPTS candidates. Miller has earned a BA in Political Science, magna cum laude, from the University of Washington, and a MA in Curriculum and Instruction from Seattle University. She has taught in the public school system since 1969. Miller's teaching was profiled in the *Seattle Times*, Pacific Magazine, (8/18/96). In 1986 and 1997, her students voted her Lake Washington High School Outstanding Teacher Award. Miller has taught staff development and has worked on research and development teams for districts and professional associations involving teacher evaluation, curriculum development and alignment, and graduation standards. Areas of special interest have included integrated instruction, technology infusion, portfolio assessment, and project-based curriculum. Nancy can be reached at njmcmiller@hotmail.com or at millern@bsd405.org

Nancy S. Perry, M.S. Ed, has served as a teacher, counselor, and Maine State Guidance Supervisor. Beginning in 1993, she managed the production and implementation of the *Get a Life@ Career Development Portfolio* for the National Occupational Information Coordinating Committee. Nancy recently retired as executive director of the American School Counselor Association (ASCA). Nancy also served in national leadership positions with ASCA, culminating with the presidency in 1991-92. She chaired the ACA (American Counseling Association) Task Force on the Status of School Counseling, was a member of the College Board Research and Development Committee, and was a member of the National Advisory Committee for the "Counseling for High Skills" project. Author of numerous publications, her latest work is *Develop Your Future I and II* – career-planning guides for middle and high school students. Nancy, who has represented school counseling throughout the world, is married and has four grown children and four grandchildren. Nancy Perry can be reached at pnperry1221@att.net

Harvey Schmelter-Davis, M.A., N.C.C., is a Senior Practitioner-in-Residence at the Heldrich Center for Workforce Development, Rutgers University. While there he has worked on a project for the USDOL to implement a training program to introduce educators to the Occupational Information Network (O*NET) and to develop and implement a Global Career Development Facilitator curriculum called *Working Ahead: The National Workforce and Career Development Curriculum.* He was lead consultant to revise and update the Improved Career Decision Making curriculum using Internet resources for the OVAE America's Career Resources Network. Previously he was the Manager of the National Occupational Information Coordinating Committee's (NOICC) Career Development Training Institute, Director of Career Services and International Education at Brookdale Community College, lead Improved Career Decision Making (ICDM) trainer for New Jersey, lead consultant to implement the AT&T Career Development Program within Bell Laboratories and senior career development consultant to the College Board. Harvey can be reached at harveysd@monmouth.com

Laura Jo Severson, M.A., is a Counselor at SeaTac Occupational Skills Center, a school that provides technical training for high school juniors and seniors from multiple school districts in the Seattle area. She has been a school counselor for students at all levels from elementary through adult. She holds a BS from Auburn University and an MA from the University of South Alabama. Laura Jo is the Past President of the Washington School Counselor Association. Laura Jo can be reached at wseverson@aol.com or at SeversLJ@hsd401.org

Christopher Simpson, Ph.D., is currently an Assistant Professor of Counseling at San Francisco State University in San Francisco, Ca. Chris holds a Doctor of Philosophy in Counseling from The University of North Texas in Denton, Texas. He is a Nationally Certified Counselor and a Licensed Professional Counselor. Specializing in working with K-12 age children and self-injurious behavior, Chris has worked in school and clinical settings. Chris is a member of several professional organizations including the American Counseling Association (ACA), the Association for Specialists in Group Work (ASGW), American School Counselor Association (ASCA), and the Association for Counselor Education and Supervision (ACES). Dr. Simpson can be reached at Christo1@sfsu.edu

Jim Whitledge, Ph.D., received his doctorate from Mississippi State University in 1993. He is the Counseling and Guidance Program Consultant for Oakland Schools, an intermediate school district that provides educational support services for 28 school districts in Oakland County, Michigan. From 1998-2001, Jim was on the faculty and coordinated the School Counseling Program at the University of Detroit-Mercy. He served as a professional school counselor for the Farmington, Michigan Public Schools until 1998. Jim has been active in leadership with professional counselor associations at the local, state, and national levels, having served as President of the American School Counselor Association (ASCA) and the Oakland Counseling Association. He is currently Chair of the Michigan School Counselor Association Ethics Committee and ASCA Representative to the American Counseling Association Governing Council. Jim is most proud of his relationship with wife Pat, daughters/sons-in-law, Julie and Curtis, Karen and Kevin, and granddaughters, Ava Rose and Lily Grace. Dr. Whitledge can be reached at jim.whitledge@oakland.k12.mi.us

Anton Wishik, M.Ed., a high school counselor in the Port Angeles School District, (90 miles northwest of Seattle on the gorgeous Olympic Peninsula), is a part-time counselor educator for City University, and has a private counseling service. Anton was the editor of the *Careers Now Activities Manual* which has been in publication since 1990 and is used in districts throughout the United States. Prior to becoming a school counselor, he served Port Angeles as a Career Specialist, founding the high school's career center and winning an award for the best Career Guidance Program in the state. He has served as president of the Guidance & Counseling Division of the Washington Vocational Association. Anton is trained as a mediator and a Challenge Course Instructor. Prior to entering education, Anton was an award-winning journalist and a paramedic. He and his wife Cindy have two grown children and are in the process of adopting a seven-year-old. Anton may be reached at Anton_L._Wishik@pasd.wednet.edu

Teresa I. Yohon, Ph.D., is an Assistant Professor at Colorado State University (CSU). With a Masters in Counseling and Ph.D. in Community and Human Resources/Vocational Education, her duties include training teacher licensure students, advising business and marketing education students, and providing leadership in educational technology. Dr. Yohon is the project director of Colorado State University's $1.1 million Preparing Teachers to Use Technology grant and manager of the Intel Pre-service Teach to the Future project. She has worked with the Colorado Institute of Technology and various business education organizations in searching for ways to increase the number of females and minorities in high-tech or information technology fields. Dr. Yohon can be reached at yohon@CAHS.Colostate.edu

Introduction

Suzy Mygatt Wakefield

Abstract

This book has been a work in progress for two years as educators around the country have contributed ideas, suggestions, resources, and programs (innovative practices) to help students with their plans after high school. Ideas range from innovations in comprehensive school counseling programs to specific activities as well as Internet delivery systems, such as the recently developed O*NET and WOIS Electronic Portfolio. The purpose of this Introduction is to give the reader an overview of the book, including societal trends and workplace issues. A thumbnail sketch of the book's eight sections is provided at the end of the chapter. A distinction is drawn between the terms *school counseling* and *school guidance*. Educators and community members are encouraged to work together to provide students with needed career guidance activities. An example of working together is when district and state graduation requirements are written to incorporate career guidance competencies through activities and projects.

Purpose of this Book

The primary intent of this book is to provide a hands-on resource for educators—school counselors, career specialists, classroom teachers, administrators, curriculum directors, career and technical education directors, school board members, and others—in an effort to help *all* students with their plans after high school. This resource book is a compilation of a broad variety of career guidance ideas, suggestions, resources, and programs. It is hoped that these suggestions and programs may be utilized by appropriate educators and others in a collaborative fashion to help students with their postsecondary plans.

Another purpose of this book is to provide educators with insights about what is occurring in our schools—such as the lack of coordinated career guidance services, the number of disengaged students, and the concerning rate of high school dropouts. A third purpose is to share insights about the changing workplace with its new configurations, with the intent of helping young people in our schools to become more informed about this new workplace, which rewards technical competencies, continuous improvement, broader responsibilities, and flexible and resilient workers, according to Feller, in his chapter in this book: *Aligning Student Planning with the Changing Workplace.* A related issue is that of the importance of teaching employability skills now *required* by employers, such as reading and following instructions carefully, being a good team member, communicating clearly, and making decisions. It is our hope that readers will find this book helpful in their own professional settings with these ideas, suggestions, resources, and programs.

The Distinction between School Counseling and School Guidance

In reading this book, it is helpful to grasp the fundamental distinction between the terms of *school counseling* and *school guidance,* as the ideas, suggestions and programs in this book fall broadly under the concept of school guidance, or, more specifically, career guidance. Some ideas, models, and suggestions in this book may be used within career guidance programs, and one model is a proposed career guidance program. (See Jensen & Madison's chapter: *Dreams Can Come True—Building a K-12 Career Development System that Inspires Hope.*)

An important concept that is often blurred in education is the distinction between the terms *school counseling* and *school guidance.* School counseling services are provided one-on-one or in small groups by credentialed school counselors trained to help students with academic, personal/social, and career development issues and barriers to school achievement. On the other hand, all appropriate educators may participate in guidance activities, including teaching developmental (age-appropriate) career guidance curriculum. As Gysbers (1990) notes, "Although counselors' responsibilities include organizing and implementing the guidance curriculum, the cooperation and support of the entire faculty are necessary for its successful implementation" (p. 16).

School counseling suggests an individual student or a small group of students sharing personal information with a credentialed school counselor to get resolution with a problem, where there is an agreement of confidentiality (unless information must be appropriately shared for student safety). School guidance, on the other hand, suggests a program or activities in which information is shared with larger groups of students. This could be information about important pre-college tests, college application deadlines, study skills, the dangers of substance abuse, AIDS education, and so forth. It is shared on an impartial basis with all students. Career guidance, therefore, is under the "umbrella" of school guidance (Myrick, 1993) and may be presented to all students by appropriate personnel, including school counselors, career specialists (a certified designation in some states), teachers, and even appropriate community members, who may serve as guest speakers. This is an important distinction to make and is a fundamental premise of this book. Myrick (1993) has defined both terms, beginning with school guidance:

> More traditionally, guidance is an 'umbrella' term which encompasses a constellation of services aimed at personal and career development and school adjustment. These services are commonly delivered by professional educators, such as teachers or counselors, although other support personnel may be involved. (p. 2)
>
> Counseling has been perceived as a process in which someone who has a problem receives personal assistance, usually through a private discussion...There is a trust relationship in which the focus is on personal meaning of events and experiences...Counseling is considered a professional endeavor by a professionally trained and certified person. (p. 3)

The distinction between school counseling and school guidance is so important that it deserves further clarification from the American School Counselor Association, which has developed *The ASCA National Model: A Framework for School Counseling Programs* (ASCA 2003). As stated in the Glossary:

> *Guidance curriculum*: the guidance curriculum component consists of structured developmental lessons designed to assist students in achieving the competencies and is presented systematically through classroom and group activities K-12. (p. 130)
>
> *Counseling*: a special type of helping process implemented by a professionally trained and certified person, involving a variety of techniques and strategies that help students explore academic, career and personal/social issues impeding healthy development of academic progress. (p. 129)

This clarification in terms is important to grasp in reading through the many ideas, suggestions and programs presented in this book, as many people (educators and appropriate community members) may need to be involved in their delivery. In the past, since school counselors have had specific training in career development, they have been asked to be the primary providers of career guidance services to all students. That is, they have been asked to bear the brunt of the responsibility. The problem, of course, has been that school counselors (often called guidance counselors) have been busy with so many other responsibilities that they have been unable to help develop and implement a career guidance program in their schools, with the result that many students have gone without much career guidance support. Understanding the distinction between the terms of school counseling and school guidance makes the issue of appropriate delivery of career guidance programs much clearer.

Inspiration for this Book

The inspiration for this book came primarily from two sources. One source was Dr. Cal Crow (an internationally renowned career consultant from Seattle) who reported at a Washington Counseling Association Conference in October, 1993, that a *Time Magazine* article (Morrow, 1993) speculated that by the turn of the century, half of all American workers would be *contingent workers* (including temps, contract, and part-time workers). The implication was that we urgently needed to train high school students to learn more about how to market their skills in what was to become an increasingly competitive workplace. The second source of inspiration was an article in *ASCA Professional School Counseling* (Granello & Sears, December, 1999), exhorting school counselors to become more centrally involved in activities (school-based learning, work-based learning and connecting activities) mandated in the School-to-Work Opportunities Act (STWOA) of 1994. The *ASCA Counselor Newsletter* (March/April 2001) published a short article entitled, *Re-thinking School-to-Work: Where do we go from here?* written by this writer, asking readers to consider a collaborative approach, particularly with state graduation guidelines support. Given the urgency to train our students to become more prepared in what was likely to be a more volatile and uncertain workplace, this writer asked, "What has caused the reluctance to set up school-based learning, work-based learning and connecting activities when the benefits are so obvious?" And the answer was:

> I believe it's been a workload issue...School counselors were inundated with responsibilities long before the school-to-work effort came along. As they will tell you virtually anywhere, school counselors already have large caseloads with myriad responsibilities within those caseloads: identifying students for special education placement, monitoring students on 504 plans, working with students who are faltering in their academic classes, intervening with students using drugs and alcohol, identifying students who might be suicidal or violent, running

support groups and helping students transition to college...The prevailing thinking is that if we would only adopt a 'comprehensive guidance and counseling model' (so well presented by Dr. Norm Gysbers of the University of Missouri) that we can work on school-to-work activities.

Clearly, spelling out a district's comprehensive guidance and counseling model K-12, 'calendaring' the activities for each level and delegating responsibilities according to prioritized needs does much to help. But it's not enough. Direction must come from the top—from the state Board of Education. Otherwise, teachers resent school-to-work activities as taking away students from instructional time. The school-to-work component must be seen as a valid graduation requirement. (p. 13)

And this book was born! Right there, right then! This writer was close to retirement and decided to put together a book, with the best ideas that could be mustered, to help students focus on their plans after high school and that could be delivered by a variety of educators and community members. So this writer, who was soon to become an editor with a project, began soliciting chapters from colleagues around the country.

In the comprehensive guidance and counseling model, Gysbers and Henderson (1994) suggest that a needs assessment be conducted with students, educators, parents, and community members (p. 193) and that a comprehensive school counseling program be developed based on identified student needs, incorporating the components of the guidance curriculum, individual planning, responsive services, and system support. But in our school, things were different. We typically did not survey student needs. We did what our administrators asked us to do, which seems to be typical for many school counselors, traditionally beginning several weeks of each school year with registering new students and balancing classes. More and more was being asked of us, and now, from the national level, school-to-work coordination. The Education Trust's report (2001a), *The Lost Opportunity of Senior Year: Finding a Better Way—Summary of Findings,* discusses counselors' large caseloads.

" In most schools, guidance counselors are overburdened and overloaded. The latest data that the Commission was able to obtain indicate that the average guidance counselor in the United States is responsible for providing career, academic, and often personal advice to about 500 students..." (p. 7).

School counselor responsibilities were burgeoning prior to the advent of the School-to-Work Opportunities Act of 1994 (STWOA). What was needed was a better understanding of the distinction between the concepts of school guidance (educators' job) and school counseling (the school counselor's unique job.) It is critically important to understand the difference between school counseling, which must be performed by credentialed school counselors, and school guidance, which can be carried out by educators and appropriate others who have specific contributions to the total effort. This distinction helps to set the stage for this book, as many suggestions and resources relate to providing career guidance for all students.

Career Guidance is an Educators' Job

Guidance curriculum can pertain to a great number of items and issues, such as teaching study skills, social skills, or decision-making skills, or teaching about the harm of substance abuse. Guidance curriculum may be taught by educators as well as by guest speakers from the community. In career guidance, once the overall design is established for the guidance curriculum, different individuals may carry out different aspects of it. Teachers may participate in what was once called "career education infusion." *Career education infusion* (Zunker, 1998) is the notion that "teachers expand their current educational objectives to include career-related activities and subjects" (p. 246). If teachers see their role as incorporating career education concepts (for example, showing how their subject content relates to the real world and how students may use what they are learning in class in their lives outside of school), they are involved in career guidance. This is a fundamental point that is often missed by educators. Career guidance is virtually every educator's job, whether it be in classroom sessions, helping students to set up and carry out internships or job shadow experiences or service learning (volunteer experiences), or helping students to set up informational or mock job interviews.

Another approach to help provide career guidance activities for *all* students is to incorporate them into district or state graduation requirements. In the state of Washington, that has happened. In October 2000, the Washington State Board of Education mandated that all students in the graduating class of 2008 would need to complete a non-credit *high school + education plan* (going one year past high school) and a non-credit *culminating project* that could conceivably be a guided opportunity to help a student explore a potential career interest (See *Washington State Minimum High School Graduation Requirements at* www.sbe.wa.gov).

With district or state support, educators can be asked to pull together and pool their resources to provide needed career guidance activities for all students. Otherwise, without district or state direction, teachers sometimes express their resentment when school counselors and others (such as career specialists, who coordinate high school Career Centers) call students out of their classes for career guidance sessions (such as college planning sessions). Teachers sometimes express that there are so many classroom interruptions that they prefer to keep students in class. This attitude can play havoc with a guidance program. For example, if students do not understand college application timelines and requirements (presented during group guidance instruction), they tend to miss deadlines, making a lot more work for the overworked school counselor and secretary, and even their parents/ guardians.

Our Climbing High School Dropout Rate

Many students drop out of school, endangering their economic survival if they do not return to school. Some do manage to complete a GED or other certificate. Some researchers speculate that our high school dropout rate could be as high as one in three (Greene, 2002; Mortenson, 2001), although that is not officially recognized. One in four students has been the more frequently stated dropout rate. According to Isaacson & Brown, (2000), "Unfortunately, as many as 25 percent leave school prior to graduation" (p. 269). The Education Trust reports a high school graduation rate with a regular diploma of 72.5 percent and a high school completion rate of 82 percent, if GED and other certificate completers are included (Education Trust, 2001b). Greene (2002) reports that many students leave school prior to reaching high school, noting that "...the vast majority of dropouts nationwide leave schools in earlier grades (usually between 9th and 10th grades)..." (p. 6). Therefore, high school graduation or dropout rates need to be observed with some caution; many students may have already left the system. According to the report *Youth at the Crossroads: Facing High School and Beyond*, prepared for the National Commission on the High School Senior Year by the Education Trust, Inc. (2001b):

> Each year, almost 1 out of every 20 youngsters leaves high school. But there are vast differences among students from different racial and economic groups...During a typical year, we lose about 1 out of 30 Whites, 1 out of 20 African Americans, and 1 out of 10 Latinos...At the same time, students from poor families are considerably more likely to leave high school than students from affluent families....By ages 18-19, data from the U.S. Census suggest that about 82% of all young people have completed high school. Of these, about 72.5% have earned a regular diploma, with another 9.8% earning a GED or other certificate. (p. 5)

The dropout rate is not necessarily the converse (or flip side) of the graduation rate as other factors may intervene, but the graduation rate of 72.5% (for students who have earned a regular diploma) gives us some sense of how many students are actually graduating on time with their peers (Education Trust, 2001b). According to the U.S. Department of Education *Consumer Guide* (March 1996), dropout rates can be reported as *event rates* (percentage of students who drop out in a single year), *status rates* (percentage of a given age range who have not completed high school), or *cohort rates* (percentage of dropouts in a cohort group, as in grades 9-12 for a given high school graduating class).

The reader may also be interested to know that the U.S. Census Bureau counts GED completers as high school graduates, while the National Center for Educational Statistics (NCES, 2002) of the U.S. Department of Education does not! This discrepancy further confounds high school graduation and dropout rates.

What Happens to Dropouts in Today's Workplace?

While our dropout rate has been climbing (Rothstein, 2002), our economy has experienced profound changes, particularly for school dropouts, in the last forty years. The Education Trust's report (2001a), *The Lost Opportunity of the Senior Year: Finding a Better Way*, reports the following:

> ...Until 1960, more than one-third of all the production jobs in the United States were held by high school dropouts. As late as 1973, in fact, education and employment were only loosely related. In that era, students with or without high school diplomas, particularly males, could get fairly decent jobs in the manufacturing economy. Widely available blue-collar jobs paid attractive wages and benefits (often with union support), supported families, bought vacation homes, and put the children of working men and women through college. Those days—and those jobs—are gone. (p. 2)

The workplace has experienced important changes as it has moved from a pyramid configuration with numerous low-skill, entry level jobs at the bottom to a diamond-shape that primarily hires technically skilled workers and has little room at the bottom for unskilled workers (Feller, 1997). Students who do not take school seriously (who do minimal work to "get by") and who do not develop a foundation for learning important technical skills will find that the only jobs available to them require two-to-three weeks of training on the job (Hoyt, 2001) in the restaurant, retail and services industries (Steinberg, 1996). These students can easily be locked into low-income wages. Students and adults in this economic trap who choose not to continue their education tend to take on two or three low-wage jobs (to boost their wages), thereby continuing this low-wage cycle throughout their lives (Ehrenreich, 2001). By intervening as educators, this is the scenario we want to prevent. A National Center for Education Statistics (NCES) report, *Dropout Rates in the United States, 1999*, further corroborates the importance of completing high school, as dropouts tend to be unemployed and, disproportionately, in prison:

> Because high school completion has become a requirement for accessing additional education, training, or the labor force, the economic consequences of leaving high school without a diploma are severe. On average, dropouts are more likely to be unemployed than high school graduates and to earn less money when they eventually secure work....The individual stresses and frustrations associated with dropping out have social implications as well: dropouts make up a disproportionate percentage of the nation's prison and death row inmates." (p. 1)

Research on "Disengaged" Students

Laurence Steinberg's book *Beyond the Classroom—Why School Reform has Failed and What Parents Need to Do* (1996) provides some of the most provocative data in the field about the actual number of disengaged students (students who do minimal work in school to get by), which he reports is about 30 percent. He also reports that about 25-30 percent of parents are disengaged in their students' lives, as far as knowing how their teens spend their free time, who their friends are, what courses they are taking in school and what progress they are making. These are troubling statistics and are based on his research of 20,000 students in nine typical school districts in two states (Wisconsin and California) during 1987-88, 1988-89, and 1989-1990. Steinberg (1996) discusses influences outside of the classroom that heavily impact student performance in the classroom: parenting styles; peer influence; work hours—especially more than 20 hours per week; emphasis on multiple non-academic activities; and healthy and unhealthy achievement attributional patterns—students seeing their achievement patterns under their control (healthy) or due merely to luck (unhealthy). The Education Trust's report (2001a) echoes Steinberg's concerns about long work hours and how they put our students at academic risk relative to their European and Asian counterparts:

The amount of time students spend at work, particularly in the senior year, is a uniquely American phenomenon. More than half of US twelfth graders (55 percent) report working three or more hours daily at a paid job, three times the international average. No other advanced country expects students to work, or permits them to work long hours at low-skill jobs just to earn spending money. (p. 6)

Conclusion

All students have the right to a comprehensive, developmental career guidance program, with many activities to help them with self-knowledge development, educational and occupational exploration, and career planning (*NCDA Guidelines*, 1989). Educators and people in the community need to work together, as they often already do, to provide career guidance activities and workplace experiences (job shadows, internships, service learning, and paid employment) for our students. It should also be noted that students can learn a lot about a career interest in a carefully chosen paying job, instead of working at a job that has no particular meaning for them.

We hope that you, the reader, can find ideas, suggestions, resources, and programs (innovative practices) to enhance your work with young people as they transition from high school to adulthood, and move into their postsecondary educational settings and workplace positions. We need to work together to help every student be well prepared and successful.

Contents of this Book

For readers who want a thumbnail sketch of each chapter, Part II is provided. This book is divided into eight sections.

In **Part I, Societal Trends and Workplace Issues**, the chapters are:

(1) *"Unfocused Kids" tend to Choose the Path of Least Resistance*—an explanation of "unfocused kids"and their typical disengaged behavior (Mygatt Wakefield);

(2) *The Importance of Career Guidance and Employability Skills for All Student*—a discussion of the importance of career guidance programs for all students, not just "unfocused" students, and the crucial importance of employability skills for workplace survival (Mygatt Wakefield);

(3) *Dreams Can Come True—Building a K-12 Career Development System that Inspires Hope*—an explanation of a hypothetical K-12 career development program, with a collaborative delivery system, to enable all students to develop a meaningful educational and career plan, portfolio, and culminating project and to participate in appropriate career guidance activities at every grade level (Jensen & Madison);

(4) *Aligning Student Planning with the Changing Workplace*—a discussion about the changing nature of the workplace from a pyramid to a diamond-shape, workers who have misinformed expectations about the workplace, and what skills they need to have to survive (Feller); and

(5) *Factors that Influence Women and Minorities to Choose High-Tech Careers*—a discussion about the under-representation of women and minorities in high tech careers and the contributing factors for this concern, including peers, parents, school, work experiences, information resources, and environmental factors (Yohon & Carlson).

In **Part II, Comprehensive School Counseling Programs,** the ASCA National Standards (student content standards in the domains of academic, career, and personal/social development) and suggestions for implementation are presented in the first two chapters:

(6) *Building a National Model*—an explanation of the *ASCA National Model: A Framework for School Counseling Programs*, its rationale, and its components (Hatch and Bowers);

(7) *School Counseling Programs: Supporting a Nation of Learners*—an explanation of the ASCA National Standards, their rationale, and a case study showing how they may be used (Dahir);

(8) *Unfocused Kids/Unfocused Counseling*—a provocative discussion about the difficulty of staying with the intended role of the school counselor in the face of so many competing demands and the rationale for having a developmental, comprehensive program (Anderson);

(9) *Career Resource Centers—Programs and Resources for all Students*— a detailed discussion about the many functions that may be provided by a school's career resource center and the varied programs its staff can help to promote (Hines & Mygatt Wakefield);

(10) *The Phantom Student*—a discussion of the importance of using a comprehensive guidance and counseling model to reach even "phantom students" who tend to get lost in the school system (Coy); and

(11) *A Model School Counseling Program Brochure: Implications for Helping Students Focus on their Plans after High School*—a template for educators to use for their own school counseling programs (including an "informed consent" brochure) (Whitledge).

Part III presents **Project-Based Career Guidance Models,** which include:

(12) *Using Projects to Teach Career Planning Skills and Tools*—a discussion about the importance of requiring all students to develop *an education and career plan*, a *career planning portfolio*, and a *culminating project* as these skills and tools can be used in the workplace (Mygatt Wakefield);

(13) *Policy—The View from on High*—a discussion about the importance of state-level career guidance graduation requirements, particularly the *high school + education plan* (going one year past high school) and the *culminating project* (L. Davis);

(14) *The False Promise of the Diploma: One District's Approach to Improving the System for all Students*—an explanation of one district's approach (the Lake Washington School District in Kirkland/Redmond,

Washington) to performance-based education in the five literacies of: Communication; Quantitative and Scientific Reasoning; Citizenship (which includes a service learning requirement); Culture; and School to Career and Life Skills (which includes an Education and Career Plan and a Field Experience) (Goldsmith);

(15) *Culminating Projects: Providing Real World Relevance and Rigor*—an analysis of 20 districts' approaches to assigning, monitoring and evaluating culminating projects with suggestions as to how to set up a program (Belasli); and

(16) *Authentic Assessment—Bridge to the Workplace*—a discussion of the role teachers play in providing authentic curriculum with real-life applications for students (Miller).

Part IV, Innovative Approaches to Workplace Training, has three chapters providing many programs and best practices (business partnerships, internships, regional occupational programs, and so forth) that educators may utilize with students to help them prepare for the workplace.

(17) *Career Preparation Programs in Secondary Education—A Sampler of Current Trends, Exemplary Programs, Model Practices and the Bottom Line*—a presentation of a detailed description of many career preparation programs and best practices around the country (including tech prep, school-to-work, and specialized high school programs)(W. Davis);

(18) *Working Connection: Business Education Partnerships that Work*—an explanation of partnerships, with many pointers about setting them up along with their benefits to educators, students, and the community, with examples such as Microsoft's DigiGirlz (Dopps); and

(19) *The Crooked Career Path*—a discussion suggesting that the best preparation is both technical and academic (with supporting internships), as students really do not know their future paths and need to be prepared for many unexpected outcomes (Severson).

Part V, Involving Parents in their Teen's Career Planning, contains two chapters:

(20) *The Important Role of Parents in their Teen's Career Development*—a discussion of what parents need to know and do regarding their teen's

career planning and how educators can encourage parents to be more involved (Sage); and

(21) *The Right Tools—Helping High School Graduates Consider all the Postsecondary Options*—a discussion encouraging parents and educators to look beyond the traditional four-year college so that they might consider community colleges, public and private technical training institutes, federally sponsored career training programs, the military, and so forth (Hoyt).

Part VI, Innovative Career Development Activities/Games, includes three chapters:

(22) *The Real Game: A Real Hook to Involvement*—an explanation of the Real Game Series ™, a hands-on career guidance approach for students, and its benefits (Perry);

(23) *Your Best Plans Should Use Your Best Strengths*—an explanation of the Dependable Strengths Articulation Model, developed by Dr. Bernard Haldane, and its application for high school students (Forster); and

(24) *Designing the Dog—Career Development Activities that Work*—an explanation of two activities for students: one hands-on activity that helps students to learn more about the old (assembly line) and new (quality circle) workplace; the other involves a 7-minute mock job interview classroom lesson plan, with 50 interview questions from employers (Wishik).

Part VII, Innovative Career Development Practices for Special Populations, includes five chapters:

(25) *Career Guidance in Rural Schools: Special Needs, Concerns, and Strategies*—a discussion of the issues of isolation and limited resources facing rural students with suggestions for remedies, such as free/inexpensive career guidance materials, technology, and community advisory committees, and school-based enterprises (Carlson and Yohon);

(26) *Career Development from a Multicultural Perspective*—a discussion of multi-cultural career development issues from the standpoint of Asian Americans, Latinos, and African Americans, as three writers each take a section (Coy, Simpson and Armstrong);

(27) *The Dream Board—A Visual Approach for Career Planning with At-Risk 8th and 9th Grade Students*—an explanation of a hands-on approach for educators to help at-risk students to grasp the connection between *Education + Skills=Job + Money=Your Future Dreams* (Jim Allen);

(28) *Career Education for Special Education Students*—a discussion of the implications of changes in the IDEA 97 (Individuals with Disabilities Education Act), requiring transition services for special education students (an ITP—Individual Transition Plan, as well as the IEP—Individual Education Plan), and the importance of professionals collaborating in delivering needed services to special needs students (Jackie Allen); and

(29) *Successful Transitions for High School Special Education Students from School to the Workplace*—a description and rationale of many targeted programs for special education students to help them prepare for both the workplace and college (Fabish).

Part VIII, Internet Delivery Systems in Career Guidance, includes two chapters:

(30) *Electronic Portfolios*—an explanation of a new program through WOIS/The Career Information System to provide site users with Internet career development services, including the Electronic Portfolio for high school students in Washington State (Palmer);

(31) *O*NET In Action—Expanding Youth Career Horizons*—an explanation, with multiple captured screens, about this new government career development program, including many specific programs within the O*NET, a revision of the DOT—much bigger and very user-friendly; available to users at http://online.onetcenter.org (Schmelter-Davis).

(32) The *Conclusion—Summing Up* asks the questions: How do we put all of this together? What needs to be done? (Mygatt Wakefield and Sage).

References

American School Counselor Association (2003). *American School Counselor Association National Model: A framework for school counseling programs.* Alexandria, VA: Author.

Education Trust, Inc. (2001a). National Commission on the High School SeniorYear. *The lost opportunity of senior year: Finding a better way— summary of findings.* Retrieved March 28, 2003, from http:// www.commissiononthesenioryear.org/Report/report.html

Education Trust, Inc. (2001b). National Commission on the High School Senior Year *Youth at the crossroads: Facing high school and beyond.* Retrieved March 28, 2003, from http: www.commissionon thesenioryear.org/Report/report.html

Ehrenreich, B. (2001). *Nickel and dimed: On (not) getting by in America.* New York: Henry Holt & Company—A Metropolitan/Owl Book.

Feller, R. (1997). Redefining "career" during the work revolution. In R. Feller & G.R.Walz (Eds.), *Career transitions in turbulent times. Exploring work, learning and careers* (pp.143-154). University of North Carolina at Greensboro: ERIC/CASS Publications.

Granello, D.H. & Sears, S.J. (1999). The School to Work Opportunities Act and the role of the school counselor. *ASCA Professional School Counseling, 3*(2), 108-115.

Greene, J.P. (2002) *Graduation rates in Washington state.* New York: Manhattan Institute for Policy Research. Retrieved December 19, 2002, from http://www.manhattan-institute.org/html/cr_27.htm

Gysbers, N.C. (1990). *Comprehensive guidance programs that work.* University of Michigan at Ann Arbor: ERIC/CAPS Clearinghouse.

Gysbers, N.C., & Henderson, P. (1994). *Developing and managing your school guidance program.* (2nd ed.). Alexandria, VA: American Counseling Association.

Hoyt, K.B. (2001). Helping high school students broaden their knowledge of postsecondary options. *Professional School Counseling, 5*(1), 6-12.

Isaacson, L.E., & Brown, D. (2000). *Career information, career counseling, and career development.* Boston: Allyn & Bacon.

Morrow, L. (1993, March 29). The temping of America. *Time.* 40-47.

Mortenson, T.G. (2001, June). High school graduation trends and patterns 1981-2000. *Postsecondary Education Opportunity*, (108), 2.

Mygatt Wakefield, S. (March/April 2001). Re-thinking school-to-work: where do we go from here? *The ASCA Counselor* [newsletter], p.13.

Myrick, R.D. (1993). *Developmental guidance and counseling: A practical approach* (2nd ed). Minneapolis, MN: Educational Media Corporation, 2-3.

National Occupational Information Coordinating Committee. (1989). *National Career Development Guidelines Worksheet.* Washington, D.C.: Author

National Center for Education Statistics (1999). *Dropout rates in the United States, 1999. Introduction.* Retrieved March 28, 2003, from http://nces.ed.gov.pubs2001/dropout/introduction.asp

Rothstein, R. (2002, October 9). Lessons: Dropout rate is climbing and likely to go higher. *New York Times.* Retrieved December 8, 2002 from http://query.nytimes.com/search/restricted/article?res=F30F1FF73A5F0C7A8CDDA90994

Steinberg, L. (1996). *Beyond the classroom-why school reform has failed and what parents need to do.* New York: Touchstone.

U.S. Dept. of Education, *Consumer Guide* (No.16, March 1996) *National Institute on the education of at-risk students: High school dropout rates.* Washington, D.C.: Author. Retrieved April 30, 2002, from http://www.ed.gov/pubs/OR/ConsumerGuides/dropout.html

Washington State Minimum High School Graduation Requirements (WAC 180-51-061), effective Fall 2004 for entering ninth graders. Retrieved fromhttp://www.leg.wa.gov/wac/
The full set of graduation requirements may be found at the (Washington State Board of Education) SBE website: www.sbe.wa.gov

Young, B.A. & Hoffman, L. (2002). *Public high school dropouts and completers from the common core data: School years 1991-92 through 1997-98*. National Center for Educational Statistics, U.S. Department of Education. Retrieved January 10, 2003, from http://nces.ed.gov/pubs2002quarterly/summer/3-5.asp

Zunker, V.G. (1998). *Career counseling—Applied concepts in life planning*. New York: Brooks/Cole Publishing Company, 246.

Unfocused Kids:

Helping Students to Focus
on Their Education and Career Plans

A Resource for Educators

Suzy Mygatt Wakefield, Editor
Howard Sage, Associate Editor
Doris Rhea Coy, Assistant Editor
Tami Palmer, Assistant Editor

Part I

Societal Trends and Workplace Issues

Part I, Societal Trends and Workplace Issues, incorporates salient societal and workplace issues impinging on high school students, such as the purported climbing dropout rate, the number of disengaged students in school, and the changing workplace configuration from the old pyramid style of corporations (with many entry level positions at the bottom) to the diamond-shaped configuration, with far fewer positions for unskilled workers.

(1) *"Unfocused Kids" tend to Choose "the Path of Least Resistance"* — Mygatt Wakefield discusses "unfocused kids" with their typical disengaged behavior and the poor choices they make as a result. She discusses several contributing factors: parental styles, achievement attributional styles, peer influence, long work hours, and participation in multiple activities.

(2) *The Importance of Career Guidance and Employability Skills for All Students* — Mygatt Wakefield emphasizes the need to work together (educators in partnership with community members) to provide appropriate career guidance activities for all students and awareness of employability skills, required for survival in today's workplace.

(3) *Dreams Can Come True — Building a K-12 Career Development System that Inspires Hope* — Jensen and Madison present a hypothetical K-12 career development program to be taught collaboratively by school counselors and teachers/advisors. They emphasize that all students need grade-appropriate career guidance activities and the opportunity to develop a meaningful *high school + education plan, career portfolio* and *culminating project*.

(4) *Aligning Student Planning with the Changing Workplace* — Feller discusses the changing configuration of the workplace from a pyramid to a diamond-shape and implications for unskilled workers, and the need to align student planning in light of this change.

(5) *Factors that Influence Women and Minorities to Choose High-Tech Careers* — Yohon and Carlson discuss the under-representation of women and minorities in high tech training programs as well as careers and the importance of their being more equitably represented.

Chapter One

"Unfocused Kids" Tend to Choose "the Path of Least Resistance"

Suzy Mygatt Wakefield

Abstract

This opening chapter offers insight into the behavior of disengaged "unfocused kids" and their issues—their apparent unwillingness or inability to focus on school, often due to peer influence; working long hours; or being overly involved in activities. Parents provide the greatest influence on teens' achievement. Different parenting styles are defined by Steinberg (1996), who suggests that disengaged parents tend to produce disengaged teens. When school becomes too difficult or they fall behind in credits, many of these teens tend to drop out of school—with the consequence of qualifying only for low-skilled, low-paying, dead end jobs. On the other hand, just going to college does not necessarily mean that teens will be successful either. It is important for educators (and parents) to provide needed one-on-one support and guidance to help teens make sound educational decisions instead of allowing them to choose "the path of least resistance".

"Unfocused Kids" and their Issues

> Two decades ago, a teacher in an average high school in this country could expect to have three or four 'difficult' students in a class of thirty. Today, teachers in these same schools are expected to teach to classrooms in which nearly half of the students are uninterested. (Steinberg, 1996, p. 184)

A purpose of this opening chapter is to describe "unfocused kids" and their prevalent issues. Fundamentally, "unfocused kids" are students who appear to have done very little purposeful thinking about why they are in school (except to socialize and "get by" with minimum effort). They also appear to have put little thought into what they want to do with their lives, as far as planning ahead. They tend to go through high school without a clear sense of educational focus or purpose. Most do at least the minimum to stay on track towards graduation, although dropout statistics tell us that many do not even do that (Bylsma & Ireland, 2002; Greene, 2002; Mortenson, 2001). They do not appear to connect what they are learning in school with what really matters to them—their lives outside of school. Many have apparently lost hope in school's value for them (Snyder, Feldman, Shorey & Rand, 2002). If they do not see value in what they are learning in terms of their personal goals, they appear to expend minimum effort, becoming academic underachievers. Brophy (1998) describes student motivation as "the degree to which students invest attention and effort in various pursuits, which may or may not be the ones desired by their teachers" (p. 3). Not only do unfocused, unmotivated students appear to invest little effort in pursuits having to do with their formal schooling, but they may also show little interest in career guidance activities, as they do not see their relevance.

There may be other reasons that students do not focus on their plans after high school or make little connection to their future. They may come from homes where preoccupied parents or guardians spend little time helping them think through their future plans, let alone take an interest in their grades, their friends, and their activities. These teens may not feel that anyone really cares; the adults around them may appear to be so busy that they do not take time to sit down with their teens and help them think through their options. Adults often counter that it's the "school's responsibility" to provide career guidance. As Schneider and Stevenson (1999) point out, parents believe that "...the major responsibility for helping adolescents select a career path and take the appropriate steps to get there rests with the school" (p.165). On the other hand, teens may be resistant or just indifferent to any efforts adults do offer to help them think about their futures. They themselves may be so busy, with going to school, involvement in after-school activities, and work responsibilities that they simply have little time left over to sit down and think about their plans, let alone talk them over with someone else. They may not even think their thoughts about their future are worthy of someone else's time so they are reluctant to discuss them. If there is no comprehensive career exploration and planning program at their school for all students, the problem is compounded.

One wonders, when looking in on a typical American classroom, why some students appear focused and purposefully occupied with the teacher and classroom activities, while others seem so unfocused and preoccupied.

They may pass notes to their friends, or stare into space, or simply sleep at their desks. In this country of remarkable opportunity, what is going on? How is it that we have so many adolescents in high school who appear so disengaged and unfocused? Even educators with many years of experience appear to be puzzled about this strange phenomenon—the increasing number of unfocused, unmotivated students.

Laurence Steinberg, in his book *Beyond the Classroom—Why School Reform has Failed and What Parents Need to Do* (1996), has provided considerable insight as to what is going on behind the scenes. His fundamental premise is that we cannot reform public school education in this country by simply analyzing and revitalizing how teachers teach and what curriculum is taught. He suggests that the forces on students *outside of school* must be considered; they usually are not. "Our findings suggest that the sorry state of American student achievement is due more to the conditions of students' lives outside of school than it is to what takes place within school walls"(p. 184). Based on extensive research involving Temple University, Stanford, and the University of Wisconsin, with two years of planning and pilot testing and four years of data analysis, a team of researchers (including psychologists, sociologists, psychiatrists, and educational researchers), studied more than 20,000 teenagers and their families in nine reasonably typical school districts (none were extreme or atypical) in two states (California and Wisconsin) during 1987-88, 1988-89, and 1989-90. The students were not necessarily high risk or exceptional in any way. They were typical of American teens everywhere.

The results of this comprehensive study of outside-of-school variables indicated that many forces may be at play simultaneously in the lives of teens. These include: the effect of *parenting styles* (i.e., authoritarian, permissive, authoritative, and disengaged or "checked out"); *students' own healthy and unhealthy achievement attributional styles* (that is, some students may see their achievements as a result of hard work and consistent effort, which is a healthy attributional style incorporating variables under their control, while others may see their occasional good grades as a result of luck, a favorable teacher, an easy assignment, or their native intelligence — that is, an unhealthy attributional style based on variables not under their control); the *positive and negative impact of peer cultures; the adverse impact of working more than 20 hours per week*; and *the constant pressure on American adolescents to be involved in many activities at the same time*, besides keeping up and/or excelling in their classes. In all, it is suggested that these variables combine to make our students far less competitive in the global marketplace than their Asian and European counterparts, who, in the aggregate, must prioritize school, take a much longer school day (including attending school on Saturdays), take more difficult academic subjects, spend more time studying, work very few hours outside of school, and limit their socializing. American teens would undoubtedly find these expectations and limitations unpleasant, if not downright intolerable.

Regarding the number of hours American high school students work, the Education Trust (2001) reports that:

> The amount of time students spend at work, particularly in the senior year, is a uniquely American phenomenon. More than half of US twelfth graders (55 percent) report working three or more hours daily at a paid job, three times the international average. No other advanced country expects students to work, or permits them to work long hours at low-skill jobs just to earn spending money (p.6).

Clearly, working long hours is a detriment to most students' ability to excel in their class work in school. Students in Europe and Asia seem to have more restricted work hours, which would contribute substantially to their being able to focus much more on academic achievement.

Steinberg (1996) discusses the construct of "engagement," which is:

> the degree to which students are psychologically 'connected' to what is going on in their classes...When highly engaged students are in class, they are there emotionally as well as physically. They concentrate on the task at hand, they strive to do their best when tested or called upon, and when they are given homework or other outside assignments, they do them on time and in good faith. They participate actively in class discussions, think about the material covered in their course, and genuinely care about the quality of their work (p. 15).

Disengaged students present quite a different picture, as many public educators in America are aware. Disengaged students do what they need to do to stay out of trouble and to get by, exerting minimum effort in class and doing little homework. Steinberg suggests that about 40 percent of students are just going through the motions of going to school: "According to their own reports, between one-third and 40 percent of students say that when they are in class, they are neither trying very hard nor paying attention" (p. 67).

The Importance of Parents on Student Achievement

The contrast between engaged and disengaged students is stark. One wonders how we have spawned an entire population of disengaged students in most of our public high schools. What forces could be operating on these adolescents? To summarize, Steinberg's major findings are that: a high proportion of students do not take school seriously; time is spent on out-of-school activities that do not reinforce what is being learned in school; the adolescent peer culture tends to devalue school, with the exception of the Asian peer culture that helps peers to succeed in school; and many American parents are just as disengaged from school as are their teens. (p. 19)

This last finding is particularly insightful as Steinberg details four parenting styles: *authoritarian* (rigid, strict, and controlling); *permissive* (accepting, indulgent, and lenient); *authoritative* (accepting, firm, and supportive of developing a child's independence); and *disengaged* (emotionally aloof, and uninvolved with their teen's progress in school, their spare time activities, or their friends). Steinberg speculates that 25-30 percent of parents are in this last category (p. 119), which results in so many students being absent from school and eventually dropping out. To determine parental attitudes, the researchers asked probing questions to assess how involved parents were in various aspects of their child's life — their spare time activities, their friends, and so forth. It is an interesting coincidence that some researchers suggest that our high school dropout rate is about 30 percent (Greene, 2002; Mortenson, 2001), reflecting almost exactly the percentage of disengaged parents determined by Steinberg. As high school counselors, teachers, or administrators, it is easy for us to assume that most parents are involved with their teens as so many seem to contact the school. In fact, some parents never do! Steinberg tells us that "only about one-fifth of parents consistently attend school programs. More than 40 percent *never* do" (p. 20). Steinberg also shares that research shows over and over, if parents are involved with their teens, their students do better in school. A key reason is that:

> ...acceptance seems to matter most for children's overall adjustment and sense of self-worth; because they feel loved, they feel lovable. As a result, children who feel valued and supported by their parents have higher self-esteem, more positive self-conceptions, and a happier, more enthusiastic outlook on life. Not surprisingly, they are more sociable and more socially skilled...(p. 109).

When parents are involved, their teens feel accepted and valued. Quattrociocchi (2000) frequently emphasizes this point in her writing and presentations to educators and parents by pointing out that "research shows that parental involvement is the single greatest factor in determining student success. Teens with highly involved families are three times more likely than their peers to earn a bachelor's degree or to complete other post-secondary programs"(p.2).

Other Influences on Achievement: Peer Groups, Work Hours, and Multiple Activities

> Nearly 20 percent of all students say they do not try as hard as they can in high school because they are worried about what their friends might think (Steinberg, 1996, p. 19).

As remarkable as this finding may appear, many educators and parents are aware of this negative peer influence on American students. Steinberg found that peer groups could have both a positive and a negative effect on student achievement, and that teens are particularly vulnerable to peer influence between the ages of twelve through sixteen. When looking at peer influence in all four predominant peer groups (Asian, White, Black and Hispanic), Steinberg found that:

> Specifically, Asian students' friends have higher performance standards (that is, they hold tougher standards for what grades are acceptable), spend more time on homework, are more committed to education, and earn considerably higher grades in school. Black and Hispanic students' friends earn lower grades, spend less time on their studies, and have substantially lower performance standards. White students' friends fall somewhere between these two extremes on these various indicators (p. 157).

Steinberg has further found that in Asian peer groups, students frequently turn to each other for academic support in their classes while this is rarely done in White, Black, or Hispanic peer groups. In fact, the opposite appears to be true for Black and Latino students, "who are far more likely than other students to find themselves in peer groups that actually devalue academic accomplishment" (p. 158). The reason is that scholastic success is equated with "selling out" one's ethnic and cultural identity to White, middle class values.

Working long hours may be detrimental to school achievement, particularly if students work more than 20 hours per week, according to Steinberg. Students who work long hours often do not have the energy left over to focus on their classes and class assignments, as educators are acutely aware. Most students do not, in fact, work to "save for college" but tend to

12

spend the money on their personal expenses. Worse, most students are not engaged in jobs that will help them explore a potential career interest. Very few jobs offer training that will be transferable to adult jobs as most teens work in restaurants, supermarkets, and retail stores. Steinberg gives a grim picture of employers' stranglehold on teenage workers, indicating that some major employers of teenagers lobby assiduously to keep child labor laws flexible; they also wage a public relations campaign "designed to convince American parents and students that adolescents somehow reap characterological, if not moral, benefits from spending their afternoons and evenings flipping hamburgers, stuffing burritos, and operating cash registers" (p. 167). Teens may receive little support from employers when asked to work longer hours than is beneficial for their progress in school, although a number of American employers may be sensitive to students' academic demands and limit their job responsibilities accordingly.

State laws may serve to restrict students' working hours somewhat. Normally a 16- or 17-year old cannot work more than 20 hours per week, without a signed variance (by a parent, a school official, and the employer), but variances for working 40 or more hours a week are granted. According to the Department of Labor and Industries in Washington State:

> For 16- and 17-year old students who want or need to work more than four hours a day and 20 hours per week, there is a special variance. The variance requires approval by the student's employer, parent, and school. The maximum is 28 hours a week, 6-hour shift lengths and limited to 16- and 17-year-olds during the school year in non-agriculture employmentÖAdditional variances may be granted by Labor and Industries. The request for a standard variance is originated by the employer. The variances can be granted up to and beyond 40 hours a week, 8-hour shift lengths and start and finish times during school and non-school weeks (Department of Labor and Industries Brochure—*Teen Workers*).

Another powerful force on teens is the pressure to participate in multiple activities. Some teens are involved in so many activities, particularly athletic activities, that their schoolwork suffers. Practice before and after school not only uses valuable study time but may leave a student exhausted and unable to concentrate on difficult academic material. Students and their coaches need to be honest about what makes up a reasonable amount of participation, although some coaches highly encourage and expect strong academic achievement, and students may be given team awards for their collective outstanding academic achievement by their local and state athletic associations. In Washington State, the Washington Interscholastic Activities Association (W.I.A.A.) makes these team awards possible. Teams with the highest cumulative grade point averages are honored by the state association. Coaches are encouraged to send in their team members grades; the cumulative grade point averages of winning teams are made known to the public, thus encouraging academic achievement throughout the sports programs (*WIAA 2002-2003 Handbook*).

American high school students are known for spending a lot of time socializing with their friends, in addition to being involved in multiple activities and/or working long hours. It adds up. The national average for time spent on homework, according to Steinberg is less than five hours per week (p. 180), hardly competitive with European and Asian adolescents. Recently in Seattle, Nathan Hale High School administrators decided to start school one hour later, from 7:45 AM to 8:45 AM, so that students could get an extra hour of sleep. However, the change ran into resistance as many were concerned that "team sports, such as baseball and fast-pitch softball, will not have enough daylight to finish their games, or that they will conflict with classes" (Jensen, 2003). Many students choose to play a sport each season. Many teams require a minimum grade point average or a passing grade in four or more classes for students to qualify to stay on the team through the season, but sports, like other activities, may take away from needed study time. It's all a matter of priorities. Further, many students feel pressured to list multiple activities on their resumes to be competitive as candidates for selective college admission. Some American high school students seem to want to do it all (sports and/or other school activities, and part-time work) at the expense of excelling in their academic classes.

Lack of Planned, Sequential Career Development Programs

Further, at school, there may not be planned, comprehensive career development programs, integrated at each grade level, to help students think about, identify, and articulate their strengths, interests, and values and to explore the many occupational options in the world of work. Or students may find that the career guidance programs are so few and far between that it is difficult to maintain a sense of continuity between one career presentation and the next. Students may be further discouraged as they may have no mechanism, such as an education and career plan or a career planning portfolio, in which to keep their assignments, papers, and notes. The career guidance program may appear disorganized in many high schools, with no clear guidelines or activities expected of all students. Gysbers (2001) addresses this concern with his vision:

My vision for guidance and counseling in the 21st Century is fully implemented comprehensive guidance and counseling programs in every school district in the United States, serving all students and their parents, staffed by active, involved school counselors. When guidance and counseling is conceptualized, organized, and implemented as a program, it places school counselors conceptually and structurally in the center of education and makes it possible for them to be active and involved. As a result, guidance and counseling becomes an integral and transformative program, not a marginal and supplemental activity. It provides school counselors with the structure, time, and resources to fully use their expertise. (p. 103)

Kuranz (2002) reports that according to ASCA (the American School Counselor Association, 2001) "the average U.S. student-to-counselor ratio is 555:1." With ratios that high, it is virtually impossible for school counselors alone, without the help of other appropriate educators, to provide substantive, systematic, and sequential career guidance activities for all students. The high student-counselor ratios demonstrate the obvious need for sharing this responsibility with appropriate others. In later chapters, several authors will discuss a number of comprehensive, integrated approaches to help students with career development. National leaders in the American School Counselor Association (Campbell & Dahir, 1997; Dahir, Sheldon & Valiga, 1998) have developed the *ASCA National Standards*, student content standards for school counseling programs in the areas of academic, career, and personal/social development. The ASCA National Standards in career development are:
   A) Students will acquire the skills to investigate the world of work in relation to knowledge of self and to make informed career decisions.
   B) Students will employ strategies to achieve future career success and satisfaction.
   C) Students will understand the relationship among personal qualities, education and training, and the world of work. (Campbell & Dahir, 1997, p. 17)

ASCA has developed the *ASCA National Model: A Framework for School Counseling Programs*, (ASCA, 2003) which incorporates a delivery system (for guidance curriculum) with integrated management and accountability systems. According to Bowers and Hatch (2002),

Historically, many school counselors spent much of their time responding to the needs of a small percentage of their students, typically the high achieving or high risk. The National Model for School Counseling Programs recommends the majority of the school counselor's time be spent in direct service to all students so that every student receives the program benefits.

It is hoped that in schools in which these standards and model are put into place that all students will be provided with age-appropriate, sequential, and meaningful career development activities. These carefully planned activities, based on the assessed needs of students, should help them with their career exploration, educational planning and goal-setting, and their academic and technical preparation for their postsecondary education and workplace endeavors.

The "Academic Middle" and High School and College Dropout Rates

In high schools across the country, many students may receive little in the way of career guidance and educational planning. Sadly, a testimony to this lack of career guidance programming is our alleged public high school dropout rate of approximately one in three students (Greene, 2002; Mortenson, 2001), or one in four (Isaacson & Brown, 2000, p. 269), depending on the source. Using the cohort group of students in grades 9-12, a dropout rate of one in three means that means that for every three ninth graders, only two will graduate from high school four years later. The national college dropout rate is about the same: one in three freshmen does not return for the sophomore year (ACT, 2002). The dropout rate in public community and technical colleges after one year is almost one in two! (ACT, 2002) These are disturbing figures, indicating that even many of our college-bound young people do not spend enough time thinking about and planning carefully for their futures, both educationally and financially.

Gray and Herr (1995) suggest that many students from the "academic middle" are encouraged to enter college when they do not really have the strength of academic preparation needed, despite the fact that they have taken "honors" classes. It seems that students in the academic middle are actually enrolled in lower level honors classes that do not really prepare them for the real rigors of college level work. These researchers attribute our high college dropout rate to the "right to try/right to fail" phenomenon that, in turn, creates a sort of massive social inefficiency.

In most countries, the idea of supporting the attendance of large numbers of youth in college who do not have the academic ability and/or preparation to be successful would be unimaginable, and dropout rates of 50% would be intolerable. But this belief is not shared in the United States, at least not yet. Why? First, until recently, the United States was perhaps the only nation that could afford these social inefficiencies. Second, this situation is tolerated because of a basic value that career development specialist Ken Hoyt (1994) calls the 'right to try' and the 'right to fail.' That '1 in 100' individuals who 'battles the odds' and succeeds despite a poor high school record seems always to be in the back of the minds of Americans. (p.34)

Gray and Herr (1995) further share that "Because of open admissions, getting into college is relatively easy, whereas graduating is not. Only about half who matriculate ever graduate in 6 years"(p.109). The other half leave college, often in debt, to look for something else. Krumboltz and Worthington (1999) offer the notion that "floundering" (when students drop out) is not necessarily bad. "Much valuable learning occurs in the trial-and-error work experiences that occur during this interval. However, the learning is haphazard and sometimes results in the learning of self-defeating attitudes and habits"(p. 314). Some students drop out of college when they run out of financial support (often with a loan obligation) and/or realize they have merely acquiesced to the wishes of others. They may realize that they need to think for themselves and make their own way, which may be to work full-time or go into the military, fundamentally to get a chance to mature and to re-evaluate their goals. These students, who have had time to align their ambitions, may return some years later with a much stronger sense of their own commitment and purpose.

Having Aligned, Misaligned or No Clear Ambitions at All

At some level, however, all of our young people do grapple with what they want to do with their lives. They do give some thought about what they want to become—what skills they would like to develop, how they want to earn money, and what sort of lifestyle and friends they would like to have. Some, who have put in a lot of time thinking about their futures, have well-defined goals and realistic plans involving the amount of education and training needed to reach their goals. Schneider and Stevenson (1999) have coined the useful term "aligned ambitions." They would describe these students as having aligned ambitions as they know what goals they want to pursue and have a realistic understanding of the educational pathways required to attain them. Others have well-defined goals but have unrealistic plans about how to achieve them. These students would be described as having "misaligned ambitions." They have articulated goals but erroneous information about how to achieve them. For example, a student who wants to become an attorney might assume that a Master's Degree is required and not understand the requirement of three years of law school, culminating with passing the state bar exam.

Still other young people have very unclear goals; some teens appear to have almost no goals or ambitions that they can articulate. From casual observation, it appears that left unattended, without guidance, this last group of young people will tend to take the "path of least resistance." They will do what makes the most sense to them in their perception of how the world works, from the way they see things. This, of course, may not be the way the world really works, but their unique (and possibly distorted) perceptions will dictate their behavior.

Limited Choice Repertoire

Capuzzi and Gross (1989) suggest that young people who make poor decisions about their lives make choices from their "limited choice repertoire." They report that it is "their selected way of coping with the myriad challenges placed in their path that differentiates at-risk individuals from their peers" (p. 11). Capuzzi and Gross add that their personal circumstances, over which they have little or no control, may impinge greatly on their ability to complete school. These circumstances might include: a dysfunctional, destructive and/or abusive family environment; low family income forcing the student to work; and/or marginal academic ability. These at-risk young people tend to choose what gives them an immediate solution, instead of considering a range of alternatives or soliciting different advice from different people. That is, they demonstrate limited decision-making ability, a lack of significant persons they can go to for help and advice, and/ or limited ability to model successful coping strategies demonstrated by others. Their limited choice repertoire is partly due to a lack of information; they are unaware of the range of choices they have and do not take adequate time to research their options.

Another term for a dysfunctional decision-making style is that of foreclosure—making choices too soon without considering enough appropriate alternatives. A purpose of career development in elementary grades, as well as in the secondary grades, is to help students "avoid premature foreclosure of choices based on inaccurate, incomplete, or biased information and stereotypes" (Herr, 1997). When disengaged, unfocused teens come to high school (which is increasingly more academically difficult for them than were the lower grades) and find that there is really nothing there for them, in terms of their own interests or goals, many choose to leave the public school system, as it is the path of least resistance. It is often reported that many students drop out in their senior year, as is true in the state of Washington, given that only 71.9 percent of seniors at the beginning of the school year in September, 2000 graduated in the spring of 2001. Bylsma & Ireland (2002) confirmed that "grade 12 experienced the largest annual dropout rate."

Reasons given for dropping out, reported in *Graduation and Dropout Statistics for Washington's Counties, Districts, and Schools Final Report, School Year 2001- 2002*, include the following: "expelled or suspended, poor grades, school not for me/stayed home, married and needed to support family, pregnant or had a baby, offered training, chose to work, or other"(Bylsma & Ireland, 2002, p. 9). By far, the greatest number of students who dropped out in their senior year reported "attended 4 years, did not continue." One can speculate why this occurs. As students realize that they have fallen too far behind in credits to graduate with their friends, they opt to leave school before embarrassing themselves with this eventuality. At least, they can get a job, earn money, and do some of the things they want to do. Hoyt (2001, p.7) reports that approximately 22 million of the anticipated 50 million new jobs between the years 1996-2006 will only require 2 to 3 weeks of short-term, on-the-job training, so low-skilled, low wage, dead end jobs abound in the American economy. The downside for young people leaving school for these jobs, if that is what they are leaving for, is that these jobs do not usually provide a living wage; students must pursue further education and training if they wish to qualify for higher paying jobs. One's level of education is closely related to a lifetime salary, as the National Dropout Prevention Center Network points out. Dropouts earn substantially less than those with some college or further training, as the following shows:

> Education is important to employees and employers. Workers without a high school diploma earn approximately $852,000 over a 40-year career. This is $672,000 less than those with an associate degree. A bachelor's degree can increase earning more than $1.9 million over a 40-year period, and a doctorate or professional degree can add more than $2.8 million. (Dolin, 2001, as cited on the National Dropout Prevention Center/ Network)

The Path of Least Resistance

Fritz (1984) gives us a conceptual framework for the path of least resistance. His insights are particularly helpful when working with these young, unfocused students. Fritz uses the metaphor of the river and suggests that, "You are like a river. You go through life taking the path of least resistance." He indicates that it is the layout of a riverbed across a terrain that determines the flow of the river.

> If a riverbed remains unchanged, the water will continue to flow along the path it always has, since that is the most natural route for it to take. If the underlying structures of your life remain unchanged, the greatest tendency is for you to follow the same direction your life has always taken... (p. 5)

This metaphor applies to unfocused young people, who tend to follow the path of least resistance unless there is some sort of intervention that changes the "underlying structure" of their lives. As engineers might excavate a new riverbed to redirect the flow of a river, so educators (and parents) need to support and redirect disengaged young people to help them take charge of the direction of their lives in more productive and positive ways.

The Relationship between an Inadequate Education and Poverty

School is academically challenging, and for many (given their state of readiness to learn), too challenging. Adelman and Taylor (2002) report disturbing findings across the country when they surveyed teachers with the question, "Most days, how many of your students come to class motivationally ready and able to learn?" Their results indicated that,

> In urban and rural schools serving economically disadvantaged families, teachers tell us they are lucky if 10 percent to 15 percent of their students fall into this group. In surburbia, teachers usually say 75 percent fit that profile. It is not surprising, therefore, that teachers are continuously asking for helping in dealing with problems. (p.235)

These are disturbing findings, showing the basis of why so many students may ultimately drop out of school, if there are no safety nets (remedial courses, small classes, alternative programs, adult mentors, tutoring, and so forth) in place to help keep them in school. Adelman and Taylor (2002) further report that, "The litany of barriers is all too familiar to anyone who lives or works in communities where families struggle with low income. In such neighborhoods, school and community resources often are insufficient for providing the basic opportunities (never mind enrichment activities) found in higher income communities" (p. 236). Dropout rates are about the same for males and females but are higher for students from different ethnic groups and for students from disadvantaged backgrounds. (U.S Dept of Education/*Consumer Guide*, 1996) According to the National Center for Education Statistics (NCES, 2001),

> In 1999, young adults living in families with incomes in the lowest 20 percent of all family incomes were five times as likely as their peers from families in the top 20 percent of the income distribution to drop out of high school.

Put another way, according to NCES, (1996):

> The annual event dropout rates for students with family incomes in the lowest 20 percent of the family income distribution range from 4.5 to 11 times the dropout rates recorded for students with family incomes in the top 20 percent of the family income distribution.

These are concerning data from NCES, clearly demonstrating the clear relationship between income and schooling. Those in the higher income brackets have a far better chance of completing their high school education. From this information, one can infer that income is a greater predictor of high school completion than is ethnicity.

The Working Poor

The New York Times (Pear, 2002) ran a headline recently declaring "Number of People living in Poverty Increases in U.S." (www.nytimes.com/ 2002/09/25/national) According to the Census Bureau, "Of the 32.9 million poor people in the United States last year, 11.7 million were under 18, and 3.4 million were 65 or older." According to this source, poor people, or the working poor, are defined in this way:

> A family of four was classified as poor if it had cash income less than $18,104 last year. The official poverty levels, updated each year to reflect changes in the Consumer Price Index, were $14,128 for a family of three, $11,569 for a married couple, and $9,039 for an individual.

It is important to make the connection between the number of students who drop out of school who then may become part of the working poor, thus contributing to the poverty rates in this country. We are presumably losing one out of three students from our public school system from grades 9 through 12 (Mortenson, 2001; Greene, 2002), although some believe that we are losing only one in four (Isaacson & Brown, 2000, p. 269), as was true about 20 years ago. Either way, we are losing *far too many* students from the public education system.

Herbert (2001), a New York Times writer, reflected on Barbara Ehrenreich's book *Nickel and Dimed: On (Not) Getting by in America,* (as cited in *Encore Magazine,* June, 2002) which captures the frustration of adults who cannot earn above the minimum wage (or poverty) level.

> The poor are pretty well hidden from everyone except each other in the United States. You won't find them in the same neighborhoods or the same schools as the well-to-do. They're not on television, except for the local crime-casts....Hiding the poor has been quite a trick, because there are still millions upon millions of them out here...(p. 7)

As is widely recognized, adults and their children living at the poverty level may not have enough food, even with food stamps, or be able to get needed medical care. They may be evicted from their housing, and their utilities may be disconnected. Many adults, locked in at minimum wages due to their low skills, must work two or three jobs, on evenings and week-ends, to try to make ends meet. This is reality for millions of adult Americans.

Boomerang Effect—"Adultolescents"

We have a relatively new phenomenon in this country—the phenomenon of "adultolescents." These are young people who choose (and are allowed) to remain with their parents or guardians, after most of their peers have chosen to be on their own. Many parents and guardians believe that if their graduating seniors "go off to college," or a postsecondary training program (assuming that they even graduate from high school), that their futures will be somewhat secure. Some parents then experience a sort of "boomerang effect"—their youngsters leave home to attend college only to return after a year or so to live at home again, while they are sorting out their priorities. Adultolescents—young adults still living at home, were featured recently in *Newsweek* (Tyre, 2002), which reports that there are four million young adults, ages 25-34, living with their parents:

Whether it's reconverting the guest room back into a bedroom, paying for graduate school, writing a blizzard of small checks to cover rent and health-insurance premiums or acting as career counselors, parents across the country are trying to provide their twenty-somethings with the tools they'll need to be self-sufficient—someday. In the process, they have created a whole new breed of child—the "adultolescent"...Relying on your folks to light the shadowy path to the future has become so accepted that even the ultimate loser move—returning home to live with your parents—has lost its stigma.(p.39)

Conclusion

Unfocused, disengaged students need extra support in developing their future plans. As suggested, some may end up as young adults, living at home long after most of their peers have moved out on their own. Unfocused young people need adults who care about them and who will take the needed time to guide them, one-on-one (this is the best form of help). While they are in school, they may need help with placing limitations on their work hours and participation in non-academic activities. They may need help with study skills and understanding that they are in control of their academic achievement. That is, their achievement level is not dependent on luck but is related to factors under their control—the amount of time they are willing to study and do their assignments, and the willingness to get help when they need it, instead of just ignoring the problem. Unfocused students need to be *encouraged* to get help when they feel they need it.

Should they choose to drop out of school, they need to understand that this choice may conscript them to working at low-skill, low-wage jobs for many years and may even lead to some becoming part of the working poor. To prevent this discouraging eventuality, students need to be encouraged to obtain further training, particularly at public or private community or technical colleges. Gray and Herr (1995) report that "technical workers are the fastest-growing and economically most promising segment in the labor force," and "the largest number and fastest growing group of jobs among technical workers can be trained for at the 2-year associate degree level" (p. 109). Even on-line "distance learning" technical training programs are available. (High Tech Learning Centers website: http://www.hightechlearning.org./overview/advisory_board.html)

Several authors in this book will present approaches to help students focus on their plans after high school. Perry will discuss the *Real Game*

Series as a "hook" to grab the interest of "unfocused kids." Forster will discuss the Dependable Strengths Articulation Model as a decision-making process based on identified strengths. Sage will explain the important role of parents in their teen's career development and planning. Hoyt will discuss the many educational options available to teens. Many useful approaches have been thoughtfully presented in this book to help educators (and parents) confront and help our growing population of disengaged, "unfocused kids" before they make costly and unfortunate decisions regarding their futures.

References

ACT National Dropout Rates, 1983 to 2002. Retrieved August 22, 2002, from www.postsecondary.org/archives/Reports/ Spreadsheets?ACT%20Natinal%20Dropo

Adelman, H.S., & Taylor, L. (April, 2002). School counselors and school reform: new directions. *Professional School Counseling, 5*(4), 235-248.

American School Counselor Association (2003). American School Counselor Association *National Model: A framework for school counseling programs.* Alexandria, VA: Author.

Bowers, J. L., & Hatch, P. A. (2002*). Draft: The national model for school counseling programs.* Alexandria, VA: The American School Counselor Association. Retrieved August 15, 2002 from http:// www.schoolcounselor.org

Brophy, J. (1998). *Motivating students to learn.* Boston: McGraw Hill Publishers.

Bylsma, P. & Ireland, L. (2002). *Graduation and dropout statistics for Washington's counties, districts, and schools. Final report, school year 2000-01.* Olympia, WA: Office of the Superintendent of Public Instruction.

Capuzzi, D., & Gross, D.R. (1989). *Youth at risk: A resource for counselors, teachers and* parents. Alexandria, VA: American Association for Counseling and Development

Campbell, C.A., & Dahir, C.A. (1997). *American School Counselor Association Sharing the Vision. The national standards for school counseling programs.* Alexandria, VA: American School Counselor Association.

Dahir, C.A., Sheldon, C.B., & Valiga, M.J. (1998). *Vision into action: Implementing the national standards for school counseling programs.* Alexandria, VA: American School Counselor Association.

Department of Labor of Industries (Washington State) (n.d.) *Teen workers have two jobs.* [Brochure] Olympia, WA: Author.

Education Trust, Inc. (2001). The lost opportunity of the senior year: Finding a better way. *Summary of findings.* Retrieved March 28, 2003, from http://www.commissionontheserioryear.org/Report/report.html

Fritz, R. (1984). *The path of least resistance.* New York: Fawcett Columbine.

Gray, C.G., & Herr, E.L. (1995). *Other ways to win: Creating alternatives for high school graduates.* Thousand Oaks: Corwin Press, Inc.

Greene, J.P. (2002). *Graduation rates in Washington state.* New York: Manhattan Institute for Policy Research. Retrieved December 19, 2002 from http://www.manhattan-institute.org/html/cr_27.htm

Gysbers, N.C. (2001). School guidance and counseling in the 21st century: Remember the past into the future. *Professional School Counseling,* 5 (2). p.103.

Herbert, R. (July 30, 2001). Unmasking the poor. (Op-ed.) *New York Times,* In *Encore Magazine,* (July 2002), 6, (Issue 4). Seattle, WA: Encore Media Group, 7.

Herr, E.L. (1997). *Career development and work-bound youth.* University of North Carolina at Greensboro, NC: ERIC/CASS (ED051199)

High Tech Learning Centers, (n.d.) *Overview of high tech learning centers program.* Retrieved February 11, 2003, from http://www.hightechlearning.org./overview/advisory_board.html

Hoyt, K.B. (2001). Helping high school students broaden their knowledge of postsecondary options. *Professional School Counseling*, *5*(1), 6-12.

Isaacson, L.E. & Brown, D. (2000). *Career information, career counseling, and career Development.* Boston: Allyn & Bacon.

Jensen, J.J. (2003, Jan. 29). Seattle high school to let pupils sleep in. *The Seattle Times.* Retrieved January 29, 2003, from http://seattletimes.nwsource.com/cgi-PrintStory.pl?document_id=134623821&zsection

Krumboltz, J.D. & Worthington, R.L. (June 1999). The school-to-work transition from a learning theory perspective. *The Career Development Quarterly, 47*(4), 312-325.

Kuranz, M. (2002). Cultivating student potential. *Professional School Counseling, 5*(3),172-179.

Mortenson, T.G. (2001, June). High school graduation trends and patterns 1981-2000. *Postsecondary Education Opportunity*, 108, (2).

National Center for Education Statistics. (1996). *Dropout rates in the United States, 1996:* Event, status, and cohort dropout rates.Washington, D.C.: US Department of Education. Retrieved November 2, 2002, from http://www.nces.ed.gov/pubs98/dropout/98250-05.html

National Center for Education Statistics. (2001). *Dropout rates in the United States, 1999.* Executive summary. Washington, D.C: U.S. Department of Education. Retrieved June 2, 2002, from http:///www.nces.ed.gov/pubs2001/dropout/introduction.asp)

National Dropout Prevention Center/Network. Career education/workforce readiness *overview (Dolin, 2001).* Retrieved February 14, 2002, from http://www.dropoutprevention.org/effstrat/careered_work/career_over.htm

Pear, R. (2002, Sept 25). Number of people living in poverty increases in U.S. *New York Times.* Retrieved November 25, 2002, from http://www.nytimes.com/2002/09/25/national /

Quattrociocchi, S.M. (2000). *Help! A family's guide to high school and beyond.* Olympia, WA: Washington State Workforce Training and Education Coordinating Board.

Schneider, B. & Stevenson, D. (1999). *The ambitious generation—America's teenagers:Motivated but directionless.* New Haven: Yale University Press.

Snyder, C.R., Feldman, D.B., Shorey, H.S. & Rand, K.L. (2002). Hopeful choices: A school counselor's guide to hope theory. *Professional School Counseling, 5,* 298-307.

Steinberg, L. (1996). *Beyond the classroom-why school reform has failed and what parents need to do.* New York: Touchstone.

Tyre, Peg. (2002, March 25). Bringing up adultolescents. *Newsweek,* 39-40. U.S. Dept. of Education, *Consumer Guide* (No.16, March 1996) *National Institute on the education of at-risk students*: *High school dropout rates.* Washington, D.C.: Author. Retrieved April 30, 2002, from http://www.ed.gov/pubs/OR/ConsumerGuides/dropout.html

Washington Interscholastic Activities Association (WIAA). 2002-2003 Handbook. Renton, WA: Author.

Chapter Two

The Importance of Career Guidance and Employability Skills for *All* Students

Suzy Mygatt Wakefield

Abstract

A distinction is made between the terms *school counseling* and *school guidance* to help clarify why career guidance is both a school and community responsibility. Students need career guidance programs to explore their strengths, interests, and career options and to learn about employability skills. Career education began as a concept in the early 1970s, followed by the National Career Development Guidelines (1989), the SCANS Report (1991) and School-to-Work Opportunities Act (1994). The SCANS Report "Personal Qualities" address employability skills—those non-technical skills that help employees be successful in the workplace. The American School Counselor Association developed the *ASCA National Standards* in 1997 (student content standards for school counseling programs in academic, career, and personal/social development) and the *ASCA National Model: A Framework for School Counseling Programs* in 2003 (a framework for delivery, management and accountability systems). A number of approaches, including state graduation requirements, are also discussed.

Career Guidance

Career guidance is a responsibility that belongs both to schools and to communities. Providing appropriate career guidance activities and teaching employability skills to all students is a daunting responsibility; no one professional (either in the schoolhouse or in the community) can do it alone. Educators need to work together and need to marshal appropriate community resources to help young people with career guidance issues. Teens need to learn about the vast array of occupational choices as well as their own strengths and interests, what jobs are really like, and what employability skills are essential to be successful in the workplace (such as communicating clearly, understanding and following instructions, being a good team member, and getting along with others). Many resources are available to provide guidelines for school career guidance programs, including the National Career Development Guidelines (1989), the SCANS Report (1991), the ASCA *National Standards* (Campbell & Dahir 1997; Dahir, Sheldon & Valiga 1998) and the *ASCA National Model: A Framework for School Counseling Programs* (ASCA, 2003). There are also Internet career development systems, such as the government-sponsored electronic revision of the DOT, the O*NET, at www.online.onetcenter.org.

Distinction between School Guidance and School Counseling

In the field of school guidance and counseling, one of the more blurred concepts is the distinction between *school counseling* and *school guidance.* Myrick (1993) draws the distinction in his text, *Developmental Guidance and Counseling: A Practical Approach* (Second Edition), in which he devotes two pages to clarifying the terms. Understanding the difference between these two terms is critical to understanding the effective delivery of career guidance programs in schools, utilizing community resources (partnerships, job shadows, internships, etc.). As Myrick (1993) indicates, guidance "is a term in education that has been flip-flopped with the word 'counseling' for more than 50 years" (p. 2). Myrick draws the distinction in this way:

> More traditionally, guidance is an 'umbrella' term which encompasses a constellation of services aimed at personal and career development and school adjustment. These services are commonly delivered by professional educators, such as teachers or counselors, although other support personnel may be involved. (p.2)

> ...Counseling has been perceived as a process in which someone who has a problem receives personal assistance, usually though a private discussion....There is a trust relationship in which the focus is on personal meaning of events and experiences. Rather than rely on general interpretations of information or behaviors, counseling focuses more on personal awareness, interests, attitudes, and goals...Counseling is considered a professional endeavor by a professionally trained and certified person. (p.3)

Conceptually, these distinctions must be understood when providing career guidance for all students, as many professional educators need to be involved in this endeavor. Traditionally, school counselors (with their burgeoning caseloads) have been asked to provide virtually the entire career guidance program for all students, because school counselor training includes at least one graduate course in career development. This coursework technically qualifies the school counselor to teach career guidance. Unfortunately for students, this perception has also led to the school counselor being seen as the *only* professional in the schoolhouse who should teach career guidance, which has led to hundreds of thousands of students who either graduate or otherwise leave the school system with little to no career guidance, unless they have come from a school system with a comprehensive guidance and counseling program, incorporating career guidance competencies. In these comprehensive programs, students may have an opportunity to complete education and career plans, career portfolios, job shadows, internships, service learning (volunteer experiences), and other hands-on career guidance activities. (It should be noted that students can also be encouraged to choose paid jobs that help them to explore a specific career interest instead of working in meaningless jobs.) All appropriate educators and community members can contribute to a comprehensive career guidance program, while school counselors can help to design it, take certain aspects of it as their own responsibility, and follow up with students with personal counseling as needed.

The History of Career Education

Career education is an effort aimed at refocusing American education and the actions of the broader community in ways that will help individuals acquire and utilize the knowledge, skills, and attitudes necessary for each to make work a meaningful, productive and satisfying part of his or her way of living. (Hoyt, 1977, as cited in Isaacson & Brown, 2000, p. 233)

In an e-mail memo (personal communication dated 3/11/03), Dr. Hoyt stated, "My definition of 'Career Education' is as follows: Career Education is the total effort of the education system and the broader community to help all persons (1) become familiar with the values of a work oriented society, (2) to integrate those values into their personal value systems, and (3) implement them in their lives in such a way that work becomes (a) possible, (b) meaningful and (c) satisfying to each individual."

As a concept, career education began about 30 years ago in this country. It was a career guidance concept in that all appropriate educators were assigned certain aspects of it. In career education, concepts were infused into the classroom curriculum, which was called *career education infusion* (Zunker, 1998, p. 246). Career education infusion required that teachers expand their educational objectives to include career-related activities and subjects in the course of teaching their regular curriculum, so that students could see the connection to the real world, particularly in relation to occupations. According to Isaacson & Brown (1997, p. 12), career education included taking field trips, having guest speakers in classrooms, establishing career internships and apprenticeships, and setting up simulated career laboratories.

Sidney P. Marland, Secretary of Health, Education, and Welfare under President Richard Nixon, is generally credited with coining the term, although Dr. Kenneth B. Hoyt is credited with popularizing the concept. According to Baker and Taylor (1998, p. 376), career education developed initially as a concept to apply early career development theory. Marland (1974, as cited in Isaacson & Brown, 2000, p. 234) described the eight elements of career education (as identified by the Center for Research in Vocational Education at Ohio State University) to include: career awareness; self-awareness; appreciations, attitudes; decision-making skills; economic awareness; skills awareness and beginning competence; employability skills; and educational awareness.

One wonders how such a well-conceived program could have lost momentum and support. Apparently, according to Isaacson & Brown (2000, p. 234), "By the mid-1980's, most of the remnants of the career education movement had been swept from American schools by the back-to-basics educational movement." Back-to-basics advocates felt that career education experiences (e.g., learning about occupations and taking field trips) took time away from the more important core subjects. In addition, there were some mistakes in the design and implementation of career education programs, including funding with "soft" money that would not be continued, added workload responsibilities for teachers, the term *career education* being confused with *vocational education* (so middle class parents were concerned that their students might be directed to a non -college goal), and sketchy local political support (Isaacson & Brown, 2000, p. 234). As a result of these earlier mistakes, there is now a better understanding that career development programs must be carefully conceptualized, planned, implemented and evaluated. Parents need to understand that the concept does not direct their students to "vocational education" or away from college (technical training is now often part of a college education).

As Quattrociocchi (2000, p. 9) suggests, if students can find out what they love to do, "what they love and do most easily will make the best careers for them." In her *Call to Parents* brochure, she adds, "When teens know what they love to do, and what they're good at, they are more likely to succeed than teens who have not explored their interests and abilities." This is a crucial point. When young people have explored their own interests, have developed some of their abilities and understand what abilities may have considerable potential, they can develop a much more focused approach to figuring out what they want to do with their lives. Teens who have not developed this foundation appear to spend a lot of time floundering.

Walz and Benjamin (1984, as cited in Isaacson & Brown, 2000, p. 235) listed several characteristics that would contribute to a systemic career development program. These characteristics recommend that the program should be: organized and planned by a team of knowledgeable professionals, parents, and community members; inclusive of age-appropriate materials and learning experiences with program delivery carefully articulated across grade levels; based on student needs; designed around clearly stated measurable objectives; prepared with an evaluation plan that measures goal achievement and the value of processes used in the program; and delivered by skilled personnel who are able to use a variety of resources and strategies to achieve program objectives. These are the suggested critical components that make up a strong and enduring career development program for students.

Baker and Taylor (1998, p. 376) note that there have been numerous efforts to translate the idea of career education into action, at times with the assistance of private and public funding. Although the concept of a national education system centered on a career development theme is not yet a reality, many examples of this can be found in local school districts. Indeed, the concept of career education has had a profound impact on the way career development is taught in American schools. Dr. Hoyt is still credited for being a vigorous advocate for the concept.

National Career Development Guidelines (1989)

According to Zunker (1998, pp. 17-18), in 1976, the National Occupational Information Coordinating Committee (NOICC) was established by an act of Congress and was supported by four federal agencies: the Bureau of Labor Statistics, the Employment and Training Administration, the Office of Vocational and Adult Education, and the National Center for Education Statistics. The NOICC had four defined functions, including: developing an occupational information system with information on employment and training programs at federal, state, and local levels; assisting in the operation of State Occupational Information Coordination Committees (SOICCs); assisting users in sharing occupational information; and providing labor market information for youth. Later the NOICC sponsored a project to establish national career counseling and development guidelines "to encourage the development of career guidance standards at the state and local levels" (p. 18).

In the late 1980s, the NOICC (National Occupational Information Coordinating Committee) funded the first phase of "the National Career Development Guideline Project, which has resulted in five extensive publications of guidelines for establishing career counseling and guidance programs in elementary schools, middle and junior high schools, high schools, and postsecondary educational institutions" (NOICC, 1989, as cited in Isaacson & Brown, 1997, p. 228). This project helped to revitalize career development programs in many schools as the whims of the school reform movement had sometimes supported and sometimes discouraged efforts to improve career development programs.

The National Career Development Guidelines provide a framework by dividing career development activities into three general areas: self-knowledge; educational and occupational exploration; and career planning. Competencies are written for the four levels of: elementary, middle/junior high school, high school and adult. Particularly in the area of educational and occupational exploration, the stated competencies (for the high school level) appear to embrace skills that students need to be successful in the workplace:

- Understanding the relationship between educational achievement and career planning
- Understanding the need for positive attitudes toward work and learning
- Skills to locate, evaluate, and interpret career information
- Skills to prepare to seek, obtain, maintain, and change jobs
- Understanding how societal needs and functions influence the nature and structure of work (from the Career Development Competencies by Area and Grade Level Worksheet—National Career Development Guidelines, National Occupational Information Coordinating Committee, 1989)

The SCANS Report (1991)

Another federal initiative, following on the National Career

Development Guidelines was the SCANS Report of 1991. According to Zunker (1998):

> In the late 1980s, the Department of Labor formed the Secretary's Commission on Achieving Necessary Skills (SCANS) to determine the level of skills required for employees to enter employment. Specifically, SCANS was to define the skills needed for employment; propose acceptable levels of proficiency; suggest effective ways to assess proficiency; and develop a dissemination strategy for the nation's schools, businesses, and homes. (p. 239).

One of the findings of the SCANS Report, according to Zunker (1998), was that "young people in general leave school without the knowledge or foundation required to find and hold jobs. In labeling job performance as *workplace know-how*, SCANS suggested that know-how has two elements: competencies and a foundation" (p. 239).

To summarize the SCANS Report (as cited in Zunker, 1998, pp.240-242), the five competencies are: *resources* (identifies, organizes, plans, and allocates time, money, materials and facilities, and human resources); *interpersonal* (participates as a member of a team, teaches others new skills, etc.); *information* (acquires, organizes, evaluates, interprets, and communicates information); *systems* (understands, monitors, and corrects performance and systems); and *technology* (applies technology to task, and maintains and troubleshoots equipment). To further summarize the SCANS Report, the foundation skills are: *basic skills* (reading, writing, arithmetic/ mathematics, listening, and speaking), *thinking skills* (creative thinking, decision making, problem solving, seeing things in the mind's eye, knowing how to learn, and reasoning), and *personal qualities* (responsibility, self-esteem, sociability, self-management, and integrity/honesty).

The Connection between the SCANS Report and Employability Skills

These foundation skills have become the essence of today's employability skills—those non-technical skills that help employees to be successful in the workplace. Kathleen Cotton (2001), in her article entitled *Developing Employability Skills* (published on the Northwest Regional Educational Laboratory website www.NWREL.org), has found that today's employers "want entry-level employees to possess an array of basic, higher-order, and affective employability skills" (p.2). Cotton reports findings from

63 documents pertaining to the topic of employability skills, which are those non-technical skills that help to make employees an asset to their employers. She found that "employers find far too many entry-level job applicants deficient in employability skills, and want the public schools to place more emphasis on developing these skills" (p. 4). This finding has important implications for educators—indicating that they need to help students understand the crucial importance of these skills in the workplace.

In her paradigm, *basic skills* would include oral communications and understanding and following instructions, basic arithmetic, and writing; *higher order thinking skills* would include problem solving and creative, innovative thinking; and *affective skills and traits* would include dependability, responsibility, positive attitude toward work and working as a team member (p. 3). One can easily see a close connection between the SCANS skills of *basic skills* (reading, writing, arithmetic), *thinking skills* (creative thinking, decision making, and problem solving), and *personal qualities* (responsibility, self-esteem, sociability, self-management, integrity, and honesty) with Cotton's suggested employability skills in the areas of *basic skills*, *higher order thinking skills*, and *affective skills and traits*.

According to Cotton (2001), "employers value these generic employability skills above specific occupational skills"(p.3). She notes that these findings apply to employers in large, medium and small companies (both public and private). She has even found that technically competent employees can be fired if they lack necessary employability skills. "One can easily see that employability skills are not merely attributes that employers *desire* in prospective employees; rather, many employers now *require* applicants to have these skills in order to be seriously considered for employment" (p. 5) Beach (1982, as cited in Cotton, 2001) cites research that shows that "fully 87 percent of persons losing their jobs or failing to be promoted were found to have 'improper work habits and attitudes rather than insufficient job skills or knowledge' " (p. 5). Clearly, employability skills are crucial to workplace survival.

> Cotton (2001) explains in greater detail this display of findings:
> For one thing, while a number of employers identified the "3 R's" and various higher-cognitive abilities as critical employability skills, virtually *all* of them named affective characteristics-particularly "dependability," "responsibility" and "positive attitude toward work"-as vital. It should also be noted that, within each of the three categories, the skills and traits are arranged in descending order according to the frequency with which each was cited in the research. Finally, when respondents cited mathematics and/or oral and written communication skills

as key employability skills, they often used qualifiers, e.g., *simple* arithmetic, *basic* reading, *brief* memo writing-and frequently noted that applicants need not be highly educated, but possess a solid foundation of these skills. (p. 3)

Basic Skills	Higher-Order Thinking Skills	Affective Skills and Traits
Oral communications (speaking, listening	Problem solving	Dependability/Responsibility
Reading, esp.understanding And following instructions	Learning skills, strategies	Positive attitude toward work
Basic arithmetic	Creative, innovative thinking	Conscientiousness, punctuality, efficiency
Writing	Decision making	Interpersonal skills, cooperation,
		Working as a team members
		Self-confidence, positive self-image
		Adaptability, flexibility
		Enthusiasm, motivation
		Self-discipline, self-management
		Appropriate dress, grooming
		Honesty, integrity
		Ability to work without supervision

Kathleen Cotton, (2001) *Developing Employability Skills.* School Improvement Research Series-Close Up #15 (SIRS) Northwest Regional Educational Laboratory, Portland, Oregon (www.nwrel.org)

In summary, the SCANS Report provided guidelines for today's employability skills. Teaching employability skills is *as* important as providing career guidance activities. Educators need to understand that both are important as they develop and expand their career guidance programs as students must be aware of the importance of *employability skills* to be successful in today's workplace. They need to be able to communicate clearly, understand instructions, solve problems, learn new skills, make good decisions, have a positive attitude toward work, and be dependable and responsible. Research on employability skills confirms their compelling importance.

The School-to-Work Opportunities Act (1994)

The federal government developed the STWOA (School-to-Work Opportunities Act of 1994) that was signed into law by President Clinton. According to Zunker (1998), it was seen as a "new approach to learning for all students in which students apply what they learn to real life and to real work situations" (p.220). It was a federally funded program (through implementation grants to the states that would then be disbursed to local school districts) to develop programs to help students connect with both the world of work and with their post high school goals. According to Perry and Ward (1997), the School-to-Work Opportunities Act (STWOA) identified "three basic components of school-to-career systems: school-based learning, work-based learning, and connecting activities, with each component further broken down into essential elements" (pp. 7-8). Further, according to Perry and Ward (1997), students were to choose a career major by the end of their junior year (p. 84). The major focus of the STWOA was to help students transition to the workplace by knowing the essential skills and competencies to be successful. The work-based learning approach was designed to help students develop skills in the areas of critical thinking, problem-solving, communications, and interpersonal relations.

At the time of the STWOA, there was much concern that our society over-valued a college education and did not give much credence to non-college bound students. According to Krumboltz and Worthington (1999), many students did not attempt college or failed in college and then spent "an average of 6 to 8 years of 'floundering' in the workforce." This resulted in an enormous loss of human potential, in terms of lost time and wages. According to Zunker (1998, p. 220), a purpose of STWOA was fundamentally to close the gap so that more youth could participate in work-based learning (career exploration, work experience, and mentoring at job sites), school-based learning (classroom instruction based on industry skill standards) and connecting activities (classroom instruction integrated with on-the-job instruction) while still in high school. Through the STWOA, students could acquire portable, industry recognized certificates, verifying mastery of designated skills. According to Lent and Worthington (1999), the STWOA was intended to help students "become more competitive for positions in their field of study, more likely to pursue meaningful work opportunities after graduation, and consequently to become more productive citizens" (pp. 292-293). Employers participating in STW programs could also expect a larger, highly skilled pool of entry-level applicants.

The STWOA was based on human capital theory, which says that workers with better educational backgrounds and training fare better in the labor market, and nations with larger pools of qualified workers would be more competitive in the global economy (Sweetland, 1996, as cited in Krumboltz & Worthington, 1999, p. 313). According to Smith and Scroll (1995, as cited in Krumboltz and Worthington, 2002), the School to Work Opportunities Act was actually designed with a human capital agenda. According to this agenda, high school students would "complete their education with an industry recognized skill certificate...as well as a high school diploma" (p. 313). In this way, students would meet the industry standards in their skill area (to earn their industry-recognized certificates) and meet the workplace needs of employers for entry-level but already highly trained workers.

Another issue was that of keeping students in school until they graduated. According to the National Dropout Prevention Center Network (NDPC/N), (www.dropoutprevention.org),

> The goal of the Act was to improve student learning, keep students in school until they graduated, and to provide relevant experiences that integrate school-based and work-based learning. The Act provided the impetus for schools and the business community to collaborate in providing real world experiences. (p. 1)

According to NDPC/N, school-based learning programs included Junior Achievement, Future Farmers of America, and Future Teachers of America. Service-learning (volunteer) projects also were considered school-based learning activities. Work-based learning activities included apprenticeships, internships and tech prep programs.

A Thumbnail Sketch of our High School Dropout Rate

The issue of keeping students in school by means of the STWOA provides a segue to the issue of the high school dropout rate, as one wonders what implications the STWOA had for student retention in our public schools. According to at least one researcher (Mortenson, 2001), our dropout rate actually increased during the years of the STWOA (1994-2001). So while it had sound intentions, some objectives were not met, the national administration changed, and its funding eventually ended in the fall of 2001.

The National Center for Educational Statistics (NCES) defines a dropout as:

> an individual who had been enrolled at any time during the previous school year, was not enrolled at the beginning of the current school year, and had not graduated or transferred to another public or private school. (p.1) (NCES, 2002, from the NCES website: http://nces.ed.gov/pubs2002/quarterly/summer/ 3-5.asp)

One of the related issues in collecting dropout data is the way the information is collected. NCES began collecting dropout data through the Common Core of Data (CCD) in 1991-92. "The CCD is a voluntary collection, and dropout statistics are published for only those states whose dropout counts conform to the CCD definition. Dropout data were reported for 12 states in 1991-92. By 1997-98, this number had increased to 37" (NCES, 2002, p. 1).

One can see the problem of obtaining accurate statistics if only 37 out of 50 states are reporting dropout data according to CCD parameters. Since voluntarily collected data are incomplete, dropout rates are not nationally representative and need to be observed with caution. For example, NCES reported that "high school 4-year completion rates were 80 percent or higher in 20 of 33 reporting states in 1997-98. (This rate does not reflect those receiving a GED-based equivalency credential.)" (NCES, 2002, p. 2) NCES does not count GED completers as high school graduates, but the U.S. Census Bureau does. NCES also does not count students in private schools. There are many confounding factors in reporting high school dropout data.

The Education Trust reports a high school graduation rate with a regular diploma of 72.5 percent and a high school completion rate of 82 percent, if GED and other certificate completers are included (Education Trust, 2001). Greene (2002) points out another issue, which is that many students leave school prior to reaching high school; he notes that "...the vast majority of dropouts nationwide leave schools in earlier grades (usually between 9th and 10th grades)..." (p. 6). Therefore, high school graduation or dropout rates need to be observed with some caution; many students may have already left the system. According to the report *Youth at the Crossroads: Facing High School and Beyond*, prepared for the National Commission on the High School Senior Year by the Education Trust, Inc. (2001):

> Each year, almost 1 out of every 20 youngsters leaves high school. But there are vast differences among students from different racial and economic groups...During a typical year,

we lose about 1 out of 30 Whites, 1 out of 20 African Americans, and 1 out of 10 Latinos...At the same time, students from poor families are considerably more likely to leave high school than students from affluent families....By ages 18-19, data from the U.S. Census suggest that about 82% of all young people have completed high school. Of these, about 72.5% have earned a regular diploma, with another 9.8% earning a GED or other certificate. (p. 5)

The dropout rate is not necessarily the converse (or flip side) of the graduation rate as other factors may intervene, but the graduation rate of 72.5% (for students who have earned a regular diploma) gives us some sense of how many students are actually graduating on time with their peers (Education Trust, 2001). According to the U.S. Department of Education *Consumer Guide* (March 1996), dropout rates can be reported as *event rates* (percentage of students who drop out in a single year), *status rates* (percentage of a given age range who have not completed high school), or *cohort rates* (percentage of a dropouts in a cohort group, as in grades 9-12 for a given high school graduating class). Greene (2002) describes how cohort rates are counted:

If we see roughly twice as many students entering high school as we see graduates four years later and we do not see a large number of students moving into or out of the school, it is reasonable to infer that the school graduates about 50% of its students. (p.3)

Understanding how dropout rates are derived (using event rates, status rates, or cohort rates) helps the reader to grasp the complexity of the dropout issue. As dropout rates can be reported in any of these formats, it is helpful to understand that there are three formats for presenting the data.

To go back to what actually happened during the years of the STWOA (1994-2001), Mortenson (2001), editor of the monthly newsletter *Postsecondary Education Opportunity,* compiled these graduation statistics for the class of 1999:

In the 1998-99 school year, public high schools awarded 2,488,605 regular high school diplomas. Four years earlier, in the fall of 1995 when these students began the ninth grade, the count was 3,704,455. Thus, 67.2 percent of those who began the ninth grade received regular high school diplomas by the end of their senior year. 1,215, 850 did not. (p.5)

Essentially, according to this statistical compilation, 1,200,000 public school students disappeared from their graduating cohort group from 1995 to 1999. We do not know what happened to them as officials in most states do not assign universal numbers to students to be able to follow them longitudinally. Mortenson (2001) further points out that over time, our high school graduation rate has been declining since 1982. "Between 1982 and 1999, the graduation rate declined from 74.5 to 67.2 percent, or by 7.3 percentage points. The decline was more gradual between 1982 and 1993, then dropped sharply between 1993 and 1999" (p. 5). It is interesting to note that the School-to-Work Opportunities Act was in place during the years 1994-2001, when the graduation rate dropped sharply, thus repudiating the belief that it helped to keep students in school.

Career Guidance Today under the ASCA National Standards & the ASCA National Model: A Framework for School Counseling Programs

The *ASCA (American School Counselor Association) Sharing the Vision: the National Standards for School Counseling Programs* (Campbell & Dahir, 1997) and the implementation document, *ASCA Vision into Action: Implementing the National Standards for School Counseling Programs* (Dahir, Sheldon & Valiga, 1998) contain *student content standards* for school counseling programs in the three domains of academic, career and personal/ social development. Comprehensive guidance and counseling programs that incorporate these three domains in their student content standards and corresponding competencies (with behavioral indicators) may provide a broad range of activities and experiences, including career guidance activities, for *all* students. According to the Introduction of the *ASCA National Model: A Framework for School Counseling Programs* (ASCA, 2003):

> The *ASCA National Model: A Framework for School Counseling Programs* is written to reflect a comprehensive approach to program foundation, delivery, management, and accountability. The model provides the mechanism with which school counselors and school counseling teams will design, coordinate, implement, manage and evaluate their programs for students' success. (p. 9)

The *ASCA National Standards* in career development "enable the student to develop a positive attitude toward work and to develop the necessary skills to make a successful transition from school to the world of work and from job to job across the life/career span" (Dahir, Sheldon &

Valiga, 1998, p.11). The three *ASCA National Standards* for career development are:

- Standard A: Students will acquire the skills to investigate the world of work in relation to knowledge of self and to make informed career decisions.
- Standard B: Students will employ strategies to achieve future career success and satisfaction.
- Standard C: Students will understand the relationship among personal qualities, education and training, and the world of work.

ASCA Vision into Action, Implementing the National Standards for School Counseling Programs "provides school counselors tools for selecting student competencies and suggestions for infusing competencies into the school counseling program" (ASCA, 2003, p. 9). This document is a particularly helpful reference as it includes: a chapter on *Design: Standards and Activities* (pp. 57-61) offering a process to help set up the standards into a comprehensive program, with a checklist of each "student competency" and the corresponding "activity/service/program" (p. 61); a chapter on *Implementation* (pp. 62-64) with a corresponding Student Competency checklist; and a chapter on *Evaluation* (pp. 65-76) with a corresponding chart to document "student competency, evaluation method, and benchmark (grade level or transitional time" (p. 70).

Further, school counselors and other educators are also encouraged to review carefully the *ASCA National Model: A Framework for School Counseling Programs* (ASCA, 2003) as they consider the delivery, accountability and management systems for their school counseling programs. Checklists are greatly expanded, such as the *Developmental Crosswalking Tools,* to help educators plan which competencies will be taught in which grades, and by whom. The Program Audit checklist in the Appendix (pp. 110-120) incorporates the following topics:

- the *Foundation*—that is, the beliefs and philosophy, the mission of school counseling programs, domains and goals; the ASCA National Standards/Competencies;
- the *Delivery System*—that is, the Guidance Curriculum, Individual Student Planning, Responsive Services; and System Support
- the *Management System*—that is, school counselor/administrator agreements, advisory council, use of data and student monitoring, use of data and closing the gap, action plans, use of time/calendar; and
- the *Accountability System*—that is, the results report, counselor performance standards, and the program audit.

For further information about the *ASCA National Standards* and the *ASCA National Model: A Framework for School Counseling Programs*, the reader is directed to the following authors and chapters in this book:

- Dr. Carol Dahir, author of *School Counseling Programs: Supporting a Nation of Learners*.
- Dr. Patricia Hatch and Judy Bowers, co-authors of *Building a National Model*, published with ASCA's permission as it appeared in the *ASCA School Counselor* (May/June 2002), Vol. 39 (5) under the title: *The Block to Build On* (pp. 12-19)

Specific Roles of School Counselors and Others in the Career Guidance Program

Thinking through the delivery system of a given school's career guidance program is crucial; it must be carefully decided who will do what. The program needs to be incorporated into the school's overall mission statement, as well as the school counseling mission statement, so that all participants (administrators, school counselors, teachers, career specialists, and community members) understand their important and complementary roles. Once developed, the career guidance curriculum may be set up so that career units are taught by school counselors or the career specialist in the Career Center, through advisories (groups of 20-25 students that meet regularly with an assigned teacher/advisor throughout the school year—if the school has that format), homerooms (if the school is set up with homerooms) or in designated classrooms.

The term "guidance" is used here to indicate that appropriate educators and even members of the community (guest speakers) can deliver portions of the school's overall career guidance program. It is not meant that school counselors will do it all! They cannot. Kuranz (2002, p.175) reports that, according to ASCA, the average student-counselor ratio is 551:1. School counselors are too busy with too many other responsibilities, but they can share responsibility for some aspects of the career guidance program. With their specialized knowledge of career development and their counseling skills, they would be available to help design the career guidance program (in collaboration with others), deliver aspects of it, and be available to provide follow-up counseling with students and parents about particular interests and concerns.

The essence of the *ASCA National Standards* and *ASCA National Model* is not so much what school counselors can do but how students are *different* as a result of what school counselors (and appropriate others) do— through their comprehensive school counseling programs, particularly through their career guidance programs. The key word here is *guidance,* which means that all appropriate educators (and community members) need to be marshaled to help.

Unfocused, Disengaged Students and Career Guidance

Career guidance is important for all high school students, as all students need to learn about themselves (their skills, interests, and values), the world of work (the vast array of ocupational options), and career management skills (writing resumes and cover letters,interviewing effectively, and building a network of contacts) to cope successfully with the workplace. Of particular concern in this chapter are unfocused, disengaged, or at-risk students, who tend to make impulsive decisions with poor or erroneous information (Capuzzi and Gross, 1989, p. 11) or who tend to foreclose on decisions too soon, without thinking through the ramifications (Herr, 1997). These students may pay a high price later for their impulsiveness by eventually dropping out of school and subsequently getting locked into entry level, low-wage, dead-end jobs with little opportunity for advancement (Hoyt, 2001). Hoyt reports that of the 50 million jobs anticipated between 1996-2006, about 22 million will require two-to-three weeks of on-the-job training, so there are many opportunities for young people to find work, whether they are still in high school or not. The problem is that without further education, teens can find themselves locked into these jobs for an indefinite period of time, with no way to improve their wages except to take on more low-paying jobs. The other alternative is to get more schooling.

Parental Reluctance to Help with Career Guidance

Parental lack of knowledge about available jobs and labor market information is frequently a reason that parents do not take more initiative in helping their teens. They are afraid to give incorrect information or advice, so they rely on school counselors, career specialists, and others to provide career guidance information. Schneider and Stevenson (1999) share that many parents express that it is the school's responsibility to provide career guidance as parents "may not know much about the field their child is considering" (p. 165). Educators do have access to a great deal of available information. In his article *The Right Tools* (March/April 2002), printed in this book with permission from ASCA, Hoyt encourages educators to inform students and parents about many postsecondary options, including high tech skills programs. "Many of the new jobs expected to be created in the next 10-20 years will require, among other things, a high level of expertise in computer usage" (p.22). Hoyt further urges school counselors to share the many postsecondary options available in addition to the four-year colleges or universities: community colleges; technical institutes; publicly supported career institutions; proprietary career-oriented institutions; federally sponsored career training programs such as the Job Corps; and the Armed Services career-oriented programs.

Four-Year College Aspirations

Hoyt (2002) explains the issue of "parental aspirations":
Statistics tell us that between 60 and 70 percent of each year's high school graduates enroll in college the next fall intending to get a four-year bachelor's degree. However, about one in four will drop out during the first year, and less than 50 percent will eventually obtain a bachelor's degree, but about 90 percent of the parents of these students want them to complete a four-year college degree" (p.19).

Hoyt exhorts educators to try to stem the flow of this needless tide by helping parents to understand that a four year college is not for everybody, as so many parents assume their students will become college graduates. Educators must help parents to understand other options.

Gray and Herr (1995) discuss the issue of weak college preparation and report that:
Nationwide, 85% of high school graduates want to obtain a 4-year college degree, but only 30% graduate with the academically advanced credentials to indicate adequate preparation for legitimate college-level academic work. The vast majority (70%) of high school graduates go on to college, most to 4-year colleges, despite inadequate academic preparation. Thus, it is not surprising to find that 50% or more have to take remedial courses sometime during their freshman year in college. Six years later, only about 50% actually graduate with a 4-year degree. (p. 81)

There is yet another issue involving the actual number of college graduates. Hoyt (2002) admonishes that "Every year, the number of students graduating from a four-year college outnumbers the available jobs requiring such degrees by 100,000- 300,000 graduates" (p.20). Thus, there appears to be a substantial over-supply of college graduates for the number of jobs requiring a college degree, depending on the source of information (Hoyt, 2001). Mittelhauser (1998, as cited in Hoyt, 2001) "reported that the Bureau of Labor Statistics expects there will be about 250,000 more college graduates with a bachelor's degree entering the labor force each year between 1996 and 2006 than there will be new college-level jobs" (p. 9). Given this information, Hoyt and many other educators strongly support parent involvement in their children's career planning, as students who go to college to please their parents may have a very expensive and unfortunate result. They may not graduate, or, if they graduate, they may find that the workplace does not need the skills they have learned. Thus, many college graduates enroll in community or technical colleges to acquire specific technical skills, so that they are employable.

Difficulty in Finding Good Jobs without Further Postsecondary Education/Training

High school graduates and dropouts who do not continue their postsecondary education may face a comparatively bleak economic future, unless they are able to follow in their family business or in a certain workplace situation. According to the Bureau of Labor Statistics (2002) regarding the high school graduating class of 2001, "Among recent high school graduates not enrolled in college in the fall, 80.6 percent were in the labor force in October 2001. Their employment-population ratio—the proportion of the population with jobs—declined from 69.7 percent in 2000 to 63.8 percent in 2001." With a weakening economy, workers with less training can find fewer employment opportunities.

A National Center for Education Statistics (NCES, 1999) report, *Dropout Rates in the United States, 1999*, further corroborates the importance of completing high school, as dropouts tend to be unemployed and, more unfortunately, disproportionately found in prison:

> Because high school completion has become a requirement for accessing additional education, training, or the labor force, the economic consequences of leaving high school without a diploma are severe. On average, dropouts are more likely to be unemployed than high school graduates and to earn less money when they eventually secure work...1.The individual stresses and frustrations associated with dropping out have social implications as well: dropouts make up a disproportionate percentage of the nation's prison and death row inmates." (p. 1)

Hoyt (2001) discusses that millions of jobs that require only 2 to 3 weeks of short-term, on-the-job training are the dead end, low paying jobs that never pay workers a substantive income.

If high school leavers seek employment without receiving postsecondary education of any kind, this is the type of job most open to them. Until and unless they obtain some kind of postsecondary education, they are unlikely to obtain what most persons would describe as 'good jobs.' (p. 7)

On that issue, so often we hear that the average age of community college students is about 29 or 30 years of age. Many of these adults, who experience so much difficulty in just finding work for their first ten years after high school, eventually choose to go back to school and learn a technical skill. In September, 1993, the U.S. General Accounting Office (GAO, as cited in McCullough, 1994) reported that about 30 percent of young people aged 16-24 lacked the skills for entry-level employment. Even more astonishing, the GAO reported that fifty percent of adults in their late 20's had not found steady jobs, documenting that so many young people at that time, ten years ago, were struggling with weak academic preparation, little career guidance, and few workplace experiences. It would appear that for many of our young people, not much has changed.

Research Supporting the Importance of Career Guidance

As noted above, without a systematic career development program in grades K-12, many students may not develop important career planning skills nor learn about many possible occupational choices. Learning about the vast array of occupational choices is, in itself, an important task for young people. Research findings demonstrate the importance of exposing teens to many career options through a systematic approach, as occurred in a week-long summer career exploration program (in a university setting) for at-risk 7th graders, called the *Career Horizons Program* (O'Brien, Dukstein, Jackson, Tomlinson, and Kamatuka, 1999):

The increase in number of careers considered signified that students were able to identify additional careers of interest to them after completion of the career exploration program...This seems particularly positive in that many students entered the program with what might be considered unrealistic career choices (e.g., to be the next Michael Jordan or president of the United States). We worked hard not to discount the dreams of students but to suggest that they develop alternative plans or 'Plan Bs,' and explained that even Michael Jordan pursued a secondary career in business to supplement his primary occupation. Encouraging students to consider an increase in number of careers is consistent with the NOICC guidelines and might contribute to increased vocational preparedness if their dream careers prove unobtainable (p. 225).

The Career Horizons Program was a collaboration of researchers and practitioners to help underachieving, at-risk 7th grade students develop efficacy in considering various career choices and in performing other tasks related to investigating, choosing, and actually implementing a career choice. The sample of fifty-seven 7th graders demonstrated significant gains from this week-long intensive summer program.

According to Swanson and Fouad (1999), Bandura's concept of self-efficacy states that "individuals' conceptions of their confidence to perform tasks (self-efficacy) mediates between what they know and how they act" (p.125). That is, individuals' beliefs about their ability to accomplish tasks may have more influence than their *actual* ability to perform a given task. The concept of self-efficacy is useful in determining student growth along specific career development parameters, as shown in this study by O'Brien, et al. (1999).

In summary, the Career Horizons Program study reported an increase in the student's sense of self-efficacy (enhancement in one's confidence) with regard to career planning and exploration activities, educational and vocational development activities, and congruence between interests and career choice. The researchers conjectured that students with a sense of heightened efficacy may have more confidence in identifying alternative career possibilities, obtaining information about careers, learning more about vocational options, and finding careers congruent with their own interests, values and abilities. (O'Brien, et al., p. 224)

Self-efficacy measures in career development have also been used by Turner and Lapan (2002), who used the Social Cognitive Career Theory (SCCT) framework "to examine the relative indirect contribution of perceived parent support...to career self-efficacy as a mediator of career interests" along with other variables. It was found that "for younger adolescents, parent support accounted for as much as approximately one third to almost one half of their children's career-task related confidence" (p. 53). These findings are important in documenting the value of intervention by educators (teachers and counselors) and by parents in helping young people with their career awareness, exploration and planning issues.

Systematic Approaches to Career Guidance—To Reach *All* Students
The Comprehensive Guidance and Counseling Program Model

The comprehensive guidance and counseling model (Gysbers and Henderson, 1994), incorporated now in the *ASCA National Model: A Framework for School Counseling Programs* (ASCA, 2003), suggests that a needs assessment be conducted with students, educators, parents, community members and selected others (p. 193) and that a comprehensive school counseling program be developed based on identified student needs, incorporating the program components of the guidance curriculum, individual planning, responsive services, and system support. So often, "the squeaky wheel gets the grease" in the school setting; only those with more pressing issues tend to be given time and attention. A great attribute of the comprehensive guidance and counseling model is that it is designed to deliver services to all students (and to their parents/guardians). As stated in *Comprehensive Guidance Programs that Work—II* (1997), "A program is not comprehensive unless counselors are providing activities to students, parents, and staff in all four program components" (p.15).

With regard to career guidance, the notion of the guidance curriculum in this model is particularly important. According to Gybers and Henderson (1997), "This model of guidance is based on the assumption that guidance programs include content that all students should learn in a systematic, sequential way. In order for this to happen, counselors must be involved in teaching, team teaching, or serving as a resource to those who teach a guidance curriculum" (p. 15). As stated earlier, school counselors need to collaborate with teachers and others to deliver a comprehensive guidance program to all students, particularly in the area of career guidance.

This is a widely utilized model in schools; the four components are easily adapted in many school settings. In this book, there are several chapters showing important applications of the comprehensive guidance and counseling model. (See chapters by Jensen/Madison, Anderson, Coy, and Whitledge for applications of the Gysbers/Henderson comprehensive school guidance and counseling model.)

Red River High School in Grand Forks, North Dakota

(This section has been written by Marilyn Ripplinger, a school counselor at Red River High School.)

An excellent example of this kind of comprehensive school counseling program can be found at Red River High School in Grand Forks, North

Dakota (Quick, Ripplinger, & Cichy, 2001). This program hinges on individual student educational/career planning conferences (SECP conferences). Each student and his/her parent/guardian are invited to participate in a 30-45 minute individual conference scheduled during the school day with their assigned school counselor on three occasions throughout high school (in grades 9, 10, and 12). The main focus of each SECP conference is to summarize and review the results of the information gathered during the career units delivered in the classroom at each grade level. This information, including various assessment results and career and postsecondary research, is then used to assist in the selection of appropriate high school courses needed for the student to achieve his/her education career goals. Parent participation in these conferences is essential to the success of this program.

It is important to note that the school counselors would not be able to perform this monumental task of the SECP conferences without the support of other staff members. A conference facilitator schedules the meetings and organizes the materials needed for the school counselor to conduct these conferences. Counselors also work on a team with career counselors, career resource educators, and the classroom teachers to create and implement both the conferences and the career units. The Grand Forks School District uses a unique blend of federal and state grant money as well as business partnerships in the community to financially support the comprehensive school counseling program at Red River High School.

Marilyn Ripplinger has been a school counselor at Red River High School in Grand Forks, North Dakota for ten years. She received a Bachelor of Science Degree in Education and a Master of Arts Degree in Counseling from the University of North Dakota. Marilyn had the opportunity to participate in a restructuring of the Grand Forks School Counseling Program over the past several years. Norm Gysbers consulted with the Grand Forks school counselors for three years to develop a comprehensive school counseling program. The Grand Forks Public Schools received the Year 2000 Exemplary Career Guidance and Counseling Program Award sponsored by the U.S. Department of Education. Marilyn Ripplinger can be reached at mripplinger@fc.grand-forks.k12.nd.us

State-Mandated Career Guidance Graduation Standards

Another example of a comprehensive and systematic approach that reaches all students is that of *state-mandated graduation standards*. The state board of education may set career development standards as part of the graduation requirement for all students. In his chapter, "Policy—The

View from on High," Davis (Executive Director of the Washington State Board of Education) explains how the Washington State Board of Education has adopted minimum high school graduation requirements (starting with the graduating class of 2008), including the performance-based Certificate of Mastery (with the requisite grade level competency tests in specified academic areas) along with two non-credit career development requirements: a *Culminating Project;* and a *High School + Education Plan* (including one year past high school). That is, all students would have the opportunity to explore a career interest (or an academic area) by means of doing an in-depth culminating project. In addition, all students would be required to develop their *High School + Education Plan.* In this statewide system, district officials would decide the "nuts and bolts" of carrying out these state mandates, but all students would be required to fulfill them. (Each building staff would need to incorporate these outcome goals in their school mission statement; staff members would decide both who would teach these projects and how student progress would be monitored.) A state-mandated career development requirement for all graduating students would pre-empt the program variability so often seen from district to district. (More information can be found from the Washington State Board of Education website: www.sbe.wa.gov and from the Washington State Legislative website http://www.leg.wa.gov/wac/-Washington State Minimum High School Graduation Requirements)

Career Resource Centers

Another example of a systematic approach to reach all students is to provide a *Career Resource Center* in every high school, so that students may easily access (in a central location) career and postsecondary information regarding colleges, universities, technical institutes, federal training programs, and the military services. According to Isaacson and Brown, (2000):

> ...the increased availability of career materials—printed, audiovisual, programmed, and computer-based—has emphasized the need for an organized system to handle these items in an orderly way. The answer in most settings has been the development of a *career resource center*, also frequently called a *career information center*. (p. 192)

Career specialists (a certificated designation in some states) or certified career counselors may be responsible for setting up and maintaining current information in the career resource centers. Some maintain a website of ongoing school and community programs to keep students, teachers, and parents updated. (See Hines/ Mygatt Wakefield's chapter on *Career Resource Centers—Information Made Available to All Students*.)

Conclusion

The distinction has been made between the meaning of the terms (or constructs) *school counseling* (in which a student shares personal information with a school counselor, with an understanding of confidentiality) and *school guidance* (an informational program provided for many students in which all appropriate personnel—educators and others—may contribute). A number of national career guidance programs or approaches have been discussed in this chapter: the career education efforts of the 1970s (infusing career development concepts into the classroom curriculum, to be taught by teachers); the National Career Development Guidelines (1989); the SCANS Report (1991); and the School-to-Work Opportunities Act (1994). Finally, the *ASCA National Standards* (1997, 1998) and the *ASCA National Model: A Framework for School Counseling Programs* (2003) provide student content standards and a delivery system for the three areas of academic, personal/social development and career development.

As our society becomes more complex, we need to expand our coverage of career guidance activities to ensure that all students learn as much as they can about themselves (self-knowledge), the world of work (educational and occupational exploration), and career planning. Students also need to learn employability skills, which include: oral communications (speaking and listening), understanding and following instructions, problem-solving, personal qualities of responsibility, dependability and punctuality, and a positive attitude toward work. As is stated in the Introduction of the *ASCA National Standards* (Dahir, Sheldon & Valiga, 1998):

> To maintain our leadership position in the global economy, education in the United States cannot accept anything less than success for all students. The demand is on schools to produce higher levels of student achievement and to reallocate educational resources to meet this objective. Today's youth need much more preparation than previous generations did. Survival and success require learning and relearning as economic and societal demands command constant change. Students need a higher level of competency to survive and succeed in the 21st century. A commitment to lifelong learning has become essential. (p.2)

That is, we must provide students with effective career guidance programs so that they can successfully manage their lives in the 21ˢᵗ century as they encounter different and ever-changing situations in the workplace. It will benefit students to become aware of recently developed Internet career guidance systems to help them with their career exploration and planning. Among these are career information delivery systems using the O*NET database and career exploration tools available through www.acsci.org. It is also helpful to know that the Labor Department offers the widely used career information and job search assistance website called Career OneStop at http://www.careeronestop,org/ and O*NET OnLine at http://online.onetcenter.org.

The world has become more complicated; this generation needs even more preparation and support than did previous generations. Educators and appropriate community members need to pull together to provide career guidance activities and opportunities (field trips, guest speakers, job shadows, internships, service learning, and paid jobs in career interest areas) for all students. Students also need to learn crucial employability skills and need to be directed to jobs that will help them explore important career interests. We want all students to be prepared and successful. A strong, comprehensive, developmental career guidance program can do much to make that a possibility for many students. The 21ˢᵗ century workplace awaits them.

References

American School Counselor Association. (2003). *American School Counselor Association National model: A framework for school counseling programs.* Alexandria, VA: Author. (See website at: www.schoolcounselor.org)

Baker, S.B., & Taylor, J.G. (June 1998). Effects of career education interventions: A meta-analysis. *The Career Development Quarterly, 46* (4). 376-377.

Bureau of Labor Statistics (U.S. Dept. of Labor). (May 14, 2002). College enrollment and work activities of the year 2001 high school graduates. Retrieved July 4, 2002, from http://www.bls.gov/news/release/gsgec.nr0.htm

Campbell, C.A., & Dahir, C.A. (1997). *Sharing the vision: The national standards for school counseling programs.* Alexandria, Virginia: American School Counselor Association.

Capuzzi, D., & Gross, D. R.. (1989). *Youth at risk: A resource for counselors, teachers and* parents. Alexandria, VA: American Association for Counseling and Development.

Cotton, K. (2001).*Developing employability skills.* School Improvement Research Series, Close-Up # 15. Portland, Oregon: Northwest Regional Educational Laboratory. Retrieved February 11, 2003, from http://www.nwrl.org/scpd/sirs/8/c015.html. See also www.nwrel.org

Dahir, C.A., Sheldon, C. B., & Valiga, M.J. (1998). *Vision into action: Implementing the national standards for school counseling programs.* Alexandria, VA: American School Counselor Association.

Education Trust, Inc. (2001). National Commission on the High School Senior Year. Youth at the *crossroads: Facing high school and beyond.* Retrieved March 28, 2003, http://www.commissiononthesenioryear.org/Reportt/report.html

Gray, C.G. & Herr, E.L. (1995). *Other ways to win: Creating alternatives for high school graduates.* Thousand Oaks: Corwin Press, Inc.

Greene, J.P. (2002). *Graduation rates in Washington State.* New York: Manhattan Institute for Policy Research. Retrieved December 19, 2002, from http://www.manhattan-institue.org/html/cr_27.htm.

Gysbers, N.C., & Henderson, P. (1994). *Developing and managing your school guidance program.* (2nd ed) Alexandria, VA: American Counseling Association.

Gysbers, N.C. & Henderson, P. (1997). *Comprehensive guidance systems that work—II.* University of North Carolina at Greensboro: ERIC/CASS. 1-15.

Hatch, T. & Bowers, J. (2002). The lock to build on. *ASCA School Counselor, 39* (5) 15.

Herr, E.L. (1997). *Career development and work-bound youth.* University of North Carolina at Greensboro, NC: ERIC/CASS (ED: 051199)

Hoyt, K.B. (2001). Helping high school students broaden their knowledge of postsecondary options. *Professional School Counseling, 5* (1), 6-12.

Hoyt, K.B. (2002). The right tools. *ASCA School Counselor,39,* (4) 19-23.

Isaacson, L.E. & Brown, D. (1997). *Career information, career counseling, and career development.* Boston: Allyn and Bacon.

Isaacson, L.E., & Brown, D. (2000). *Career information, career counseling, and career development.* Boston: Allyn and Bacon.

Kuranz, M. (February, 2002). Cultivating student potential. *Professional School Counseling. 5* (3), 172-179.

Krumboltz, J.D. & Worthington, R.L. (June 1999). The school-to-work transition from a learning theory perspective. *The Career Development Quarterly, 47* (4), 312-325.

Lent, R. W. & Worthington, R. L. (1999). Applying career development theories to the school-to-work transition process. *The Career Development Quarterly, 47* (4), 291-293.

McCullough, L. (1994). Legislation enhances school-to-work initiatives. *ACA Guidepost, 36,* p.1.

Mortenson, T.G. (2001, June) High school graduation trends and patterns 1981-2000. *Postsecondary Education Opportunity,* 108, p.5.

Myrick, R.D. (1993). *Developmental Guidance and Counseling: A practical approach* (2nd ed.). Minneapolis, MN:Educational Media Corporation, 2-3.

National Center for Education Statistics (1999), U.S. Department of Education. *Dropout rates in the United States, 1999. Introduction.* Retrieved March 28, 2003, from http://nces.ed.gov.pubs2001/dropout/introduction.asp

National Center for Education Statistics (2002), U.S. Department of Education. *Public high school dropouts and completers from the common core data: School years 1991-92 through 1997-98.*Young, B.A. & Hoffman, L. Retrieved January 10, 2003, from http://nces.ed.gov/pubs2002/quarterly/summer/3-5.asp

National Dropout Prevention Center/Network. *Career education/workforce readiness overview.* Retrieved February 14, 2003, from http://www.dropoutprevention.org/effstrat/careered_work/career_over.htm.

National Occupational Information Coordinating Committee (1989). The National Career Development Guidelines, *Worksheet.* Washington, D.C.: Author.

O'Brien, K.M., Dukstein, R.D., Jackson, S.L., Tomlinson, M.J., & Kamatuka, N.A., (March 1999). Broadening career horizons for students in at-risk environments. *The Career Development Quarterly,*47(3), 215-229.

O*NET OnLine. (2002). Website: http://online.onetcenter.org (Web-based viewer that provides easy public access to O*NET information from any Web browser.)

Perry, N. & Ward, L. (1997). *Helping students plan careers — A school-to-careers guide for counselors.* Alexandria, VA: American Vocational Association.

Quattrociocchi, S.M. (n.d.) *A call to parents.* [Brochure]. (Published in collaboration with the Washington State Tech Prep Directors Association). Bellevue, Washington: Bellevue Community College Printing Services.

Quattrociocchi, S.M. (2000). *Help! A family's guide to high school and beyond.* Olympia, Washington: Washington State Workforce Training and Education Coordinating Board.

Quick, J., Ripplinger, M. & Cichy, N. (May 22, 2001). *The four p's — plan, pathway, portfolio, and project.* Paper presented at the Pierce County Consortium, Tacoma, Washington. (For further information, contact mripplinger@fc.grand-forks.k12.nd.us)

Schneider, B. & Stevenson, D. (1999). *The ambitious generation—America's teenagers: motivated but directionless*. New Haven: Yale University Press.

Swanson, J.L. & Fouad, J.A. (1999). *Career theory and practice—learning through case* studies. Thousand Oaks: Sage Publications, 125.

Turner, S. & Lapan, R.T. (2002). Career self-efficacy and perceptions of parent support in adolescent career development. *The Career Development Quarterly, 51*(1), 44-55.

Washington State minimum high school graduation requirements (WAC 180-51-061). Effective Fall 2004 for entering ninth graders. Retrieved from http://www.leg.wa.gov/wac/ The full set of graduation requirements may be found at the Washington State Board of Education (SBE) website at www.sbe.wa.gov

Zunker, V.G. (1998). Career counseling: Applied concepts of life planning. (6th ed.). New York: Brooks/Cole Publishing Company.

Chapter Three

Dreams Can Come True—Building a K-12 Career Development System That Inspires Hope

Christine M. Jensen and Mark A. Madison

Abstract

There are striking changes in the workplace, in the "clientele" of schools, and in the capacity of K-12 systems to respond effectively to these changes. The authors suggest practical models for changing our thinking for how educators meet the needs of a unique generation facing unknowable challenges. Topics include: shifting from a linear model of school counseling to one in which all members of a community participate in providing career guidance; motivating the unmotivated student; and building a coherent approach to career development, K-12, that is essential to a district's mission for improving student achievement. Included in this chapter are specific outcomes and detailed strategies for ensuring that this generation, otherwise known as the "Millennials," can and will be successful in activating their dreams. The chapter culminates in a detailed model that responds to legislated educational reform in the context of a research-based, developmental approach to career development—one that relies on parent participation and support by all educators.

Part I: The Dream—A Wake-Up "Call"

Suppose you are a welfare recipient in New Jersey who uses a toll-free number to call the state welfare office for information. According to a report aired by National Public Radio on March 20, 2002, you would be connected to someone in India to answer your questions. Apparently, not even the welfare office hires locally! Through a privatized service, thousands of people in India are paid $3 an hour for what would otherwise cost $15 an hour for a resident of New Jersey. Do *you* know the geographical location of the person you talk to when you dial a toll-free number? Does it matter?

Few students, let alone their parents, would name telephone operator as a career dream. Yet, considering many high school freshmen and sophomores leave school before graduation, what else will they be equipped to do? The National Center for Education Statistics reports that for the 1999-2000 school year more than 18 percent of the freshmen class left their Chicago high schools, 26.8 percent left in Cleveland, over ten percent stopped attending in Atlanta, and ten percent dropped out in Albuquerque (NCES, 2002a). In the shrinking labor market of unskilled jobs, few choices remain. Of those that are available, few pay enough to support a family.

At the other end of the continuum are students with high aspirations for professional careers. They know that white-collar professions offer the best opportunity for income and advancement—the surest path to social mobility. But has anyone told these ambitious students and their eager parents that "six times more adolescents want to be doctors and five times more want to be lawyers than there are projected to be openings in these professions" (Schneider and Stevenson, 1999)? Projections made by the National Center for Education Statistics forecast that between 1999 and 2011 there will be 20 percent more students enrolled in degree-granting institutions and 18 percent more bachelor's degrees (NCES, 2002b). Already the number of students graduating with four-year degrees exceeds the jobs requiring those degrees by 100,000 to 300,000 (Hoyt, 2002). Will career dreams and aspirations become museum pieces in the emerging economy of the 21st century?

To protect the dreams of children and teens will require more than wishful thinking and individual striving; it will take an entire system of informed parents, educators, and business/industry members to create a coherent, developmental sequence of planned activities and experiences for young people to engage in their learning, to see the relevance of schooling to their futures, and to posses essential knowledge and skills to succeed in the workplace. This chapter will present a case for moving forward in a K-12 career development system: Part One presents an overview of the issues, including elements for working with disengaged learners; Part Two describes in detail a model for integrating career development throughout a K-12 school system.

In Search of Dreams

This chapter will offer school personnel and parents a model for helping students develop a life plan—*one that integrates career dreams in the context of labor market realities.* To increase the probability of success in adulthood, life plans transform ambitions to everyday goals; they "provide adolescents with a sense of order, encourage them to engage in strategic effort and to sustain high levels of motivation, and help them to use familial and organizational resources" (Schneider and Stevenson, 1999). Such a personalized plan communicates a student's uniqueness, documents growth, displays patterns of interests and aptitudes, and fuels energy and commitment to hold fast to dreams while accepting legitimate limitations.

Dreams are starting points not just for students—they must be starting points for the helpers, guides and mentors as well. In fact, the whole K-12 educational system must embrace a dream of every high school student graduating with a life plan that is personally invigorating and responsive to change, one that yields sufficient income to meet at least minimal needs, and one that satisfies an individual's basic need to do "good" work on behalf of self and society.

Seasoned educators know how elusive this dream for a K-12 career development system can be. School counselors and vocational teachers on the brink of retirement can describe their efforts to implement career education in the 1970s and 1980s. They can recall their quest to institutionalize elements of school-to-work during the 1990s. As they look around their schools in the 21st century, they still find gaps of understanding and appreciation for students' need for career planning. In spite of extensive and enthusiastic support from the business and industry community, in spite of what seems like common sense, and in spite of anecdotal and research-based data that confirm a linkage between success in school and work and career planning, the gap persists between good intentions to provide career development and follow-through in a coherent, systematic way. Career guidance remains spotty, haphazard, out-of-date and reserved for high school juniors and seniors who express an interest in going to college. Because many educators, parents and policy makers do not recognize the benefits of career planning as a significant contributing factor to student achievement, career guidance activities continue to lose ground to a narrow view of basic skills and preparation for high-stakes testing.

Adults know first-hand how inefficient, let alone costly, trial and error career planning can be. In a 1999 Gallup Poll commissioned by the National Career Development Association, findings confirmed that most adults (69%) believe they did not receive sufficient or satisfactory career guidance. If they could repeat adolescence, they would insist on comprehensive career guidance, personal time with a guidance counselor, and resources to explore and field-test career ideas. Instead, only 13 percent met with a high school counselor; most got information about careers from friends and family members (National Career Development Association, 2000). The challenge that the education community faces is how to guarantee effective career development to *all* students, regardless of socioeconomic status and parental aspirations; size, resources and location of the school district; and prevailing state and national politics. Dreams *can* come true, as the reader will see in the model proposed later in this chapter and detailed in the appendix.

Putting Humpty Dumpty Back Together Again

To build a functional system that supports life planning for all students, it will take all members of the larger educational community to pool their wisdom and energy to overcome the three deadly pitfalls that lead to system disintegration: fragmentation, marginalization and competition for scarce resources. Some school staffs are beginning to recognize that to optimize learning, education must be delivered through collaborative relationships that cut across disciplines and that link to personally relevant purposes, i.e., contextualized. Yet, in many large districts, counselors, psychologists, social workers, and career specialists are often organized into separate units with different supervisors, thereby exacerbating fragmentation (Adelman and Taylor, 2002). Although student support staff usually deal with the same "common barriers to learning (e.g., poor instruction, lack of parental involvement, violence and unsafe schools, inadequate support for student transitions), they tend to do so with little or no coordination, and sparse attention to moving toward integrated efforts" (p. 236).

School counselors know full well that up to half of their students may manifest learning, behavioral, and emotional problems (p. 236). Even with a strong desire to deliver an effective comprehensive guidance and counseling program to meet the needs of this volume of at-risk students, if the program is not viewed as essential, implementation gets pushed to the side (marginalized) and considered expendable in the next round of budget cuts. In this era of high-stakes testing, educational support activities for personal/social/career development take a backseat to instruction, even though educators experience first hand the challenge of trying to engage students who are distressed. And, "distressed" students can be those who are doubtful about their futures in a changing economy, those who are underestimating or overestimating the amount of preparation their career goal may require, and those who are befuddled about how to pay for their post-secondary choice.

Worse yet, as available resources shrink and public demands increase, a comprehensive guidance and counseling program may have to compete with other "non-essential" programs, such as music and art. Who is in a position to make that kind of decision for any child and according to what criteria? With site-based management practices, decisions which should be centralized are often relegated to principals, who may or may not perceive that a comprehensive guidance and counseling program adds value to their overall educational program.

Fortunately, comprehensive guidance and counseling programs are becoming the norm for how counselors organize their activities and spend their time. Counselors, however, need to be wary of fragmentation and marginalization within the program itself (Herr, 2001; Gysbers and Henderson, 2001). The components of the framework—individual student planning, guidance curriculum, responsive services, and system support—are often understood as independent elements, when in fact they are deeply interconnected. Without responsive services and a guidance curriculum, individual student planning is weak and ineffective; without a guidance curriculum and responsive services, school climate at the systems level cannot be adequately addressed; and without individual student planning, the other components begin to lose relevance. Furthermore, individual student planning, guidance curriculum and responsive services all require an infrastructure, so these efforts are dependent on the system itself. To illustrate this point, consider the following diagram:

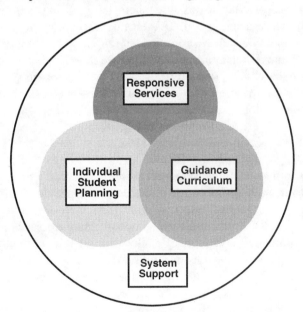

Figure 1.1   A systems/view of a comprehensive guidance and counseling program

What is different about this perspective is that the guidance and counseling "program" is not a linear model; it is one where activities are interconnected, which means that what happens in one affects what happens in the others. This view also recognizes that what goes on in a counseling program happens within a system, which is part of another system, and so on. The reverse is also true: what happens in the larger system of national, state, community, district, and school affects the counseling program. The system in which school counseling takes place must be fundamentally integrated in the larger system of the school and school district and must be viewed as essential to the "business" of the schools: curriculum, instruction and assessment. (See Figure 1.3.)

In the era of educational reform, this has never been truer than it is today. For example, legislators in the state of Washington passed the Education Reform Act of 1993, requiring standards-based curricular and instructional practices in all grades and performance-based assessment at the fourth, seventh and tenth grades. Then, in 2000, the Washington State Board of Education expanded graduation requirements to include a high school + education plan and a culminating project. In the meantime, counselors across the state were attempting to implement a comprehensive guidance and counseling program, K-14. Even now, the two efforts are not capturing the kind of synergy possible when energy from multiple sources is harnessed towards a single aim. In the authors' opinion, now is the best of times for school counseling programs—a real opportunity to contribute to student outcomes in meaningful and visible ways and to create a complete K-12 system in which all members and units contribute to career development, thereby increasing the relevance of coursework, the meaning of a high school diploma, and the likelihood of realized dreams.

It's About Time!

Building or remodeling a system is labor intensive and just plain hard work. However, both authors have witnessed busy people challenge and remove barriers that they had previously perceived as immovable or impenetrable. For at least the past decade, school counselors have struggled to reach recommended levels of time allocation in each component of a comprehensive school counseling program. What if they thought differently about time itself? First of all, effective programs are not about time: they are about meeting identified student needs and demonstrating measurable impact on important student outcomes. Secondly, because time is unanimously voted as the biggest barrier to any desired change, what if counselors said to themselves that they have all the time they need? Busy people, regardless of their role, often complain that they don't have time to think about time!

Yet, **NOW** is the only time there is; the rest is psychological time spent in remembering the past, often with anger or hurt, or worrying about the future, which translates to fear and anxiety (Tolle, 2000). According to Ekhart Tolle, the only time that matters is this moment—a moment of clock time in which we act on a choice that is congruent with our intentions; to spend time any other way confounds progress and leads to stress, disappointment, frustration, cynicism, and ultimately to burn out. Busy school counselors can ask themselves periodically if the barriers they perceive are real, in which case they can confront them with a plan and action steps, or imagined in psychological time, in which case they can let them go and refocus on what is at hand.

Reaching Students Who Can But Won't

As the graphic above suggests, there may be ways to maximize the use of time. Consider the area of overlap among individual student planning, guidance curriculum and responsive services. The authors hypothesize that this area of the Venn diagram includes students with motivation problems. Seasoned educators confirm that the proportion of students who can (have necessary knowledge and skills) and will (are motivated and compliant) is shrinking; the population that seems to be growing fastest are those students who are capable but disinterested and/or disengaged from learning. In some schools, teachers report that only 10 % to 15 % of their students "come to class motivationally ready and able to learn" (Adelman and Taylor, 2002).

One way to think about motivation is to consider the following approaches to meeting the needs of four types of students: 1) those with ability and motivation (Can and Will); 2) those with ability but not motivation (Can but Won't); 3) those who lack skills but are motivated (Can't but Will); and 4) those who lack both skills and motivation (Can't and Won't).

Students Who Can and Will:	Students Who Can but Won't:
• Challenge them to take advanced classes • Provide leadership opportunities, such as natural helpers, mentoring, and tutoring other students • Encourage extracurricular activities • Teach tolerance and empathy • Help them learn how to accept mistakes as part of learning • Help them realize elements of a balanced life, including techniques for stress management	• Identify the root cause of the motivation issue • Provide leadership opportunities, such as natural helpers, mentoring, and tutoring other students • Make learning relevant and meaningful • Identify obstacles to motivation • Help them see "big" picture by connecting school to life • Provide opportunities for goal setting and action planning
Students Who Can't but Will:	**Students Who Can't and Won't:**
• Consider testing for learning disabilities • Organize a tutoring program to assist, e.g., buddy system • Implement a Sustained Silent Reading (SSR) Program • Help them identify and explore their strengths • Teach them how to monitor their own growth • Modify learning so they experience success • Focus on one skill or one segment of an assignment at a time • Identify their "intelligences" and incorporate in lessons	• Present options for alternative programs • Provide training on social skills, with an emphasis on personal responsibility • Ensure they experience success and provide recognition • Build relationships so they feel visible and valued • Discover what activities bring them pleasure and find avenues for them to express their strengths and unique intelligences

Table 1: Strategies for Engaging Students
(Developed by Dr. Christine Jensen, October, 2001)

The *system* that supports all four types of students must itself have several features:

1. Active and constructive *relationships* among key stakeholders—parents, teachers, counselors, administrators, school boards, and the business/industry community.
2. A clear and compelling mission among stakeholders to encourage as well as challenge **every** student to excel and to provide

educational supports to those who need them.

3. School cultures that support student belonging and success and that personalize education.

4. Concrete plans and specific actions that each stakeholder commits to performing on behalf of students. (See Appendix A.)

5. Recognition and acceptance by all stakeholders of the importance of career development in motivating all students to be engaged in their learning, regardless of their level of ability or degree of motivation.

6. Clearly stated outcomes and measures for career development, K-12, that are addressed through an integrated curriculum, one that is willingly and ably presented by teachers and counselors.

7. A sequence of planned events, K-12, which help students meet desired career guidance outcomes in developmentally appropriate ways, including school-to-career opportunities. (See Appendix B.)

Attitudes Shape Behavior

Life planning is a deeply personal endeavor, one that is best conducted within a supportive network of counselors, teachers and parents. Students need to be able to think out loud about who they are, who they want to be, and how they think they can get there. An element of career development that is all too often absent in schools is the annual conferencing that invites reflection, appreciation of growth, and mid-course correction when actions are not aligned with dreams. (See Figure 1.5.) To personalize education, the importance of this conference cannot be overstated.

Yet, building a personalized educational system that supports *all* types of students will require us to challenge our own thinking and perceptions. Because attitudes shape behavior, as professionals we must be willing to ask difficult questions, such as do we really believe that all students can learn? Or do only some students—those of a particular socioeconomic group or those of a particular ethnic/racial group or those from a particular type of family—have the potential to succeed? Data compiled and disseminated by the Education Trust (www.edtrust.org) suggests a pattern of underperforming students that can be traced to low expectations on the part of counselors and teachers, inequitable access and/or distribution of information and resources, and ineffective teaching—not poverty or race or family structure (House and Hayes, 2002).

As human beings, we have a natural tendency to judge, which can easily lead us to placing blame for why students are not as successful as we would like them to be—or so we say. But as data from Education Trust point out, school personnel may need to look inward and challenge some closely held and often hidden assumptions. In accepting responsibility for creating the conditions for student success in schools, counselors and teachers can begin by refining their own skills in differentiating between skill deficits and motivation issues of the students with whom they work.

Going one step further, school personnel need to devise strategies for re-engaging learners with specific motivation challenges. Table 2 presents six typical problems of unmotivated learners. The suggestions are based on the notion that students will expend effort when they expect to perform a task successfully, when they value the rewards, and when they have an opportunity to actually engage in the task. This formula, *effort = expectancy X value*, is a general principle of motivation (Brophy, 1998). In other words, for students to exert effort, they must value the task and see its relevance to them now or in the future, they must feel confident in their ability to meet the demands of the task, and they must have opportunity to do so.

Another key element of motivation that is relevant here comes from the work of Csikszentmihalyi, who studied the experience of "flow." "Flow experiences" are those in which we become so absorbed in what we are doing that we forget about time. According to Csikszentmihalyi, people experience flow during challenging activities that are within their ability to perform—a combination of perceived challenge and perceived skill.

Table 2. Motivational Issues and Strategies to Eliminate Them
Based on Brophy (1998).

Type of Issue	Indicators	Strategies to Eliminate
Limited Ability	Has difficulty keeping up; has low expectations and accepts failure; may withdraw into passivity or become a behavior problem; frustrated when can't handle tasks	Reduce difficulty; use lessons that are short, multisensory, and familiar; model "thinking out loud;" find a tutor; help student set realistic goals; make frequent eye contact; provide extra credit work; grade individual effort and production
Failure Syndrome	Gives up quickly; believes failure is due to lack of ability, not effort; low expectations of being successful	Provide successful experiences; recognize effort; help student to set reasonable goals; teach coping skills

Self-Worth Protection	Does things to please teacher or impress peers; distracted by being preoccupied with image; seeks to avoid humiliation	Orient student to learning goals, not performance goals; provide safe learning environment; offer cooperative learning; discover areas of curiosity; communicate belief in student's ability; link effort and self-worth; avoid competitive situations; teach student how to ask for help
Committed Under-Achievers	Avoids responsibility; sets unrealistic goals; socially immature and/or impulsive; oppositional	Use escalating learning contracts; avoid nagging and threatening comments; help student develop occupational plans; acknowledge accomplishments
Alienated	Doesn't find school learning meaningful or worthwhile; doesn't engage; may resist overtly or covertly; displays negative reactions to school	Use learning contracts and collaborative goal setting; build relationship through sincere interest and active listening; discover/build on existing interests; encourage honest communication about feelings and preferences
Chronically distracted or burnt-out	Displays uncharacteristic fatigue and/or lack of enthusiasm; cannot focus or concentrate; does not meet important deadlines; looks and acts depressed or withdrawn; avoids contact with previously important adults; grades decline, often suddenly	Refer to counselor immediately; acknowledge hard work and dependability; show empathy and understanding; teach stress management skills; accept student's need to slow down and incorporate self-care

I Think I Can, I Think I Can...

As transition planning with students and their parents becomes institutionalized, counselors and teachers are noticing that some students may be lacking more than skills and/or motivation. They may, in fact, be experiencing a sense of hopelessness and despair about their futures. C. R. Snyder, a clinical psychologist at the University of Kansas, has studied the phenomenon of hope and believes it is more than a "cross your fingers and hope for the best" attitude (Snyder, 2002). His reconceptualized view of hope is "not as a passive emotional phenomenon that occurs only in the darkest moments, but as a process through which individuals actively pursue their goals" (p. 299). According to Snyder, hopeful thinking is composed of three elements: goals, pathways thinking (planning to meet goals), and agency thinking (goal-directed determination).

Goals are those hoped-for ends that are "targets of mental action-sequences" and that "anchor purposive behavior" (p. 299). They may be long term or short term, they may be large or small, and they may be attainable through great or minimal effort. Snyder proposes that goals are hierarchical: they can be global and general, such as intending to live a happy and meaningful life; they can be domain-specific, such as desiring to complete a bachelor's degree or graduating from high school or getting a good job; or they can be goal-specific, such as wanting to get an "A" in Algebra (p. 299-300).

Before initiating a behavior sequence to achieve the outcome, however, students must engage in two more cognitive functions: they must construct plans (pathways) and they must feel energized and optimistic about taking action (agency). The two cognitions are inseparable—a plan without action and action without a plan lead nowhere. Embedded in this three-part process is an ability and willingness to "re-goal" (p. 302). Students need to learn how to discriminate between goals they value and goals valued more by others; they need to have courage to develop back-up plans when they do not become professional athletes, as twelve percent of younger students expect to become (Csikszentmihalyi, 2000); and they need to be skilled at setting new goals that inspire pathways and agency thinking.

The millennial generation, or as some refer to as the "tapas" generation because this group prefers information in bite-sized pieces (Gregory, 2002), will apparently face a particularly difficult challenge when it comes to being hopeful. Snyder and his colleagues believe that the development of hope begins during infancy, when children learn that they can effect change in their environment in order to get their needs met. The most hopeful people are those who experienced a dependable relationship in which basic needs were satisfied and in which they were allowed to establish a sense of self (Snyder, 2002). If uncertainty was dealt with satisfactorily in early childhood, more than likely it will be dealt with satisfactorily in the future.

In the aftermath of the terrorist attacks on September 11, 2001, and in recognition of changes in the workplace due to technological and economic events, the sense of predictability and certainty is greatly diminished for the generation born in the early 1980s and who are still in school. Perhaps more than any previous generation since the industrial age, this group of students must have strong support and effective strategies for remaining hopeful about their futures. And, their caregivers will require a great deal of information so they can provide useful guidance. School counselors, in particular, are well positioned to help students identify their true values and interests (in short, their dreams), to devise action plans that will allow them to live congruently, and to experience confidence and competence in reaching a career goal. Following is a detailed plan, the Alpha Model, for providing K-12 experiences that help students achieve all three elements of hope: goals, action planning, and initiative.

Part Two: The Blueprint—The Alpha Career Guidance Model

As mentioned earlier, the state of Washington recently passed legislation mandating High School+ Education Plans and Culminating Projects as graduation requirements to reflect student exploration, understanding, planning, and preparation for future career and education options. In response, school districts have been looking for tools to aid them in their design and implementation of K-12 career guidance programs that align with and support student preparation for these new requirements. The Alpha Career Guidance Model in Appendix B was created to meet this need, and provides a framework and model from which effective career guidance programs could be developed. What follows is an overview of the core elements of the model: conditions for success, exit outcomes and developmental targets, assessment tools (career portfolio and education plan), and a process for career guidance instruction.

Conditions for Success

Before outlining the details of the Alpha Model, it is important to discuss the systemic conditions in which such a model should be implemented. As a seed will either germinate or die depending upon the conditions of the soil in which it is planted, so to the success of any career guidance program is dependent upon the certain conditions within the education system in which it is developed. The fact that one could fill a library with the countless career guidance models in schools throughout the nation, yet be hard pressed to find a handful of programs that have been fully implemented and survived the test of time and changing administrations, testifies that there is more to a successful program than a good model. In the experience of many counselors, while efforts at creating models for career guidance have been quite fruitful, attempts to implement, sustain, and gain district support for such programs have not been as successful.

The successful development, implementation, and sustainability of the Alpha Model requires the following five core conditions within the host school district:

- Career development outcomes are endorsed as part of the district's overall mission and goals, and are supported by all key stakeholders.
- The K-12 career guidance program is perceived and supported by all key stakeholders as valuable and essential in addressing district outcomes in a real and effective way.
- The task of addressing career development outcomes is perceived as a shared responsibility among all key stakeholders.
- Sufficient time and resources are allocated to ensure that career development outcomes are fully addressed at each grade level.
- Education Pathways are clearly developed, supported, and utilized by the school district to aid students in their education planning.

The importance of these conditions cannot be overstated. Consider for a moment the scenario of a superintendent determining the district budget for the upcoming school year. Overall, student scores on the statewide assessment have been low and there is increasing pressure from the community, state, and school board to increase student performance. Further complicating the decision is the fact that resources are decreasing due to a struggling economy. Given these variables, the superintendent is faced with the challenge of maximizing existing resources to meet the mission and goals of the district.

Suppose for a moment that a career guidance program is developing within the superintendent's district, but the five conditions listed earlier do not exist. In evaluating the allocation of resources to support the guidance program, the superintendent approaches this task from the perspective that the district's sole mission is to increase student achievement and perform well on the state assessments. As illustrated in figure 1.2, this narrow mission creates the perception that the developing career guidance program is disconnected from the goals and outcomes of the district. From this perspective, the superintendent would logically conclude that allocating resources to the guidance program in light of a diminishing budget would not be a prudent investment.

Figure 1.2 – Career Guidance in a system lacking the five core conditions

In contrast, now apply the same scenario to a district where all five conditions are in place. Operating from a broader definition of student outcomes within the district's overall mission, the career guidance program is perceived much differently. As illustrated in figure 1.3, the program is now viewed as fully integrated and essential to the district's overall mission and goals. From this perspective, the superintendent would logically conclude that allocating resources to the program in light of a diminishing budget would be a prudent investment since the program is tied directly to the district's outcomes.

Figure 1.3 – Career Guidance in a system with the five core conditions

Comparison of the two scenarios illustrates the importance of creating such conditions within the education system as part of successfully implementing a career guidance program. While these conditions do exist in some districts, many counselors unfortunately find themselves in districts where these conditions seem quite elusive, and student performance on statewide assessments has become the narrow focus of the system's mission. For counselors in these systems, increasing their influence and involvement in shaping the district's mission, goals, and decisions is extremely critical.

Exit Outcomes and Developmental Targets

As with all effective programs, the Alpha Model is, first and foremost, outcome driven. These outcomes provide focus for the overall career guidance program, serve as standards for evaluation and, as mentioned earlier, should be fully integrated into the district's overall mission and goals. The Alpha Model is built around the following three exit outcomes:

- *All students will exit high school competent in the academic and technical skills required for success in post-secondary education and the workplace.* This outcome emphasizes the importance of guiding students toward greater intellectual achievement and skill development in light of the expectations from employers and post-secondary institutions, as well as highlighting the importance of addressing areas of deficit.
- *All students will exit high school in pursuit of a specific post-high school goal toward which their education experience has been aligned.* This outcome emphasizes the importance of increasing awareness of career and education options, goal setting and education planning, establishing a purpose to learning, and pursuing education pathways in alignment with personal interests and ambitions.
- *All students will exit high school as responsible managers of their learning, planning, and preparation toward their educational and career ambitions.* This outcome emphasizes the importance of student reflection on their learning, self-directedness, and ownership of preparation and life direction.

In addition to addressing student needs for development of goals, action planning, and personal agency, these outcomes also provide a framework from which a scope and sequence of developmental targets can be developed throughout the K-12 continuum. As illustrated in Appendix B, the Alpha School District Model defines career developmental targets for grades K-3, 4-6, 7, 8, 9, 10, 11, and 12.

Assessment Tools: The Student Portfolio and Personal Education Plan

In addition to defining exit outcomes, the Alpha Model includes a means for assessing student progress in relation to these outcomes and the developmental targets designated at each grade level. The Alpha Model maintains that outcomes and assessments are interdependent, and to include one without the other creates significant problems for implementation. On the one hand, outcomes without assessments create programs that cannot be measured or evaluated. On the other hand, assessments without outcomes result in activities and tools for which students and staff cannot articulate a purpose. In the Alpha Model, two assessment tools are used throughout the K-12 system to assess student success in relation to the exit outcomes and developmental targets: the Student Portfolio and Personal Education Plan.

The purpose behind the Student Portfolio in the Alpha Model is to serve as a vehicle demonstrating academic achievement, career exploration, and education planning throughout a student's K-12 educational experience. As illustrated in Appendix B, the required elements of the portfolio are determined at each grade level by the developmental targets, and include such items as report cards, assessment data, career information, personal reflections, honors, and awards. In addition, over time the portfolio demonstrates developmental patterns and becomes a valuable tool for the purpose of post-secondary planning. The Student Portfolio may take any of a variety of forms including notebooks, file folders, compact discs, and digital folders on a server.

The second assessment tool used in the Alpha Model is the Personal Education Plan (PEP), which is used to demonstrate evidence of student goal setting, management of learning and preparation, and thoughtful and purposeful educational planning. As with the Student Portfolio, the PEP is initially developed in grades K-3 and continues to evolve as the student progresses through the elementary, middle, and high school years. As detailed below, the elements of the PEP are defined for each grade level, and become more and more complex as the student continues toward graduation:

Elements of the Personal Education Plan in Grades K-3
- A personal goal and strategy for the school year
- A reading goal and strategy for the school year
- A school habit/behavior goal and strategy for the school year

Elements of the Personal Education Plan in Grades 4-6
  • A personal goal and strategy for the school year
  • A reading goal and strategy for the school year
  • A school habit/behavior goal and strategy for the school year
  • Academic performance goal and strategy for the school year
  • Academic improvement goal and strategy for the school year

Elements of the Personal Education Plan in Grade 7
  • A personal goal and strategy for the school year
  • A school habit/behavior goal and strategy for the school year
  • Academic performance goal and strategy for the school year
  • Academic improvement goal and strategy for the school year
  • Scope and sequence of 8th grade courses and learning experiences aligned with student goals and interests.

Elements of the Personal Education Plan in Grade 8
  • A personal goal and strategy for the school year
  • A school habit/behavior goal and strategy for the school year
  • Academic performance goal and strategy for the school year
  • Academic improvement goal and strategy for the school year
  • Tentative post-high school career goal/interest
  • Tentative post-high school education goal
  • 4-Year scope and sequence of high school courses aligned with post-high school goals.

Elements of the Personal Education Plan in Grade 9
  • Academic performance goal and strategy for the school year
  • Academic improvement goal and strategy for the school year
  • Tentative post-high school career goal/interest
  • Tentative post-high school education goal
  • Tentative Education Pathway interests/goal
  • 4-Year scope and sequence of high school courses aligned with post-high school goals.

Elements of the Personal Education Plan in Grade 10
  • Academic performance goal and strategy for the school year
  • Academic improvement goal and strategy for the school year
  • Tentative post-high school career goal/interest
  • List of post-secondary schools of interest
  • Education Pathway interests
  • 4-Year scope and sequence of high school courses aligned with

post-high school goals and education pathway.

<u>Elements of the Personal Education Plan in Grade 11</u>
- Academic performance goal and strategy for the school year
- Academic improvement goal and strategy for the school year
- Post-high school career goal/interest
- Specific Post-secondary school to which to apply
- Selected Education Pathway (s)
- Culminating Project topic interest
- 4-Year scope and sequence of high school courses aligned with post-high school goals and education pathway.

<u>Elements of the Personal Education Plan in Grade 12</u>
- Academic performance goal and strategy for the school year
- Academic improvement goal and strategy for the school year
- Post-high school career goal/interest
- Specific Post-secondary schools where accepted or awaiting notification
- Financial Plan for post-high school plans
- 4-Year scope and sequence of high school courses aligned with post-high school goals and education pathway.

Quality of Outcomes Reflect Quality of Instruction

Complementing the importance of clear outcomes and effective assessments is the need for a quality career guidance instructional process. As a skilled teacher takes students through a process that naturally leads to demonstrations of desired learning objectives, so too must the deliverer of career guidance craft a process that brings about demonstration of the outcomes of the program. In the Alpha Model, the quality of the instructional process is measured by:
- The degree to which Student Portfolios contain all the required elements, and are used for goal setting and development of the Personal Education Plan

- The degree to which Personal Education Plans address all required elements, and are coherent with the student's stated goals and aspirations

To illustrate the importance of the instructional process and its relationship to these two outcomes, let us consider for a moment the following freshman career development activities common to many high school career guidance programs. The activities take place in a required semester class to ensure that all students have opportunity to participate in the career guidance unit. Since only one half of the students take the class during the fall semester, the other half of the freshman class will complete their career unit later in the spring. The unit begins with students completing an interest inventory that generates a list of careers matching their reported interests. From this list of career areas, students are asked to complete a research paper on a career of interest, addressing such topics as training requirements, salary, projected employment, work duties, and personal impressions about the field. At the completion of the unit, the report and information from the assessments are added to the student's portfolio.

In early March, about two months prior to the spring semester career unit, students receive a 50-minute registration orientation from their guidance counselors in their English classes. During this orientation, students receive their registration materials and are asked to select courses for the following school year while outlining a four-year plan of courses that correspond to their career interests, post-high school goals, and the school's graduation requirements. Students are encouraged to utilize the information found within their portfolios to aid them in this process. While more time is needed to answer all the student questions, time is limited due to the fact that the English teacher has so much content to cover. At the end of the short orientation, students are instructed that they will have one week to have these materials completed, signed by a parent, and returned to the counseling office to meet the registration deadline.

Following the registration deadline, counselors begin the painstaking and time consuming process of cleaning up schedules for the 60 percent of students whose registration forms were in error, incomplete, missing a parent signature, or absent altogether. Furthermore, examination of student four-year plans reveals a pattern of random and inappropriate selection of courses, avoidance of difficult courses, and education plans misaligned with the requirements for stated future ambitions. Using the Alpha Model's criteria for a quality instructional process, this career program receives a failing grade.

For purposes of comparison to the Alpha Model later in our discussion, we will identify the instructional process described in this scenario as "The Traditional Process". As illustrated in figure 1.4, the traditional process consists of five distinct instructional phases:

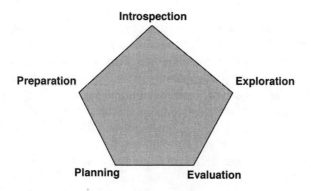

**Figure 1.4 – The Traditional Process for Career
Guidance Instruction**

Introspection: Characterized by student exploration of personal interests, goals, values, needs, and resources through self-assessment exercises and tools and formation of cognitive framework for education planning and vocational goal setting.

Exploration: Characterized by identification and investigation of multiple vocational options using career interest and information tools and resources, and creation of a list of potential career interests.

Evaluation: Characterized by prioritizing education and career interests by taking time to reflect upon personal preferences and how those are perceived to be satisfied or frustrated within the environments of various educational and occupational interests.

Planning: Characterized by creating a Personalized Education Plan which maps out the scope and sequence of courses, learning experiences, and steps reflecting the most effective strategy and path toward one's goals.

Preparation: Characterized by personal engagement in implementing one's plan through registration for courses, development of a portfolio, application to post-secondary schools, and participation in selected learning experiences.

Close examination of our scenario demonstrates the progression of these phases throughout the career guidance instructional process. In the freshman units, students were asked to identify their interests (introspection), explore career options (exploration), evaluate their perceptions about the career fields researched (evaluation), develop education plans (planning), and register for courses (preparation). On the surface, this process appears to be very logical and sound, which is likely the reason it is so prevalent in many guidance programs today. In reality, however, the traditional process described in this scenario has two extremely significant flaws.

Personalizing Student Planning

The most significant weakness of the traditional process, and where much of the poor outcomes can be attributed, is its reliance on students to figure out on their own how to translate their learning and aspirations into education plans that are coherent, aligned with future goals, and engaged through the registration process. While those who apply this approach are hopeful for quality outcomes, their hopes fail to align with the reality that the selection of courses by many high school students more often reflects avoidance of difficult courses and recommendations of teachers by friends than attention to future goals. It is also the experience of this author that many students have difficulty identifying and putting together the appropriate scope and sequence of courses and experiences to meet their goals, and need guidance to avoid creating schedules that are misaligned with their intended focus.

Unfortunately, this reliance on students to go it alone with regard to education planning is becoming an all too common trend among our nation's schools. In a recent study conducted by Ferris State University (2002) of career decision-making and planning patterns among high school students, over 50 percent of students surveyed reported they could not identify anyone in school helpful in advising them on preparing for post-high school career and education options. Furthermore, while most students viewed their parents as being the most helpful in preparing for their future, their conversations with parents about career planning were limited to about three hours or less over the past few months. In short, students are struggling to find the support and guidance they need to effectively plan for the future.

The Alpha Model seeks to address this need by infusing advising and personalized attention to planning within the career guidance instructional process. As illustrated in figure 1.5 below, the Alpha Model adds an additional phase to the instructional process called Conferencing to serve as a bridge between the Evaluation and Planning phases.

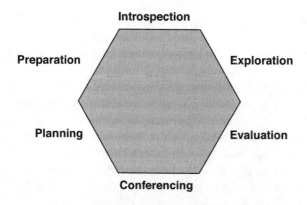

**Figure 1.5: The Alpha Model Process for Career
Guidance Instruction**

In the Conferencing phase, students and their parents meet with an advisor to review their portfolio while discussing their goals, strategies, and concerns with regard to learning and future planning. At the elementary school level, this conference occurs with the student's classroom teacher as the advisor and focuses on identifying personal goals and those related to academic growth and improvement. During middle school, students, parents, and advisors address personal goals, strategies for academic growth and improvement, and high school planning and transition. At the high school level, these conferences take on a post-secondary focus and include identifying preferences and concerns, clarifying post-secondary aspirations, and identifying effective strategies and education pathways to reach post-high school goals.

Key to the Conferencing phase is the dialogue that takes place between the student, parent, and advisor. To facilitate this communication, students and parents are given specific prompts prior to their scheduled conference that serve as focal points of conversation with their advisor. In addition, advisors are trained in advance in the use of these prompts to assist parents and students in this process. The following are examples of prompts used in the Alpha Model's Conferencing phase:

Sample Conference Prompts for Grades K-6:
- From your portfolio, what work are you most proud of? Why?
- What activities in school do you feel you do well?
- What activities in school would you like to become better at?
- What grades would you like to earn this year?

- How many books would you like to read this year?
- What do you feel are your good habits?
- Are there habits you would like to change?
- Do you have any concerns about school and your learning?

Sample Conference Prompts for Grades 7-8:
- From your portfolio, what work are you most proud of? Why?
- In what subjects do you believe you do well?
- In what subjects would you like to improve your performance?
- What grades would you like to earn this year?
- How do you feel about your study habits? Are there habits you would like to change?
- What careers most interest you at this time?
- What courses available in high school interest you the most?
- What would you like to do after high school?
- Do you have any concerns about school, your learning, and transition to high school?

Sample Conference Prompts for Grades 9-12:
- From your portfolio, what do you see as your strengths and skills?
- What are your career interests and values?
- What is your current goal for the year following graduation?
- What courses in high school are of greatest interest to you?
- In what subjects are you doing well?
- In what subjects do you need to improve?
- How do you feel about your study habits? Are there habits you would like to change?
- Do you have any concerns about school, your learning, and preparing for the future?
- Additional questions related to post-high school planning, financial planning, senior project, and academic performance as appropriate.

In this expanded instructional process, the Planning phase extends naturally from the Conferencing phase as advisors, students, and parents close their conference by translating the content of their dialogue into a Personal Education Plan. In stark contrast to the Traditional Process, the student's Personal Education Plan is developed collaboratively and is carefully crafted to meet the student's individual learning needs, ambitions, and personal concerns. The culmination of the Conferencing and Planning phases is marked by parents, students, and advisors signing off on a Personal Education Plan that all parties agree is appropriate and coherent. Once completed, the PEP is used as the basis for student registration, resulting in the elimination of many of the unwanted outcomes generated by the traditional process described earlier.

Attention to Scheduling and Sequencing of Phases

A second problem related to our career guidance scenario is the issue of scheduling career activities to ensure that all students complete the phases of the career guidance instructional process in the proper sequence. As you may recall, because of the way career units were scheduled according to semester classes and the timing of registration, the experience of those students completing career units during the fall semester was quite different than those enrolled in the spring semester course. As illustrated in table 1.3, using the phases of the traditional approach as a context for evaluating the experiences of both groups of students reveals the problems with this approach to career guidance delivery:

	Fall Semester Class	Spring Semester Class
Fall Semester	Introspection Phase Exploration Phase Evaluation Phase	
Registration	Planning Phase Preparation Phase	Planning Phase Preparation Phase
Spring Semester		Introspection Phase Exploration Phase Evaluation Phase

Table 1.3: Comparison of Groups in the Traditional Process Scenario

As can be clearly seen from the above table, only the fall semester group had the opportunity to experience the phases of introspection, exploration, and evaluation prior to the assigned tasks of planning and preparation associated with the scheduling of the registration period. As a consequence, even if students were able to translate their preferences and aspirations into effective education plans and course selections without the intervention of personalized advising, only 50 percent of the entire freshman class would have had the career guidance experiences necessary to be ready for the task. Furthermore, those students completing their career planning activities in the spring would be unable to actually apply their learning to the planning and preparation phases until registration for the 11th grade year!

As demonstrated in appendix B, the Alpha Model takes into consideration the importance of planning activities according to the required phases of the instructional process as opposed to convenience of time. At the elementary level, particular attention is paid to the scheduling of Parent/Teacher Conferences that are used for the Conferencing, Planning and Preparation phases. At the secondary level, activities are scheduled according to the period of registration, at which point students must be ready to implement their Personal Education Plans as part of the Preparation Phase. By paying attention to these key events, the Alpha Model ensures that all students complete each phase of the instructional process in sequence and at the appropriate times.

Redefining the Role of the School Counselor

In responding to presentations of the Alpha Model, counselors often express much concern with regard to their role and the time required in implementing the model. As if by automatic response, many are quick to point out that such a model is completely unrealistic and impossible to implement due to the counselor's large student loads and responsibilities. Such individuals often cite the Conferencing phase and personalization of planning as the focus of their criticisms. How could counselors, they argue, possibly meet with each and every student and parent within their caseload and continue to manage all of their other responsibilities?

Such criticisms often reflect two assumptions common to the thinking of many counselors, and which need to be carefully examined if true progress is to be made in helping students develop the goals, action plans, and personal agency required for hopeful thinking. The first concerns the perceived role and responsibility of the counselor in relation to his or her peers, the second the issue of time and priorities. Both are described in the following example of syllogistic thought, and demonstrate the significant impact these assumptions have on the success or failure of a career guidance program.

"Due to their training, knowledge, and access to planning materials, school counselors are the only qualified individuals in the school system to be responsible for providing the guidance and advising my students need to effectively plan and prepare for their future" (*Assumption regarding the role and responsibility of counselor and non-counselor peers*)

"Because of their student load and the amount of responsibilities and activities requiring their time and attention, there is no possible way counselors can find the time to provide the personalized guidance and advising that students need" *(Assumption regarding time and priorities)*

"Therefore since counselors are the only qualified individuals to provide the personalized guidance and advising students need but lack the time to do so, students cannot receive the guidance and advising they need to effectively plan for their future and will need to figure this out on their own"

(Logical conclusion and outcome)

It is important that we not underestimate the power of such beliefs and assumptions in relation to the problems we seek to address. As illustrated in previous line of thinking, beliefs about the counselor's role, responsibility, use of time, and priorities are critical elements to be addressed in implementing a career guidance program that will truly be benefit students. Consequently, attention needs to be given to these beliefs.

Since the issue of counselor beliefs about time and priorities has been addressed earlier in this chapter (see "It's about Time"), we will limit our discussion to those assumptions concerning the counselor's role and responsibility in relation to non-counselor peers. First of all, the authors agree that counselors do have specialized training, knowledge, and resources with regard to career and education planning beyond that possessed by most educators within the education system. Furthermore, these authors agree that school counselors are truly qualified to provide career guidance and advising to students. Therefore, at issue is the question as to whether or not the counselor is the *only* one qualified to provide such guidance and direction.

According to the assumption, the status of counselors as the only qualified persons to provide guidance and advising to students in their career planning is based solely on their level of specialized training, knowledge, and resources in relation to their non-counseling peers. Assuming that having a certain level of training, knowledge and resources can equip someone to be an effective advisor, certain questions logically arise:

What level of training, knowledge, and resources are needed to effectively advise the average student in his/her educational planning?

If such training, knowledge, and materials were provided to non-counselors, could they not then become qualified to serve as effective advisors?

With appropriate training, knowledge, and resources, could not the

85

responsibilities of the Conferencing and Planning phases be shared and distributed between teachers and other non-counseling professionals?

Would not the sharing of these responsibilities provide a more efficient and manageable approach to providing personalized guidance to all students than that of the counselor as the sole provider of such services?

If school counselors were no longer the sole providers of student advising, what role would they play in the education system?

Such questions raise serious challenges to the traditional beliefs about the role and necessity of the counselor as sole advisor to students, and are quite naturally perceived as very uncomfortable and threatening to the counseling profession. Yet, the authors believe that unless such questions are addressed, and new ways of thinking about the role, responsibility, time, and priorities of the counselor are developed, students will continue to report the failure of the education system in meeting their needs for guidance and direction in future planning. The time has come for all educators to insist upon a career guidance program where students' needs for personalized guidance are truly met, and where the meeting of needs of students is viewed as a shared responsibility.

Non-counselors can and should be trained and utilized as advisors in the educational planning process of students. The Alpha Model incorporates this perspective by utilizing teachers as trained advisors in the implementation of the Conferencing, Planning, and Preparation phases. Furthermore, in applying this approach the Alpha Model redefines the role of counselors from sole advisors to students to managers of the career guidance program and advising process. Consequently, counselors align their time and priorities to facilitate delivery of learning experiences to support all phases of the instructional process, supply training and materials to support building advisors, provide intervention and advising for students and parents with complex educational planning needs, and offer ongoing consultation and staff development.

In conclusion, the Alpha model provides a significant departure from the paradigm of traditional career guidance models and approaches applied in many schools today. It requires new ways of thinking about how we look at students, determine our outcomes and mission, evaluate our success, define our roles within the education system, and involve parents. It challenges our assumptions, and forces us to question the practices and paradigms that have kept us from achieving what we know we need to accomplish. For many counselors, it provides a radical, uncomfortable, and perhaps threatening alternative to the current approach. For students, however, it offers a refreshing opportunity for hope, meaning, and inspiration.

Appendix A. Role of School Personnel and Community Members in a Developmentally Based Career Guidance Program

Counselors	• Implement a highly visible, outcomes-based, data-driven comprehensive program. • Accept a leadership role in school improvement efforts. • Coordinate services with other student support personnel. • Contribute to grade-level and/or curricular teams. • Provide resources to teachers and deliver effective professional development in-services.
Teachers	• Recognize the value of developmental guidance. • Use subject areas to assist students in developing personal/social, career, and learning competencies. • Work as team members to plan and implement guidance activities essential to the overall development of students.
Students	• Provide student perspective on curriculum, resources and career development needs. • Take responsibility for completing high school + plans, career portfolio, and culminating project that demonstrates knowledge and skills.
Parents/ Guardians	• Participate in annual conferences with student and counselor for career planning and course selection. • Become an advocate for the student. • Take an active and supportive interest in the academic progress of their student. • Participate on the guidance committee that will facilitate implementation of the Developmental Guidance.
Director of Curriculum	• Works with guidance staff to plan, implement, and evaluate the comprehensive developmental guidance program. • Ensures guidance program directly supports district outcomes. • Helps counselors know how and when to integrate guidance lessons in content areas. • Facilitates development, administration, analysis, and dissemination of data collected from guidance needs assessments.

District Administrator	• Views all school personnel as having a part to play in an articulated developmental guidance program. • Recognizes and publicly supports career development as essential to student learning and achievement. • Requires accountability and evaluation of progress toward goals, objectives, and student outcomes.
School Board Member	• Supports policies for delivering the guidance program as an integral part of the total educational process so that all students' development needs are met in academic, career, and personal/social domains.
Postsecondary Staff	• Arranges for seamless transition from high school to postsecondary. • Coordinates post-secondary course offering with secondary curriculum. • Exchanges information with secondary staff.
Business and Industry Staff	• Provides up-to-date labor market information, co-op and apprenticeship sites, and mentorship for all students. • Participates in career day events and serves as guest speakers for classroom guidance lessons.
Local Career and Technical Director	• Participates in planning, implementing, and evaluating the guidance program. • Coordinates school-to-career opportunities. • Provides technical support for Individual Student Planning, including resources for career development materials.
Psychologist Social Worker School Nurse	• Are involved in planning, implementing, and evaluating the Developmental Guidance Program so that all students receive systematic guidance based on academic, career, and personal/social needs.

Adapted from *Career Development Counseling Action Plan* by Roger H. Lambert, Center on Education and Work, University of Wisconsin-Madison. (printed with permission)

APPENDIX B – The ALPHA Career Guidance Model
(Developmental Targets for Grades K – 12)

	Grades K-3 Requirements	Grades 4-6 Requirements	7th Grade Requirements	8th Grade Requirements
Introspection	• Identify your current likes and dislikes. • Identify your work habits. • Identify your personal achievements.	• Identify your current interests and hobbies. • Identify your learning strengths and needs. • Identify your personal achievements.	• Using Career Clusters, Identify the types of activities that would be of interest to you in a career. • Identify your learning strengths and needs. • Identify your personal achievements. • Create a list of careers matching your identified career cluster interests.	• Using Career Clusters, Identify the types of activities that would be of interest to you in a career. • Identify your learning strengths and needs. • Identify your personal achievements. • Update your list of careers matching your career cluster interests.
Exploration	• Identify and describe occupations found within your family and school. • Explore courses and extracurricular opportunities within grades 1-4.	• Identify occupations found within your community. • Explore courses and extracurricular opportunities within grades 5-7	• From your list of possible career interests, investigate the activities and post-high school requirements for specific careers. • Explore 8th grade courses and extracurricular opportunities.	• From your list of possible career interests, investigate the activities and post-high school requirements for specific careers. • Explore community college and university learning opportunities and entrance requirements. • Explore high school course, program, and extracurricular offerings
September to March				

89

	Grades K-3 Requirements	Grades 4-6 Requirements	7th Grade Requirements	8th Grade Requirements
Evaluation	• Select annual learning goals, including goals addressing areas needing improvement.	• Prioritize your list of careers within your community according to your interest. • Select annual learning goals, including goals addressing areas of need. • Identify courses and opportunities that allow you to explore your interests and reach your identified goals.	• Prioritize your list of careers based on your current interests. • Select 8th grade learning goals, including goals addressing areas of need. • Identify 8th grade courses and opportunities that allow you to explore your interests and reach your 8th grade goals.	• Prioritize your list of careers based on your current interests. • Select a post-high school goal that will put you in the best position do what you want to do. • Identify high school courses that are required for graduation, prepare you for the state assessment, allow exploration of your career interests, and meet the requirements for your post-high school plan
Conferencing	• Discuss your interests and goals with your parent and advisor during annual conference. • Review previous year's Personal Education Plan • Discuss your academic progress and concerns, and identify resources and strategies to address your learning needs. Education Plan•	• Discuss your interests and goals with your parent and advisor during annual conference. • Review previous year's Personal Education Plan • Discuss your academic progress and concerns, and identify resources and strategies to address your learning needs.	• Discuss your interests, 8th grade goals, courses of interest, strengths, needs, and concerns with your parent and advisor during annual pre-registration conference. • Review previous year's Personal Education Plan • Discuss your academic progress and concerns, and identify resources and strategies to address your learning needs.	• Discuss your career interests, post-high school goals, HS class interests, strengths, needs, and concerns with your parent and advisor during annual pre-registration conference. • Review previous year's Personal Education Plan • Discuss your academic progress and concerns, and identify resources and strategies to address your learning needs.

September to March

	Grades K-3 Requirements	Grades 4-6 Requirements	7th Grade Requirements	8th Grade Requirements
Planning	• In collaboration with your parent and advisor, update your Personal Education Plan that aligns with your goals, academic needs and interests.	• In collaboration with your parent and advisor, update your Personal Education Plan that aligns with your goals, academic needs and interests.	• In collaboration with your parent and advisor, update your Personal Education Plan to reflect your 8th grade goals, and align with your academic needs and interests.	• In collaboration with your parent and advisor, develop a High School+ Education Plan (PEP) which meets HS graduation requirements, and align with your academic needs, career interests, and post-high school plan.
Preparation	• In accordance with your Personal Education Plan (PEP), implement strategies for each school year. • Add to Your Portfolio: • Personal Education Plan (PEP) • List of likes and dislikes • Report cards/Grades • Record of awards. • Selected Work Samples	• In accordance with your Personal Education Plan (PEP), implement strategies for each school year. • Add to Your Portfolio: • Update Personal Education Plan (PEP) • List of Interests and Hobbies • Prioritized list of occupations within community • Report cards/Grades • Record of awards. • Selected Work Samples	• In accordance with your Personal Education Plan (PEP), register for 8th grade courses • Add to Your Portfolio: • Updated Personal Education Plan (PEP) • Career Interest Assessment Data • List of Career Interests • Report cards/Grades • Record of awards. • Selected Work Samples	• In accordance with your High School+ Education Plan (PEP), register for 9th grade courses • Add to Your Portfolio: • Initial High School+ Education Plan (PEP) • Career Interest Assessment Data • Prioritized List of Career Interests • Report cards/Grades • Awards and Service-learning activities • Selected Work Samples
March +				

	9th Grade Requirements	10th Grade Requirements	11th Grade Requirements	12th Grade Requirements
Introspection	• Further clarify the types of activities that would be of interest to you in a career. • Identify your learning strengths and needs. • Identify your personal achievements. • Update your list of career interests.	• Identify the work values that would be important to you in a career. • Identify your learning strengths and needs. • Identify your personal achievements. • Update your list of career interests.	• Identify your temperament and the types of settings that best match your temperament. • Identify your learning strengths and needs. • Identify your personal achievements. • Update your list of career interests.	**Finalizing High School+ EducationPlan): (September to February)** • Specify your post-high school plan for the year following graduation. • Specify the schools/training programs you are pursuing and to which you will apply. • Specify the career area(s) you are preparing for through your post-high school training. • Specify the majors/programs of study you plan to pursue, Conferencing with Advisor (September to February) • Review previous year's Personal Education Plan
Exploration	• From your list of possible career interests, investigate activities and post-high school requirements for careers not yet researched. • Explore career opportunities available through community college, technical college, university, apprenticeship, military, and post-HS employment. • Explore high school course, program, Pathway, and extracurricular offerings.	• From your list of possible career interests, investigate how your work values are supported within these careers. • Investigate and identify specific post-secondary schools and training programs that align with your current post-high school plan. • Explore high school course, program, Pathway, and extracurricular offerings	• From your list of possible career interests, investigate how your temperament is supported within these careers. • Explore and Identify post-high school majors that align with your career interests and ambitions. • Explore high school course, program, Pathway, and extracurricular offerings	

September to March		Final Planning and Preparation (September through June)

92

	12th Grade Requirements
Final Planning and Preparation (September through June)	**Conferencing with Advisor (September to February)** • Discuss your High School+ Education Plan (PEP) with your advisor in preparation for transition to post-secondary goals. • Discuss your academic progress and concerns, and identify resources and strategies to address your learning needs **Preparing for Post-Secondary Education:(September to February)** • Visit colleges and/or training sites. • Complete applications and essays. • Complete entrance examinations. • Secure letters of recommendation • Complete scholarship applications • Complete FAFSA

	9th Grade Requirements	10th Grade Requirements	11th Grade Requirements
Evaluation (September to March)	• Update your list of careers that best match the types of activities that most interest you. • Select a post-high school plan that will put you in the best position do what you want to do. • Identify high school courses that are required for graduation, prepare you for the state assessment, allow exploration of your career interests, and meet the requirements for your post-high school plan	• Prioritize your list of career interests based on those careers that seem to best align with the activities and work values that most interest you. • Specify the post-high school plan that will serve as the focus of your preparation for grades 11-12. • Identify high school courses and Pathways that meet graduation requirements, satisfy the requirements for your post-high school goal, and provide opportunities to explore career interests.	• Prioritize and modify your list of possible post-high school education institutions based on majors and personal preferences. • Prioritize your list of career interests based on those careers that seem to best support the activities, work values, and temperament that are important to you. • Finalize the post-high school plan that will serve as the focus of your preparation for 12th grade.
Conferencing	• Discuss your career interests, post-high school goals, class interests, strengths, needs, and concerns with your parent and advisor during annual pre-registration conference. • Review previous year's Personal Education Plan • Discuss your academic progress and concerns, and identify resources and strategies to address your learning needs.	• Discuss your career interests, post-high school goals, class interests, strengths, needs, and concerns with your parent and advisor during annual pre-registration conference. • Review previous year's Personal Education Plan • Discuss your academic progress and concerns, and identify resources and strategies to address your learning needs.	• Discuss your career interests, post-high school goals, class interests, strengths, needs, and concerns with your parent and advisor during annual pre-registration conference. • Review previous year's Personal Education Plan • Discuss your academic progress and concerns, and identify resources and strategies to address your learning needs.

	9th Grade Requirements	10th Grade Requirements	11th Grade Requirements	12th Grade Requirements
Planning	• In collaboration with your parent and advisor, update your High School+ Education Plan (PEP) to meet graduation requirements and align with your academic needs, career interests, and post-high school plan.	• In collaboration with your parent and advisor, update your High School+ Education Plan (PEP) to meet graduation requirements and align with your academic needs, career interests, and post-high school plan.	• In collaboration with your parent and advisor, update your High School+ Education Plan (PEP) to meet graduation requirements, reflect culminating project goals, and align with your academic needs, career interests, and post-high school plan.	Preparing for Employment: (September to June) • Complete Resume and Cover Letter • Secure References • Complete Mock Interview
Preparation / **March +**	• In accordance with your High School+ Education Plan (PEP), register for 10th grade courses. • Add to Your Portfolio: • High School+ Education Plan (PEP) • Career Assessment Data • Updated List of Career Interests • Initial Resume and Cover Letter • Report cards/Grades • Record of awards and community-based learning activities • Selected Work Samples	• In accordance with your High School+ Education Plan (PEP), register for 11th grade courses• Add to Your Portfolio: • Updated High School+ Education Plan (PEP) • Work Values Assessment Data • Updated List of Career Interests • Certificate of Mastery • Report cards/Grades • Record of awards, work experience and community-based learning activities • Selected Work Samples	• In accordance with your High School+ Education Plan (PEP), register for 12th grade courses • Add to Your Portfolio: • Updated High School+ Education Plan (PEP) • Temperament Assessment Data • Updated List of Career Interests • List of Colleges and Post-HS interests • Pathway Certificates if applicable • Report cards/Grades •Record of awards, work experience and community-based learning activities • Selected Work Samples	Preparing for Graduation: (February to June) • Prepare Portfolio: • Include evidence of education planning • Add College Essays and list of colleges receiving applications. • Add Pathway Certifications • Add record of awards, work experience, and community based learning activities. • Add Final Resume, Cover Letter, and References. • Prepare and present a Culminating Project • Submit Final High School+ Education Plan

Final Planning and Preparation (September through June)

94

References

Adelman, H.S. & Taylor, L. (2002). School counselors and school reform: New directions. *Professional School counseling, 5*, 235-248.

Bridges, W. (2001). *The way of transition: Embracing life's most difficult moments.* Cambridge: Perseus Publishing.

Brophy, J. (1998). *Motivating students to learn.* Boston: McGraw Hill.

Csikszentmihalyi, M. & Schneider, B. (2000). *Becoming adult: How teenagers prepare for the world of work.* New York: Basic Books.

Ferris State University Career Institute for Education and Workforce Development (2002). Decisions without direction: Career guidance and decision-making among American youth [Electronic version]. Retrieved June 22, 2002, from http://www.ferris.edu/careerinstitute/ncds.htm

Gregory, R. (2002, June 19). A faster-reading rolling stone? *Seattle Times,* E3.

Gysbers, N.C. & Henderson, P. (2001). Comprehensive guidance and counseling programs: A rich history and a bright future. *Professional School Counseling, 4,* (4) 246-256.

Herr, E.L. (2001). The impact of national policies, economics, and school reform on comprehensive guidance programs. *Professional School Counseling, 4,* (4) 236-245.

House, R, M., & Hayes, R.L. School counselors and school reform: New directions. *Professional School Counseling,* 5,(4), 249-256.

Hoyt, K.B. (2002). The right tools: Helping high school graduates consider all the post-secondary options is your job; making the most of the options is theirs. *ASCA School Counselor,* 39:4, 19-23.

Lambert, R. (1992). *Career development counseling action plan.* Paper presented at the Tech Prep & Counseling Workshop for the Center on Education and Work, Chicago, IL.

Lapan, R.T. (2001). Results-based comprehensive guidance and counseling programs: A framework for planning and evaluation. *Professional School Counseling, 4,* 289-299.

National Career Development Association. (2000). *Career connecting in a changing context: A summary of the key findings of the 1999 national survey of working America.* Paper presented.

National Center for Education Statistics, (2002a). *1999-2000 Percent dropouts in 100 largest school districts.* Retrieved June 24, 2002, from http://nces.ed.gov/pubs2001/100_largest/table16.asp

National Center for Education Statistics, (2002b). *Projections of education statistics to 2011,* Retrieved from June 24, 2002, from http://nces.ed.gov/pubs2001/proj01/highlight.asp

Schneider, B. & Stevenson, D. (1999). *The ambitious generation: America's teenagers, motivated but directionless.* New Haven: Yale University Press.

Snyder, C.R., Feldman, D.B., Shorey, H.S., & Rand, K.L. (2002). Hopeful choices: A school counselor's guide to hope theory. *Professional School Counseling, 5,* 298-307.

Tolle, E. (1999). *The power of now: A guide to spiritual enlightenment.* Novato, CA: New World Library.

Chapter Four

Aligning Student Planning with the Changing Workplace

Richard W. Feller

Abstract

What one believes best helps students plan for success within the changing workplace has much to do with the lens used to understand "the kids" and the "changing workplace." Feller contends that most enter the workplace "nervously employed" with misinformed expectations about the relationships between going to school and preparation for work. His review of the school-to-work research, analysis of the workplace, and suggestions for improved planning help close the gap for students.

Helping students best plan for their future has much to do with the lens used to understand the changing workplace. Daily experience with high school students allows educators to influence their hopes and fears as they prepare for post high school transitions. Career development and school reform legislation can influence this as well. Yet, most educators have limited experience as private sector employees, managers or owners. This chapter suggests that closing the gap between student planning and workplace realities is needed regardless of student focus, opportunities or backgrounds.

Uncertain Futures

Whether China's cloning breakthroughs dominate the next economy, the hydrogen economy redistributes the world's opportunities, or promises of school reform to "leave no student behind" becomes reality, the vast majority of students will continue to graduate. Will they work for themselves within a *Free Agent Nation* (Pink, 2001), take advantage of *The War for Talent* (Michael, Handfield-Jones & Axelrod, 2001) or benefit from an

Impending Crisis: Too Many Jobs, Too Few People proposed by Herman (2003)? It is hard to determine. Only time will tell how youth will experience the globalization of goods and services, deregulation, technological advances and instability created by terrorism. Regardless, too few depart high school with the agility, self-reliance, and character commitments needed to adapt to a future demanding lifelong learning, and personal accountability for career development within the workplace.

Many enter college hoping time will accelerate career exploration, clarify focus and enhance personal responsibility. Unfortunately, too many drop out of high school before crossing the stage. Most dropouts flounder within the secondary labor market with little opportunity of attaining livable wages until finding a second chance leading to postsecondary education and/or marketable skills. Both dropouts and completers enter the workplace "nervously employed" with misinformation about the relationship between that which is rewarded in school and what makes up successful workforce behaviors.

Misaligned Ambitions

When asked "What do you want to do after high school?" most students state either "I'm going to college" or "I don't know." North America's individualistic society creates a challenge offering an unlimited number of occupations from which to choose. Yet youth are generally insulated from work beyond retail, service and manual labor. While most hold high career expectations and know skills needed for more than a "teenage job" are required to move to adult status, too much planning is left to chance, is shaped by peer pressure, or influenced by subjective parental wisdom.

Schneider and Stevenson (1999) report that over 90 percent of high school seniors expect to attend college, and more than 70 percent expect to hold professional jobs regardless of income or background. School counselors and faculty hesitate to confront this "silent dream" held by parents knowing the difficulty of suggesting anything which could deny access to the state university, even though career and academic maturity is often not congruent. Soon many students find themselves without the math or science needed in technical programs or the basic verbal, reading and math skills necessary for postsecondary completion. Altered ambitions occur as students drop from college realizing their goals require more time in school, and more classes than they are prepared to complete. As a result, youth often navigate through school with misaligned connections to educational plans and career paths.

Gray and Herr's *Other Ways to Win: Creating Alternatives for High*

School Graduates (1995), Gray's *Getting Real: Helping Teens Find Their Future* (2000), and Hoyt and Maxey's *Counseling for High Skills: Responding to the Career Needs of All Students* (2001) sounded alerts particularly for students in the academic middle. Federal initiatives such as the School-to-Work Opportunities Act (passed in 1994) tried to address this misalignment but failed to create sustainability beyond local scale. While equipping youth for employment, lifelong learning and career advancement continues to receive interest, it faces many local challenges (Feller & Davies, 1999). This is especially true when the economy experiences downturns or labor demand fails to create entry level work to meet expectations.

How Is The Workplace Changing?

Anticipating and adapting to change has increasingly become a requirement for youth to succeed as adults. Just as basic skills and agility are essential to lifelong learning, response time to change, and identifying and solving problems (in a way that adds value) are essential to financial and personal success. This cannot be overstated considering the changes shaping how, when and where work takes place. As personal balance becomes a goal, the need for career development competencies and a career management paradigm becomes even greater.

While opinions vary about the degree of workplace change youth will encounter, the U.S. Department of Labor Bureau of Labor Statistic's *Working in the 21st Century* (2002) lists the following general trends:
- The labor force is growing more slowly and is becoming older
- More women are working today than in the past
- Minorities are the fastest growing part of the labor force
- Immigrants are found at the high and low ends of the education scale
- Education pays
- Some jobs with above-average earnings do not require a bachelor's degree, but most require substantial training
- Workers with computer skills are in demand
- The ten occupations to generate the most jobs range widely in their skill requirements
- Benefits account for more than one-quarter of total compensation
- Retirement plans are changing
- Workers will be supporting more Social Security recipients
- Years spent with an employer are down for men and up for women
- The temporary help industry has grown rapidly
- The most common alternative employment arrangement is an

independent contractor
- Most mothers work
- Married couples are working longer
- The workplace is becoming safer

This report further forecasts that one-third of the 30 jobs projected to grow the fastest this decade are in technology. Half are in human health care; the rest are in education, fitness and animal health care. Government, security, finance and defense will continue to experience strong demand as well. The list of fastest-growing occupations reflects the emergence of technology in virtually every area of life, the aging of the baby boom generation, and an increase in security issues.

Such general trends offer insight to help focus and design student careers. However, to make a livable wage, it is critical to understand that learning has become a job requirement. Motivating unfocused students to remain flexible, mobile, and able to live with less security is a daunting task when they need to focus on improving academic performance, gaining occupational skills and demonstrating career development competencies for transition to adulthood.

Getting Focused While Staying Agile

The workplace requires skills and competencies necessary to ensure future employability without consistent employer support. Being able to manage new work and life realities, find a work-life balance, and feel a sense of economic viability within a less stable global labor market is a necessity for workers regardless of age.

Increasingly the "new workplace" is more dynamic, entrepreneurial, and less patient with workers unable to add value quickly. The responsibility for obtaining basic skills, training, and postsecondary education needed for job longevity has shifted to the employee. Agility, innovation, and a willingness to redefine one's job description is the only "employment security" the workplace offers. More competitive, global, and technical advances challenge employee tenure and vertical mobility. The primary labor market's less skilled and inexperienced youth are expected to be more competent in communication, math, computer technology, self-management, and decision-making skills as the economy centers on information flow, knowledge creation and a culture of constant innovation.

Workers formerly tied to jobs matching "wages with ages." Highly educated and traditionally credentialed employees have learned that merged and evaporated companies, local economies, and stockholder decisions have little interest in past contributions. All jobs now experience transitional casualties as entrepreneurs and deregulated industries see the entire world as one marketplace. Students without direction are subjected to the same consequences and have been negatively and disproportionately affected by the difficulty of obtaining apprenticeships and the loss of manufacturing jobs, now at the lowest level in 40 years (U.S. Department of Labor, 2002).

Career Assumptions Need to Shift

Many students believe that employers can guarantee lifetime employment. In the past, high school diplomas were the minimal requirement for many livable wage jobs, and postsecondary education was absent from job requirements or seen as necessary only for professional or managerial jobs. In return for loyalty, endurance, and hard work, employers were expected to provide a paycheck and upward mobility tied to personal networking and one's ability to follow hierarchical orders.

Large and established employers were seen as safe havens for continuous employment. However, transportation, satellite transmission, and communication connectivity have reduced the importance of an employer's name or geographic location. The world labor force offers abundant and cheap labor, not job security, permanent positions, or stepladder career paths. In the past, traditional workplaces honored the top 15-25 percent of their workers, in a pyramidal paradigm (Feller,1995), as the professional managerial class made the decisions and exerted control. The 85 percent of blue collar workers (filling in the lower area of the hypothetical pyramid) took direction, followed orders, and were rewarded for leaving their brains, heart, and soul at the door. By fulfilling very narrow job descriptions with stable skill requirements, there were ample entry-points for students leaving high school. Beginning and low skilled workers were welcomed as human robots on manufacturing lines, clerical office pools, and as agriculture hired hands.

Work designed for performing a small number of routine operations did not demand significant thinking or teamwork skills. Self-management and self-directed learning were seen as having limited value, and self-advocacy was interpreted as resistance. With little interest and few expectations about what non-college bound students knew or thought, employers prized a worker's ability to conform, tolerate repetition, and respond to hierarchical supervision. North America dominated the world economy, and its competitive advantages created jobs for low skilled but middle wage workers who saw little value in postsecondary education. Through seniority, collective bargaining, and continuous economic growth, workers could obtain more than average wages in the traditional triangle or pyramid-shaped workplace (Feller, 1995).

As the workplace became more global and characterized by unprecedented technological change and mobility, competition crossed borders. Management's many layers became cost prohibitive, making way for the PC and Internet to disseminate "real time" information. As a result, assumptions about traditional jobs, workplaces, school-to-work programs, career transitions, and student options were transformed (Feller & Walz, 1996; Feller & Davies, 2002). Increasingly, the workplace became home to fewer living wage jobs for unskilled and young workers. More work followed workers due to technical "connectivity," and traditional 9-5 work expectations changed. Employment opportunities noticeably shifted from larger to smaller organizations where cross-training became a necessity.

An Emerging Workplace Design

In an emerging diamond shape model (Feller, 1996) the workplace rewards different skills, broader responsibilities, and more flexible workers. Far fewer supervisors increasingly "coach" more broadly skilled workers seeking alignment within an organization's most profitable and core competencies. Rewarded by adding value to a company's core mission more than by accumulating degrees and titles, workers began seeing the value of developing core competencies through self-directed learning, risk taking within new projects, and technical and postsecondary education options. Students striving to become core workers are those who acquire the technical skills, "intellectual capital," and personal strengths (Clifton & Anderson, 2002) critical to a unit's competitive advantage.

To the degree it exists, job security is much more vulnerable as all work demands constant learning as a job requirement for those seeking livable wages. Workers are now encouraged to focus on traits of globally competitive high performance organizations, such as: sustained market success or achievement of organizational objectives; customer focus and continuous improvement; a focus on added value; innovation in quality and customer satisfaction; product or service differentiation; use of self-managed work teams; clear links between training, development and organizational objectives; and support for organizational and individual learning.

In the new global workplace, continuous improvement, international quality standards, self-management, teamwork and transferable skill expectations are the norm. Intense global competition, time-compressed distribution and product development, and process innovation has transformed work roles, job titles, and organizational structures. In terms of job options, the emerging diamond shaped workplace requires fewer managers or supervisors. What is crucial for high school students to understand is that fewer primary, entry-level, livable wage jobs are available to youth or new workers lacking basic skills. The inability to access and gain occupational proficiencies, current information through technology, and the inability to remain motivated and self-directed handicaps all workers, particularly young workers starting out in the workforce.

Young people need to understand that economic fluctuations influence employment as well as support for learning and development options. Skills and competencies tied to adding value increasingly determine the quality of jobs, length of employment, and future opportunities to learn and develop on the job. As the workplace becomes more service based, changes in consumer spending can quickly impact job growth, job security, and employment options.

No One Left Behind—at School, Work or Beyond

Schools enjoy success when educating students from backgrounds that prepare them to come to school ready and motivated to learn. *The 34th Annual Phi Delta Kappa/Gallup Poll of the Public's Attitudes Toward the Public Schools* (Rose & Gallup, 2002) confirms parents approve of the school their oldest child attends. Equal support exists for the government's most recent comprehensive promise to deal with critically important school problems of those touched by poverty within the *No Child Left Behind Act*, signed into law by President Bush on January 8, 2002. Hopefully, motivations declaring that "all children can learn" will provide the support necessary to overcome the fact that not all students can learn to the same level, given the same amount of time and resources. Agreeing that no child should be left behind is simple; getting agreement that students do not start at the same place is a complex political issue. Because students come from poverty does not mean they will not be successful, but it does mean that on-demand remediation is a wise investment. As *America's Children: Key Indicators of Well-Being 2002* (Interagency Forum on Child and Family Statistics, 2002) illustrates, children face many challenges impacting their view about school, work and community role.

Most acknowledge that the skills needed for postsecondary success are also required for lifelong learning and training for livable wage jobs. However, the relationship between schooling and a community's economic health has been overstated. While the report *A Nation at Risk* (National Commission on Excellence in Education, 1983) debased public schools for the inability to overcome declining global competitiveness, no such relationship was prized during the "golden economy" of the 1990's.

Those advocating for career preparation at the expense of preparing students for other life roles should temper blind enthusiasm for "training" and focus enthusiasm on higher goals that serve students for learning, work and being a good citizen. More than ever, communities need to educate students with character commitments to resist the ploys leading to corporate scandals and political corruption undermining trust in institutions. Career plans of students need to include an apprenticeship in democracy (Goodlad, 2002), a strong foundation of developmental assets (Search Institute, 1997), and competencies needed to be self-reliant career managers (Blueprint for Life/Work Designs, n.d.) regardless of how much the workplace will change in the future.

Lessons Learned from School-to-Career Efforts

Few opportunities exist to learn job-specific skills within high schools. Secondary career-technical education has lost its power to move students directly to livable wage jobs. Without resources to expand high school career-technical education, it has too often become a prescription for individualized education plans for special needs students and potential dropouts. The School-to-Work Opportunities Act followed debates between vocational preparation purists and college preparation elitists that left students without basic skills and the potential to learn in context. Now that the Act has run its course and funding has been terminated, researchers try to distill its impact. Like other reforms trying to improve academic achievement and workforce preparation, it has led to lessons learned. Hughes, Bailey and Karp (2002) report:

Our conclusion is that the research so far has found generally positive results: the school-to-work strategy does benefit students, teachers, and employers. Although critics of this educational approach feared that it would weaken academic achievement and divert students to low-skilled jobs, truncating their opportunities for college and further study, the growing body of evaluation work–even at the most rigorous and definitive levels– has turned up almost no evidence that such fears were justified (p.273).

Having reviewed over one hundred studies their conclusions include five key points about school-to-work:

- It supports academic achievement in a variety of ways, such as reducing the dropout rate and increasing college enrollment
- It teaches skills and abilities useful in careers and helps students think about and plan their future
- It appears to help students mature and develop psychologically

- It encourages more varied types of contact between students and adults, including teachers and work-site mentors
- Teachers and employers are positive about school-to-work (p. 277).

These points offer encouragement to those dedicated to helping youth plan a smooth high school transition. School-to-work/career strategies deserve support as education seeks a clearer lens to close the gap among misaligned career expectations, academic expectations, and successful work behaviors. With the lens I use to understand the changing workplace, school-to-career innovations have clarified the need to:

- Expand higher level basic skills for all students
- Broker access to occupational skills within high performance organizations that connect youth to helpful adult role models
- Accelerate career exploration programs that help students identify strengths and experience how interests can be tied to solving problems at work
- Expand vertical articulation so competencies are valued along with coursework
- Promote "focused effort" through contextual learning as a way to build talent
- Expand work-based learning through community partnerships so that students can have success in real life experiences
- Provide opportunities where learning is the constant, and time is the variable, so that all students reach higher expectations
- Take advantage of the predictive power of hope (Snyder, Feldman, Shorey & Rand, 2002) by expressing confidence about the future

Best Bets for Creating Alignment

As Posner (2002) states, "It is a tricky business trying to guess what experiences will motivate an individual to intellectual achievement or what skills or bits of knowledge will wind up being important in a person's life" (p.316). Yet educators hold beliefs about preparing youth for the changing workplace, beliefs which often rest unexamined. Regardless, educators want students to improve, to do well, and to be successful in the workplace. This chapter suggests that student planning improves when educators use language which explains how the workplace is changing. It also suggests youth should be brave and humble in a world of uncertain futures.

Regardless of the level of focus, high school students can decide to discipline themselves to do what they do not like to do. They can get more of what they want out of career and life roles. They can work toward what

Seligman calls *Authentic Happiness* (2002). Educators can close the gap between student planning and the changing workplace's needs as they expose students to options, excite them about their potential, and model confidence about the future. Students learn from experiences that allow them to evaluate trade-offs, and they grow when personal freedom comes from assuming responsibility and taking action. They are happiest when they use their strengths, do what they do best, and engage in activities that cause them to forget themselves, lose track of time, stop worrying (Csikszentmihalyi, 1991) and, I suggest, do not realize they are learning. These are the mental tools which can help students align their planning with the realities of a changing workplace which, in the end, will allow them to experience success in lifelong learning and employment.

References

Clifton, D. O., & Anderson, E. (2002). *Strengths quest: Discover and develop your strengths in academics, career, and beyond.* Washington, D.C.: The Gallup Organization

Csikszentmihalyi, M. (1991). *Flow.* New York: Harper and Row.

Feller, R. W. (1995). Action planning for personal competitiveness in the "broken workplace". *Journal of Employment Counseling, 32,* 154-163.

Feller, R. W. (1996). The future of work. *Vocational Education Journal, 71,* 24-27.

Feller. R. W., & Walz, G. R. (1996). *Career transitions in turbulent times: Exploring work, learning and careers.* Greensboro, NC: ERIC/CASS.

Feller, R. W., & Davies, T. G. (1999). Career Development for All. In A. Pautler, (Ed.), *Workforce education: Issues for the new century.* Ann Arbor, MI: Prakken.

Feller, R.W., & Davies, T. G. (2002). Changing the career planning context. In T. Harrington (Ed.), *Handbook for career planning for students with special needs* (3rd ed.). Austin, TX: Pro-Ed.

Goodlad, J. I. (2002). Kudzu, rabbits, and school reform. *Phi Delta Kappan, 84,* 1, 16-23.

Gray, K. C., & Herr, E. L. (1995). *Other ways to win: Creating alternatives for high school graduates.* Thousand Oaks, CA: Corwin Press.

Gray, K. C. (2000). *Getting real: Helping teens find their future.* Thousand Oaks, CA: Corwin Press.

Herman, R., Olivo, T., & Gioia, J. (2003). *Impending crisis: Too many jobs, too few people* Winchester, VA: Oakhill Press.

Hoyt, K. & Maxey, J. (2001). *Counseling for high skills: Responding to the career needs of all students.* Greensboro, NC: CAPS Publications.

Hughes, K.L., Bailey, T. R. & Karp, M. M. (2002). School-to-work: Making a difference in education. *Phi Delta Kappan, 84,* 4, 272-279.

Interagency Forum on Child and Family Statistics. (2002) *America's children: Key indicators of well-being.* Retrieved December 31, 2003, from http://www.childstats.gov/americaschildren/

Michael, E., Handfield-Jones, H., & Axelrod, B. (2001). *The war for talent.* Boston, MA: Harvard Business School Press.

National Commission on Excellence in Education. (1983). *A nation at risk: The imperative for educational reform.* Washington, DC: Government Printing Office. Retrieved December 31, 2002, from http://www.childstats.gov/americaschildren/

National Life/Work Centre. (n.d.) *Blueprint for Life/Work Designs.* Retrieved December 31, 2002, from http://www.blueprint4life.ca

Pink, D.H. (2001). *Free agent nation: The future of working for yourself.* New York: Warner Books.

Posner, D. (2002). Education for the 21st century. *Phi Delta Kappan, 84,* 4, 316-317.

Rose, L. C., & Gallup, L. M. (2002). The 34th annual Phi Delta Kappa/Gallup poll of the public's attitudes toward the public schools. *Phi Delta Kappan, 84,*1, 41-58.

Schneider, B. & Stevenson, D. (1999). *The ambitious generation: America's teen-agers—motivated by directionless*. New Haven: Yale University Press.

Search Institute. (1997). *The asset approach: Giving kids what they need to succeed*. Minneapolis, MN: Author.

Seligman, M.E. (2002). Authentic happiness: Using the new positive psychology to realize your potential for lasting fulfillment. New York: The Free Press.

Snyder, C.R., Feldman, D.B., Shorey, H.S. & Rand, K.L. (2002). Hopeful choices: A school counselor's guide to the hope theory. *Professional School Counseling*, 5,5, 298-307.

U.S. Department of Education. (2001). *No Child Left Behind*. Washington, DC: Author.

U.S. Department of Labor, Bureau of Labor Statistics. (2002). *Working in the 21st Century*.Retrieved December 31, 2002, from http://www.bls.gov/opub/working/home.htm

Chapter Five

Factors that Influence Women and Minorities to Choose High-Tech Careers

Teresa I. Yohon and Laurie A. Carlson

Abstract

While our nation's schools are educating a larger percentage of our population and at a higher level than ever before, concern exists about the ability of our schools to adequately provide students with the knowledge, skills, and competencies to function successfully in a technological society. Various studies indicate that everybody should have computer fluency. Despite the need for technology skills, statistics clearly indicate that women and minorities are under-represented in technology classes and fields.

This chapter focuses on the key factors or systems that influence young people in general, and specifically women and minorities, to choose high-tech careers. Six factors will be examined: (1) peers, (2) parents, (3) school (including counselors and teachers), (4) work experiences, (5) information resources, and (6) environment (which includes socio-economic status and cultural background). Suggestions on how these factors can be mobilized to help women and minorities enter technology careers will be summarized.

Globally, technology is changing the basic occupational requirements for jobs as well as adding new jobs and careers to the employment landscape. According to the Spring 2000 *Occupational Outlook Quarterly's* special issue entitled "The 1998-2008 Job Outlook in Brief," computer and high technology careers expect an above average growth in the projected ten year time frame. The need for Information Technology (IT) workers continues despite the current United States economic downturn. A study by the Computing Technology Industry Association (CompTIA) found the average number of open IT service and support positions in U.S. companies has more than tripled since 1999 (Pastore, 2001). The 2001 study, "Ongoing Crisis in IT Management," stated that IT managers believed staffing and training to be their biggest challenges (Pastore, 2001).

Because of this, adding a technology focus to young people's career paths may increase their employment potential. However, concern exists about the failure of our schools to adequately provide students with the knowledge, skills, and competencies to function successfully in a technological society, even though our nation's schools are educating a larger percentage of our population and at a higher level than ever before (Sanders, n.d.). Pamela Haage, from the American Association of University Women Educational Foundation (AAUW), states that it is imperative that everybody, particularly girls who are underrepresented, have computer fluency (Mayfield, 2000).

Statistics clearly indicate that women are under-represented in technology fields. In a report discussed by Mayfield (2000), women make up only 20 percent of information technology professionals and receive less than 28 percent of the computer science degrees.

Additionally, the makeup of the U.S. workforce is shifting. According to U.S. Bureau of the Census projections, from 1995 to 2050 the workforce is expected to change from 12 to 14 percent African-American, 10 to 24 percent Hispanic, 4 to 9 percent Asian, and from 74 to 52 percent non-Hispanic White (National Science and Technology Council, 2000). It appears that females and non-White groups will need to be tapped to fill businesses' increasing need for high-tech skills.

Many factors influence the movement of young people into high-tech careers. This chapter summarizes those factors, including unique factors that influence females and minorities to choose technology-related careers. Once these factors are understood, teachers and counselors can adapt their teaching and counseling strategies as well as their interactions with their students' environment (parents and peers).

Factors that Influence Movement of Young People into High-Tech Careers

Six factors influence young people in making career choices: (1) peers, (2) parents, (3) school—including counselors and teachers, (4) work experiences, (5) information resources, and (6) environment—including socio-economic status and cultural background. Career decision-making is a complex process, and the relative weight of each factor on career decisions varies from person to person.

Peer Influences

Peer influences are key factors to how initial career choices are made. Peer groups can support or temper achievement strivings, depending on

110

particular group norms (Epstein, 1983). Some research suggests that the concerns of female peer groups with romantic relationships can influence the value attached to achievement and can divert a woman's interest from preparation for a career (Eisenhart & Holland, 1992). According to Dr. Richard Tapia, a Rice University engineering professor (who won the 1996 Presidential Award for Excellence in Science, Mathematics, and Engineering Mentoring), his daughter's peer group changed her from a 7-year-old who liked computers to a girl more interested in lipstick, make-up, and going to the mall (Zuniga, 1997). Dr. Tapia suggests that a girl's peer group dictates what girls are supposed to be like and maintains the strongest pressure on career choice.

In high school, girls often have a negative or jaded view of the information technology career field. The prevalent image is that information technology careers are for "geeks, gadgets, and greed." Girls typically see technology-focused people as "unambitious" and "not connected to daily problems" (Kuhl, 2000). Focus groups commissioned by the American Association of University Women Educational Foundation showed that girls did not describe themselves as "computer-phobic" but were "computer reticent," i.e. disenchanted with computer careers and culture (*Tech Savvy*, 2000). In observing boys and their interactions with technology, girls felt that boys just want to take things apart instead of building relationships with people (Kuhl, 2000).

Parents

Parents can be allies in promoting career planning by providing job opportunities through their contacts and practical advice about their own careers and organizations. However, parental influence can also have a dampening effect on the diversity of career choices (Jacobsen, 1999). If parents are not fully informed of career opportunities, all possible career alternatives will not be explored in a family career discussion. Parents may also limit their children's career choices by either pushing their sons or daughters into careers in which they have no interest or by narrowing career pathways based on personal biases and cultural influences.

Nauta and Kokaly (2001) found that parents were the most influential in academic and career decisions made by college students. Thirty-nine percent of the students indicated that their mother had been most influential, and 24% indicated that their father had been most influential. Same-gender friends represented an additional 12% of the influences. According to Otto (2000), eleventh grade students indicated that they turned to their mothers for career advice and that their career aspirations were similar to their parents.

Parent expectations of their daughters affect girls' self-efficacy (Blevins-Knabe & Musun-Millie, 1991). Further, parental expectations for technical and scientific careers for their sons are chief motivating factors for boys, while girls must be more self-motivated to choose courses in math and science. In the report *Women and Minorities in IT* (1999), many women and minorities stated they didn't have positive "home" experiences, which would encourage them to pursue IT careers.

School Experiences

With school counselors.

Career counseling must take place within the cultural context without making assumptions that all individuals in a culture have the same values, goals, and experiences (Kerka, 1998). Counselors' personal attitudes affect students and the careers they choose. According to Herr and Cramer (1996), women seem to receive less encouragement from career counselors and others; therefore expectations of personal efficacy, or the ability to deal with prospective situations seen as challenging, ambiguous, unpredictable or stressful, tend to be weakened for women.

Career counseling systems generally consist of the following pieces: (a) clarifying work values and developing planning skills, (b) providing occupational and career information, (c) encouraging training, goal setting, and decision making related to a tentative career path, and (d) integrating academic and career skills in a school curriculum (Herring, 1998). Obviously multiple intervention points are available to introduce high-tech information, experiences, and skill building opportunities.

With teachers.

Students of all ages spend much more of their time with the classroom teacher than the guidance counselor. The teachers' role in career counseling tends to center on providing students with activities focusing on career development. Areas of career development include job-hunting skills, career and occupational research, and industry research ("Career Activity," 1998). Many such activities use the Internet as a tool to provide up-to-date information and current trends.

Teachers do influence students' confidence and experience in technology, math and science courses. Erickson (1987) found that the confidence of students in their math ability is related to their perception of teacher encouragement, which is particularly true for girls and students of color. In earlier studies, Kirk (1975), Matthews (1981), and Treisman (1982) indicated that students of color found it academically useful for teachers to provide additional help, explain things carefully, and provide encouragement.

The report *Tech Savvy: Educating Girls in the New Computer Age* (2000) indicates that male and female teachers perceive their students' computer interests differently. Male teachers perceived that male students were more interested in the "mechanics" of technology (71% versus 1% of the female students) and 36% believed that male students like computer experiences more than females. On the other hand, female teachers find the male and female students are about equal in terms of which group uses technology more frequently. In general, female teachers see girl students as more technically competent than do male teachers.

According to Brown (2001), teachers inadvertently allow boys to have more computer "time." Since boys are often more aggressive when computer time is available, they push the girls away from technological tasks. Research also indicates that females believe that computer science courses are frustrating and poorly taught (*Tech Savvy*, 2000).

Work Experiences

In an attempt to bridge that gap between school curricula and the labor needs of high-tech industries, national legislation has led to school-to-work reforms. These programs are collaborative efforts between secondary and post-secondary educational institutions, businesses and a variety of connecting activities that include career counseling services. Many school-to-work programs are designed to provide technical and academic preparation, and often certification programs, needed to increase the supply of high-tech workers. A key component to these programs is work-based learning, with experiences ranging from job shadowing to internships and apprenticeships. One contribution of school-to-work reform is the emphasis on academic competence, which is critical since academic proficiency is related to educational and occupational aspirations (Mau & Bikos, 2000). While only time will determine the long-term success of these programs, initial research has demonstrated positive results.

Information Resources

Research states that students get career information from a variety of sources including teachers, counselors, family, and peers. The Internet is becoming a standard for job searches and career information. The most popular sources for occupational trends are the *Occupational Outlook Quarterly* and *Occupational Outlook Handbook* (http://www.bls.gov/oco). Counselors and teachers use the *Dictionary of Occupational Titles* (DOT) or O*NET (http://online.onetcenter.org), both published by the Department of Labor (DOL), as tools for matching people with jobs. The current DOT provides narrative descriptions of tasks, tools, duties, and working conditions for about 12,000 distinct jobs. O*NET allows for occupation and skill searches and specific occupational information. The U.S. Department of Labor's Employment and Training Administration (http://www.doleta.gov) sponsors America's Career Kit, a set of national web-based resources that includes America's Job Bank, America's Learning Exchange, and America's Career InfoNet.

States also provide rich career resources. The Association of Computer-Based Systems for Career Information (ACSCI) provides a summary of career information resources by state (http://www.acsci.org/acsci_states.asp). States also have Career Information Delivery Systems (CIDS) that provide a wealth of state information about career opportunities and career resources that are available for counselor and teacher use. America's Career InfoNet provides a CIDS list by state at http://www.acinet.rog/acinetlibrary.htm?category=1.6#1.6.6.

Many students, particularly female and minority students, are unaware of labor and career projections, especially in the job market for computer engineers, systems analysts, and webmasters (*Tech Savvy*, 2000). Additionally they have a "distasteful and masculine" view of computer careers (*Tech Savvy*, 2000). According to Brown (2001), giving female and minority students career information is meaningless if it is not accompanied by real-world experiences of observing or talking with people in these career fields.

Environment
  Socioeconomic factors.
  According to Tichenor, Donohue, and Olien (1970), "as the infusion of mass media information into a social system increases, segments of the population with higher socioeconomic status tend to acquire the information at a faster rate than the lower status segments, so that the gap between these segments tends to increase rather than decrease" (pp. 159-160). Therefore, lower socioeconomic segments that include many minority groups generally have less data availability for decision-making. Other research findings indicate that high school students' aspirations are positively associated with the family's socioeconomic status (Mau, 1995), the father's occupational status (Smith, 1991), and the educational level of the parents (Wilson & Wilson, 1992). According to Leong (1995), family socioeconomic status is probably the best predictor for an individual's occupational status.

Economics also influences the level of Internet and computer availability. Only 32 percent of high school graduates own personal computers, compared to 68 percent of college graduates (National Telecommunications and Information Administration, 2000). Only 32 percent of all U.S. Internet users in 2000 had a high school education or less (Lenhart, 2000). The NTIA (2000) estimated that only 31 percent of U.S. households with incomes less than $30,000 had Internet access, while 78 percent of households with incomes of $75,000 or more had access.

Cultural factors.

Cultural background plays a key role in the career path decisions of adolescents and adults. Career counseling must take place within the cultural context, with counselors being aware of their own and others' cultures (Kerka, 1998). Race (such as EuroAmerican or Hispanic) and ethnicity (Mexican or Latin American) must be considered in its interaction with gender and socioeconomic class (Herr & Cramer, 1996). As stated in the prior section, family socioeconomic standing heavily influences career aspirations and should first be considered, and then ethnicity. It is also important to understand that the students' acculturation (the acceptance of a society's values and beliefs) and ethnic identification (the level of adherence to an ethnic group's norms) provides the context for career decisions (McFadden, 1996).

In the broad sense, the idea of "career" may not be culturally sensible to certain people (Kerka, 1998). Kerka (1998) found that minority students have higher ethnic identity and vocational maturity (i.e. readiness to make educational and vocational choices) at an earlier age than the rest of the student population. This higher vocational maturity of minority students falls behind the rest of the student population by 11th grade, which may be due to greater ethnic identity that has led to a greater awareness of potential career barriers. According to Leong (1995), minorities often have to become bi-cultural to function in their families, communities, and mainstream institutions.

Values, educational aspirations, and educational attainment are all variables that are influenced by ethnicity (Leong, 1995). According to Leong's research, Asian American students had the highest college and occupational aspirations, whereas Hispanic students had the lowest. For Asian Americans, academic success is considered a source of pride. For Hispanic students, financial pressures and language difficulties may lead to premature dropout from school. Furthermore, female students had significantly higher occupational and educational aspirations than did male students (Mau & Bikos, 2000).

Some cultures value the family role over the work role. Individuals with these cultural influences have a hard time going into careers that would cause a disturbance in the home-family relationship (Lee & Richardson, 1991). Culturally related factors that can impact the career development and occupational behavior of Hispanics include: acculturation level, ethnic identity, race, and the experience of discrimination (Leong, 1995). The impact of these factors is moderated by the person's socioeconomic background and recency of immigration. It is also important to note that recent immigrants from Latin American countries tend to experience a decline in occupational status due to language and credentialing issues (Herring, 1998). Thus, educational attainment may be a more accurate indicator than socioeconomic status.

For Hispanics, gender roles are clearly defined and individuals are socialized to behave accordingly (Lee & Richardson, 1991). Boys are expected to be independent and to perform outside the home. Girls, on the other hand, are taught to be selfless and to sacrifice. As Hispanic women strive to define themselves, they are subjected to family pressures and societal oppression. This conflict creates self-doubts in their ability to manage it all and to "fit" into the world.

In looking at female versus male cultures, females have lower expectations for themselves in math than do boys (Stipek & Granlinski, 1991) and lack the self-confidence to stay in the sciences when their GPAs are higher than their male counterparts (Seymour, 1993). Additionally females who see math as a male activity do not succeed as well in math courses than girls who see it as appropriate for both genders (Armstrong, 1980).

Women and Minorities in High-Tech Careers: Specific Influencing Factors

Women

According to the Bureau of Labor Statistics, as stated in "Women and Minorities in IT" (1999), women represent 46% of the total workforce, but women hold only 25% of the professional information technology workforce jobs and only 10% of the top information technology jobs. The majority of women and girls still plan to enter occupations that are traditionally dominated by women (Eccles, 1994).

In viewing the undergraduate population in U.S. colleges and universities, only 1.1% of women choose IT-related disciplines compared to 3.3% of male undergraduates ("Women and Minorities in IT," 1999). In the workplace, 28% of computer analysts and scientists and 31% of computer programmers are women.

Even though females are taking math and science courses at the same rate as males, they opt not to move into technology courses. The factors that lead to this invisible, but personal, barrier to high-tech career choice are often in place by eighth grade. By eighth grade, girls tend to lower their career expectations and decide they aren't interested in technical subjects that may be considered "unfeminine" (Mayfield, 2001). Eccles (1994) suggests that females actively choose alternatives that their socialization prepares them to see as desirable and generally explore careers from a narrower set of career options than do boys. Girls learn early which occupations are suitable for them and which ones are not.

Farmer and associates (1997) theorized that young women's values are shaped against different expectations than young men's values. Young women hear "Do what you want to do and be happy" while young men hear the message "Get good grades so you can get into the best schools and be successful in a career." Young women are continually faced with the impact of their choices in their educational and working roles on their future home-family role.

Another factor that influences a girl's choice of technology as a career is how technology is currently embedded in the younger generation. Girls aren't afraid of technology. However, boring video games, dull programming classes, and the perceived lack of social interactivity in technology careers turns them off (*Tech Savvy*, 2000). Girls are interested in "high-skill, not high kill" (Mayfield, 2000). Part of the problem seems to be the computer "culture." Girls prefer to interact with people, not inanimate objects like computers (Kuhl, 2000). In a 1997 survey of college-bound high school students for the Garnett Foundation, 50 percent of both males and females felt that "computer science" is more geared toward men. Females indicated that computer work is tedious, sedentary, and antisocial (*Tech Savvy*, 2000).

In general, studies in computer science at secondary and university levels have found that female students are more interested than male students in the "social context" of computing (Genderwatchers, n.d.). The Computer Science Department at Carnegie Mellon University's study showed that 44% of women interviewed (versus 9% of the males) linked their computer science interest to other arenas, such as medicine and the arts. Women stated the importance of connecting computer science to "real problems."

Role models also are keys to successful movement into high-tech fields. In a study of 12 women successfully employed in nontraditional, technology-related professions, many reported being encouraged by a male in their personal lives or by a teacher in their educational experience (Smith, 2000).

Girls want both achievement and affiliation. Miller and Stiver's (1993) self-in-relation theory provides one view of the conflict between achievement and relationships. This theory suggests that (a) women thrive in situations where relationships can be maintained and (b) they avoid situations that force them to separate themselves from significant others.

Given the relative isolation that women feel in male-dominated careers such as engineering and information technology, women struggle with resolving work-relationship conflicts even though they are technically competent.

Females lack the essential information that permits them to consider high-tech careers. According to Karan Eriksson, CEO of Women in Technology International, "The biggest issue facing women is communication: getting women to know that there is a huge market of jobs and careers open to women in technology professions" (Arent, 1999). According to *Tech Savvy* (2000), females need to: (a) know more about technology career options, (b) have a more complex, realistic view of jobs available (i.e. that many technology jobs emphasize communication, collaboration and creativity), and (c) get a balanced view of technology careers in terms of how these careers meet both economic and social goals. Additionally counselors need to reinforce behaviors that lead to enhanced exposure to and experience of nontraditional occupations (Herr & Cramer, 1996).

Another study, as cited in "Women and Minorities in IT" (1999), examines the issue of why women and minorities are underrepresented in this field at both the national and state levels and at all areas of the workforce pipeline. Factors listed were:

- Lack of computer equipment in public schools prevents access to technology for many economically underprivileged minority children, households, and schools.
- Few K-12 teachers and counselors are knowledgeable about the wide variety of career paths and opportunities in IT and do not have sufficient backgrounds to counsel their students about these careers.
- Minorities attend college in much lower percentages than whites do, so there is a smaller pool of students to enter the computer science pipeline.
- Women have not been encouraged to pursue high school courses in mathematics and science (AP calculus and physics) that are requirements for degree programs in computer science and computer engineering.
- Girls are not encouraged to take things apart and put them back together on their own, a skill which is useful in many IT computer careers.

Minorities

African Americans, Asian Americans, Hispanic (Latino/Latina) Americans, and Native American Indians constitute the major ethnic minority groups in the United States. Contrary to the uniformity suggested by their labels, each of these groups subsumes a highly heterogeneous mix of peoples and subcultures, and each is growing faster than the majority population, with the implication that the U.S. workplace is becoming increasingly diverse and will continue to do so.

Despite these facts, minorities make up only 3% of all technology positions (Barron, n.d.). Of engineers, Hispanics of both sexes amounted to only 3.3% in 1995 and Blacks made up another 4.7 % (Zuniga, 1997). Only 2.8% of the mathematical and computer scientists were Hispanic and 7.2% were Black, both percentages far below their percentages in the population (Zuniga, 1997). According to the Bureau of Labor Statistics table, "Employed Civilians by Occupation, Sex, Race, and Hispanic Origin, 1983 and 1995," only 2.5% of workers in professional specialties were Hispanic, and in 1995 the share had grown only slightly by more than one percentage point. A variety of statistics with different percentages exists, but all percentages indicate a significantly lower percentage of minorities in high-tech fields versus in the labor force or total population.

In schools, minorities are underrepresented in science education at every level from elementary to graduate school (Clark, 1999). Lack of preparation in science among under-represented minority groups in the early elementary grades undermines enrollment and success in secondary-level school programs and, ultimately, in college and career choices later in life. Although African Americans demonstrated significant progress during the decade from 1980 to 1990, in both science and math courses taken and in student achievement, they continue to be underrepresented in the science and engineering labor forces (Clark, 1999).

Advanced Placement exams also indicate the lack of minorities preparing for high-tech careers. In the 1999 Advanced Placement Computer Science exam, 65% of the exam takers were white, 22% Asian American, 5% African American, 5% Hispanic, and 3% "other" (*Tech Savvy*, 2000). African American women took the AP exam at a higher rate than African American males. African American women scored "1" on the exam (a score of 1 means that the student will not be recommended for advanced placement) at more than twice the percentage for all women (83% versus 41%). The most disturbing statistic is the low numbers of Hispanics who took the exam. For example, only seven Hispanic girls took the computer science AP exam in California in 1999, despite their large numbers in the California population.

Factors contributing to unequal participation of minorities in science and mathematics education include: understaffed and under-equipped schools–usually found in minority communities, tracking, judgments about ability, number and quality of science and mathematics courses offered, access to qualified teachers, access to resources, and curricula emphasis (National Science Foundation, 1994). Schools, particularly secondary schools, in urban areas with a high proportion of economically disadvantaged or a high proportion of minority students offer less access to science and mathematics education (Clark, 1999).

Complicating this problem is that for some minority groups, language and access to resources (e.g. the Internet) are barriers. Approximately 69% of all Web pages are in English (Abbott, 2001), which may restrict access to minorities whose English skills are limited. In terms of Internet access, the National Telecommunications and Information Administration survey (2000) reported that 34% of Hispanics had Internet access from home or work whereas 33% of African Americans, 56% of Caucasians, and 66% of Asian/Pacific Islanders had access either at home or work.

Research suggests that students from minority families may have fewer out-of-school learning opportunities that promote knowledge of and preparation for careers (Clark, 1999). It also suggests that students from minority families may express fewer occupational choices, and may personally know fewer role models in higher status positions (Fouad & Kelly, 1992; Palmer, 1993).

For minorities, parents are among the most important sociocultural factors influencing career development, especially in areas such as expectations for achievement and teaching about the world of work. Johnson (1986) found that parental encouragement to study math and science showed up as a key factor in the decisions of talented students of color to pursue careers in math and science fields. In studies of eighth grade girls, Koballa (1988) determined that for most Hispanic and African American girls, the mother was the person most likely to convince them to take physical science courses in high school. However, MacCorquodale (1980) found that many Latino parents were unable to provide information and encouragement for their children because they themselves lacked awareness of course offerings and requirements at the high school and college levels.

Little occupational material exists that is specifically targeted to ethnic minorities. Finding useful and culturally relevant occupational information in printed materials is harder for ethnic minorities than for their White, middle-class counterparts (Herring, 1998). Numerous websites (such as http://www.imdiversity.com/ or http://www.diversitycareers.com/) or web pages supported by various technology-oriented professional organizations

120

(such as http://www.amstat.org/careers/minorities.html or http://www.nbif.org/links/4.1.php) target minorities. However, access to the Internet may not be available to the minority population. A survey of 1,350 adults conducted by the Gallup organization for the National Career Development Association (NCDA) (Brown et al., 1991) found that ethnic minorities were more likely than non-minorities to report that they needed help getting information about jobs. Ethnic minorities were also less likely to find the information that they needed.

Understanding all the cultural and economic influences for minority individuals is a key factor in educating them about high-tech career opportunities. Marsella and Leong (1995) recommend that counselors locate each client on a continuum of ethnocultural identity, identifying the relative importance of personal or cultural values to an individual. For example, for a fully acculturated person, personal values or personality may be more relevant, where for a more traditional person, personal cultural mores have more influence. Leong (1995) suggests that career choice issues will be different for members of particular minority groups depending upon their socioeconomic level, i.e. a Latino coming from a middle-class background versus a low-socioeconomic background.

Lay and Wakstein (1985) reported that self-esteem was more potent than actual achievement in influencing the aspirations of African Americans. Additionally, many African Americans are drawn to careers that offer direct service to their communities (Herr & Cramer, 1996). For technology to be appealing, technology-related careers must be tied to cultural values.

The Gallup Organization conducted a 1989 telephone survey of adults for the National Occupational Information Coordinating Committee and the National Career Development Association as reported in "Multicultural Career Development: Central Perspectives-Part 2" (Marino, 1999). The results of this survey list problems that minorities have encountered in the career guidance process:

- 27% of African Americans said they took the only jobs that were available to them, compared with 19% of Asian Americans, 17% of Hispanics, and 10% of European Americans.
- 27% of all respondents said they needed additional assistance in finding information about jobs, with African Americans reporting the highest need (44%) and European Americans the least (25%) among ethnic groups.
- 53% of the respondents said public high schools are not providing the training in job-seeking skills for students who are not going to college.
- 40% of the respondents said high schools are not providing enough

help to students to choose careers.

- 19% of Asian Americans and 15% of African Americans reported they needed assistance in the labor market. For European Americans, the figure was 6%, and for Hispanics 8%.

Conclusion

High-tech positions do exist. A shortage of qualified people to fill those high-tech positions also exists. This brief look into how young people begin their career exploration demonstrates what factors influence their career choices. It also demonstrates the unique aspects of women and minorities in high-tech career development, which, hopefully, should provide direction to parents, teachers and counselors who are the major influencers in their career choices. Clearly, high-tech employment opportunity is knocking on the career doors of female and minority students. The question is – will they enter?

References

Abbott, J. P. (2001). Democracy @ Internet.Asia? The challenge to the emancipatory potential of the Net: Lessons from China and Malaysia. *Third World Quarterly, 22*, 99-114.

Armstrong, J. M. (1980). *Achievement and participation of women in mathematics: An overview.* Report.(ERIC_NO: ED184878).

Arent, L. (1999). Wanted: Women in tech. *WiredNews.* Retrieved May 15, 2001, from http://www.wired.com/news/print/0,1294,20116,00.html.

Barron, J. J. (n.d.). Careers in assistive technology: Win-win situations go wanting. *High Technology Careers.* Retrieved August 31, 2001, from http://www.hightechcareers.com/doc500/assistive500.html

Blevins-Knabe, B. & Musun-Mille, L. (April,1991). *Parental beliefs about the developmental of preschool children's number skills._* Paper presented at the Biennial meeting of the Society for Research in Child Development, Seattle, WA. (ERIC No.: ED338379)

Brown, B. L. (2001). *Women and minorities in high-tech careers.* ERIC Clearinghouse on Adult, Career, and Vocational Education. (ERIC Digest no. 226.)

Brown, D., Minor, C. W., & Jepsen, D. A. (1991). The opinions of minorities about preparing for work: Report of the second NCDA national survey. *Career Development Quarterly, 40,*5-19.

Career activity: Technology and career development. (1998). Stillwater, OK: Oklahoma Dept. of Vocational and Technical Education, Guidance Division. (ERIC Online Document: ED426338).

Clark, J. V. (1999). *Minorities in science and math.* ERIC Clearinghouse for Science, Mathematics, and Environmental Education: Columbus, OH. (ERIC No: ED433216).

Eccles, J. S. (1994). Understanding women's educational and occupational choices. *Psychology of Women Quarterly, 18,* 585-609.

Eisenhart, M. A. & Holland, D. C. (1992). Gender constructs and career commitment: The influence of peer culture on women in college. In T. L. Whitehead & B. V. Reid (Eds.). *Gender constructs and social issues* (pp. 142-179). Chicago: University of Illinois Press.

Erickson, F. (1987). Transformation and school success: The politics and culture of educational achievement. *Anthropology and Education Quarterly, 18*(4), 335-56.

Epstein, J. L. (1983). The influence of friends on achievement and affective outcomes. In J. H. Epstein & N. L. Karweit (Eds.) *Friends in school* (pp.177-200). New York: Academic Press.

Farmer, H. S. (Ed.). (1997). Diversity and women's career development: From adolescence to adulthood. Vol.2 of *Women's Mental Health and Development Series.* Thousand Oaks, CA: Sage.

Fouad, N. A., & Kelly, T. J. (1992). The relation between attitudinal and behavioral aspects of career maturity. *Career Development Quarterly, 40,* 257-271.

Genderwatchers. (n.d.) How science and technology academic programs can attract girls and women. Genderwatchers. Retrieved August 22, 2001, from http://www.genderwatchers.org/Legend/SceinceTech.html

123

Herr, S. H. & Cramer, E, L. (1996). *Career guidance and counseling through the life span: Systematic approaches.* Boston, MA: Addison Wesley Longman, Inc.

Herring, R. (1998). *Career counseling in schools: Multicultural and developmental perspectives.* Alexandria, VA: American Counseling Association.

Jacobsen, M. H. (1999). *Hand-me-down dreams. How families influence our career paths and how we can reclaim them.* New York: Crown Publishers. (ERIC_NO: ED437504).

Johnson, S. T. (1986). *Career choices in science and mathematics among talented minority graduates.* Paper presented at the Twelfth Annual Conference on Research on Women in Education.

Kerka, S. (1998). *Career development and gender, race and class.* ERIC Digest No. 199. (ERIC No: ED421641)

Kirk, B. A. (1975). *Factors affecting young women's direction toward science-technology- mathematics.* (NSF Grant No. GY-11311). Berkeley, CA: Management Technology.(ERIC Document Reproduction Services No. ED 1435 292).

Kuhl, C. (2000). Girls just wanna' have fun. *Communication Engineering and Design.* Retrieved August 22, 2001, from http:www.cedmagazine.com/ced/0006/june7.htm

Lay, R. & Wakstein, J. (1985). Race, academic achievement, and self-concept of ability. *Research in Higher Education, 22,* 43-64.

Lee, C. C. & Richardson, B. L. (Eds.). (1991). *Multicultural issues in counseling: New approaches to diversity.* Alexandria, VA: American Counseling Association.

Lenhart, A. (2000, September 21). *Who's not online.* Washington, D.C.: Pew Center for the People and the Press. Retrieved June 21, 2001, from http://www.pewinternet.org/reports/toc.asp?Report=21

Leong, F. T. L. (1995*). Career development and vocational behavior of racial and ethnic minorities*. Mahwah, NJ: Lawrence Erlbaum Associates, Inc.

MacCorquodale, P. (1980).*Psycho-social influences on the accomplishments of Mexican-American students*. Paper presented at the meeting of the American Association of School Administrators, Chicago, IL. (ERIC Document Reproduction Service No. 2000 355.)

Marino, T. (Ed.). (1999). Multicultural career development: Central perspectives-part 2. *Career Counseling and School Counseling,2*(2). Retrieved August 21, 2001, from http://www.counseling.org/enews/volume_2/0202a.htm

Marsella, A. J. & Leong, F. T. L. (1995). Cross-cultural issues in personality and career assessment. *Journal of Career Assessment, 3*(2), 202-218.

Matthews, W. (1981). Influences on the learning and participation of minorities in mathematics. *Journal of Social and Behavioral Science, 27*, 88-92.

Mau, W. C. (1995). Educational planning and academic achievement of middle school students: A racial and cultural comparison. *Journal of Counseling and Development, 73*, 518-526.

Mau, W. C. & Bikos, L H. (2000). Educational and vocational aspirations of minority and female students: A longitudinal study. *Journal of Counseling and Development, 78*(2), 186-194.

Mayfield, K. (2000). Why girls don't compute. *WiredNews*. Retrieved May 15, 2001, from http://www.wired.com/news/print/0,1294,35654,00.html

Mayfield, K. (2001). Girls into science, not computers. *WiredNews*. Retrieved August 20, 2001, from http://www.wired.com/news/print/0,1294,42210.00.html

McFadden, J. (1996). Values and career development through transcultural counseling. In R. Feller, G. R. Walz, & D. W. Engels (Eds.), *Career transitions in turbulent times: Exploring work, learning, and careers*. (pp. 57-66). North Carolina: ERIC/CASS Publications.

Miller, J. B. & Stiver, I. P. (1993). A relational approach to understanding women's lives and problems. *Psychiatric Annals, 23,* 424-431.

National Science Foundation. (1994). *Request for proposals.* Washington, D.C.: U.S. Government Printing Office.

National Telecommunications and Information Administration (NTIA). (2000). *Falling through the Net: Toward digital inclusion.* Washington, D.C.: U.S. Department of Commerce, National Telecommunications and Information Administration. Author.

National Science and Technology Council. (2000). *Ensuring a strong U.S. scientific, technical, and engineering workforce in the 21st century.* Retrieved October 13, 2001, from http://www.ostp.gov/html/workforcerpt.pdf

Nauta, M. M. & Kokaly, K. (2001). Assessing role model influences on students' academic and vocational decisions. *Journal of Career Assessment, 9*(1), 81-99.

Occupational Outlook Quarterly. (2000, Spring). *A special issue: The 1998-2008 job outlook in brief, 44*(1). Washington, D.C.: U.S. Department of Labor.

Otto, L. B. (2000). Youth perspectives on parental career influence. *Journal of Career Development, 27*(2), 111-118.

Palmer, T. (1993). The athletic dream—but what are the career dreams of other African American urban high school students? *Journal of Career Development, 20,* 131-145.

Pastore, M. (2001). IT worker shortage continues. *New Media.* Retrieved October 13, 2001, from http://www.newmedia.com/nm-print-ns.asp?articleID=3112

Sanders, M.G. (n.d.). Schools, families, and communities: A partnership for student success. (Online monograph). National Association of Secondary School Principals. Retrieved August 13, 2001, from http://www.nassp.org/pdf/schls_fmles_cmntes.pdf

126

Seymour, E. (1993). Lecture. *Why are women leaving?* NECUSE Conference, Brown University.

Smith, L. B. (2000). The socialization of females with regard to technology-related career. *Meridian: A Middle School Computer Technologies Journal, 3*(2). Retrieved August 22, 2001, from http://www.ncsu.edu/meridian/archive_of_meridian/sum2000/career/index.html

Smith, T. E. (1991). Agreement of adolescent educational expectations with perceived maternal and paternal educational goals. *Youth and Society, 23*, 155-174.

Stipek, D. & Granlinski, H. (1991). Gender differences in children's achievement-related beliefs and emotional responses to success and failure in mathematics. *Journal of Educational Psychology, 83*(3), 361-371.

Tech-savvy: Educating girls in the new computer age. (2000). AAUW Educational Foundation Commission on Technology, Gender, and Teacher Education. Washington, D. C.: American Association of University Women Educational Foundation.

Treisman, P. (1982). *Helping minority students to excel in university-level mathematic and science courses.* Unpublished manuscript. University of California Professional Development Program: Berkeley, CA.

Tichenor, P. J., Donohue, G. A. & Olien, C. N. (1970). Mass media flow and differential growth in knowledge. *Public Opinion, 34*, 159-170.

Wilson, P. M. & Wilson, J. R. (1992). Environmental influences on adolescent educational aspirations: A logistic transform model. *Youth and Society, 24*, 52-70.

Women and minorities in information technology forum. (1999). Sandy, M., Principal Investigator. Funded by National Science Foundation Transition for Childhood to Workforce grant. Retrieved June 21, 2001, from http://www.vsgc.odu.edu/html/gender/forum.html

Zuniga, J. A. (1997). Helping girls move into technology careers. *Hispanic Engineer and Information Technology.* Retrieved August 22, 2001, from http://www.crpc.rice.edu/CRPC/newsArchive/hisp_eng_oct_97.html

Part II

Comprehensive School Counseling Programs

In Part II, Comprehensive School Counseling Programs, the ASCA National Standards (student content standards in the domains of academic, career, and personal/social development) are presented in two chapters: (6) *Building a National Model* (Hatch and Bowers) and (7) *School Counseling Programs: Supporting a Nation of Learners* (Dahir).

(8) *Unfocused Kids/Unfocused Counseling*—Anderson presents a provocative discussion about the difficulty of staying with the intended role of the school counselor in the face of many competing demands; he urges the use of the comprehensive guidance and counseling model as shown in the *ASCA National Model: A Framework for School Counseling Programs.*

(9) *Career Resource Centers—Programs and Resources for All Students*—Hines and Mygatt Wakefield discuss the many functions that may be provided by a school's career resource center (staffed by a career specialist and an instructional aid) to enhance a school's career guidance program, with information about postsecondary educational options, testing programs, in-school career programs, website updates, and program enrollment support.

(10) *The Phantom Student*—Coy discusses the importance of using a comprehensive guidance and counseling model to reach "phantom students" who tend go unnoticed and become virtually lost in the school system. She presents several guidance lessons that counselors and teachers may use to help students with analyzing their skills and interests and with goal-setting.

(11) *A Model School Counseling Program Brochure: Implications for Helping Students Focus on their Plans after High School* –Whitledge provides a template for a model *school counseling program brochure* for educators to use in their own districts to publicize their counseling program to students, teachers, parents, and community members. He also provides a template for an *informed consent brochure*, so that parents and students are aware of the services provided in a school's guidance and counseling program, and may have the opportunity to ask for needed clarification.

Chapter Six

Building a National Model*

Trish Hatch and Judy Bowers

Abstract

ASCA has developed *The National Model: A Framework for School Counseling Programs* (ASCA, 2003) which includes the ASCA National Standards. The model is intended to address historical concerns and current challenges within the profession and to provide a framework for the practicing school counselor in planning for the future of their programs. ASCA brought the leaders in the school counseling profession together and created the common lens for all counselors, *One Vision, One Voice.* The ASCA National Model maximizes the full potential of the standards documents and reflects current education reform movements, including the No Child Left Behind legislation, which mandates that all federally funded programs are accountable and directly connected to student learning and student improvement. The model provides the mechanism with which school counselors and school counseling teams may design, coordinate, implement, manage and evaluate their programs for students' success.

*This chapter is being reprinted with the permission of the American School Counselor Association. It first appeared in the *ASCA School Counselor*, 39 (5), May/June 2002, 12-19.

As we head further into the 21st century, school counselors continue to define new directions for the profession. Recently, the American School Counselor Association (ASCA) released its National Model: A Framework for School Counseling Programs (ASCA, 2003). Before looking to the school counseling profession's future, it's crucial to understand its past. At the turn of the 20th century, school counselors didn't exist. Instead, teachers used a few minutes of their time to offer vocational guidance to students preparing for work in a democratic society.

The school mission of 2002 is not altogether different than in the 1900s. Today, in a world enriched by diversity and technology, school counselors' chief mission is still supporting the academic achievement of all students so they are prepared for life beyond school. However, school counselors no longer work in isolation; instead, they are professionals, integral to the total educational program. This evolution from teachers spending minutes a day to full-time trained professionals implementing a comprehensive school counseling program did not take place without professional scholars and counselors having the vision, knowledge and determination to move forward (Gysbers, 2001).

School counseling training programs have had conflicting and varied theoretical perspectives. Consequently, within the field we have programs that have trained counselors differently. School counselors began as vocational counselors nearly 100 years ago, and the profession has evolved to address all children in the comprehensive domains of academic, career, and personal/social development (Miller, 1968; Campbell & Dahir, 1997). During this evolution, differing philosophical perspectives developed between and among academic counselors, career counselors, and personal/social or mental health counselors regarding their role and function, purpose, and focus. Lacking clear role definition as a profession, school counseling became a "house divided by controversy" between those who focused on vocational guidance (which later became educational guidance) and those who attended to the personal-social foundational needs of students in education (Aubrey, 1986). While procedures were similar in counseling, methods varied. Counseling could be either directive or non-directive – two somewhat opposing methods of delivery. In directive counseling, the focus was on intellectual interpretation and was counselor directed, while non-directive counseling was client-centered and focused on the release of feelings and the achievement of insight. One was delivered by the counselor; the other was discovered by the student. Warters (1946) reported that most vocational counselors during this time were directive, while social workers, mental hygienists, and child-guidance clinicians were more non-directive.

In the 1960's, the directive approach to counseling was encouraged by the National Defense Education Act. However, coinciding with this movement was Carl Rogers' non-directive approach to counseling. Counselors trained in programs rooted in psychological and clinical paradigms differed greatly in practice from those rooted in educational paradigms. These changes and varying models confused school counselors and school administrators, teachers, and parents. As Cunnan & Maddy-Berstein (1998) wrote: "When schools fail to clearly define the counselor's role... school administrators, parents with special interests, teachers or others may feel their agenda ought to be the school counseling program's priority. The results often lead to confusion and criticisms when they are disappointed."

Over its history, the counseling and guidance movement has been characterized by a proliferation of competing methodologies which focused more attention on the technique of counselors and the process of counseling and less on the content and objectives of the program. This alteration in counseling methodology led to changes in substance and the priority which guidance programs were given (Aubrey,1986). "The focus was on a position (counselor) and a process (counseling), not on a program (guidance) (Gysbers & Henderson, 1997, p. 1). Consequently, guidance became an ancillary support service and not a program integral to the total educational program of student success. The result was that counselors were more likely to be saddled with administrative tasks and clerical duties (Roeber et al., 1961).

In the 1970's and 80's, several attempts were made to unify the profession. Emerging from this movement were several theoretical models of comprehensive programs, many of which were based on the expansion of the career guidance model. Norm Gysbers and Patricia Henderson developed and trained educators in districts and states in comprehensive guidance programs models (1997, 1998). C. D. "Curly" and Sharon Johnson (1991) focused on results-based school counseling programs, and Robert Myrick (2003) wrote on planned developmental guidance programs. Despite the impact of these visionary thinkers, the role of the school counselor and the school counseling program remained one of concern.

Current Challenges

In 1992, Phyllis Hart and Marilyn Jacobi wrote *From Gatekeeper to Advocate: Transforming the Role of the School Counselor.* It served as an anchor document in The Education Trust's design and development of the Readers Digest-DeWitt Wallace Foundation effort to transform the training of school counselors. One of the chapters in the book discusses the six problems in school counseling programs. They are summarized here:

1. Lack of basic philosophy: Few counselors are guided by a well developed philosophy or belief system, one that indeed drives the entire program and the behaviors of the school counselors within the program. Rather, they tend to work independently and are often reactive.

2. Poor integration: School counseling remains ancillary rather than a core component of K-12 education. School counselors must connect with

other stakeholders in the school system as an integral partner in the total educational program.

3. Insufficient student access: Student-to-counselor ratios are high. Many students do not have the opportunity to see their school counselors. High ratios are only part of the problem. Another problem is that some counselors still insist on focusing more on individual counseling rather than ensuring that every student receives school counseling services through a school- wide guidance curriculum.

4. Inadequate guidance for some students: Poor students and students of color are often denied access to rigorous academic curriculum. Parents' and students' ignorance of the system contributes to this problem. Counselors are often the gatekeepers and must reach out to encourage high expectations for all students.

5. Lack of counselor accountability: A common understanding does not exist as to what constitutes accountability and in what way school counselors are to be held accountable.

6. Failure to utilize other resources: School counselors themselves cannot make up the entire counseling program. Rather, school counselors are encouraged to collaborate with other stakeholders to better utilize school and community resources to create networks, referral opportunities and to meet a variety of student needs.

For decades, the school counseling profession has responded to the question, "What do counselors do?" However, that question only served to confuse our profession, depending on which model one was trained. In addition to listing myriad counseling related duties (e.g., guidance lessons, group counseling, academic planning, individual counseling, consultation, collaboration, etc.), school counselors have complained throughout their history about "doing" a variety of quasi-administrative and non-counseling duties. Just as pre-service trainings have varied for school counselors, so too have administrative expectations based on administrative pre-service training (or lack of it) with regard to school counseling programs (Olson, 1979). Consequently, the school counseling profession has continued to struggle with this issue while attempting to institutionalize the appropriate role of the counselors. As a result, school counselors have often been assigned additional responsibilities, such as:

- Master schedule duties: Many counselors, instead of administrators, develop the school's master schedule. Certainly, school counselors would want to participate as consultants in the process, but unfortunately, in many schools, they carry the bulk of the responsibility in this area – therefore diminishing school counseling services for students.

- Testing coordinators: In a world of increased high stakes testing, more and more school counselors are called on to assist in the preparation for testing, when the appropriate role for a school counselor is to interpret the results of these tests and to analyze them in conjunction with multiple measures of student achievement.
- Classroom coverage: In the absence of a teacher or other certificated staff, school counselors often are directed by their administrator to cover classrooms, thus taking the counselor away from his or her planned counseling activities. School counselors are team players and understand they sometimes need to assist when emergencies arise. The problem in this area occurs when school counselors are turned to regularly and first in order to cover classes. This is an inappropriate use of counselors' time and skills.
- Discipline: School counselors are not disciplinarians and most do not possess the appropriate credentials for disciplining students. Their appropriate role is: to provide counseling for students before and after discipline; to determine the causes of students' behavior that leads to discipline; to provide school-wide curriculum for the deterrence of behaviors that lead to discipline; and to collaborate on school leadership teams which work systemically to create policies which promote appropriate behavior on campus.
- Clerical responsibilities: The school counseling program contains many areas in which clerical assistance is necessary to perform functions that are outside of the school counselor's appropriate job description. Many districts employ guidance assistants to provide this service so that school counselors can spend more of their time in direct service to students.

Rather than answer the question of "What do school counselors *do*?" and only focusing attention on listing activities performed by the school counselor, the new and more important question is: "How are students different *because* of what school counselors do?" School counselors can no longer ask the principal on the first day, "What would you like me to do?" Instead, school counselors must be trained and educated both to inform the administrator of the contributions they plan to make to all of the students in the school, and to collaborate with administrators on areas of needed improvement.

Current Trends

Current issues in education are familiar to us all: the reform movement, accountability, the standards-based movement, high-stakes testing, achievement gap issues of equity and access, the increase in legislation supporting student retention, the funding of new programs through block grants, the use of technology and data to drive decisions and effect change, school safety issues, and the movement from an educational culture of entitlement to one of performance.

Current trends in the school counseling field have included the development of the American School Counselor Association's (ASCA) *National Standards* which contain the student content standards used to design competencies for students in the areas of academic, career and personal/social development (Campbell & Dahir, 1997). Other trends include the *Transforming School Counseling Initiative* (Martin & House, 1998) and the more current *Met Life School Counselors Training Initiative* (The Education Trust, 2002) which challenges school counselors to be leaders, advocates and systems change agents in an effort to reduce the effects of environmental and institutional barriers impeding student academic success. These trends have contributed to the work of state departments, school districts and school counselors to develop state and local models, and to an increase in legislative activity to promote school counseling programs for students (Hanson, Whitson, & Meyers, 2002).

Nonetheless, questions remain unanswered by many school counselors nationwide:
- What is the purpose of your school counseling program?
- What are your desired outcomes?
- What is being done to achieve these results?
- What evidence is there that the objectives have been met?
- Is your program making a difference?

One Vision One Voice

As the next logical step to the introduction of the *ASCA National Standards*, ASCA's Governing Board, at its March 2001 meeting, agreed to develop a national program model. The *American School Counselor Association National Model: A Framework for School Counseling Programs* (ASCA, 2003) maximizes the full potential of the standards documents and reflects current education reform movements, including the No Child Left Behind legislation, which mandates all federally funded programs be accountable for and directly connected to student learning and student improvement.

The decision to hold a National Summit to create an ASCA National Model was a decision ASCA made to bring the leaders in the field together and create *One Vision, One Voice* for all school counselors. ASCA moved forward to develop the model to address the historical concerns and current challenges, and to assist practicing school counselors in planning for the future of their programs and the profession through one common lens. The model provides the mechanism with which school counselors and school counseling teams will design, coordinate, implement, manage and evaluate their programs for students' success.

The *American School Counselor Association National Model: A Framework for School Counseling Programs* (ASCA, 2003) is written to reflect a comprehensive approach to program foundation, delivery, management and accountability. It provides a framework for the program components, the school counselor's role in implementation, and the underlying philosophies of leadership, advocacy and systemic change. School counselors switch their emphasis from service-centered for some of the students to program-centered for all students. It not only answers the question: "What do school counselors do?" but further, it requires us to respond to the question, "How are students *different* as a result of what we do?"

School counseling programs are designed to ensure that *every* student receives the benefits of the program. Historically, many school counselors have spent 80 percent of their time responding to the needs of 20 percent of their students, typically the high-achieving or high-risk. The *ASCA National Model* recommends 80 percent of the school counselor's time be spent in direct service to all students so that *every* student may receive the program benefits.

The *ASCA National Model* incorporates school counseling content standards and competencies for every student, which serve as the foundation for the program and focus the direction for an organized, planned, sequential and flexible school counseling curriculum. The model uses disaggregated data to drive program and activity development, thus enabling school counselors to design interventions to meet the needs of all students and to close the gap between specific groups of students and their peers. The model emphasizes an organizational framework and accountability systems to determine how well students have met the standards or have achieved intended outcomes. The school counseling program reduces confusion, aligns goals and objectives with the school's mission, and ultimately leads to student achievement as demonstrated by results data.

The *ASCA National Model* serves as a template for the development of a school counseling program; it is not meant for exact replication. Because attention to local demographic needs and political conditions are necessary for effective school counseling program development, the *ASCA National Model* is meant to integrate with and adapt to the school's current program. There is no one "ideal program" that can or should be used as a cookie cutter throughout the nation. Rather, ASCA's goal is to provide school counselors with a document that will institutionalize the framework of a comprehensive school counseling program.

Leadership skills are critical to the successful implementation of new or remodeled programs at the school, district and state levels. School counselors are change agents, collaborators and advocates. As school counselors become proficient in retrieving and analyzing school data to improve student success, they ensure educational equity for every student. Using strong communication, consultation and political skills, school counselors collaborate with other professionals in the school building to influence systemic change and advocate for every student.

Learning from the past is critical in developing a new school counseling program. The *ASCA National Model* provides a program audit which, when completed by members of the school counseling team, assists them in analyzing their current program so that areas of improvement can be identified. Looking at recent and current achievement and achievement-related data in the school will illuminate performance trends. This analysis is imperative as school counselors can use this data to recognize if program changes are needed – and they must be prepared to make them – no matter how comfortable the status quo or how difficult or uncomfortable that change may be.

Model Development

From the first stages of development, the *ASCA National Model* called upon the expertise of national leaders and practicing school counselors. Development began with a Summit held in June 2001, where the framework was developed. The resulting model included the basic content of the four major components: the foundation, delivery system, management system and accountability system. The themes of advocacy, leadership, collaboration and systemic change are woven throughout the model. Finally, suggestions for administrators are included as they provide the strong support necessary for successful implementation of the *ASCA National Model*.

The first draft version model was unveiled during ASCA's national school counselor conference in Miami in June, 2002. Keynote conference speakers included leaders in the school counseling field who attended the initial model development summit meeting: Norm Gysbers, Ph.D., University of Missouri; Clarence "Curly" Johnson, Ph.D., retired; and Robert Myrick, Ph.D., University of Florida. Several conference sessions were devoted to providing an overview of the model. The authors of the ASCA National Model (Judy Bowers and Trish Hatch, Ph.D.) also provided an intensive three-hour workshop on implementing the model in their districts. ASCA sought national public comment for the four- month period following the conference and received an overwhelmingly positive response. School counselors and counselor educators nationwide provided praise, helpful constructive criticism and suggestions for improvement. The final document was published in early 2003.

The *ASCA National Model* is expected to become the standard of training in counselor education programs on a national level, and current school counselors are encouraged to begin aligning or transforming their programs. Engaging administrators early in the process is important, as they will be a partner in program design and development. As the school counseling department moves forward with implementation, it will be important to keep the school board, staff and stakeholders informed and involved. Remember, the school counseling program belongs to the school, and the support of all team members is vital.

References

Aubrey, R.F. (1986). Excellence, school reform and counselors. *Counseling and Human Development, 19,* 1-10.

American School Counselor Association (2003). *The ASCA national model: A framework* for school counseling programs. Alexandria, VA: Author.

Campbell, C.A. & Dahir, C.A. (1997). Sharing the vision: The national standards *for school counseling programs.* Alexandria, VA: American School Counselor Association.

Cunnan & Maddy-Bernsten. (1998). *In vision into action: Implementing the national standards for school counseling programs.* PowerPoint presentation.

The Education Trust (2002). *National school counselor initiative.* Met Life Foundation. Washington, DC: Author.

Gysbers, N. C. (2001). School guidance and counseling in the 21st century: Remember the past into the future. *Professional School Counseling, 5*(2), 96-104.

Gysbers, N.C. & Henderson, P. (1997). *Comprehensive guidance programs that work*-II. Greensboro, North Carolina: ERIC/CASS Publications.

Hart, P.J., & Jacobi, M. (1992*). From gatekeeper to advocate: Transforming the role of* the school counselor. New York, NY: College Entrance Examination Board.

Hanson, C., Whitson, L.& Meyers, P. (2002). California's core. *ASCA School Counselor, 39*(5), 23-27.

Johnson, C.D. & Johnson, S.K. (1991). The new guidance: A system approach to pupil personnel programs. *CACD Journal, 11.*

Martin, P.J. & House, R.M. (1998). Transforming school counseling. (In *the transforming school counseling initiative).* Washington DC: The Education Trust.

Miller, F.W. (1968*). Guidance principles and services* (2nd ed). Columbus, Ohio: Charles E. Merrill Publishing Company.

Myrick, R. D. (2003) *Developmental guidance and counseling: A practical approach.* (4rded.) Minneapolis, MN: Educational Media Corporation

Olson, L. (1979). Lost in the shuffle: A report on the secondary guidance system: A *report on the guidance system in California secondary schools.* Open Road Issues Research, Citizens Policy Center: Santa Barbara, CA.

Roeber, E.C., Walz, G.R & Smith, G.E. (1969). *A strategy for guidance: A point of view* and its implications. Ontario, Canada: The McMillan Company.

Warters, J. (1946) *High school personnel work today.* McGraw Hill, New York.

Chapter Seven

School Counseling Programs: Supporting a Nation of Learners

Carol A. Dahir

Abstract

School counselors play an increasingly important key role in preparing students to meet the complex demands of our society that require significantly higher levels of knowledge and skills to succeed in the 21st century. As part of an educational team, school counselors, too, must accept the challenge of preparing every student to meet the expectations of rigorous academic standards and to develop educational and career goals that will lead to a successful future.

Not every student is ready, willing, or able to rise to the level of academic expectations now required in all 50 states. Students who are unmotivated, disabled, from poverty, frustrated or angry also need to receive a quality education. School counselors, committed to implementing the National Standards for School Counseling Programs (ASCA, 1997), provide a comprehensive program that systematically delivers activities, strategies, programs and services that will ensure that "no child will be left behind".

It is recognized, even by the federal government, that we have a genuine national crisis. More and more, we are divided into two nations: one that reads, and one that doesn't; one that dreams, and one that doesn't (Bush, 2002. p.1). The recent educational reauthorization *The No Child Left Behind Act* (2001) has as its primary purpose to close the achievement gap between disadvantaged students and their peers. Specifically goals 4 and 5 require all educators to address the importance of providing safe and drug free environments that are conducive to learning and ensure that all students will graduate from high school. These two goals speak to the heart and soul of school counseling to assure that all students have equitable access to educational opportunities. School counselors must see themselves as critical players to help students successfully negotiate and graduate from high school with all options available to them for the next phase of their post-secondary plans (Stone & Dahir, in press).

Merely legislating a change in expectations for students will not produce the desired outcomes. Far more needs to be done. The federal, state, and local emphasis on accountability essentializes the need for school counselors to demonstrate how the school counseling program contributes to the school improvement agenda and how school counselors, too, are committed to closing the gap.

Providing Equitable Opportunity

The data on the low socio-economic status of minority children and their families is cause for alarm. The U.S Bureau of the Census (2000) tells us that 13.8% of all families of all races had incomes below the poverty level. The percentage increased dramatically for families of color. McLoyd (1998) reminds us that African-American and Hispanic children are more likely to experience persistent poverty, and continue to live in areas of concentrated poverty. The rise in the numbers of students of color has also increased the proportion of children living below the poverty line. Children who live in high poverty communities have different life exposures, which can include: limited access to public services and quality health care, poorly equipped schools, street violence, homelessness, drug racketeering, etc.

Studies have shown that high SES students stay in school longer and have higher levels of achievement (Garrett, Ng'andu, Ferron, 1994; Conger, Conger, & Elder, 1997; McLoyd, 1998). Students who are caught in the cycle of poverty are also caught in the cycle of low expectations. These cycles do perpetuate themselves unless there is direct intervention on the part of educators to focus their efforts on both the obvious and the underlying symptoms. McLoyd (1998) also speaks to several other contributing factors such as low expectations, learned helplessness, peer influences and resistance cultures and tracking. Each of these concerns offers additional insight and opportunities for school counselors. Students from poverty may not wear the "trendy" clothes that other young adolescents and teens consider as essential to their wardrobes and may have little or no experience with cultural icons such as museums, theatres, and public libraries. This can result in insecurity about jumping into classroom discussions or an inability to participate in field trips resulting in a lack of self-confidence and low self-esteem. Students caught in the cycle of poverty may not see education as a viable opportunity for success in the future. They may feel intimidated to conform and perform to standards that seem far above their reach.

Researchers have linked socio-economic status as the most important single indicator of a child's educational plans. A longitudinal study conducted by the National Center for Education Statistics (Sanderson, Dugoni, Rasinski, & Taylor, 1996) showed that student educational aspirations were formed at an early age, and higher levels of aspiration were linked to higher levels of socio-economic status. Students must be made aware at an early age of the importance of an education and its potential economic payoff. Students need to be apprised of the financial supports that are available to help them achieve their educational goals and dreams. Higher levels of student achievement will not result in a better educated and prepared workforce without an assurance of equitable student access to postsecondary programs and assistance in transitioning from high school to college.

Education and economic success are inextricably entwined. School counselors are ideally situated to identify policies and practices that can stratify student opportunities (Stone & Clark, 2001) by denying access to quality educational experiences and the necessary support services to help every child achieve success. This requires examining behaviors and focusing efforts towards the common goal of providing every student with access to a quality education. School counselors can rise to this challenge and accept the responsibility of supporting academic achievement, sharing the pressures of school improvement and advocating for every student to experience success. School counselors must be seen as critical partners to ensure that "no child will be left behind" (U.S. Dept. of Education, 2001).

The School Counseling Agenda in School Improvement

Until recently, the voice of the school counselor, and the acknowledgment of the contributions of counseling programs in schools had not been heard in the educational arena. The history of the school counseling profession is replete with chastisement and dictates from external forces. The continued omission of school counseling in the educational reform agenda of the 80's and early 90's was the impetus for the American School Counselor Association (ASCA) to take action and to focus its efforts and resources to establish school counseling programs as an integral component of the educational system.

Sharing the Vision: The National Standards for School Counseling Programs (Campbell & Dahir, 1997) brought attention to the content of school counseling programs and to the manner in which programs in schools are designed and delivered. The development of the *National Standards for School Counseling Programs* (ASCA, 1997b) offered school counselors, administrators, teachers, and counselor educators a common language and characteristics similar to other educational programs including: a scope and sequence, student outcomes or competencies, activities and processes to assist students in achieving these outcomes, professionally credentialed personnel, materials and resources, and methods of accountability. The national standards connected school counseling to school improvement by clearly delineating what students should know and be able to do as a result of the school counseling program (Stone & Dahir, in press). In this era of increased educational accountability, school counselors must demonstrate their contribution to prepare students to meet the increasingly complex societal demands that are needed to succeed in the 21st century.

The National Standards: What Students Should Know and Be Able To Do

The national standards identified the attitudes, knowledge, and skills that students should acquire in a proactive and preventive manner through a broad range of experiences. The adoption and implementation of the national standards has changed the way school counseling programs are designed and delivered across our country. The emphasis is on academic success for all students, not only those students who are motivated, supported, and ready to learn. Implementing the national standards is an important step in engaging school counselors and stakeholders in a national conversation about the attitudes, knowledge and skills in academic, career and personal-social development that every student should acquire as a result of participating in the school counseling program (Dahir, 2001). The national standards, linked to the mission of the school, encourage school counselors to evaluate and assess the impact of the program on student achievement and success in school.

The nine national standards are based on the three widely accepted and interrelated areas of student development as described in the counseling literature and research: academic, career and personal/social development.

Academic Development

The three standards for academic development guide school counselors as they implement school counseling program strategies and activities to support and maximize student learning. Academic development includes students acquiring attitudes, knowledge, and skills that contribute to effective learning in school and across the lifespan; employing strategies to achieve success in school; and understanding the relationship of academics to the world of work, and to life at home and in the community. The academic development standards are:

Standard A. Students will acquire the attitudes, knowledge, and skills that contribute to effective learning in school and across the life span.

Standard B. Students will complete school with the academic preparation essential to choose from a wide variety of substantial postsecondary options, including college.

Standard C. Students will understand the relationship of academics to the world of work, and to life at home and in the community.

Career Development

The standards for career development guide school counselors as they implement school counseling program strategies and activities to assist students in acquiring attitudes, knowledge, and skills to successfully transition from grade to grade, from school to post-secondary education, and ultimately to the world of work. Career development activities include the employment of strategies to achieve future career success and job satisfaction, as well as fostering understanding of the relationship between personal qualities, education and training, and future career goals. The three career development standards are:

Standard A. Students will acquire the skills to investigate the world of work in relation to knowledge of self and to make informed career decisions.

Standard B. Students will employ strategies to achieve future career success and satisfaction.

Standard C. Students will understand the relationship between personal qualities, education and training, and the world of work.

Personal-Social Development

The standards for personal-social development guide school counselors as they implement school counseling program strategies and activities to provide personal and social growth experiences to facilitate students' progress through school and make the transition to adulthood. Personal-social development contributes to academic and career success, and includes the acquisition of attitudes, knowledge, and skills to help students understand and respect self and others, acquire effective interpersonal skills, understand safety and survival skills, and develop into contributing members of society.

The three personal-social development standards are:

Standard A. Students will acquire the attitudes, knowledge, and interpersonal skills to help them understand and respect self and others.

Standard B. Students will make decisions, set goals, and take appropriate action to achieve goals.

Standard C. Students will understand safety and survival skills.

Sharing Responsibility for Student Success

School counselors are challenged to demonstrate accountability, document effectiveness, and identify school counseling's contributions to the educational agenda. School counseling programs defined by statements of what students should know and be able to do are seen as accountable, viable, and visible in the eyes of school stakeholders.

School counselors coordinate the objectives, strategies, and activities of a comprehensive school counseling program to meet the academic, career, and personal-social needs of all students (ASCA, 1997a). Once the school counseling program has an organization and structure like the other disciplines in school, it is no longer perceived as ancillary but as an integral component directly linked to student achievement and school success. When guidance and counseling is conceptualized, organized and implemented as a program, it places professional school counselors at the heart and center of education and makes it possible for them to be active and involved (Gysbers, 2001).

Comprehensive and developmental national standards-based school counseling programs solidify our presence and will continue to shape our future (Campbell & Dahir, 1997).

How do we deliver nine standards and student competencies as the heart and soul of a school counseling program? We do this by focusing our efforts on student accomplishment of competencies and the standards and by connecting our efforts to student success and school improvement. We do this by engaging others in a school-wide effort that supports affective education and student growth in academic, career and personal-social development. We do this by organizing our efforts around the very same delivery methods (individual student planning, responsive services, system support, guidance curriculum) used in the comprehensive, developmental and results-based models.

Random acts of guidance are no longer acceptable in 21st century schools (Bilzing, 1997). School counseling programs and the primary methods of delivery are determined by the degree of the academic, career, and personal–social developmental needs of students. The counselor is in a key position to identify the issues that impact student learning and achievement by becoming involved at the core of school planning, by developing programs, and, thereby, impacting school climate. This cannot be accomplished unilaterally. It is important to create meaningful conversations among school counselors, school administrators, teachers, parents, and representatives of business and community about expectations for students' academic success and the role of counseling programs in supporting and enhancing student learning (Dahir, Sheldon & Valiga, 1998). Community members can see that school counseling programs do produce the results they are expecting and that school counselors desire the same levels of success and positive results as do parents, teachers and administrators. Student success in school depends upon the cooperation and support of the entire faculty, staff, and student services personnel.

The school counselor, in implementing a national standards-based school counseling program, uses a collaborative model as a springboard for success. Counselors do not work alone; all educators play a role in creating an environment, which promotes the achievement of identified student goals and outcomes. The counselor facilitates communication and establishes linkages for the benefit of students, with teaching staff, administration, families, student service personnel, agencies, businesses, and other members of the community. Student success in school depends upon the cooperation and support of the entire faculty, staff, and student services personnel.

Program delivery consists of the many ways that professional school counselors provide services to students including: individual and group counseling, large and small group guidance, consultation, management of resources, and coordination of services. The school counselor utilizes a variety of strategies, activities, delivery methods, and resources to facilitate student growth and development. In order to accomplish this, the school counselor must possess a solid knowledge of what he/she needs to know and be able to do to serve as a student advocate, provide direct and indirect services, and demonstrate the belief that all children can learn and achieve and do so by her/his actions.

Hope Is Not a Strategy: Cassie's Story

Students experience differentiated educational pathways. Readiness, ability grouping, placement, tracking, retention and promotion are commonplace terms. School careers are further defined by special education, gifted education, bi-lingual education, alternative, and vocational education. If students see academic success as unattainable, they protect themselves by deciding school is unimportant (Comer, 1988). The overarching vision for higher levels of achievement for all students lies in the creation of equitable opportunities to learn. This requires that appropriate support systems must be put into place when necessary, (i.e., extended time, learning tools, and differentiated instruction) so that all students can meet the same academic standards. Every student needs help to rise to the challenge of higher expectations. Every student can benefit from acquiring attitudes, skills and knowledge based on the nine national standards. Let's apply this ability to benefit to Cassie's situation.

Cassie's parents divorced when she was 8 years old, and neither parent remarried. She lives with her mother, who works nights at a department store. She visits her father, a factory worker, on weekends. Cassie is the youngest of four children and since Cassie was 10 years old she "watched herself" because she refused to stay with a babysitter.

Cassie attended public school until the sixth grade. Her second-grade and fifth-grade teachers had suggested that she be tested for ADHD, but based on feedback from the family and several observations conducted by the school psychologist and the family pediatrician, it was felt that ADHD was not really the problem. During the fifth grade, Cassie had also been tested for special education placement, but she did not meet the criteria for learning disabilities (her academic scores were not quite low enough) or behavior disorders (her behavior was not quite difficult enough). Halfway through the sixth grade, Cassie was suspended for telling a teacher to take a book and "shove it". Her parents, concerned that her behavior was deteriorating, decided that she needed a different environment and agreed to an alternative middle school program placement.

Cassie's academics improved significantly in the alternative setting and currently she is functioning on grade level in every subject. However, her grades sometimes suffer because she refuses to do homework or "loses" class assignments. She continues to be occasionally defiant to the faculty and staff, and she refuses to participate in any school activities. But other times, she shows herself to be a pleasant, fun-loving teenager and often engages teachers and other students in interesting conversations.

The school counselor at the alternative school believed it was in Cassie's best interest to return to the public high school. The purpose of the case conference, therefore, was to prepare a transition plan for Cassie to attend 11th grade in the high school next semester.

When I met with Cassie privately after the team meeting, I assured her that all of her teachers believed she would have no difficulties with the curriculum and achieving good grades. Then I presented the personal-social development standards to her. I explained that jointly creating a transition plan will help her to "...make decisions, set goals, and take necessary action to achieve the goals" (Campbell & Dahir, 1997, p. 17). Together we discussed Cassie's goals for this school year, for her senior year, and for after high school graduation. We developed a plan to help her meet her short term goals of adjusting to her new school and her long term goal of going away to a four year college. Cassie and I agreed to meet weekly to assess her progress. I reassured her that it is the "taking action component" that will help her achieve her goals for this year and for the future. Most importantly, we further discussed the importance of acquiring the attitudes, knowledge, and interpersonal skills to help her better understand and respect herself and others. This will not only help her to become socially successful in her new school setting but also will ensure that she can get along with her new teachers and not find herself in an adversarial position, as has happened in the past. I explained to her that we would work on these skills as part of our comprehensive national standards-based school counseling program in which every high school student participates.

I left the transition meeting and the conference with Cassie knowing that hope alone would never be enough. Specific strategies to further Cassie's success relied upon the acquisition of attitudes, knowledge, and skills that would help her successfully negotiate her way through the day-to-day stresses of high school. Cassie would leave our school knowing that we provided her with a solid academic preparation and the affective competence to prepare her to successfully transition to the world of postsecondary education and the challenges of the 21st century. We would ensure that Cassie would not be caught in the gap and the cycle of frustration and failure.

Conclusion
Making Connections: What Counselors Need to Know and Be Able to Do

School counselors utilize a variety of strategies, activities, delivery methods, and resources to facilitate student growth and development. In order to accomplish this, the school counselor must possess a solid knowledge of what he/she needs to know and be able to do to serve as a student advocate, provide direct and indirect services, and subscribe to the belief that all children can learn and achieve.

Goals 2000: The Educate America Act (1994), the subsequent national standards movement, and the *No Child Left Behind Act* (2001) presented the opportunity to establish the role of school counseling programs in the American educational system. Implementing comprehensive school counseling programs, based on the national standards, challenges school counselors to demonstrate the impact of such programs and their relationship to student achievement. Communities can see that school counseling programs do produce the results they are demanding and that school counselors desire the same levels of success and positive results as do parents, teachers and administrators. As an integral part of the total school program (Clark & Stone, 2000), school counselors can no longer rely on their reputations and good intentions as dedicated helpers; they must be accountable for their efforts (Johnson, 2000). As part of an educational team, school counselors must accept the challenge of preparing students to meet the expectations of higher academic standards and to become productive and contributing members of society.

The current school reform agenda acknowledges the issue of equitable access to educational opportunities, and seeks to create educational settings in which all children are held to high expectations and are given fair opportunities to achieve this goal. As members of the learning community, school counselors understand and accept the fact that schools do respond to complex social and personal issues on a daily basis. However, it is increasingly more imperative than ever before for school counselors to play a proactive role in identifying and responding to the issues, policies and practices that stratify student opportunity (Stone & Dahir, in press). School counselors who focus their attention on improving student results will contribute to raising the level of aspiration for every student. This commitment to help to close the achievement gap that tends to exist among unmotivated students, poor students and students of color demonstrates our willingness to partner with education professionals to improve schools.

The 21st century presents an array of opportunities to share responsibility for school improvement and to identify our profession's contributions to the educational agenda. The "new vision" for school counseling emphasizes the relationship and interactions between students and their environment with the expressed purpose of reducing the effect of the environmental and institutional barriers that impede student academic success (Education Trust, 1997). The comprehensive, national standards-based school counseling programs are integral to the successful educational experience of all students. The contributions of school counselors may now ensure that every student will progress through school and emerge more capable and more prepared than ever before to meet the challenging and changing demands of the new millennium.

References

American School Counselor Association (2003). *American School Counselor Association national model: A framework for school counseling programs.* Alexandra, VA: Author.

American School Counselor Association. (1997a). *Definition of school counseling.* Alexandria, VA: Author.

American School Counselor Association. (1997b). *Executive summary: The national* standards for school counseling programs. Alexandria, VA: Author.

Bilzing, D. (1997). *School counseling updates.* Paper presented at the meeting of State Department Consultants for Guidance and Counseling, American School Counselor Association, Dallas, TX.

Bush, G.W. (2002). *No child left behind.* Washington, D.C.: U.S. Department of Education

Campbell, C., & Dahir, C. (1997). *Sharing the vision: The national standards for school counseling programs.* Alexandria, VA: American School Counselor Association.

Clark, M., & Stone, C. (2000). The developmental school counselor as educational leader. In J. Wittmer (Ed.), *Managing your school counseling program: K-12 developmental strategies* (2nd ed., pp. 75-81). Minneapolis, MN: Educational Media.

Comer, J. (1988). Educating poor minority children. *Scientific American. 259,* 46.

Conger, R.D., Conger, K.J. & Elder, G. (1997). Family economic hardship and adolescent academic performance: Mediating and moderating processes. In G. Duncan & J. Brooks-Grunnan (Eds.). *Consequences of growing up poor.* (pp. 288-310). New York: Russell Sage Foundation.

Dahir, C. (2001). The national standards for school counseling programs: Development and implementation. *Professional School Counseling, 4 (5),* pp. 320-327.

Dahir, C., Sheldon, C., & Valiga, M. (1998). *Vision into action: Implementing the national standards for school counseling programs.* Alexandria, VA: American School Counselor Association.

Education Trust. (1997). *Working definition of school counseling.* Washington, DC: Author.

Garrett, P., Ng'andu, N., & Ferron, J. (!994). Poverty experiences of young children and quality of their home environment. *Child Development, 65,* 331-45.

Gysbers, N. C. (2001). School guidance and counseling in the 21st century: Remember the past into the future. *Professional School Counseling, 5,* 9-105.

Johnson, L.S. (2000). Promoting professional identity in an era of educational reform. *Professional School Counseling, 4,* 31-40.

McLoyd, V.C. (1998). Socio-economic disadvantage and child development. *American Psychologist, 53*(2).185-204.

Sanderson, A., Dugoni, B., Rasinski, K. & Taylor, T. (1996*). National Center for Education Statistics: Descriptive summary report with an essay on access and postsecondary choice.* Washington, DC: US Department of Education Office of Educational Research and Improvement.

Stone, C. B., & Clark, M. (2001). School counselors and principals: Partners in support of academic achievement. *National Association of Secondary School Principals Bulletin, 85* (624), 46-53.

Stone, C. & Dahir, C. (in press). *Introduction to school counseling: The new vision.* Prentice Hall: Columbus, Ohio.

U.S Bureau of the Census. (2000). Home computers and the Internet use in the United *States*: August 2000. Washington, DC: Current Population Survey.

U.S. Department of Education. (2001) No Child Left Behind Act of 2001 (H.R.1).Washington, D.C: Author.

U.S. Department of Education. (1994). *Goals 2000: The Educate America Act.* Washington, DC: Author.

Chapter Eight

Unfocused Kids/Unfocused Counseling

Keith Anderson

Abstract

The issue of focus is an issue that school counseling has yet to master. Education reform, technology and a rapidly changing world make the issue of focus even more difficult. School counselors must begin to find ways to limit the myriad expectations brought upon them. They must create a system that can positively impact the achievement of every student. This chapter is intended to provoke your thinking and challenge your assumptions. Our students will remain "unfocused kids" as long as we remain "unfocused counselors."

In the summer I fish, commercially, in Alaska. Bristol Bay has the largest sockeye salmon run in the world, and it's only a few weeks long. This means that, when the fish are running, we fish non-stop, without sleep, for several days. On the other hand, when the fish are not running and the boat and gear are all ready – we wait, long hours and days on "the dock of the bay."

If you are close to my age or into blues music, you might remember this Otis Redding song. Having many days away from home and hours to sit and think has its positive consequences. You learn to appreciate the things you miss. There's time to think, review and evaluate what's really important, or how you could have done things differently, or how you will do them next time.

So what does this have to do with school counseling? As I get mentally ready for the school year to begin my anxiety goes up. I don't know why it should. I've been at it for more than 25 years. I should feel pretty secure about what I'm doing, but I have my anxieties about what I'll be able to do and what I'll be able to accomplish. I have goals for the year – things I want to do, but it never fails – as soon as school starts, my priorities are challenged and my goals are questioned. I have administrators who believe that what I should do is be more a part of the "administrative team." I have parents who want me to do more "therapy." I have students who use me for a "pass back to class." I have teachers who want me to make no more schedule changes except for the students they don't want in their classes. I have authorities telling me there's a new role for counselors and an association that tells me there's a role for counseling in everything from violence to college applications. I have a district that wants me to make sure we have 504 Plans so that we won't get a lawsuit. I have a comprehensive program with a guidance curriculum which says there are things I must accomplish, and I have a personnel evaluation that doesn't seem to have anything to do with any of this. I have a million and one things to do and too many bosses.

When I think about all this, I am reminded of those long hours and days away from home. I remember "the dock of the bay." Then I think of Otis Redding and a line from this song, "I can't do what ten people tell me to do – so I guess I'll remain the same." And I think that maybe remaining the same isn't so bad – if remaining the same means letting the needs of students continue to drive my priorities. Maybe remaining the same is still OK, if it means I can apply my skills as a counselor to individual and group counseling to help students meet their goals and be successful. Remaining the same could be the right thing to do if it means helping one student succeed. Maybe I can remain the same if, in spite of too many bosses, I'm fulfilling the role of counselor which teachers and administrators cannot and are not trained to do. Maybe I would have fewer anxieties if I just knew that being a counselor means you don't have to be a teacher too, you don't have to make administrators jobs easier for them, and it's not your responsibility to make students happy.

For this next school year, I think I'll be a counselor – neither a teacher nor an administrator. I think I'll be a professional and have an opinion and make decisions for myself. I've decided – "I can't do what ten people tell me to do – so I guess I'll remain the same."

If I have no agenda for what I do, someone will give me theirs. This has led to a career of seeking how to set priorities for myself as a professional counselor as well as a means to let me know if I have accomplished anything useful to students and their success.

My formal research began as I looked at what the literature had to say about school counseling and counseling programs (Anderson, 1987). At the same time that I began this adventure, I started counseling at a different school (Anacortes High School in Washington State). I had come from a small school (250 K-12 students) to a mid-sized comprehensive high school.

I felt overwhelmed by the expectations brought on by years of counseling history and confusing roles. I had a great need to bring order out of what I thought was chaos. We have been somewhat successful.

In the winter of 1985, after a review of what existed regarding counseling program planning, we developed a counseling advisory committee made up of representatives from the student body, parents, staff, and the community. Our first task was to explain what a counseling program looked like and what it was we were trying to do. This was difficult because we were unsure of what and how to develop this program. The research indicated that we should develop some means of assessing the needs of our students. We ended the first year with our advisory committee's mission as developing such an instrument. In addition, it was established by the committee that the counselors needed a full-time secretary. The counselors did a time-task analysis to determine how much of their time was spent on counseling, guidance and clerical (non-guidance) activities. Our pie charts showed that too large a portion of our time was spent not in providing direct service to students, but in doing a large amount of work that could be done by a clerical person – even a student aide. Our administration responded by providing a full time secretary the next school year.

In subsequent years we developed a program and philosophy for counseling that was driven by the assessment of students' needs as they were expressed through various means. This included a survey and all tests which addressed the counseling needs of students. We developed a presentation for our school site council as we sought their approval. The document outlined the program components as well as the results of all assessment information we had available to us. (You can view and download this document from the Anacortes High School Counseling Center website [2003a].)

The process of our program followed these steps. We began with an advisory committee that directed the formal student needs assessment (as mentioned above). From the results, we developed our program to meet these identified needs. As the literature developed, we articulated our program using Gysbers' and Henderson's model (Gysbers & Henderson, 1994; Henderson & Gysbers, 1998; Gysbers & Henderson 2000). Counselors were either directly involved or provided leadership in the following program components: Individual Planning, Responsive Services, Guidance Curriculum and System Support. The next programmatic step was developing an implementation strategy.

Implementation was intended to include resources from school staff as well as the community. All school personnel were expected to participate in the guidance efforts of the program. Much of the guidance curriculum was delivered through two semester courses in health and career planning. (The guidance curriculum of our program can be viewed on the AHS Counseling Center website by following the "guidance curriculum" link [Anacortes High School Counseling Center, 2003a].)

The fifth phase of the program model was the evaluation process. For evaluation we used several methods. One was a re-assessment of the student counseling needs using the advisory committee's formal needs assessment survey. As we compared these results to the prior survey's results, we drew inferences regarding the program's success as well as information to redirect the program's emphasis.

As the program developed, we established criteria for student performance on each component of the guidance curriculum. These criteria can be viewed by following the "learning to work," "learning to learn" and "learning to live" links of our website (Anacortes High School Counseling Center, 2003a).

Counselors in our district have generic personnel evaluation forms which have little to do with improving counseling skills or performance. To assist us in understanding the effects we have on students, our website makes it possible for students, parents, school staff and members of the community to evaluate their experience with a counselor (Anacortes High School Counseling Center, 2003b).

This program model has helped us provide more focus for what we do with students. It has helped us to gain a clearer picture of our role within the school setting. However, we have not developed research into the effectiveness of what we do in relation to student achievement. Our goal, now that the American School Counselor Association (ASCA) has developed standards for school counseling programs (Campbell & Dahir, 1997) and a model for school counseling programs (American School Counselor Association, 2003), we hope to work with our advisory committee to establish a program that uses these two documents as guidelines.

Counseling Program Implementation

The Counselor's Role

When I present the counseling program for our school, I always begin the presentation with a brainstorm. I ask the participants to give me their expectations of what the counselor should be doing in the school. The audience is always surprised at the length of the list. What is not so predictable are the items of the brainstorm. Parents, the counseling advisory committee, and staff members have very different expectations. (I have yet to try this with students alone. It would be interesting to learn what their expectations are.) The response is predictable in one sense. This plethora of expectations, from my point of view, is the fundamental problem for school counseling and the implementation of a school counseling program. When determining the role of the school counselor, what within the school culture is not somehow related to what people expect of the counselor? Currently, some of those expectations are school safety, crisis response, harassment and bullying, dropout prevention, as well as student achievement as measured on some form of high stakes test. At the same time, nothing from the accumulated role of school counseling has been eliminated. That includes college admissions counseling, scholarships, tracking credits, attending to "at risk" students, working with 504 Plans and special education, etc. Where do we put a limit to this amassing of expectations? First we must define, again and more clearly, what guidance and counseling are.

Guidance and Counseling

Am I a guidance counselor? What is guidance and what is counseling? For me, the two are separate and distinct. Guidance is everyone's responsibility.

In our school, we have defined guidance as

> . . . both **process** and **program**. The guidance process helps individuals unify all of their learning activities and experiences. Guidance programs are devoted to (1) learning about individuals and their needs and the effects of educational experiences on them, and (2) facilitating improvements and changes in the learning program and environment to better meet individuals needs efficiently and humanely.
>
> Guidance is also a **program** consisting of activities and services that aid the individual in choices, decisions, and problem solving as these relate to personal values and life objectives. The program is aimed at helping the person achieve a self-identity and personal adequacy. (Anacortes High School Counseling Center, 2003a)

We have attempted to define counseling and the counselor more specifically to clarify the role of the counselor and its relationship to guidance.

> **Counseling** is often incorrectly used synonymously and interchangeably with **guidance.** It provides a direct personal way of helping the individual in a one-to-one or small group basis. Counseling operates on a more intense level than guidance and focuses on the specific needs of an individual. The counseling process utilizes various counseling techniques and

tools which assists an individual in sorting through alternatives, making decisions, and solving problems. (Anacortes High School Counseling Center, 2003a)

To clarify the role of the counselor in relation to guidance we have used the following definition.

The **counselor** is the person on the staff who has special training for assessing the specific needs of each student and for coordinating an appropriate guidance program in the educational, career and personal-social domains. While **guidance is a function of every member of the educational team**, the responsibility for leadership of the guidance program is one of the primary functions of the counselor. The counselor has been trained in various helping skills and is prepared to work closely with individuals in assisting them with **normal** developmental concerns, decisions, sorting through options, problem solving, and planning, as well as coping with crisis. The counselor may perform individual or small group counseling, large group guidance, consultation with parents, faculty and other professionals and coordinate a variety of guidance and counseling related services. (Anacortes High School Counseling Center, 2003a)

Indeed, as cognitive psychology and technology influence education, each teacher will become a facilitator, a guide, for students. This would replace the twentieth century role of teacher as font and purveyor of knowledge. Myrick (1993, pp. 219-242) helps with a definition and activities related to large group guidance. "In times past, when there were no school counselors, students were dependent upon classroom teachers and classroom guidance for any personal help that they might receive." He goes on to explain that "after counselors were employed in the schools, teachers continued to think of their personal work with students as guidance or advisement instead of counseling" (pg. 219). My experience has been different. Just a few months ago, at a faculty meeting, our administrators introduced the idea that teachers, during their class time and advisory periods, should relate students' course work and course selection with each student's plans beyond high school. The response of one teacher, and supported by the head nods of others, was: "Isn't that the counselor's job?" The times have changed. Guidance and counseling have become an amalgam that appears to be inseparable in the minds of everyone, including counselors. The American School Counselor Association has provided excellent documents to help educators in schools and districts to design and implement school counseling programs. However, in *ASCA's National Model: A Framework for School Counseling Programs*, the terms for *school guidance* and *school counseling* curriculum are used interchangeably on the same page (American School Counselor Association, 2003, pg. 40), without intending any confusion, to describe the same concept. In the glossary, counseling is defined, but guidance is not. The differences between guidance and counseling are enormous. The unconscious use of these terms synonymously is fundamental to the confusion as to what counselors are expected to do. From the beginning, we must clearly define these terms and outline who is responsible for the outcomes of guidance and the outcomes of counseling.

Accountability

The counseling program is important. The national agenda for education is accountability in terms of student achievement. The *No Child Left Behind Act of 2001* (Public Law 107-110) has one focus – accountability. The Federal Government has defined student achievement and told states how to measure it. For elementary schools, students must show incremental improvement on state 4th, 7th and 10th grade testing in reading and mathematics each year until 100% of the students reach mastery. This is to be accomplished by the year 2014. High schools will need to improve graduation rates incrementally each year with success being measured as an 85% graduation rate. Educators will need to show how students are achieving through a process of Adequate Yearly Progress (AYP). If schools are not showing progress, there will be a system of steps to improvement which could end in a "Plan for Alternative Governance." Someone other than the local school district will take over. Without funding counseling programs or even mentioning school counseling, expectations for the school counselor may include interpreting high stakes testing and helping students find ways to meet the standards. At the high school level, the burden of helping students find appropriate placement for success and achievement will fall on the counselors. Counselors will need to, and should, show evidence of how their work relates to student achievement, or schools will have to find someone else who will.

The American School Counselor Association (ASCA) has developed a *National Model: A Framework for School Counseling Programs* (American School Counselor Association, 2003a). To help in dissemination of this model, ASCA's website provides an online, downloadable, Microsoft PowerPoint® presentation (American School Counselor Association, 2003b).

The presentation explains the historical problems for school counseling and the development and rationale for a national model for school counseling programs. The model presents a paradigm shift "From: Not only monitoring process and measuring services delivered. To: Focusing also on and measuring the results of our programs and services." The presentation goes on to outline the *National Model* and shows how research can be used to describe the effects, in terms of student achievement, as a result of the implementation of a comprehensive counseling program.

The *ASCA National Model* will provide us with a means of implementing a comprehensive counseling program as well as guidance for outcome-based research and accountability. Although we have been implementing an evolving comprehensive program in our school, outcome-based research is obviously missing. This lack of research, in part, is caused by insufficient time; research takes focus away from implementation of a program that is to impact every student. A third element, which will be discussed later, is the impact of supportive administrative leadership.

Program vs. the People

We have three certified counselors in our high school. The total enrollment of all students ranges from 900 to 1100. By some standards this is a good counselor-to-student ratio. As department chair, I have taken the responsibility for developing a 9-12 comprehensive program (Anacortes High School Counseling Center, 2003b). The other counselors assist in designing and implementation. This program's design and implementation take a considerable amount of time. With only 180 days of student contact and 7.5 hours a day, each moment counts. The program work must be done, for the most part, beyond the school day, on weekends and in the summer.

There is a very fine balancing act for counselors. While in a "paradigm shift," we continue "to be all things to all people." Now we add the role of counseling program leadership in an atmosphere that holds school counseling and the counselor in a marginal position — relative to the total school agenda. Two of the sources of confusion I have had in regard to my professional role have been: (1) being seen in school stakeholders' minds as an administrator; and (2) being seen as a teacher. The balancing act requires us to manage a program (administrator) and implement a curriculum (teacher). We must maintain our professional identity as school counselors or we will lose the contact and regard of the most important members of the school and the counseling program, i.e. the students. Whatever we do, we must vigilantly protect our role as counselors because, I have learned, it is one role no one else in the school can duplicate in a professional manner. Students are our focus and our curriculum. Student success and achievement, however they are measured, are the result of that focus. I have learned that we can do nothing in a vacuum. We need the support of others, especially those who are given legitimate power and resources.

Leadership, Politics and Advocacy

I have known the power of supportive leadership. At that time, our high school counseling program was recognized by the Washington School Counselor Association as "an exemplary program." The later result of this leadership brought us national recognition from ASCA through an "honorable mention as an exemplary counseling program." We received these awards because of the support and involvement of building and district leadership. I have no illusion that our counselors worked harder than any other counselors in the nation. I am certain that the initiation and maintenance of the school counseling program structure came from our administrative leadership. We were given the freedom and support to design and implement our program. I have learned that, without this leadership, we customarily are left to the traditional crisis-oriented, reactive model of the past.

We must have resources and understanding leadership to allow us to form advisory committees, work collaboratively with teachers, consider and meet the staffing needs of the program, and provide time to implement a program which includes outcome- based research. But administrators are not the sole ingredient to accomplishing the mission of the counseling program. As I stated in the *ASCA Professional School Counseling Journal* (June 2002, pp. 321-322):

> I may be extreme, but I believe counselors must realize their role in the school building is as important as any other professional. Counselors are not in the building to "serve" others; they are in the school to implement a program and apply the distinct skills and knowledge that only they possess.

> Counselors must be more involved in the political process. This requires that they have a clear vision of the counselor's role and the counseling program within the school's mission. This requires the courage to take risks and participate in building, district, state and national politics. It requires a belief that what counselors and counseling programs do in the school is so important that, without them, the school could not meet its mission and the needs of all students.

> The power of politics is always personal and most powerful at the interpersonal level. Many counselors would rather not become involved in these activities. Baker (2001) was right. We need charismatic leaders, but we can't wait for one to show

up in our building. We must be the charismatic leaders. We make a difference in people's lives. We must know our boundaries. We must take the risk of saying "no" to some expectations held for us. Then we can say "yes" to the things we have the knowledge and skills to do. (Anderson, 2002)

We must advocate for ourselves as we teach our students to advocate for themselves. If we do not, we will be consumed by the whirlpool of change going on around us. We may lose our jobs, but it won't be from not doing our jobs. We will lose our jobs because we cannot advocate for ourselves and show the effects of our work in a world of rapid change.

Change in the Field of School Counseling

The American School Counselor Association focused one of its *Professional School Counseling* journals on the past, present and future of school counseling (American School Counselor Association, 2001). A dominant theme in these articles was the concept of change: in society, in culture, in the labor market and economics, as well as changes in education. The articles also called for a change in how counselors do their business. A shift in focus from the *counselor providing services* to a *counseling program focused on every student*, aimed at student achievement, was recommended. Evaluation of both individual counselor and overall program performance will become a higher priority as states adopt national teaching certification standards and evidence-based accountability. To survive, counselors must show how what they do affects student achievement through outcome-based research. A very common and pervasive theme of the journal was the discussion of the counselor's role. The discussion ranged from expanding the role (Green and Keys, 2001) to clearly defining and limiting the role of school counselors (Paisley and McMahon, 2001).

The impact of technology has changed the entire world as well as the realm of school counseling. Not only are rapid changes brought about by technological advances, but there are also profound social and cultural changes. Technology is becoming more available to more people, but a "digital divide" remains that allows access to some, but not all citizens in our democratic society (Green and Keys, 2001; Paisley and McMahon, 2001). What are those changes that can help counselors reach more students and make counseling and education more available to every student and their family?

Technology

Anacortes is a small city in northwest Washington. It is an island— the staging point to the San Juan Islands and Victoria, British Columbia. We might consider ourselves isolated from the many challenges of big and inner city life. It is conceivable that most high school students could walk or ride a bike to school. Most don't. Technology and economics have changed our student parking lot. Many students own newer cars than do the staff. Many also have cell phones, hand-held computers and laptops. We don't need to teach the slide rule anymore. We have calculators that can do nearly any math problem. We have distance education labs where students can take high school or college courses online. Students can download movies from the Internet. Just twenty years ago very few people knew what "download" even meant. Indeed, our language has changed, dramatically. Our students install hard drives, upload data, FTP (file transport protocol) and write to a CD-ROM (read only memory). E-mail and instant messaging are common practice. And setting up your own website is taught to middle school students. We have changed, and so must school counseling.

Technology is helping to replace some of the clerical work of high school counselors. Computer programs can count credits more efficiently than a counselor trained at the master's level. Computer guidance systems can assess students' abilities, interests and work values. In the not-too-distant future, computer programs will be able to collate enough information on each student that counselors, if given the chance, will have more time to work with individuals and small groups.

Examples of Technology in School Counseling Programs

There are many problems that will arise with the use of technology, including those associated with ethical use and the critical thinking skills of the users. Here are examples of how a counselor, a counseling program, a school district and a state department of education have made excellent use of the technology on the World Wide Web.

Millard South High School in Omaha, Nebraska (Millard South High School, 2003) has developed an extensive counseling center website for their high school. The site is well laid out and easy to use. One of the elements that impressed me most is a Microsoft PowerPoint® presentation they have added entitled "For Prospective MSHS Students - a PowerPoint Presentation." It is easy for new and returning students and parents. They can access basic information regarding graduation requirements, school activities, athletics and more. Although the initial development of this information must have taken many hours, once the website and presentations were completed, it would relieve the school counselor of the task of repeating critical but routine information. Referring students and parents to the website would help parents and students independently prepare for what is expected at high school.

Bob Torba's Cyber Guidance Office (Torba, 2003) is another example of counselor use of technology. Torba is a counselor at Stanton College Preparatory School in Duval County, Jacksonville, Florida. This site is unique in that Torba has created a system of databases that help to track students in terms of the college preparation. The site offers general links and information to colleges, financial aid, and testing. What is unique, in addition to the database systems, is the "cyber counseling" that is used. The cyber counseling includes e-groups, bulletin boards, and Internet counseling services.

An outranking example of a school district's application of the *ASCA National Model* and the use of technology is Marino County Unified School District (2003) and their counseling website. Marino County Unified School District has made implementing the *National Model* easier for counselors in the district. If you review the site, you will notice that an accountability system, which follows the *ASCA National Standards,* is implemented. Necessary forms are available for counselor use. Microsoft PowerPoint® presentations are available for others to review, and a very orderly system for implementing the *ASCA National Model* is provided.

Another site of note, as an example of a state's implementation of the *ASCA National Model* and technology, is the Arizona Department of Education (2003). Arizona provides the "Arizona Comprehensive Competency Based Guidance" handbook for counselors to use in the implementation of the ASCA model in Arizona's schools. In narrative form, Arizona has provided all the information that educators in a school need to implement ASCA's model.

Conclusion

As counselors, we must find the balance between technology and human interaction. Technology is a tool to help counselors meet the needs of more students. There is a new language that has developed as a result of technology. We must be fluent in it. Students use e-mail, chat rooms and instant messaging as a regular part of their life. Counselors must get ahead of their students or learn from them. It is not useful to polarize our activities in terms of "I'm involved in human interaction" and "I'm interested in technology," or vice versa. Our students are using both. We must be proficient in both. In terms of technology we cannot become the leaders who will one day say, "There they go and I must hurry, for I am their *counselor.*"

Education reform has been in process for many years. Counseling has been overlooked. I argue that counseling does not need reform. Counseling needs revolution. It is not a revolution of the counselor's role. I take issue with those whom I have heard say that counseling "reform" means that counselors must get out of their offices and into the classrooms. This is not reform. This is just another role for counselors. The comprehensive program model for counseling, as I see it, leaves role definition to educators in the local building. The revolution I'm talking about is this: School counseling can no longer be represented by the person of the counselor. School counseling must become a program with the goal of measurable outcomes related to student achievement. In the eighteen years I have worked to implement a counseling program, the greatest hurdle I have yet to clear is this understanding. The misunderstanding is as rampant among counselors as it is among all the other stakeholders in the school. The needs of every student should drive what the counseling program is and what the counselors do. Developing a program will help avoid the myriad "add-ons" that befall counselors and will allow counselors to focus on helping each student to achieve.

The *ASCA National Model* is a hopeful answer to meeting the challenges of a society so enmeshed in change. It is flexible in implementation. It shares the responsibility for guidance with everyone including parents, students and the community. This is a revolution.

Dr. Terry Bergeson, Washington State Superintendent of Public Instruction, has a vision for education. She mentions the traditional ingredients of education as curriculum, instruction and assessment. She adds that there is a missing piece and that piece is guidance. Bergeson is working to develop a model for education reform that includes guidance being as fundamental to student achievement as curriculum, instruction and assessment. When guidance is used this way, the school counselor is not only included; the school counselor must become a leader in the process. When guidance is viewed this way, providing personal meaning to each student's education, it will help us eliminate the "unfocused kids."

References

American School Counselor Association, (2001) *Professional School Counseling.* 5, 2.

American School Counselor Association. (2003a) *ASCA national model: A framework for school counseling programs.* Alexandria, VA: Author.

American School Counselor Association. (2003b) *National model: A framework for school counseling programs.* Retrieved March 2, 2003, from http://www.schoolcounselor.org

Anacortes High School Counseling Center. (2003a). *Comprehensive guidance and counseling program.* Retrieved March 1, 2003, from http://ahs.asd103.org/counseling/ guidance.htm

Anacortes High School Counseling Center. (2003b). *AHS counseling center.* Retrieved February 27, 2003, from http://www.ahs-counseling.org.

Anderson, K. A. (1987). Guidelines for K-12, comprehensive counseling programs. (Doctoral dissertation, Seattle University, 1987). *Dissertations Abstract International,* 48, 1657-A.

Anderson, K. A. (2002). A response to common themes in school counseling. *Professional School Counseling. 5 (5),* 315-321.

Arizona Department of Education (2003). *2002 AZ CCBG Handbook.* Retrieved February 23, 2003, from http://www.ade.az.gov/cte/api

Baker, S. B. (2001). Reflections on forty years in the school counseling profession: Is the glass half full or half empty. *Professional School Counseling.* 5, 75-83.

Campbell, C. A. & Dahir, C. A. (1997). The national standards for school counseling programs. Alexandria, VA: American School Counselor Association.

Green, A. & Keys, S. G. (2001). Expanding the developmental school counsciling program: Meeting the needs of the 21st century student. *Professional School Counseling,* 5, 84-95.

Gysbers, N. C. & Henderson, P. (1994). *Developing and managing your school guidance program* (2nd ed.) Alexandria, VA: American Counseling Association.

Gysbers, N. C. & Henderson, P. (2000). *Developing and managing your school guidance program* (3rd ed.). Alexandria, VA: American Counseling Association.

Henderson, P., & Gysbers, N. C. (1998). *Leading and managing your school guidance program staff.* Alexandria, VA: American Counseling Association.

Marino Valley Unified School District. (2003). Student Services. Retrieved February 23, 2003, from http://www.mvusd.k12.ca.us

Millard South High School (2003). *Millard South Counseling Center.* Retrieved January 3, 2003, from http://www.esu3.org/districts/millard/south/guid/msguid.html

Myrick, R. D. (1993). *Developmental guidance and counseling: A practical approach.* Minneapolis, MN: Educational Media Corporation.

Paisley, P. O. & McMahon, H. G. (2001). School counseling for the twenty-first century: Challenges and opportunities. *Professional School Counseling*, 5, 106-115.

Public Law 107-110. No Child Left Behind Act of 2001. *Elementary and Secondary Education Act of 1965* (20 U.S.C. 6301 et seq.).

Torba, B. (2003). *Cyber Guidance Office.* http://cyberguidance.net/

Chapter Nine

Career Resource Centers—Programs and Resources for *All* Students

Yvonne Hines and Suzy Mygatt Wakefield

Abstract

Using the guidance approach that all appropriate educators and community members need to be involved in the school's career guidance program, Career Resource Center staff members contribute by providing information and resources for all students to help them prepare for living, learning and working in the 21st century. The program is driven by the school's mission statement and school counseling program goals. Activities may include: teaching career units in classrooms, homerooms or advisories; organizing career fairs and career days; providing outreach luncheon programs for parents and students, providing job listings; hosting college representative visits; hosting career speakers; organizing workplace tours; updating the school's website; and enrolling students in specialized career and technical programs (e.g., High Tech Learning Centers) and pre-college programs (e.g., Washington State's *Running Start* Program). Career pathways are also discussed. With a comprehensive approach, *all* students are ensured access to the school's highly visible career guidance program.

Career Resource Centers

The increased availability of career materials—printed, audiovisual, programmed, and computer-based—has emphasized the need for an organized system to handle these items in an orderly way. The answer in most settings has been the development of a *career resource center*, also frequently called a *career information center*...In the last decade there has been considerable growth of career resource centers. Such centers assemble materials and a professional and paraprofessional staff whose responsibility is to develop in-house and outreach programs. (Isaacson and Brown, 2000, p. 192)

Isaacson and Brown (2000) note above that Career Resource Centers came into being at least a decade ago. They outline the basic criteria of Career Resource Centers (synonymously called Career Centers in many high schools): accessibility; attractiveness; ease of operation; and adaptability. The Career Center needs to be centrally located, with a location well known to all students. (This issue can be aided, for all new students, with a tour of the Career Center during orientation activities at the beginning of each school year.) The materials need to be attractively displayed, with well-defined areas for different categories of information, such as university, college and community college catalogues; military services brochures; standing occupational files; miscellaneous handouts for students; and available computers for career search activities. Ease of operation refers to the easy readability and accessibility of different types of materials, so that the reader may find what he or she is looking for without help. According to Isaacson and Brown (2000), "If clients find that what they want is simple, they are likely to explore further" (p. 193). Finally, the Career Center staff needs to be sensitive to student needs and be able to adjust with the changing concerns of students and their parents, so that information is current, timely and appropriate.

Isaacson and Brown (2000) also discuss the components of a Career Resource Center: responsibility (who will be responsible for developing and maintaining it and what materials will be incorporated); staff (the professionals and paraprofessionals assigned to provide services); facilities (appropriate student furniture, shelf space, computers, standing files, display racks, and so forth); location (hopefully, centrally located in the school, with a room of adequate size to hold a classroom of students); security (of materials and student records); budget (a specified line item allocation in the district's budget, and supplemental career development funds from the district or state); publicity (through use of the school's website and school newsletters); and operating policies (checkout procedures posted for all to see, particularly on the use and loan of materials) (pp. 194-196). If scholarship files are lost, for example, subsequent students cannot access application forms and other information kept in a particular scholarship folder. It is, therefore, imperative that users understand the rules and limitations of the checkout system.

The Career Resource Center may be utilized as the hub of a school's career guidance program. Zunker (1998) suggests that "more emphasis in many career centers has focused on pre-placement services, such as general information about educational programs, outreach programs, cooperative education and internships, part-time jobs, and computerized career guidance and information systems" (p.244). Zunker also suggests that faculty members as well as students utilize the Career Resource Center. "It is also a place where instructors can meet with groups of students or entire classes for a variety of career guidance objectives. Finally, the entire professional staff is encouraged to use the center as a resource for ongoing projects" (p.172).

The Career Center as an Extension of the School Counseling Program

School counselors, in collaboration with administrators, teachers, and career specialists, are responsible for organizing the comprehensive career guidance program—consistent with the school's mission statement and the school counseling program's statement of philosophy, goals and student competencies. School counselors are encouraged to refer to the American School Counselor Association's *Vision into Action: Implementing the National Standards for School Counseling Programs* (Dahir, Sheldon & Valiga, 1998) as they determine student content standards for career development. They are also encouraged to review the *ASCA National Model: A Framework for School Counseling Programs* (ASCA, 2003) as they develop the delivery, accountability and management systems for their career guidance program.

The delivery system for the career guidance curriculum is an important issue to consider and needs to be incorporated into the school's mission statement so that the personnel involved (school counselors, career specialists, teachers, and community members) all understand their important and complementary roles. The career guidance curriculum may be set up so that career units are taught by the school counselor or career specialist in the Career Center, or by teachers in their advisories or homerooms, or by classroom teachers in designated classrooms, after being trained on the content of career guidance units. Community members may serve as guest speakers and may provide sites for student job shadows, short internships and service learning (volunteer) experiences. The Career Center staff can provide considerable support to the school counseling program, as a great variety of career information resources (including online resources) can be made available to students and parents through the Career Center.

What Should be in the High School Career Center

Ideally, if a school has a Career Center, it should be large enough to hold at least 32 students so that an entire class may participate in career guidance units, led either by school counselors or by the career specialist. Materials should be organized so that students may see how careers relate to classroom subjects. One approach is to organize career materials into six career pathways that are color-coded in standing files that are easily accessible. Many schools in Washington State use this approach in helping students register for their classes—with six suggested career pathways, based on the Holland Code (from WOIS/The Career Information System), or a variation:

1) Arts
2) Business Communications
3) Business Operations
4) Science
5) Social Service
6) Technical (from WOIS/The Career Information System, www.wois.org/online/indices/occs_capraths.cfm

As part of the *Individual Student Planning* program in the Franklin Pierce School District (in Tacoma, Washington), students choose a career path before 9th grade and may change it annually with parent input. This is from their website: www.fp.k12.wa.us.

(This career pathway model is called a "hybrid" in that it presents a slight variation from the WOIS original.)

The Career Paths, followed by Post-secondary Options, in the Franklin Pierce School District are:

- Arts & Communication
- Business & Marketing
- Health & Human Services
- Engineering & Technology
- Science & Natural Resources

Post-Secondary Options

- Employment
- Apprenticeship Program
- Technical College
- 2-Year Community College
- 4-Year College
- Advanced Degree (5+ years)
- Military

Different school staffs may use different configurations of the career pathways or career clusters. Occupations in each pathway or career cluster are then organized into three educational levels: entry, skilled, and professional. The entry level is for students who plan to finish high school and then go to work; the skilled level is for students who plan to attend a program at a technical or community college; and the professional level is for students who plan to attend a four-year college or university.

Using the WOIS/The Career Information System, an Internet user can browse the www.wois.org website, obtain a guest password, and then choose one pathway (such as Arts) click on the appropriate level, and find a listing of occupations. Using the career pathway model (some schools do and some do not), a school counselor, career specialist, or homeroom/advisory teacher might help students to further explore interest areas by helping them to explore one of these career pathways. For example, if a student enjoyed history and working with people, then he/she might be encouraged to look at the Social Service careers; if a student considered being a politician or a social worker, then he/she might be directed to courses in government, history and psychology.

Printed materials and many other resources are available in the Career Center. According to Zunker (1998, pp. 178-179), some resources typically found in Career Centers across the country are: the Dictionary of Occupational Titles (now replaced with the O*NET on the World Wide Web at www.online.onetcenter.org [Ed.]); the Encyclopedia of Careers and Vocational Guidance; Guide for Occupational Exploration; Vocational Biographies, Inc.; Occupational Outlook Handbook; U.S. Industrial Outlook; Military Careers; The U.S. Army Career and Education Guide; Navy Career Guide; various college catalogues for 2-year and 4-year institutions (such as Peterson's Guide to 2-4 Year Colleges); business journals, newspapers and other resources. Another important resource often found in Career Resource Centers is the *Occupational Outlook Quarterly, now available on-line at* www.bls.gov/opub/ooq/ooqhome.htm

Other electronic resources are often available. Video tapes may be available in the high school Career Center (to watch on-site or to check out) on colleges and universities, and skill areas such as rèsumè writing, job interviewing and so forth. Some high schools are equipped with in-house TV networks so that students may watch programs in their classrooms (when they are linked to the same channel). They also can be a part of national or global satellite workshops. The television and VCR are very useful tools for viewing a virtual library of videos.

Career resource center staff members can help students become aware of the career information delivery system using the O*NET database and career exploration tools available through www.acsci.org. It is also helpful to know that the Labor Department offers the widely used career information and job search assistance website called Career OneStop at http://www.careeronestop,org/ and O*NET OnLine at http://online.onetcenter.org

Career Center Computers and Website

The Career Center staff may be responsible for maintaining the school's website—to maintain current information about activities throughout the school, particularly in the academic and career development areas. Computers are very important in the Career Center for students to use in researching their future plans, both in terms of exploring their own interests (with online Internet career interest assessments and online career outlook projections and job descriptions) as well as exploring the many postsecondary options available (such as college-search programs, online college applications, financial aid information, and much more). Much of this information may be linked to the high school's homepage that is accessible to students via the Internet at home, at school or in the public library.

Career Counseling Bulletin

The school's website homepage may include a bulletin called the "Career Counseling Bulletin." An example in the State of Washington is Lake Washington High School's website which has such a "bulletin," which is continually updated: http://wwwlwhs.lkwash.wednet.edu This bulletin may list all of the college visits that will be made to a given high school or to schools in the surrounding area. The bulletin may also give students information on enrichment opportunities, such as college summer workshops, job internships, SAT-preparation classes, extracurricular activities, etc. There may also be a bulletin link to local, collegiate, and national scholarships. With the Internet, students have unlimited opportunities at their fingertips.

Computer Technology

Technological proficiency on the computer is virtually a requirement for all students in the 21st Century. Many students appear to be reasonably proficient in using a computer but may need some guidance in navigating the Internet and locating specific information needed in career planning. It is helpful for the Career Center to have several computers for use by walk-in students. During an actual classroom career unit presentation, students can be scheduled in the school's computer lab (if the school has one) for the purpose of providing instruction on Internet navigation and on using career assessment tools.

Computer-Assisted Career Guidance Systems

According to Zunker (1998), using computers for career counseling has been welcomed by the career development profession, largely due to the proliferation of occupational information. "The fast-paced development of both hardware and software systems has created very attractively designed programs for different populations and for different purposes." Three prominent, nationally recognized career-guidance systems are: DISCOVER (American College Testing Program); SIGI (System of Interactive Guidance and Information), and SIGI Plus. (It is beyond the scope of this chapter to discuss these computerized career guidance systems other than to mention that they provide a needed service in helping students with career planning.)

In the state of Washington, the Washington Occupational Information System (WOIS), now called WOIS/The Career Information System, (available on the Internet at www.wois.org), is an example of a Career Information Delivery System (CIDS) that is customized for a given state. Administrators in high schools throughout the state have the option to purchase a site license, which then allows all students (and their parents/guardians) in that school (or district) to have access to the WOIS system. While in classroom career units, students are asked to fill out the WOIS/CLUES questionnaire to determine (based on their expressed preferences) which occupations would provide the best match. A total of 349 occupations are included in the system. Depending on how students answer the questions, occupations are eliminated through a negative template sort, leaving students with those occupations that provide the most congruent match with their stated preferences. Students may ask for a print-out on any occupation of their choice. In this way, students may obtain more detailed information about various occupations, including: job descriptions, working conditions, projected labor market information, salaries, places of employment, and so forth. (If their school system requires an education and career plan and/or a career planning portfolio, students may incorporate this information in their plan or portfolio.) The information needs to be updated as students explore additional occupational options.

A Tentative Model for Career Exploration Units

Career exploration units for grades 9, 10, 11 and 12 should be organized according to a given district and school's overall mission statement and/or the school's counseling program statement of goals, philosophy, and competencies. School counselors, the career specialist, and/or advisory, homeroom, or classroom teachers may be assigned to teach various career units. Here is a hypothetical example of a sequence of career units in grades 9-12 in which students would be asked to:

Grade 9:
- Begin to develop their education and career plan (or continue with one already initiated)
- Complete at least one career interest inventory and produce a list of suggested careers
- Explain the characteristics of and qualifications for three careers of personal interest
- Explain how personal interests and skills match career choices
- Describe career pathways and courses that would best match one's tentative career choice

Grade 10
- Begin to develop the career planning portfolio (or continue one already initiated)
- Complete the WOIS/ The Career Information System CLUES interest inventory
- Complete a job application
- Complete a resume and cover letter and add them to the electronic portfolio
- Continue to develop the education and career plan; share it with the school counselor, career specialist, and/or homeroom/advisory teacher, *and* with parents

Grade 11
(Presentation of this unit should be scheduled just prior to registration of classes for the senior year.)
- Review the education and career plan and, if needed, revise current career goals/path
- Review postsecondary educational options and determine post high school plans
- Learn about university and community/technical college

application procedures
- Select senior classes supportive of the education and career plan
- Update information in the career planning portfolio

Grade 12
- Review the education and career plan; make tentative post high school choices
- Update the education and career plan in light of additional occupational exploration
- Continue to add materials to the career planning portfolio (both hard copy and electronic)
- Update the Career Planning Portfolio to prepare for transition to a postsecondary setting
- Learn about projected labor market supply/demand and salaries in career interest areas
- Develop, plan, research, write, and present the culminating (senior) project, under the guidance of an assigned mentor (in school or in the community)
- Participate in a community-based field experience (shadow or internship) and/or a service learning (volunteer) experience, as required for graduation

Students who complete this sort of integrated, comprehensive guidance program model will have experienced many aspects of preparing for their postsecondary plans. By the time they graduate from high school, they will have completed: an education and career plan, a career planning portfolio, and a culminating (senior) project. They will have explored a number of career options (at least on paper, if not in the field), may have written a resume and cover letter, and often will have completed at least one field experience and service learning experience. In many ways, students exposed to these high school experiences, as part of their school counseling program, will have developed some preparation for the workplace and for their postsecondary educational plans.

Career Seminars

One of the most important aspects of a career guidance program is to expose students to a great many careers or occupational options. Career Seminars allow students to see and hear workers in specific (often unknown to them) career areas. Throughout the school year, seminars representing many occupations may be planned. Students will need to be excused from their regular classrooms to attend seminars. One suggestion is that in September, all high school students be surveyed to find out their career interests—up to three interest areas per student. Once the data is processed (processing may be done, for example, at no cost by a sponsoring local business with the "Learning for Life" Explorer/Boy Scouts Program), the Career Center staff may plan the seminars around the most frequently indicated career interests. Ideally, each student would attend at least one seminar a year that is related to his/her career of interest. (The speakers at these seminars may be arranged by the "Learning for Life" Explorer Program.) All speakers are volunteers and are instructed to be sensitive to the concerns and needs of high school students. Speakers will allow students to ask them questions about training, salary and benefits.

The seminar presentation may be a great eye-opener to many students who may not have had contact with people actually working in many different careers. An additional benefit is that students may obtain a personal contact in their particular field of interest–to begin to develop their own network of contacts. People who make up a student's personal network of contacts may later be available to set up a subsequent field experience–a job shadow or an internship experience, or even a part-time paid job. In some cases, an adult may become a mentor (or field expert) and guide a student for a period of time through a specific career interest.

Workplace Tours

Business people are often amenable to cooperating with high school staff members in arranging tours of their businesses. Many business personnel will even ask their employees to allow students to join them in their offices and provide a one-on-one informational interview of their job.

Workers are really honest with students, and students get a firsthand impression of their position. Some businesses have even provided lunch for students. Some may even set up a formal business luncheon to give students an understanding of the professional etiquette required in today's workplace.

Field Experiences—Job Shadows and Internships

A suggested goal in high school is for all students to have field experiences (job shadows and internships), and service learning (volunteer) experiences. Conley (2002) recommends that educators "determine whether local businesses are willing and able to enter into partnerships that allow students access to school-to-career experiences." These hands-on paid or unpaid experiences can be very valuable for students, as they explore career options. In her publication entitled, *Smart Choices about Teen Jobs*, Quattrociocchi (1995, p. 19) urges students to choose jobs that make good use of their time and will help them relate their work to their career interests. She further points out that good jobs "allow contact with more skilled workers and management, provide interaction with different aged workers, [and] provide mentors" so that students can learn about different aspects of an occupation. Often, students work just to make money to buy a car or other items they want to have, and not to explore serious career interests. Quattrociocchi urges parents and educators to encourage students to choose jobs that will provide them an opportunity to explore career interests. Carefully chosen jobs may provide valuable opportunities to help students gain much information about a specific career area, and such jobs may pay as well as jobs that have no particular career exploration value.

Career Fairs

A career fair may be a large event, often organized by the career specialist and assistants, that is usually held once a year (in a large area, such as the school's gym) to give students firsthand information about careers, as students are provided with an opportunity to speak with many workers from different fields. There is a sort of festive atmosphere as students walk from booth to booth (or table to table) speaking with different representatives. Incentives may be built into the experience for students to speak with a number of workers. For example, students may each be given a "passport" which they must have stamped by three different job representatives so that at the end of the Career Fair experience, they are eligible for door-prize drawings, such as free pizza! These contacts may be the only ones students will have had with people who actually work in different occupations, so students are able to gain valuable information about what the work is really like. Students may also be given business cards so that they may follow up with informational interviews or actual job interviews.

Job Placement and Community Volunteers

Part-time paid jobs or volunteer jobs can be coordinated through the Career Center. All job listings that are called into the high school should be screened by a school employee, and employers may be asked to give permission to list their jobs on the school's website homepage. Therefore, if the school has its own website, students may have access to these job contacts via the Internet. These contacts may be updated daily by the Career Center staff. Students may come into the Career Center and access the Internet, or they may access the listings from their home computer. People from many businesses and organizations often call the high school Career Center to advertise volunteer jobs or internship opportunities for students. (These contacts may also be listed on the school's web site.)

The Innovative "Cyber Cafe" Outreach Program for Students and Parents

As an institution, the high school may appear to be uninviting, if not foreboding, for some parents and guardians. As an innovative practice, staff members may try to improve this perception and bridge the gap between the school, parents and students by providing a monthly interactive lunch program, such as the "Cyber Cafe." Contacts from the business world may be invited to join school counselors, the career specialist, teacher advisors, students and parents to discuss their respective careers, highlighting specific educational pathways and programs. The purpose of the Cyber Cafe is to provide information and interaction between students, parents, counselors, teachers, and Career Center staff members. A sponsor in the community (a business representative or military recruiter) may even provide a free box lunch! (It is suggested that about 20 students and 20 parents attend each session, as that number will fill the Career Center.)

Students and parents may also be given a packet of information both in hardcopy form and on the Internet on the school's website homepage to help them learn more about career and college planning. According to Steinberg (1996) and Quattrociocchi (2000), research has demonstrated that parents have more influence on their child's decision-making than anyone else, including teachers, counselors and peers; parents are the experts when it comes to knowing their teen. Quattrociocchi (2000) further reports that:

> Research shows that parental involvement is the single greatest factor in determining student success. Teens with highly involved families are three times more likely than their peers to earn a bachelor's degree or to complete other postsecondary programs. (p.2)

Financial aid and scholarship information is also very important for parents to obtain. The Cyber Cafe, or similar outreach program, may help parents find both scholarship information and financial aid contacts. This information will assist them in helping their student plan for post-secondary education. In our experience, parents have commented that they really appreciate having all of this information at their fingertips and can access it all at home via their Internet browser. Parents have also reported that they enjoy the opportunity to be able to talk directly to school counselors, the career specialist, and/or other staff members over the casual and friendly lunch setting. Questions can be easily answered and specific files, such as the Scholarship File, can be pointed out. Further, parents can learn the location of brochures, college catalogues, and so forth.

College Courses Offered to Students While in High School

The Running Start Program of Washington State
The Career Center staff may be involved in helping students to consider enrolling in several college credit programs. One example is Washington State's Running Start Program in which 11th and 12th grade students are allowed, if they qualify by passing the pre-college assessment and are 16 years of age, to enroll in college-level courses in local community colleges while still attending high school (*Lake Washington High School Planning Guide and Course Description Catalogue, 2002*). By law, the tuition is paid for by the student's home school district. (Only college-level courses qualify, so students may have to pay for special interest courses with course numbers below "101.") These college-credit courses are then dually posted and counted, both on the high school transcript (toward graduation) and on the community college transcript, as a college course. These courses will then transfer to four-year universities. Students must pay for their books, materials, lab fees, and transportation. Although only a small portion of students may choose to attend from each high school (about 10 percent of each high school class), in the aggregate, a great many students do participate in this innovative program that has been in place for about a decade. "During the 2000-01 school year, 13,442 students—about 10 percent of the state's 11th and 12th graders—participated in this program statewide" (Conley, 2002). The Running Start Program is part of the Choices Legislation, enacted by the Washington State Legislature in 1993, giving students choices other than staying in high school full-time as they pursue graduation requirements.
Other college credit courses are: *College in the High School*, in which articulation agreements have been set up between designated advanced courses in high school and equivalent college courses, yielding both high school and college credit; *Advanced Placement courses and exams*, developed by the College Board, to allow students to move forward in their college curriculum, based on test scores they earned on Advanced Placement

tests while in high school; and *Tech Prep* credit, in which there are articulation agreements between designated vocational high school courses and specific courses at the community or technical college level, allowing students who have earned a grade of B or better to move forward in the college curriculum when they arrive on campus. After two years in the designated community or technical college program, students completing the program will receive a certificate and/or an associate degree.

Job Skills in Cooperative Vocational Classes (NEVAC)

The Career Center staff may help students to consider enrolling in a local cooperative vocational training program, such as the local NEVAC (Northeast Vocational Area Cooperative) Program located on the "Eastside" of Seattle, with information packets available for students. Students must attend an orientation session to determine if they really want to attend a specific class and then must fill out the necessary paperwork, get a parent signature, and document that they can provide their own transportation. NEVAC was begun as a sort of "school without walls," established about 20 years ago by a local school counselor named Jim Cairns. According to the Lake Washington School District *Student Profile* (2002), this highly successful program is a consortium of nine school districts (30 high schools). Students in this consortium may attend these career and technical education courses in neighboring school districts without paying tuition. In this particular cooperative vocational program, students attend their home high school part of the day and spend the balance of their day in their NEVAC class. With some exceptions, most classes are a year-long and meet for two hours a day. Further, in the NEVAC classes with a Tech Prep notation, students may earn college credit while in high school at no additional cost. When they enter an articulated Tech Prep program at the community college level, they will be moved ahead, according to their earned level of competence, in the college curriculum. Students gain advanced training, employment preparation, and experience in a career field, while obtaining occupational education credits (which meet a specific high school graduation requirement). Often, students also earn an industry-based certificate, documenting their training.

Examples of these two-hour technical programs are: Auto Collision Technology, Radio and TV Broadcasting, Media Production Technology, Carpentry/Construction Technology, Fire Service Training, Horticulture, Health Care Occupations, Restaurant/Hotel Management, CISCO Networking Essentials, and Digital Imaging/Video Production (*Career and Technical Education*, Lake Washington School District [brochure], p. 17). Students must be 16 years old and provide their own transportation. They are allowed an hour a day to commute to their class. They must be of junior standing in high school so that they have their driver's license.

High Tech Learning Centers

Career Center staff members can help students enroll in the High Tech Learning Center program. In order to deal with the shortage of skilled high tech employees in the greater Seattle area, the Lake Washington School District, in cooperation with the NEVAC Consortium, has also created online "High Tech Learning Centers" in each of the district's high schools, where students can take classes from their home high school via Distance Learning, and work at their own pace at home. This program increases the eligibility of these students to enroll in post-secondary Information Technology (IT) training programs (and employment) and simultaneously earn an industry-based technology certificate. According to the *Mainfunction Resource Database*,

> The High Tech Learning Centers (HTLCs) deliver state-of-the-art Information Technology (IT) education to high school students that leads to industry certification and/or accelerated placement in higher education creating a skilled IT workforce in the most productive way. The HTLC offers students who attend a school which is part of the Northeast Vocational Area Cooperative (NEVAC) the opportunity to earn high school and college credit through a variety of technology courses including animation, multimedia, networking, programming, and web authoring. Students can take advantage of these classes via online courses or through the HTLC's distance learning program. The HTLC also helps student obtain mentorships, internships, and job shadowing opportunities.

The HTLCs are located in 25 high schools in participating school districts. According to the www.hightechlearning.org website, over 10,000 students have taken HTLC's classes. Further, according to this website, "by building a college transcript in high school, the HTLCs not only increase the supply of high-tech students, they also reduce the time and expense of achieving a post-secondary information technology (IT) certificate or degree." Obviously, this distance learning program has met with great success and has helped to minimize the shortage of qualified IT workers.

Summary—Programs/Services in the High School Career Center
- Career Center resource materials (college, vocational, military, job postings, and more)

- Technology exposure—online computer experience with CIDS (Computer Information Delivery Systems, such as WOIS/The Career Information System)
- Career Exploration
- Career Seminars
- Workplace Tours
- Arrangement of field experiences—job shadows and internships through business partnerships within the community
- Career Fairs
- Job Placement and placement in community volunteer (service learning) experiences
- Outreach (Cyber CafÈ) Sessions for students and parents
- Coordination of enrollment in a pre-college program (such as Running Start)
- Coordination of enrollment in cooperative vocational classes (such as NEVAC)
- Coordination of High Tech Learning Centers (industry-based technology certification)
- Coordination of Tech Prep classes—college credit posted through the Career Center
- Sessions with technical college, community college and university representatives
- Scholarship applications and awards—through the filing system and online information

Conclusion

Career Resource Center staff members (the Career Specialist and instructional assistant) in high schools may do much to enhance the school counseling program, as they may offer a wide variety of career guidance services and programs to all students, often in collaborative partnerships with people in the community. The programs and services provided should be in alignment with the district's and school's mission statement and school counseling program goals.

The personnel responsible for the delivery of these career guidance programs and services may include: school counselors (who help to design and implement the school's program), career specialists and their instructional assistants, homeroom/advisory or classroom teachers and appropriate community members. That is, others can do much to extend the work of the school counselor, who has traditionally been seen as the primary provider of career guidance in high schools. With the guidance model of career development programs (where everyone does their part) as well as the utilization of a centrally located Career Resource Center, *all* students may then have equal access to the many career guidance programs and services that are visibly offered all year long. With strong program development and all appropriate educators and community members involved, *all* students may then easily participate in a school's comprehensive career guidance program.

References

American School Counselor Association (2003). *American School Counselor Association national model: A framework for school counseling programs.* Alexandria, VA: Author.

Conley, David T. (April, 2002). Preparing students for life after high school. *Educational Leadership,* Vol. X, 60-63.

Dahir, C.A., Sheldon, D.B., & Valiga. M.J. (1998). *Vision into action: Implementing the national standards for school counseling programs.* Alexandria, VA: American School Counselor Association

Franklin Pierce School District (n.d.). *Individual student planning.* Tacoma, WA: Author. Further information may be obtained from the district website at: http://www.fp.k12.wa.us

High Tech Learning Centers Website, Retrieved February 18, 2003, from http://www.hightechlearning.org/overveiw/default.html

Isaacson, L.E., & Brown, D. (2000). *Career information, career counseling, and career development.* Boston: Allyn and Bacon, 192-196.

Lake Washington School District. (n.d.) *Career and technical education, connecting education* to careers.[brochure] Redmond, WA: Lake Washington School District Printing Center

Lake Washington High School planning guide and course description catalogue, 2002-*2003.* Academic opportunities for advanced HS students—Running Start. Redmond, WA: Lake Washington School District Printing Center, 4.

Lake Washington High School Website, Kirkland Washington. Retrieved October 8, 2002, from http://wwwlwhs.lkwash.wednet.edu

Mainfunction Resource Database, *Curriculum.* Retrieved February 17, 2003, from http://educators.mainfunction.com/Resources/interchange/Preview/asp? PeerID=2484

O*NET OnLine. (2002). http://online.onetcenter.org (Web-based viewer)

Quattrociocchi, S. (1995). *Smart choices about teen jobs: A guidebook for students, parents, educators, and employers.* Eugene, Oregon: Steve Laing Communications.

Quattrociocchi, S. (2000). *Help! A family's guide to high school and beyond.* Olympia, WA: Washington State Workforce Training and Education Coordinating Board Publications, 2.

Lake Washington School District (2002). *Student profile: Curriculum framework for secondary education.* Redmond, WA: Author.

Steinberg, L. (1996). *Beyond the classroom—why school reform has failed and what parents need to do.* New York: Touchstone.

WOIS/The Career Information System. Occupations by career path. Retrieved February 18, 2003, from http://www.wois.org/online/incides/occs_carpaths.cfm

Zunker, V. G. (1998). *Career counseling: Applied concepts of life planning.* Pacific Grove, CA: Brooks/Cole Publishing Company, 171-192.

Chapter Ten

The Phantom Student

Doris Rhea Coy

Abstract

Five types of students have been identified by Good & Power (1976). Each needs to benefit from the school experience. However, the phantom student, who is rarely noticed or heard from and often seems to fade into the background, could benefit greatly from the guidance component of the comprehensive developmental school counseling program. This article offers suggestions for reaching all students—including phantom students, who, according to research, comprise sixty percent of the student population. In addition, this chapter reviews the rationale for a needs assessment, a school counselor job description, a board-approved school counseling program and curriculum, and the role of the school counselor.

Introduction

Good & Power (1976) in their article, *Designing Successful Classroom Environments for Different Types of Students,* identify five different types of students. Those types are: successful, social, dependent, alienated, and phantom. They describe each type of student in the following manner.

- The successful student is task oriented and academically successful. These students create few if any discipline problems, participate in lessons, and their homework, which is turned in on time, is usually correct and complete. These students are liked by both teachers and peers. Difficult questions are directed to them by the teacher because they are usually prepared with the correct answer.
- The social student is not task oriented but person-oriented. Socializing with friends is more important than working on homework assignments. While popular with their peers, their teachers see their socializing as creating management problems.

They are called on fairly often to keep them involved in the assignments, and most questions directed to them by the teacher can be answered by them.

- The dependent student needs support and encouragement from the teacher. They tend to be socially immature and are often rejected by their peers. While they are frequent hand-raisers, their level of achievement is low. Teachers do what they can to help this student because of their low level of achievement.
- The alienated student is seen as a potential dropout. School and anything associated with it is often rejected by them. They are often seen as hostile, disruptive, aggressive and defiant. Peers often ignore them, and teachers' attitudes toward these students range between indifference to rejection (Good & Power, 1976, p 268).

While the school counselor should develop a comprehensive developmental school counseling program that addresses the needs of all students, the students identified as phantom students are often overlooked or ignored because they appear to become invisible.

What are phantom students? According to Good & Power (1976), these students are rarely noticed or heard from and seem to fade into the background. They further note that these students do not tend to be involved in public service, yet are viewed as average in most areas. They can vary from being shy or nervous to quiet, independent workers of average ability. In addition, these students are rarely involved actively in group activities because they do not volunteer. They work steadily on their assignments, but because they never create disruptions, they are not known very well by teachers or peers (p 268).

One way to reach all students is to utilize a comprehensive developmental school counseling program model that reaches all students, including the phantom student. Otherwise, they can easily graduate from or leave school without the benefit of having experienced the three domains of the counseling program: personal/social, educational, and career development. These students need to learn the skills (and demonstrate the competencies) offered in these three domains to better prepare them for a productive and responsible life.

The successful, social, dependent, alienated and phantom students will benefit from the innovative practices to help students focus on their plans after high school that are included in other chapters of this book.

Providing Guidance and Counseling Services to Students

It has been suggested that phantom students may make up at least 60% of a school's population. Goodnough & Dick (1998) note that the thrust toward a comprehensive developmental program developed as a reaction to the tendency of "traditional" counselors spending too much time with students at either end of the continuum of student performance (troubled students at one end and very able, college-bound students on the other). Left out were the majority of students in the middle (p. 15).

At the elementary and middle school levels, counselors have more access to students, so it is easier for them to deliver services to all of the students unless they are overburdened with non-counseling assignments or the counselor-student ratio is unreasonable. The secondary school counselor, however, is often burdened with excess paper work, testing assignments, and administrative tasks. The students they often see are the successful students who are task oriented and academically successful, the dependent students who look to teachers and counselors for support and encouragement, and the alienated students who are referred by teachers, parents, or principals. The phantom student is often left to take care of him/herself.

Providing individual counseling services to students is difficult at the secondary school level. Pulling a student from a class for individual counseling is not viewed in a positive manner by most secondary teachers, and group counseling is often available only before or after school. How to see a student and provide him/her with the services he/she needs becomes a major problem. Classroom guidance or educational guidance is one method for the school counselor to deliver services to the majority of students. This may involve various teachers giving up a class at least once or twice a year. It is, therefore, important that the school counselor provide data demonstrating the importance of providing this service and that students, teachers, and parents be involved in providing information (through a needs assessment) for developing and delivering the comprehensive developmental school counseling program.

Rationale for a Needs Assessment

Students, teachers, and parents need to provide information for developing the components of the comprehensive developmental school counseling program so that it can be used to reach the students. To do this, the school counselor must obtain data on the services or information needed by conducting a needs assessment with students, teachers, and parents. This should be conducted at the end of the school year so the appropriate areas identified can be incorporated in the school program the following year. Many areas require attention each year such as: test taking skills, critical thinking, post-secondary education, scholarships, financial aid, career consideration, course selection, goal setting, decision-making, alcohol and drug abuse, conflict resolution and self understanding. However, if they have been identified as concerns from the needs assessment, the following additional areas are worthy of addressing: alerting students to warning signs associated with suicide, eating disorders, physical and sexual abuse, self-mutilation or self hurt, sexually transmitted diseases, bullying and date rape. While many might argue that these should not be addressed in the school but in the home, we find that these topics are not being addressed in the home and therefore the student is uninformed or misinformed about the topic of concern to him/her. By conducting a needs assessment, these topics are identified by students, parents, and teachers and not by the school counselor.

Rationale for a School Counselor Job Description and Board-Approved Program

By developing a board of education-approved school counselor job description, school personnel and community members, as well as students, are aware of the role of the school counselor. The responsibilities usually involve counseling (individual and group), classroom guidance, consulting with others, coordinating the school counseling program, referring students to outside resources for long-term therapy and providing feedback on the various appraisal instruments students take. The school counselor's role also includes leadership and student advocacy.

A board-approved comprehensive development school counseling program should be built around the mission of the school. By so doing, it becomes an integral part of the educational program rather than ancillary. It provides administrators, teachers, and parents with an awareness of the goals of the program and the measurable expected outcomes (change in students' knowledge, skills, values, or dispositions). It also provides a means of systematically addressing the personal/social, educational, and career needs of all students. The program should be evaluated, revised and updated on an annual basis with input from students, teachers, and parents.

Rationale for the School Counseling Curriculum

The school-counseling curriculum is not an ancillary part of the school educational program. It should be an integral part of the total educational program and central to the mission of the school. The building administrator should provide the leadership for implementing the program, but it also requires a commitment of full and explicit support by the entire school community. The actions of the principal determines to what degree the school counselor plays a role in the school's mission: as a minor player or as a professional who is the primary agent to advocate for and help students.

The school counselor works with students to help them:

1. develop aspirations of a personal and career nature;
2. address goals with a plan and responsibility by exploring and acting on them;
3. become aware of how their growth and development is facilitated by understanding how course work and curriculum options are known and used systematically;
4. understand how future opportunities connect with present academic courses; and
5. gain self-esteem, confidence, effective interpersonal skills, and academic focus by achieving goals they have set for themselves (Herr, 1998).

To implement the comprehensive developmental school counseling program, three methods are suggested by Goodnough & Dick (1998). They are: 1. Training teachers to infuse the guidance curriculum into the existing subject areas by combining the guidance curriculum with the teaching objectives and providing an integrated curriculum for the students (p.18); 2. Collaboration between the counselor and teacher for the curriculum occurring in the classroom with the presentation meeting the goals of both the subject area and the guidance curriculum (p.18); 3. Delivery by the counselors to large or small groups of students (p. 19).

Role of the School Counselor

The school counselor is trained to provide several helping processes:

1. Counseling is a process of assisting a student, parent, or teacher in making decisions. The focus is on a specific concern that includes making a plan to address the concern and acting on the plan. Counseling is intended to be a confidential working relationship.
2. Consultation is a process which is cooperative in nature and the counselor as consultant assists the parent, teacher or others to think through problems and develop skills that make them more effective in working with (a) student(s).

3. Coordination is the process of organizing and managing the comprehensive developmental school-counseling program so that it is in harmony with the school's educational program.
4. Referral is the process of referring an individual to professionals in other agencies. This usually occurs when the concern is beyond the expertise of the school counselor or the amount of time needed to address the concern is beyond what the school counselor can provide.
5. Appraisal is the process of gathering and analyzing information, drawing accurate conclusions, and making recommendations to address the concerns of students and others (Baker, 2000; Herr, 1998; Schmidt, 1999).
6. Guidance, as viewed by the writer, is the process of providing information of an educational nature to a classroom, or a large or small group. It is not confidential in nature but informational.

Tammie Radd (1998) provides the following outline of the necessary components of a comprehensive, developmental competency-based school counseling program. She states that goals, competencies, and outcomes are integral within each system and program component (p. 94).
1. Goal – this statement indicates the long-term outcome in each general and specific area and reflects purpose and philosophy.
2. Competency – in each general and specific area the desired proficiency is stated.
3. Outcome – what will be seen when the competency is met.

An example of this can be found in the ASCA publication, *Counseling Paints a Bright Future – Student Competencies a Guide for School Counselors* (Coy, 1990). In this booklet, the authors developed student goals under each of the three areas of counseling: personal/social, educational, and career. They then developed student competencies, by grade level, to implement the student goals. The purpose of developing long-range goals is to help students become effective learners, responsible people, and productive workers. The booklet covers student outcome from pre-school through postsecondary and can serve as a guide for those developing or re-evaluating a comprehensive developmental school counseling program (Coy, 1990).

Example: Student Developmental Goals

Career Goals: Students will be Analyzing Skills and Interests

Kindergarten	Describe what they like to do.
First grade	Identify skills they have.
Second grade	Recognize activities that interest them and those that do not.
Third grade	Realize that people are influence by interests \and abilities.
Fourth grade	Recognize different methods of evaluating "progress."
Fifth grade	Describe the meaning of "value" and how values influence goals.
Sixth grade	Analyze the relationship between interests and abilities.
Seventh grade	Analyze various methods of monitoring their progress toward a goal.
Eighth grade	Describe their present skills and predict their future skills.
Ninth grade	Describe their skills, abilities, interests, and aptitudes.
Tenth grade	Assess their ability to achieve past goals and integrate this knowledge into future planning.
Eleventh grade	Evaluate the importance of having laws to protect workers from discrimination.
Twelfth grade	Conduct an assessment of their current skills, abilities, and career prospects.
Postsecondary	Develop a realistic picture of their skills and interests.

School Counseling
Guidance Lesson Plan

It is suggested that the school counselor develop guidance lesson plans that address each of these outcomes for each grade level. The following example is an outline of the form used by students in the writer's (university) Secondary School Counseling class.

195

Topic:	Career
Title:	**Analyzing skills and interests**
Grade level:	Kindergarten
Materials needed:	Magazines, scissors, paste, large sheets of paper, markers

Time limit:	20 minutes
Goal:	Analyzing skills and interests.
Competency:	Students will describe what they like to do.

Activity:	Provide each student with magazines, scissors, paste, a large sheet of paper, and markers. Instruct students to cut out of a magazine what they like to do and then paste it on their piece of paper. Students may draw what they like to do with their marker on their piece of paper. Demonstrate by cutting out a picture of what you (the counselor) like to do. Draw of picture of what you (the counselor) like to do. Tape each piece of paper around the room at the end of 10 minutes. Have each student describe his/her picture by saying, "This is what I like to do. I like to ...
Evaluation:	Each student produces a large piece of paper with pictures pasted on the paper or pictures drawn on the paper. Each student describes what she/he likes to do.

Prepared by:	Dr. Doris Rhea Coy 10-7-02

Activities of this type permit each student to share in the lesson and provide information to the counselor about the student. The phantom student, as well as the successful, social, dependent, and alienated student, is given an equal opportunity to take part in, and learn from, the experience.

Students in the writer's Secondary School Counseling class have a number of group projects. Katrina Miles, Jennifer Shaw, Rhona Rosenthal and Jamie Walton (2001) developed the following school-wide guidance unit composed of five guidance lessons on "Goal Setting for Students in

Transition." Permission has been granted by them for the unit to be included in this article.

School Counseling Guidance Lesson Plan

Topic:	Goal setting
Title:	Goal Setting for Students in Transition
Grade level:	7 – 12

Introduction:

Goal setting is essential in the lives of adolescents. It allows them to recognize the importance of preparing for the future. By establishing goals, young people are more apt to remain focused throughout their adolescent and adult lives. Goals are a tremendous motivating force. They not only give people the motivation to strive for success but also allow an individual to detect when certain behaviors are not in line with the targets previously set. Clearly, adolescents deserve the opportunity to be taught the steps needed to develop academic, vocational, and personal aspirations. Through this goal-setting unit, adolescents are provided early on with the appropriate tools necessary to effectively plan for a fulfilling life.

Lesson I:

Topic:	Goal-setting
Title:	**Direction Puzzle Example**
Objective:	Helping students realize that having a goal makes achieving that goal easier.
Materials needed:	One puzzle for each 2 – 4 students.
Time:	30 – 45 minutes
Procedures:	1. Break students into groups of 2 – 4.
	2. Have students clear their desks.
	3. Provide each group with puzzle pieces.
	4. Do not provide the picture of the puzzle.
	5. Have students attempt to put the puzzle together.
	6. Students will begin to complain that they need the picture to complete the puzzle.
	7. Compare the need for the puzzle picture to the need or necessity of having a large vision or idea to work toward.
	8. Have students discuss their goals.
Developed by:	Miles, Shaw, Rosenthal & Walton 10-01

Lesson 2:

Topic   Goal-setting
Title: **Direction Activity**
Time: 30 – 45 minutes
Objective: To make students aware that there are all kinds of obstacles that we may have to overcome to reach our goal; but having a vision of where you are going makes achieving your goal easier.

Materials needed: Three blindfolds, moveable furniture, a goal

Procedure:

1. Find a place where you have lots of room.
2. Decide on a place/thing for the students to focus on; that object is their "goal" (where they want to go).
3. Ask for 5 volunteers and remove them from the room.
4. Have the remaining students rearrange the room.
5. Volunteer #1, no blindfold and no student obstacles.
6. Volunteer #2, no blindfold, and with student obstacles.
7. Volunteer #3, blindfolded and no student obstacles.
8. Volunteer #4, blindfolded, and with student obstacles.
9. Volunteer #5, blindfolded, with student obstacles, with verbal help.
10. With no blindfold or obstacles (clear path to goal) ask 1st volunteer to walk to the goal.
11. With no blindfold and with student obstacles, ask 2nd volunteer to walk to the goal.
12. With blindfold, and no student obstacles, ask 3rd volunteer to walk to the goal.
13. With blindfold and student obstacles,

ask 4th volunteer to walk to the goal.

14. With blindfold, student obstacles, and verbal help, ask 5th volunteer to walk to the goal.

15. Discuss activity by comparing volunteers with a vision (no blindfold) to those without a vision (blindfold). Point out how there are all kinds of obstacles that we have to overcome to reach our goals, but having a vision of where you are going makes achieving your goal easier.

Developed by: Miles, Shaw, Rosenthal & Walton 10-01

Lesson 3:

Topic: Goal-setting
Title: **Types of Goals**
Time: 30 – 45 minutes
Objective: To differentiate between short-range goals and long range goals; realistic goals and unrealistic goals.
Materials needed: Large piece of paper (1 for every 5-6 students), markers, masking tape, overhead projector, screen
Procedure: 1. Using the overhead and screen, place the following on the overhead. A. What is a goal? Have students answer. Then show: B. A goal is something you intend to do – the end that you strive for.

2. Overhead # 2: Two types of goals A. Short-range goal: (have students give examples) then show the definition: Something you intend to do which can be done in a time period of one year or less.

3. Overhead # 3: B. Long-range goal: (have students give examples) then show the definition: Something you intend to do which can be done in a time

199

period from one year through a lifetime.

4. Divide students into groups of 5-6 and direct them to write on the paper A. short-range goals B. long-range goals.

5. Have students listen as you explain, using the overhead projector, what realistic goals are – A. facing facts as they really are – those things that can be done. B. Specific behaviors – those things you can do to reach a goal.

6. Writing S.M.A.R.T. Goals (overhead)

    a. Specific – state exactly what you're aiming at. Goals are not vague or confusing. Example: My goal is to buy a stereo set.

    b. Measurable – state what and when you want it. Example: My goal is to buy a stereo system six months from today.

    c. Action-oriented – spell out exactly HOW you will achieve the goal. What will you do? Example: My goal is to buy a stereo system six months from today. I'll save $75 a month from my part-time job.

    d. Realistic – realistic goals are possible. They may be hard, but they are not just a wild dream. Example: My goal is to buy a stereo system six months from today. I'll save $75 a month from my part-time job; however, that's the total amount I make each month which means I can't buy anything else; therefore, I will save $50 a month for the stereo and keep $25 for other things I might want to do or buy.

    e. Timely – give yourself enough time to achieve your goal but not too much. Example: My goal is to buy a stereo system six month from today. I'll save $50 a month and in six months I will have saved $300 –enough for a good mini stereo system.

7. Have the students return to their piece of paper. Have them select one goal and apply the S.M.A.R.T. Goal principle to it. Use the backside of their piece of paper. Take turns explaining their goal according to the S.M.A.R.T. principle to the rest of the class.

8. Have each student write down a person goal using S.M.A.R.T. Goals. The goal needs to be achieved before the end of the year. Give each student an envelope and have him/her place his/her name on the envelope. Ask them to place what they have written in the envelope and seal the envelope. Give the envelope to the instructor. It will be returned to the student at the end of the year to see if he/she was able to achieve his/her goal.

9. Short-term goals for the week (overhead).

   A. Personal – anything that applies to you. Write down no more than 3 personal goals for the week.

   B. Academic – anything that applies to school. Write down no more than 3 academic goals for the week.

   C. Interpersonal – relationship issues. Record no more than 3 interpersonal goals for the week.

10. Things to Remember (overhead).

   A. Setting goals that are unreachable will only make you lose your motivation for reaching other goals.

    B. Setting too many goals may make you confused.

    C. Set realistic limits for achieving goals.

    D. Revise and update your goals as your needs, wants, and desires change.

11.   Remember: Goals Give You Control Rather Than Leaving Them to Chance (overhead).

Developed by: Miles, Shaw, Rosenthal & Walton   10-01

Lesson 4:

Topic:	Goal-setting
Title:	**Direction**
Time:	30-45 minutes
Objective:	To have students identify what exactly they want and how they are going to get there.
Materials needed:	Overhead, screen, handout.
Procedure:	Have students complete the following handout.

DIRECTIONS:

In what areas of your life can you say right now: "I know exactly what I want, why I want it and I know how I am going to get there."

In the spaces below, for each area of your life, write: WHAT you want, WHY you want it, and HOW you are going to get it.

1. Family:
   What I want:
   Why I want it:
   How I'm going to get it:
2. School:
   What I want:
   Why I want it:
   How I'm going to get it:

3. Activity:
   What I want:
   Why I want it:
   How I'm going to get it:
4. Relationships:
   What I want:
   Why I want it:
   How I'm going to get it:
5. Work/Service:
   What I want:
   Why I want it:
   How I'm going to get it:

Give each student an envelope. Have him/her write his/her name on the envelope. Place the completed DIRECTION handout into the envelope. Seal the envelope. The instructor collects the envelopes to return to the students near the end of the school year.

Developed by: Miles, Shaw, Rosenthal & Walton   10-01

Lesson 5:

Topic:	Goal-Setting
Title:	**Writing a Mission Statement**
Time:	30-45 minutes
Objective:	To make students aware that the process of writing a mission statement involves answering a series of questions.
Materials needed:	Overhead projector, screen, handout
Procedure:	Prepare the following as an overhead: The Process of Writing a Mission Statement Involves Answering a Series of Questions:

1. What things do I want that I feel are important?
2. What am I about?
3. What are the qualities of character that I would like to emulate?
   4. What legacy do I want to leave?
Have the instructor give his/her answers.

Pass out the handout, which is
identical to the overhead, and have
the students complete it. After 5-10
minutes ask if anyone would like to
share what he/she has written.

Developed by: Miles, Shaw, Rosenthal & Walton   10-01

Conclusion

Classroom guidance appears to be one way for school counselors to
meet with and provide information to all students. Teachers can also assist
in the process by presenting the unit instead of the counselor; however, if
the counselor conducts the presentation, the teacher should remain in the
classroom if possible. By remaining in the classroom, the teacher is aware
of the services provided by the counselor. Whether being presented by the
school counselor or the classroom teacher, classroom guidance provides an
opportunity to address those topics of interest or concern to the majority of
students whether it addresses personal/social, academic/education, or career
areas. These topics can be identified by conducting a "needs assessment"
by students, parents, and teachers. Classroom guidance can then address
the varying needs of the successful students, the social students, the
dependent students, the alienated students and the phantom students.

References

Baker, S. (2000). *School counseling for the twenty-first century (3rd ed.).*
Upper Saddle River, NJ: Prentice-Hall.

Coy, D. (1990). Counseling paints a bright future: Student competencies
K-12. In Coy, Cole, Huey, & Sears (Eds.) *Toward the transformation
of secondary school counseling.* Ann Arbor, MI: ERIC.

Good, T. & Power, C. (1976). Designing successful classroom environments
for different types of students. *Journal of Curriculum Studies 8,* 45-60.

Good, T. & Brophy, J. (1995).*Contemporary educational psychology* (5th
ed.). White Plains, NY: Longman Publishers.

Goodnough, G. & Dick, J. (1998). The school counselor's curriculum at the secondary school level. In C. Dykeman (Ed.) *Maximizing school guidance program effectiveness*. Greensboro, NC: ERIC Clearinghouse on Counseling & Student Services.

Herr, E. (1998). Why should school administrators care about school counseling? In C. Dykeman (Ed.) *Maximizing school guidance program effectiveness*. Greensboro, NC: ERIC Clearinghouse on Counseling & Student Services.

Radd, T. (1998). Designing an outcome based school counseling system and program. In J. Allen (Ed.) *School counseling: New perspectives and practices*. Greensboro, NC: ERIC Clearinghouse on Counseling and Student Services.

Schmidt, J. (1999). *Counseling in schools* (3rd ed.). Boston: Allyn and Bacon.

Chapter Eleven

A Model School Counseling Program Brochure: Implications for Helping Students Focus on their Plans after High School

Jim Whitledge

Abstract

School counselors are responsible for providing programs that contribute to student achievement. Graduation should signify that every student has a plan and focus for what they will do in the future.

School counselors should develop and distribute a school counseling program brochure that provides information for students, parents, and others to make informed choices about student participation in the school counseling program. The model school counseling program brochure that is described in this chapter provides a framework that practicing school counselors may modify and adapt to the level, needs, and characteristics of their students, school, and district.

When school counselors market, inform, and define how their program improves student success, students will have a plan and focus in place when they graduate from high school. Parents, teachers, administrators, and the community will know what is available to students and be supportive of school counseling programs that will improve student success.

Introduction

It is important for students to have both a plan and a focus when graduating from high school. This is of particular importance because of the way that students and society are impacted by both an expanding global economy and enhanced technology. While there may be many approaches, activities, and methods for assisting students in learning about themselves (establishing their priorities and enhancing their strengths), it is important that students know what is available through their school counseling program.

Often, students graduate from high school without their educational and career development needs met throughout their K-12 educational experiences. Time after graduation is then spent on those career and educational development activities that are needed in order to develop a plan and a focus for what the student will do in the future. That time should have been spent on these career development activities while the student was still in high school.

School counselors are in a position to deliver career, educational, and personal/social development components to students through their comprehensive school counseling programs. This position is consistent with the competencies stated in the *National Standards for School Counseling Programs* (Dahir, Sheldon, & Valiga, 1998).

Comprehensive guidance and counseling programs should focus on the career and educational activities and opportunities for students (Gysbers & Henderson, 2000; Myrick, 1997; Schmidt, 1999). Students (and parents) should have knowledge of those programs in order to make informed decisions about their participation in them. It seems that having a vehicle for marketing and informing about school counseling programs, and how students benefit in developing a plan and focus by the time they graduate from high school, will enhance the learning environment and provide successful achievement for students.

A Vehicle to Provide Information about How School Guidance and Counseling Programs Help Students Plan for Life after Graduation

The Michigan School Counselor Association (MSCA) Ethics Committee developed a model informed consent brochure for school counselors' use at the high school level (Michigan School Counselor Association, 2000). Informed consent implies that the school counselor provides information to students so they can make informed decisions about participating in the school's counseling program. It is suggested that school counselors develop their own unique brochure, based on the model framework, the needs of students, and the characteristics of their school or district. Thus, the model brochure does not provide a "cookie cutter" tool in which the school counselor may simply take the model and use it in his or her school or district. Rather, the model serves as a framework from which the school counselor may modify and develop a school counseling program brochure, based upon the needs of the school or district. Although the model brochure focuses on the secondary level of education, it may be easily modified and adapted to the elementary and middle school levels as well.

The model school counseling informed consent brochure is supported by the ethical codes of the American School Counselor Association (ASCA) and the American Counseling Association (ACA). The format of the model brochure is based on one developed and used in Yakima, Washington (at A.C. Davis High School, n.d.). Overall, the informed consent brochure provides students with the opportunity to learn about the guidance and counseling program and make informed decisions about their participation.

Why Have a School Counseling Program Brochure?

This section addresses the question, "Why should the school counselor develop and distribute a school counseling program brochure?" The following background information and rationale are offered to answer this important question. The terms "informed consent" and "disclosure" are used interchangeably.

The MSCA Ethics Committee was requested to develop a model school counseling program informed consent brochure by its Governing Board in September, 2000. The request to develop such a statement of disclosure about one's program is consistent with both the ethical and legal responsibility of school counselors. Counselees have a right to know about the potential outcomes and risks, as well as the process that will take place in connection with the guidance and counseling program in which they (and their parents) choose to participate. The brochure provides opportunities for school counselors to discuss and enhance their working relationship with students and others in the school, providing students with increased awareness, accurate perceptions, and an opportunity to learn more about the process and their expectations of the school counseling program.

Ideally, all school counselors have a written comprehensive guidance and counseling program in their school setting, based on MSCA's *Michigan Comprehensive Guidance and Counseling Program* (Michigan School Counselor Association, 1997) model (or other state model) and one that adheres to the *ASCA National Standards for School Counseling Programs* (Dahir, Sheldon, & Valiga, 1998). These two documents complement each other and reinforce the premise that students have a right to be informed about the school counseling program in which they choose to participate, as well as about their school counselors who are responsible for implementing the program. Integral to that program are the educational, career, and personal/social development components that will enable students to have a plan and focus for after high school.

Furthermore, the ASCA *Ethical Standards for School Counselors* (American School Counselor Association, 1998) provides guidelines for professional school counselors to provide information to counselees so that they make informed choices about whether to participate in the counseling program. These guidelines challenge school counselors to define who they are, what they do, and how they do it, in language that is understood by students and parents. The Preamble to the Ethical Standards emphasizes that, "Each person has the right of choice and the responsibility for goals reached." Section A.2 (a) focuses on informing "the counselee of the purposes, goals, techniques, and rules of procedure under which she/he may receive counseling at or before the time when the counseling relationship is entered." This section further emphasizes that issues of confidentiality, and exceptions to confidentiality, must be clearly defined and shared with counselees through a disclosure statement that is both written and shared.

Since most counselees are minors, the school counselor has a responsibility to parents that may be addressed through the disclosure statement as well. Section B.2 (a) (American School Counselor Association, 1998) states that the counselor "Informs parents of the counselor's role with emphasis on the confidential nature of the counseling relationship between the counselor and counselee." Parents rights and responsibilities, as well as ways that school counselors work with parents, are emphasized in Section B and may be referenced and communicated in a disclosure statement.

In addition, the *ACA Code of Ethics* (American Counseling Association, 1997) supports, and is consistent with, what is included in *ASCA's Standards*. Section A.3 of the ACA Code specifically indicates, "When counseling is initiated, and throughout the counseling process as necessary, counselors inform clients of the purposes, goals, techniques, procedures, limitations, potential risks and benefits of services to be performed and other pertinent information."

From a legal standpoint, a model school counseling program informed consent brochure may serve to describe the counselor to students, parents, faculty, administration, and the community. The counselor is held accountable on the basis of the informed consent and whether they are practicing within their scope of practice (Keel & Brown, 1999). School counselors have traditionally offered only verbal informed consent by talking to counselees about their practice, confidentiality and its limits, and what to expect from the counseling relationship and program. This oral approach, however, can be disputed from a legal standpoint. The student or parent can say that informed consent never happened in the case of a potential lawsuit that is dependent on whether informed consent was obtained (Kaplan, 1996).

The model school counseling program brochure can be perceived as a marketing tool. It is a tool that enables the school counselor to advertise his/her program and inform students, parents, faculty, and administration about what it is that they do as professional school counselors (Kaplan, 1996).

Many school counselors in Michigan and other states are licensed as a Licensed Professional Counselor (LPC). This LPC credential generally requires that one have a personal disclosure statement on file as part of the application process. Disclosure statements are seen as of part of the credentialing requirement process.

In terms of the content of an informed consent brochure, Kaplan (1996) suggests that information about the counselor's interventions, techniques, theories, and general approach to counseling be included in such a disclosure statement. Other areas that should be addressed in the disclosure statement include information about confidentiality and its limits, the counselor's educational background and training, procedures for seeing the counselor, and an acknowledgment section of the program brochure. As an option, this acknowledgment section is signed by the student (and parents of minor students), acknowledging their agreement to enter into counseling, to participate in the counseling program, and confirming their understanding of both. An example of the acknowledgment section is provided below in Figure 1. This acknowledgment section is considered optional because it may not be a consistent fit with the scope of practice and policies in all schools and all school districts. If it is used, it is suggested that the acknowledgment section and call for signature be included at the end of the school counseling program informed consent brochure.

The MSCA Model School Counselor informed consent brochure includes the essential features that have been suggested by Kaplan, (1996). The model brochure is provided in Figure 2 below and is based upon a school that ideally has a school counseling program that is comprehensive and developmental in nature and consistent with the new *ASCA National Model: A Framework for School Counseling Programs* (American School Counselor Association, 2003). The *National Model* features programs that focus on the school counselor's role in leadership, advocacy, and using specific data to determine how school counseling programs make a positive difference in the achievement of students.

Figure 1. Example of acknowledgment section option:

Acknowledgment
(Please complete)

I have read and understand the information stated in the Model High School Guidance and Counseling Program Information Brochure. I received clarification on any points that I did not initially understand and had my questions answered as needed. I am willing to fully participate in the guidance and counseling program at MHS and agree to abide by the guidelines set forth in this brochure as indicated by my signature.

_____

(Student Signature)
(Date)

_____

(Parent Signature)
(Date)

The model brochure is based upon the *Model High School* (MHS), includes customizing directions, and is provided on a floppy disk kit which MSCA members may purchase and adapt to their own school situation. The disk contents are formatted in Microsoft Word in a tri-fold brochure. A welcome section, mission statement and counselor assignments are included on the front page. Other sections include information about the school's counseling program and biographical information about the school counselors and their individual approaches to counseling.

A section defining confidentiality, counselor appointments, additional points about the program, reference to the ASCA and ACA codes of ethics, and credits to MSCA comprise the rest of the model brochure. It is suggested that school counselors using the kit may wish to reduce the amount of text that they use in their brochure and that they may use their own logos and clip art. The clip art that is available in the model brochure kit is one of the MSCA logos; it is general in nature and references pine trees and sun.

Figure 2. School Counseling Brochure about the School Guidance and Counseling Program

---

Model High School (MHS)

Guidance and Counseling Program
Information Brochure

Welcome to the MHS Guidance and Counseling Program. We appreciate the opportunity to provide you with a guidance and counseling program to benefit your successful educational experience at MHS. This brochure was developed to provide you with information about the program so that you make an informed decision about participating in it. Please write questions you may have so that we can discuss them during our first meeting.

Mission Statement: The MHS Guidance and Counseling Program assures that all students will acquire and demonstrate competencies in career planning and exploration, knowledge of self and others, and educational/career-technical development as they learn to live, work, and learn over their lifetime.

Counselor Assignments:

Ms. Doe: (A-H)	(555-5555)
Mr. Jones: (I-P)	(666-6666)
Dr. Smith: (R-Z)	(777-7777)

The Guidance and Counseling Program is a comprehensive one that is designed to meet the developmental needs of all students. Its purpose is to contribute to the overall success of student learning.

Our program adheres to both the *National Standards for School Counseling Programs* and the *Michigan Comprehensive Guidance and Counseling Program*. The Standards are based on providing success through activities designed to ensure students' academic, career, and personal/social development. The program is delivered through individual counseling, small group counseling, large group guidance, consultation, and coordination.

The Guidance and Counseling Program is composed of four programmatic components. First, through *Guidance Curriculum*, counselors teach, team teach, or assist with learning activities on a large group basis. These activities are for all students and include such topics as study skills, career awareness, decision-making, personal responsibility, and personal safety.

Individual Planning is the second component, consisting of activities that assist students to plan, monitor, and manage their academic, personal, and career

---

Figure 2 cont.

development. The counselor plans and directs activities relevant to student appraisal, advisement, and placement. Topics include college selection, financial aid, interest surveys, course selection, career exploration, and portfolios.

Third, *Responsive Services* consist of activities to meet immediate student needs and involves personal or crisis counseling, consultation, information, and referral. This component is often initiated by students.

Component four is *Systems Support* in which counselors manage activities that enhance the total guidance and counseling program. It includes counselors' participation in professional development activities, serving on school/community advisory committees, communicating with staff and community, coordinating community resources, and gathering information to enhance students' success.

Counseling Approaches/Backgrounds

Ms. Doe, Mr. Jones, and Dr. Smith are counselors who have graduate degrees in school counseling. They are certified teachers, endorsed as school counselors, and committed to delivering a comprehensive guidance and counseling program to students. Additional information about them is provided below:

Ms. Joan Doe, M.A., School Counselor: Joan joined MHS as a math teacher in 1991 and became a counselor in 1996. She believes that her teaching experience is beneficial to her role as a counselor in delivering classroom guidance lessons to students. She earned her Master's Degree from Western Michigan University in 1993, is a National Certified School Counselor (NCSC), and a Licensed Professional Counselor (LPC). Joan believes that her role as a counselor is one of being a facilitator, helping students to explore information about themselves, explore options, and make decisions for which they take responsibility. Joan emphasizes concepts and methods inherent to Reality and Cognitive Therapy which she feels are effective ways of working with students in the school setting.

Mr. Slade Jones, Ed.S., School Counselor: Slade is a graduate of MHS and returned as a counselor after receiving his Education Specialist Degree from Wayne State University in 1998. Previously, he served as a teacher at Melvin Middle School. He has training in cognitive and behavioral counseling and has experienced extensive training in conflict resolution and mediation. Slade prefers a practical approach to solving problems and tries to find out what will work best for each student in addressing their needs. He assists students in realizing their potential by identifying and utilizing their personal strengths and sources of support within their families and community. He serves on the Guidance and Counseling Advisory Board for Eastern Michigan University. He is credentialed as an LPC and NCSC.

Figure 2 cont.

Dr. Dorothy Smith, Ph.D., School Counselor: Dorothy received her Ph.D. in Counselor Education from Mississippi State University in 1993. She has 25 years of experience as a teacher and counselor and is a past president of the American School Counselor Association. She is an LPC and NCSC and is active in the Oakland Counseling Association and the Michigan School Counselor Association, currently serving as Ethics Chair. She believes that students measure their success in school and life by believing in themselves. Dorothy specializes in the solution-focused brief counseling approach, believing that it is efficient in working with students at the high school level. She conducts brief counseling workshops and is a visiting lecturer at the University of Detroit Mercy.

Confidentiality

Confidentiality means that the privacy of information that you share with your counselor belongs to you. You may share information with others as you wish, but we understand that you have a right to privacy. We will guard that privacy as much as is permitted by the law, ethics, and school rules. We recognize the legal rights and responsibilities of parents in doing what is in the best interest of their children. If you ask that information be shared with others, you and your parents will be asked to sign a release form. We will send only information you request unless mandated by law or ethics. You should know that there are exceptions where we are obligated to break confidentiality, including: potential harm to you or someone else; state laws that mandate reporting of child abuse; or a court of law that requires testimony or student records. Counselors occasionally consult with other school professionals, but in such cases only information necessary to achieving the goals of the conference will be shared. In addition, counselors keep informal notes regarding conferences, notes that are stored in a secure, locked drawer and treated confidentially.

Counselor Assignments and Appointments

Students are assigned alphabetically to counselors. It is best to sign up for an appointment in advance. There are times when counselors are available on a walk-in basis, such as before or after school, or during lunch. Check in the Counseling Center for appointment information and your counselor's calendar, which indicates her/his schedule in implementing the guidance and counseling program. Parents are encouraged to call for an appointment.

Figure 2 cont.

Additional Points

As professional school counselors, we adhere to standards of practice that support your:

- right to respect and dignity as a unique human being
- access to a guidance and counseling program without prejudice or discrimination as to person, character, belief, or practice
- right to self-direction
- right to choice and responsibility for your decisions
- expectation of receiving guidance and counseling services that are within the accepted scope of practice relative to the training, education, and professional credentials of counselors
- right to privacy and to our compliance to laws, policies, and ethical standards relative to confidentiality

We recognize and abide by the American School Counselor Association *Ethical Standards for School Counselors* (1998) and the American Counseling Association *Code of Ethics and Standards of Practice* (1997).

Format for this model brochure was provided by the Michigan School Counselor Association. MSCA is a state branch of the American School Counselor Association and a division of the Michigan Counseling Association

www.mich-sca.org

Summary

School counselors have a responsibility to provide opportunities for students to enhance their school achievement through the school counseling programs in which they participate. An opportunity that applies to every student in every high school has to do with the ability to have a plan and focus in place for after high school at the time the student graduates from high school.

It is recommended that professional school counselors develop and distribute a school counseling program brochure that is specific to their school and provides information about their school counseling program. The brochure provides information for students, parents, and other publics to make informed choices about participating in the school counseling program in ways that improve student achievement and enable students to be prepared for that "next step" as they transition through life.

Professional counseling association codes of ethics provide support for such disclosure so, in essence, it is the "ethical" thing to do. The model school counseling program brochure is simply a framework that practicing school counselors may modify and adapt to the level, needs, and characteristics of their students, school, and school district.

When school counselors make the effort to market, inform, and define how their school counseling program improves student success, only good things can occur to enhance that success. Students will be prepared and have a plan and focus in place when they graduate from high school. Parents will know what is available to their children and be supportive of school counseling programs that are aimed at improving their students' success. Teachers, administrators, and support staff will have an understanding of the school counseling program, know how it will benefit themselves and students, and be supportive of the program. The community will be in the position of being aware of the school counseling program and its benefits.

In addition, the professional school counselors will be intrinsically motivated to continue to evaluate and provide improved school counseling programs to their students. Programs will not only benefit students, but will benefit school counselors as well. There will be more opportunities for quality feedback on the school counseling programs when more people are aware of the programs and the benefits that are derived from them.

References

A. C. Davis High School. (n.d.). *A.C. Davis High School counseling services disclosure pamphlet* [Brochure]. Yakima, WA: Author.

American Counseling Association. (1997). *Code of ethics and standards of practice*. Alexandria, VA: Author.

American School Counselor Association. (1998). *Ethical standards for school counselors*. Alexandria, VA: Author.

American School Counselor Association. (2003).*American School Counselor Association national model: A framework for school counseling programs*. Alexandria, VA: Author.

Dahir, C. A., Sheldon, C. B., & Valiga, M. J. (1998). *Implementing the national standards for school counseling programs.* Alexandria, VA: American School Counselor Association.

Gysbers, N. C., & Henderson, P. (2000*). Developing and managing your school guidance program.* Alexandria, VA: American Counseling Association.

Kaplan, D. M. (1996, April). Developing an informed consent brochure for secondary students. *The ASCA Counselor, 39,* 3.

Keel, L.P., & Brown, S.P. (1999, July). Professional disclosure statements. *Counseling Today, 42,* 14, 33.

Michigan School Counselor Association. (1997). *Michigan comprehensive guidance and counseling program.* Grand Rapids, MI: Author.

Michigan School Counselor Association. (2000). *Model school counselor informed consent brochure.* [Kit/brochure] Grand Rapids, MI: Author.

Myrick, R. D. (1997).*Developmental guidance and counseling.* Minneapolis, MN: Educational Media Corporation.

Schmidt, J. J. (1999).*Counseling in schools: Essential services and comprehensive programs.* Needham Heights, MA: Allyn and Bacon.

Chapter Twelve

Using Projects to Teach Career Planning Skills and Tools Incorporating the ASCA National Standards as Guidelines

Suzy Mygatt Wakefield

Abstract

This chapter addresses the importance of teaching students career planning *skills* that, once mastered, can become *tools* that can be used throughout their lifetimes to navigate the changing workplace. Educators need to provide developmental, systematic, and comprehensive approaches to career guidance for all students. By working together, educators can design and provide career planning curriculum (through classrooms, homerooms, or advisories) as part of a school's overall mission. The *ASCA National Standards* provide student content standards in the academic, career, and personal/social domains; *The ASCA National Model: A Framework for School Counseling Programs* provides a framework for delivery, management and accountability systems. Student competencies may be checked off as students complete components of their *education and career plans, career planning portfolios,* and *culminating projects*, with each project incorporating a number of skills (such as writing a résumé and cover letter), in the safety of the shool setting.

Career Planning Skills and Tools for All Students

Middle and secondary school students need strong connections with adults, preferably many of them, to guide them as they explore options for school, postsecondary education, and work. Beginning in the middle school years, students and adults might develop a "learning plan," a formal but flexible outline of what

the student hopes to accomplish in young adulthood. Written into this plan would be education, work, and service experiences that can best help the student to attain those goals. Also included would be ways to signal trouble ahead and timelines for taking "dry runs" of college and employment placement tests so that students could identify their strengths and weaknesses and work to strengthen the latter before taking the tests for real.
(National Commission on the High School Senior Year, The Education Trust, 2001, p. 7)

The Education Trust provides an excellent idea as to how we can help young people, particularly "unfocused kids," with setting up a "learning plan" (as they call it) early in their school years, as early as middle school, so that they do not feel so unfocused. As we consider approaches to providing career guidance curriculum to *all* students, we might consider teaching them specific career planning *skills* so that, once mastered, they may become *tools* to be utilized over their lifetimes. Whether they are clear about their goals or not, *all* students need support with educational and career planning, or career development. According to Starr & Gysbers (1992, as cited in O'Brien et al., 1999), "career development is an on-going, lifelong process in which students must accomplish a series of tasks appropriate for their developmental level, to progress successfully in vocational decision making" (p. 216). From a developmental standpoint, it is suggested that specific career planning skills and tools be taught through comprehensive career development projects, such as an *education and career plan (the Education Trust's "learning plan")*; a *career planning portfolio*; and a *culminating project*. Each of these projects would be carried out over a period of time. The *education and career plan* could be initiated in the 8th grade and continued through high school. The *career planning portfolio* could be started in the 9th grade and continued through graduation. The *culminating project* (which could have a strong career exploration emphasis) usually is assigned in the 11th or 12th grade and normally must be completed for graduation. These projects would provide a systematic way for various embedded career development competencies to be checked off, or systematically monitored. Monitoring student progress against given competencies can be time-consuming, so having students assigned the same comprehensive projects would facilitate monitoring their progress systematically. In a large high school, systematic monitoring is a necessity, as students would be progressing at different rates in completing these school-wide projects.

Scope and Sequence: Begin the Education and Career Plan in the 8th Grade

In her booklet for students and parents, *Did Somebody Say College?*, Quattrociocchi (1999) urges young teens to do three things: "Get focused, get skilled, and get connected." She encourages students of 13 and 14 years of age to begin making connections to their future by volunteering in a work setting in which they might have a career interest, such as in a hospital if they are interested in the health care industry, or contacting a writer if they want to explore the field of writing:

> Maybe you want to be a writer. Then write to one. You'd be amazed how many writers respond to letters from aspiring writers. Try it...Think of adults as points on a vast web of information. Start anywhere, with any adult, and let that person lead you to another who can help you. (pp. 13-14)

Educators, with appropriate curriculum training, could appropriately teach 8th graders how to formulate an **education and career plan** (also called a *"high school + education plan"*) through advisories, homerooms, and/or classrooms (such as in Social Studies or Language Arts classes). Teachers would need to be educated as to their expectations with career guidance activities. School counselors would likely be responsible for helping to design and teach some career guidance units; they would also be available to meet with students and their parents to discuss their education and career plans in more detail. In some high schools, career specialists are available to lend informational support to students and their parents/ guardians.

Scope and Sequence: Begin the Career Planning Portfolio in the 9th Grade

In the ninth grade, teachers could follow up with each student's "education and career plan" (again through an advisory, homeroom and/or designated classroom, according to the school's mission statement) as well as begin each student's **career planning portfolio**, which would follow the student through high school (grades 9-12 or 10-12). This portfolio could be kept at home by the student and could be done both in hard copy and online (see www.wois.org in Tami Palmer's chapter, *The Electronic Portfolio*). The student would then have an ongoing portfolio for recording, revising, and keeping his or her career and education plans, goals, résumé and cover letter, interview experiences, and so forth. (An Internet-based electronic portfolio would be accessible from any computer, with password access, for updating as needed.) The student's letters of reference, transcripts, tests scores, exhibits of academic and art work, and other documents could also be kept in this portfolio, or scanned in electronically. Also, the written reports by the student of his or her field experiences (shadows and internships) and service learning (volunteer) experiences could be included, along with guidelines for mock job interviews and informational interviews, carried out in the safety of the classroom setting.

Scope and Sequence: Implement the Culminating Project in the 11th or 12th Grades

By the time a student was a senior in high school and asked to complete a **culminating project** for graduation (typically at least 60 hours spent, under the guidance of a mentor during the junior and/or senior year, on a proposal, written research paper, short internship and follow-up oral presentation before a panel), he or she would have begun to develop virtual "career planning tool kit" with which to navigate the workplace. Going through the protracted experience of doing the culminating project would teach the student both time and resource management skills, important skills according to the SCANS Report (1991, as cited in Zunker, 1998) as well as interpersonal and research skills. It is true that often culminating projects have an academic and not a career focus. However, students generally may choose their own topic, and the culminating project would provide an excellent opportunity for a student to explore a serious career interest. In the process of spending the required 60 hours on a culminating project, the student would have considerable opportunity to learn more about a career interest from Internet sites, books, periodicals, brochures, actual job shadow visitations, interviews, and videos.

Monitoring and "Checking off" Project Competencies

Here's how the career guidance program could work. The *career planning portfolio* (assigned in the 9th grade, if not earlier), for example, would be made up of various components or competencies: written reports of service learning (after participating in volunteer experiences), completed job applications, a résumé and cover letter (both electronic and hard copy) written reports of completed mock job interviews and informational interviews, and even the research-based senior (culminating) project itself.

As each project was completed, proof of completion could be checked off manually by an appropriate school employee (perhaps an instructional assistant or secretary), and then entered into a computer database. Management of competency completion is a complicated issue and would need to be part of the overall comprehensive career guidance plan, as it was initially being set up by a team of educators.

Normally, students in business and other vocationally funded classes are often assigned specific career guidance projects (such as writing a résumé and cover letter and conducting mock job interviews), but in this suggested career development curriculum design, all students would be required to complete specific projects. Current practice often allows students in Business Education and other vocationally funded classes to receive an excellent exposure to concepts such as: a career planning portfolio, field experiences, job applications, a résumé and cover letter, and mock job interviews. Typically, however, students in mainstream academic classes do not get the benefit of these career development experiences.

ASCA as a Resource for Career Guidance Projects

School counselors are encouraged to work collaboratively with administrators, teachers, career specialists (and selected members of the community) in a team effort to organize and deliver the comprehensive career guidance program, consistent with the school counseling program's goal statement, and the school's and district's mission statements. Educators will find a great resource in the American School Counselor Association (ASCA) implementation document *Vision into Action—Implementing the National Standards for School Counseling Programs* (Dahir, Sheldon, & Valiga, 1998) as they determine the career development student competencies for students in their own school. The *ASCA National Standards* are premised on the notion that "the school counseling program enables all students to achieve success in school and to develop into contributing members of our society." The three *ASCA National Standards* (p. 11) for career development are:

- Standard A: Students will acquire the skills to investigate the world of work in relation to knowledge of self and to make informed career decisions.
- Standard B: Students will employ strategies to achieve future career success and satisfaction.
- Standard C: Students will understand the relationship among personal qualities, education and training, and the world of work.

According to the *ASCA National Model: A Framework for School Counseling Programs*, (ASCA, 2003):

> The school guidance curriculum component consists of a written instructional program that is comprehensive in scope, preventative and proactive, developmental in design, coordinated by school counselors and delivered, as appropriate, by school counselors and other educators. School guidance curriculum is designed to facilitate the systematic delivery of guidance lessons or activities to every student consistent with the school counseling program's statements of philosophy, goals and student competencies. (p. 40)

A practical example is the *education and career plan*. Specific competencies are provided from the *ASCA National Standards* (Dahir, Sheldon, and Valiga, 1998, p.12) in the career development domain. Under Standard A (above), in the area of *develop career awareness*, related competencies are that students will:

> ...develop skills to locate, evaluate, and interpret career information; learn how to make decisions; learn how to set goals; understand the importance of planning, [and] learn how to balance work and leisure time. (p. 12)

Also under Standard A, in the area of *develop employment readiness*, students are to:

> ...acquire employability skills, such as working on a team, problem solving, and organizational skills; apply job readiness skills to seek employment opportunities;...understand the importance of responsibility, dependability, punctuality, integrity, and effort in the workplace; and utilize time and task management skills. (p. 12).

These competencies would be appropriate in an education and career plan. Under Standard B (above) in the area of *acquire career information*, suggested student competencies are to "apply decision-making skills to career planning, course selection, and career transitions" with specific supporting activities articulated across the 9-12 grade levels. (The reader is encouraged to look at Appendix H, **Action Plan** of *ASCA's Vision into Action, Implementing the National Standards for School Counseling Programs*, [Dahir, Sheldon & Valiga, 1998, p. 119], to see how supporting activities might be written in for each competency, along with the parameters of "when, who, and expected results for students".) Another suggested competency is to "identify personal skills, interests, and abilities and relate them to current career choices" (p. 13). When assigning career guidance projects for all students, the manageability of tracking completed competencies by students can then be systematized.

ASCA National Model: A Framework for School Counseling Programs

School counselors and other educators are encouraged to review the *ASCA National Model: A Framework for School Counseling Programs* (ASCA, 2003) as they consider the delivery, accountability and management systems for their career guidance program. Checklists are greatly expanded, such as the *Developmental Crosswalking Tools,* to help educators to plan which competencies will be taught in which grades, and by whom. As shown in the *ASCA National Model: A Framework for School Counseling Programs* (ASCA, 2003), the Program Audit checklist in the Appendix (pp. 110-120) incorporates the following topics:

- the *Foundation*—that is, the beliefs and philosophy, the mission of school counseling programs, standards and goals, the ASCA National Standards/Competencies;
- the *Delivery System*—that is, the Guidance Curriculum, Individual Student Planning, Responsive Services, and System Support;
- the *Management System*—that is, school counselor/administrator agreements, advisory council, use of data and student monitoring, use of data and closing the gap, action plans, use of time/calendar; and
- the *Accountability System*—that is, the results report, counselor performance evaluation, and the program audit.

The essence of the *ASCA National Standards* and *National Model* is not so much what school counselors do but how students are *different* as a result of what school counselors (and appropriate others) do–through their comprehensive school counseling programs. Rhodes (2003) notes that, "The standards and model are program-centered, and they clearly demonstrate a focus on student development throughout the academic, career, and personal/social domains" (p.11). According to Hatch and Bowers (2002), in their article in the *ASCA School Counselor*, "The Block to Build On," the *National Model for School Counseling Programs* is "written to reflect a comprehensive approach to program foundation, delivery, management and accountability. School counselors switch their emphasis from service-centered for some of the students to program-centered for every student"(p. 15).

An excellent example of school counselors and teachers working together to deliver career development activities can be found in the ASCA *National Model Appendix (pp. 104-105): The XYZ Middle School Guidance Curriculum Action Plan* (www.schoolcounselor.org). It is suggested that school counselors, administrators and teachers work together to develop the school's guidance curriculum, and then decide in which classes/subjects (i.e., Social Studies, Language Arts, Science, etc.) the lessons or career guidance concepts would be taught. Thus, through advisories, homerooms and/or classroom settings, *all* students would be systematically taught selected career development competencies.

Template for a Career and Education Plan

A template for an education and career plan would need to be utilized. Students may not only be meeting a graduation requirement (if it were required) in developing and completing their *education and career plan* but they would also be learning a life skill. As adults, they would find that knowing how to revise a career plan would be useful so that they could find a new job in the same field or even be able to switch fields. According to a recent article in *U.S. News and World Report*, (Schneider, 2003, March 3), "Finding Work,"

> Unemployment is still pretty high, and in some fields—technology, publishing, and investment banking—layoffs and closings have left plenty of walking wounded...Yet those same professionals are often in the best shape to find other good jobs, especially if they are willing to switch fields. Dumped dot-commers can take their computer skills to the healthcare industry, for example, or former human resource managers, with retraining, can become educators." (p. 80)

Once a person learns how to develop and revise an education and career plan, the potential for utilizing that skill is significant, helping the worker to re-tool and find a new place in the workplace. The skill of writing and revising an education and career plan may become a lifelong tool that can be utilized, as needed, with the vagaries of the workplace.

There are several excellent examples of templates for an education and career plan. One such example is the *Individual Career Plan Form: High School Level (National Career Development Guidelines: Local*

Handbook for High Schools, 1989, NOICC, as cited in Isaacson & Brown, 2000, pp. 283-285), which provides sections, by grade level, for the student to outline his/her interests, skills and abilities, hobbies and recreational/ leisure activities, favorite school subjects, and preferred careers, and so forth, by grade level. Another example is the *ASCA Get a Life Portfolio— My Personal Career Plan* (Perry & Van Zandt, 1993), which also incorporates an education and career plan and helps a student to work logically through these important aspects:

> self knowledge; awareness of the world of work; career assessment information; linking self-knowledge with the world of work; career exploration; career options; career decision; career plan; training; training decision; job-seeking skills; [and] employability skills..." (*ASCA Get a Life Portfolio—My Personal Career Plan.*)

A third example of a career and education plan (along with a portfolio and a culminating project) is from the Franklin Pierce School District in Tacoma, Washington. Below it is shown in the context of student advisories in which the plan, along with the student portfolio, is monitored by the advisory teacher. Note the emphasis on parent support in this *Individual Student Planning* program.

Franklin Pierce School District
Individual Student Planning - High School

Individual student planning (ISP) consists of ongoing activities that help students plan, monitor, and manage their educational and career development. Franklin Pierce School District encourages cooperative effort of the student, parent and educators in developing the student's personalized plan. This plan is developed through guidance curriculum during advisory, student portfolios, and individual parent-student conferences finalizing as a culminating project.

Advisory

Advisory is a means to present guidance curriculum to all students and to help students complete portfolio requirements. These activities and lessons will enable students to successfully utilize their portfolios to lead/ conduct quality Individual Student Planning (ISP) conferences with parent & teacher/counselor. Each high school has an advisory coordinator and a team leader for each grade level.

Student Portfolio/Planner

High School + Education Plan/ Portfolio

Through guidance activities each student will develop a portfolio that includes interest assessments, transcripts, credit checks, standards-based works, high school plan for success, post-secondary choices & plans and career goals. The portfolio is a showcase that exemplifies what is best about the student. It will enable the student to keep records of progress in the areas of learner, citizen and worker.

Career/Educational Pathways

Using information obtained from interests, achievement, guidance and other assessments, students develop a sequence of courses that may lead to further education and training. Educational pathways are flexible and may be changed based upon student and parent rationale. Franklin Pierce School District has five career paths from which to choose: Arts & Communication, Business & Marketing, Health & Human Services, Engineering & Technology, and Science & Natural Resources.

Parent Involvement

As part of the district's commitment to prepare students for success during and beyond high school, Franklin Pierce School District hosts annual individual student-parent conferences. The outcome of the ISP Conference will enable the student with parent/guardian assistance to prepare for a relevant high school career and post secondary education leading toward successful future goals. Students and parents meet individually with a counselor, educator, or district administrator. The student will lead the conference using his/her portfolio as a guide for discussion. Topics will pertain to the student's current academic status, plans for success for remainder of high school, educational opportunities, career path, plans for beyond high school. Pre-registration for the following school year is completed at this conference.

Culminating Project

Effective with the graduating class of 2004, all seniors must complete the individual student plan. Students must present this plan to a panel of community and district staff members prior to graduation. This culminating project documents the student's competence in academic areas, demonstrates their ability to plan for post-secondary education and training, and demonstrates their citizenship qualities. Students not completing the essential elements of this plan prior to their senior year will take a remedial course in student portfolios their senior year. (Updated 11/18/02)

Further information may be found at the Franklin Pierce School District (in Tacoma, Washington) website at: www.fp.k12.wa.us

---

Possible Delivery Systems for a Career Guidance Program

In presenting career guidance skills and tools, we must consider appropriate delivery systems. Typically, school counselors have been given the primary role of providing career guidance for virtually all students, but the responsibility is too large and too complicated for only one type of professional educator to be involved. Kuranz (2002) reports that the average school counselor-to-student ratio, according to ASCA, is 1:551.

There are several possible venues for the career guidance curriculum in high school. One is the classroom advisory, in which 20-25 students are assigned to a teacher (who is paid a stipend for this additional responsibility) for an entire school year for each of the high school years. (The same students stay with the same teacher, possibly throughout high school.) Another venue could be the homeroom, still in use in many high schools. Gray and Herr (1995) explain the homeroom in this way.

> Most high schools begin the day with something called homeroom period. Homeroom is truly a unique phenomenon because it is probably the only circumstance, other than lining up alphabetically for graduation, in which the school does something that results in bringing high school students together on an egalitarian basis, independent of course selection, intellectual ability, athletic prowess, family income, or even race. More needs to be done to promote this intermingling among students of differing academic characteristics. (p.155)

The non-threatening, non-academic nature of the advisory or homeroom make them ideal for the presentation of career guidance projects, such as the education and career plan, the career planning portfolio, and the culminating project. If those venues are not available, then the classroom is appropriate, as is the Career Center.

229

The delivery system for the career guidance curriculum needs to be incorporated into the school's mission statement, so that the personnel involved (school counselors, administrators, teachers, and career specialists) all understand their important and complementary roles, whether they are designing, planning and/or actually teaching or implementing the career guidance units. The curriculum may be set up so that career units are taught by the school counselor or career specialist in the Career Center, teachers in advisories or homerooms (if the school is set up with advisories or homerooms), or by classroom teachers, school counselors or career specialists in designated classrooms. School counselors, with their specialized knowledge of career development and their counseling skills, would normally help to design the career guidance program (in collaboration with others), teach some aspects of it, and be available, one-on-one, to provide follow-up support with students and their parents about particular interests and concerns.

Skills that, once mastered, may become Career Planning Tools

In summary, in an effort to develop needed skills (competencies) and, ultimately, career planning tools, students could be asked to demonstrate that they are able to successfully complete three projects:
- an **education and career plan** (or a "high school + education plan")
- a **career planning portfolio** (also called "student portfolio")
- a **culminating (senior) project** (may be required instead in the junior year)

Students could also be asked to demonstrate that they can successfully complete the following career planning and exploration activities, depending on a school's mission statement and/or school counseling program's philosophy statement:
- Arrange one-day **shadow experiences, longer internships, and service learning (volunteer) experiences,** and **possibly a mentorship.**
- Fill out **job applications** for several job openings.
- Write a **cover** , based on the needs of the situation presented.
- Conduct an **informational interview** (with pre-arranged questions).
- Conduct a **mock job interview** (with pre-arranged questions and coaching).
- Build a **network of personal contacts** to help explore the world of work.

- Be proficient in using the computer **to communicate by email** and to **explore career websites on the Internet.**

Conclusion

Early planning and career exploration comprise a key concept in this chapter. Students need to be started as early as middle or junior high school to think about their future plans — what they want to do in their lives, and how they need to prepare for their goals. Unfocused kids, in particular, need one-on-one support from adults (parents, school counselors, teachers, career specialists, and others) in thinking about and planning for their future. Students who do not get started early in this process may not get started at all, as some will drop out between the ninth and tenth grades (Greene, 2002). So, it is imperative to develop comprehensive career guidance programs beginning in middle school or junior high school, at least the *education and career plan.*

These projects would ideally be introduced sequentially in a manner that is consistent with the district's and school's mission statement and the school counseling program goals statement: the *education and career plan*; the *career planning portfolio* (incorporating the cover letter and resume, job applications, interviews, along with school records, exhibits of academic work, and written reports of service learning and field experiences); and the *culminating project* (possibly exploring a serious career interest). Components of these projects, once they were practiced activities, would provide skills and tools that could become a student's virtual "tool kit" in the workplace. When it came time for a student to leave or graduate from high school, he/she would have at least some mastery over the expectations that would soon develop. He/she would have acquired important job seeking skills, including: mock job interviewing, informational interviewing, Internet job searches, résumé

With appropriate career planning skills and tools, young people would be more likely to take charge of their resources, direction, and focus. These three career guidance projects are designed to help them develop that responsibility. Appropriate educators in advisories, homerooms, classrooms, or the Career Center may assist all students to develop their goals and consciously choose their path, with specific career planning skills and tools. Then, when these teens graduate, their well-practiced "career planning tool kit" would be available for them. Hopefully, these practiced skills and tools would help teens to have a firm sense of control about their future. They would then be able to take a focused, purposeful, planned and confident path toward their postsecondary plans and goals.

References

American School Counselor Association. (2003). *ASCA national model: A framework for school counseling programs.* Alexandria, VA: Author.

Dahir, C.A., Sheldon, C.B., & Valiga, M.J. (1998). *Vision into action: Implementing the national standards for school counseling programs.* Alexandria, VA: American School Counselor Association

Education Trust, Inc. (2001). National Commission on the High School Senior Year. *The lost opportunity of the senior year: Finding a better way.*(p.7). Retrieved March 28, 2003, from http://www.commissionon thesenioryear.org/Report/report.html

Franklin Pierce School District (n.d.). *Indivdiual Student Planning.* [website presentation] Tacoma, WA: Author. Further information may be obtained from the district website at http://www.fp.k12.wa.us

Gray, C.G. & Herr, E.L. (1995). *Other ways to win: Creating alternatives for high school graduates.* Thousand Oaks: Corwin Press, Inc.

Greene, J.P. (2002). *Graduation rates in Washington State.* New York: Manhattan Institute for Policy Research. Retrieved December 19, 2002. from http://www.manhattan-institute.org/html/cr_27.htm

Hatch, T., & Bowers, J. (May/June 2002).The block to build on. *ASCA School Counselor, 39(5),*15.

Isaacson, L.E. & Brown, D. (2000). *Career information, career counseling, and career development.* Boston: Allyn and Bacon.

Kuranz, M. (February, 2002). Cultivating student potential. *Professional School Counseling. 5 (3),* 172-179.

National Occupational Information Coordinating Committee (1989). The National Career Development Guidelines. [Worksheet] Washington, D.C.: Author.

O'Brien, K.M., Dukstein, R.D., Jackson, S.L., Tomlinson, M.J., & Kamatuka, N.A. (March, 1999). Broadening career horizons for students in at-risk environments. *The Career Development Quarterly, 47*(3), 215-229.

Perry, N. & Van Zandt, C.E. (1993). *ASCA get a life portfolio—my personal career plan*. Alexandria, VA: American School Counselor Association.

Quattrociocchi, S. & Cripps, J. (1999). *Did somebody say college? Or how to* reduce the high costs and high risks of after-high school education. Bellevue, WA: Bellevue Community College Printing Services, 13-14.

Rhodes, G.R. (2003). Hand in hand. *ASCA School Counselor, 40(3)*. 11-13.

Schneider, J. (2003, March 3). Finding work. *U.S. News and World Report, 134* (6), 80.

Zunker, V.G. (1998). A SCANS Report for America 2000—What work requires of schools. *Career Counseling: Applied concepts to life planning*. Pacific Grove: Brooks/Cole Publishing Company, 239-242.

Chapter Thirteen

Policy — A View From On High

Larry Davis

Abstract

In October, 2000, the Washington State Board of Education (SBE) adopted revised state minimum high school graduation requirements. The new requirements take effect with the graduating class of 2008 (ninth graders in the fall of 2004). Two new requirements, in particular, will help students bring greater focus on their plans after high school – a "culminating project" requirement and completion of a "high school+ education plan." How these two requirements came about and how they will make a difference for students' post-high school experiences are the subject of this chapter.

Policy is one of the fuels that drives the engine of government and policy development is very much a journey through a web of egos, competing interests, and differing philosophies. The "story" that follows makes use of an onion, fabric, a Chinese proverb, the *Wizard of Oz*, Bob Dylan, vision, leadership, purpose, a shovel, a balance scale, statesmanship, and the decathlon. What do these seemingly unconnected items and concepts share in common? My "view from on high" is that each is a piece of the state-level policy puzzle. More specifically, these puzzle pieces are used to illustrate the process of state-level policymaking on an important public policy issue – state minimum high school graduation requirements.

Policy: State Government Context

What is policy and why is it important? The *Merriam-Webster Collegiate Dictionary* defines policy as: "a definite course or method of action selected from among alternatives and in light of given conditions to guide and determine present and future decisions; a high-level overall plan embracing the general goals and acceptable procedures especially of a governmental body." In short, policy is a declaration of intent or requirements, or both, on a given issue. Policy establishes the position on, priority for, and commitment to the issue by the body setting it. Policy defines for those affected by it the expectations and requirements for dealing with the particular issue.

At the state level, policy-setting bodies include: the Legislature, which creates policy by passing bills (laws) that are codified in the Revised Code of Washington (RCW); the Governor, who signs bills into law and also establishes policies through Executive Orders; state agencies, like the State Board of Education, that implement laws through policies adopted in the form of rules that are codified in the Washington Administrative Code (WAC); and the Washington State Supreme Court, which can set or shape policy through its legal decisions.

Who makes policy is as important as what policy is made. The structure for K-12 education governance in Washington State includes the following policymakers, shapers, and influencers:

Governmental Body	# Statutory Members
Legislature	147
Governor	1
Superintendent of Public Instruction (SPI)	1
State Board of Education (SBE)	11
Academic Achievement and Accountability (A+) Commission	9
Professional Educator Standards Board (PESB)	20
Workforce Training and Education Coordinating Board (WTECB)	9
Educational Service Districts (ESDs; 7 or 9 member boards)	9 ESDs
School Districts (SDs; 5 member boards, except Seattle with 7)	296 SDs

NOTE: The State Superintendent is a member of the SBE, A+ Commission, PESB, and WTECB.

NOTE: The list above is exclusive of other significant policy-influencers, such as lobbyists for various professional education associations, the state business community, and parents.

These bodies are like an **onion** in that they operate at different layers of the policy environment. The outer layer represents enacted education laws that set the basic policy direction or requirements (the Legislature and Governor). The second layer represents state agencies responsible for implementing laws, usually requiring some degree of more detailed policy specification through the adoption of implementing rules (SBE, SPI, A+ Commission, PESB, and WTECB). The third layer represents further implementation detail through policies adopted by the local school board. The last layer, not always present, represents school-level decisions that reflect final tailoring of the original policy direction to the conditions and culture of the school building.

The challenge of policymaking for an agency such as the State Board of Education is to develop policy that is "uniformly" applicable statewide, yet appropriately and responsibly respects the fact that no two communities, districts, schools, or people are exactly alike. The policy has to be "common" statewide. However, when it takes effect at the local level it does so taking into account the practical realities of structural and human diversity in the system.

The following data is from the 2001-02 school year (unless otherwise noted) and can be thought of as the interconnecting threads of **fabric**:

- 296 school districts
- 1,482 local school board members
- 2,172 schools
- 3,824 administrators (district-level and building-level; 2000-01 data)
- 35,051 classified staff
- 58,919 teachers (2000-01 data)
- 1,010,167 public school students (and at least that many parents)
- 82,310 private school students
- 20,433 homeschooled students (2000-01 data)

Each thread is critical to the overall structural integrity of the fabric. The threads must be woven in a properly aligned manner to provide strength, flexibility, and resiliency in support of the purpose of the fabric.

Policy: Setting Direction

Policy does not exist in a vacuum. Given the focus of this book, a brief look back at a key point in Washington State history is necessary. Legislative interest in the early 1990's, in charting a new direction for public education, culminated with the passage and signing into law of The

Education Improvement Act of 1993 (commonly called "House Bill 1209," after the number of the House bill signed into law.) (Education Improvement Act, Washington State Legislature, 1993) This new state education policy launched Washington State on an education reform journey that continues today. The new direction remains appropriate for reasons reflected in:

> "Do not confine your children to your own learning, for they were born in another time."
>
> (Chinese Proverb)

> "Toto, I have a feeling we're not in Kansas anymore."
>
> (Dorothy in *The Wizard of Oz*)

In 1993, a new millennium was on the horizon and fast approaching. We can and should learn from the past, but do not have the option of living there (at least until time travel is invented).

These pieces of the policy puzzle underscore the need for policymakers to align policy with the conditions that exist, or can be reasonably expected to come into existence. As Bob Dylan wrote and sings, *"The times they are a-changin'."* Consequently, it is important that public policy remain in step.

HB 1209 modified the original goal of the state's 1977 Basic Education Act. The revised basic education goal reflects a "true north" vision for the state's public education system that is not inherently new, but is now formally expressed:

> "The goal of the Basic Education Act for the schools of the state of Washington...shall be to provide students with the opportunity to become responsible citizens, to contribute to their own economic well-being and to that of their families and communities, and to enjoy productive and satisfying lives."
> (Revised Goal of Basic Education and Student Learning Goals, Washington State Legislature, 1993)

The revised 1993 goal goes on to require that "...the goals of each school district, with the involvement of parents and community members, shall be to provide opportunities for all students to develop the knowledge and skills essential to..." meet the four student learning goals. The heart and soul of the 1993 policy are the following statewide Student Learning Goals:

1. "Read with comprehension, write with skill, and communicate effectively and responsibly in a variety of ways and settings;

2. Know *and* apply the core concepts and principles of mathematics; social, physical, and life sciences; civics and history; geography; arts; and health and fitness;
3. Think analytically, logically, and creatively, and to integrate experience and knowledge to form reasoned judgments and solve problems;
4. Understand the importance of work and how performance, effort, and decisions directly affect future career and educational opportunities."

The most significant shift in state policy of these learning goals, especially Goal 2, is that it is no longer sufficient for students to merely know the subjects. They must now be able to demonstrate that they can apply the knowledge and skills they have acquired.

The Student Learning Goals (SLGs) are the foundation for the Essential Academic Learning Requirements (EALRs), (Essential Academic Learning Requirements, Washington State Legislature, 1993) a defined set of content standards for what a student needs to know *and* do in each of the eight subjects identified under the learning goals (reading, writing, communication, mathematics, social studies, science, health and fitness, and arts).

Policy: The State Board of Education
And Graduation Requirements

By law, the State Board of Education has the policy mandate to establish statewide minimum high school graduation requirements. (Authority to set Graduation Requirements, Washington State Legislature, 1997). In 1997, honoring its statutory obligation to "...periodically reevaluate the graduation requirements...," the Board established a Graduation Requirements And Diploma (GRAD) Committee. The committee was directed to review the Board's current graduation requirements and make recommendations about what changes might be necessary to align them with the evolving performance-based education system. The fundamental question was, "What do all students statewide need to know and be able to do, at a minimum, in order to graduate from high school?"

In exercising this policy responsibility, the State Board followed a path most closely aligned with the following definition of **leadership**: "As for the best leaders, the people do not notice their existence. When the best leader's work is done, the people say we did it ourselves." (Lao-Tzu, 6th century Chinese Taoist philosopher). No other state-level education governmental body is perhaps more able to say that when its "...work is done, the people say we did it ourselves."

The State Board of Education is "the people." It is a lay citizen policy body created by the Legislature, itself a lay body elected by citizens statewide. State Board members are elected by citizens (9 members are elected regionally by local school boards, whose members in turn are elected by the citizens in those communities; 1 member, the Superintendent of Public Instruction, is elected by the citizens statewide; and 1 member is elected by private school board members, who in turn are selected by the citizens who avail themselves of this learning option for their children).

Policy: Purpose

Every policy has a purpose. The State Board of Education has defined the purpose of graduation requirements to include: supporting the continuing refinement of the standards and performance-based system of education; encouraging and facilitating local innovation; aligning the requirements with the goal of the Basic Education Act; assuring that the EALRs are taught in the high school curriculum; assuring that students are aware of the connection between their education and potential career opportunities; and assuring that students are provided the opportunity to effectively prepare for the secondary Washington Assessments of Student Learning and earn the Certificate of Mastery (COM), recognizing that the COM, along with other state and local graduation requirements, represents attainment of the knowledge and skills that are minimally necessary for high school graduation. (Purpose of Graduation Requirements, Washington State Legislature, 2000)

Additionally, in adopting the new requirements, the State Board sought to appropriately balance: State-wide public expectations for all graduating students; high, meaningful, and fair requirements every student can meet; and recognition that some students' educational plans may not include college or may include application for admission to a postsecondary institution one year or more after being granted a high school diploma.

Policy: Seeking Balance

This is the balance scale of state-level governance in Washington State: state control on one side, local control on the other. In the public policy arena the tension often involves determining toward which side the balance should tip. The changes adopted by the State Board reflect a thoughtful balance of bringing the graduation requirements into greater alignment with the ongoing emergence of a performance-based education system, while not changing so much as to unduly shake up traditional comfort zones of doing the business of high school education. Finding the right balance in developing good policy is like seeking treasure. If you are not having success, it really just means that you have not yet found with your shovel the right place to dig for the answer. Time and patience will be rewarded.

The more complex the policy issue, the more time should be taken before enactment or adoption. The quality of legislation or rules can suffer when the length of time given to the policy creation process does not afford the kind of in-depth analysis that is warranted. When the motivation to pass a policy exceeds the patience to be more deliberative in developing it, "The impulse to do something...may outweigh the obligation to do the right thing." (David L.Shreve, and Scott A. Liddell (May 1992), *The GM School of Reform*, State Legislatures). Good policy reflects taking the time that is necessary to get it right. It also requires seeking broad public input.

In the case of revising graduation requirements, the stakes for students, parents and educators was too high not to take the necessary time to get it right. Part of the Board's formula for getting it right was to make sure citizens, educators, and students had an opportunity to provide meaningful input. In the Fall of 1997, with work on the EALRs essentially complete, the State Board began a review of its current graduation requirements to determine how, if at all, they should change to align with the state's ongoing education reform effort. In October 2000, the State Board adopted the new graduation requirements and policies following a very open process that included multiple opportunities for public input prior to adoption of the new requirements:

- Eighteen months of GRAD Committee work (the committee met a total of ten times from late 1997 to early August 1999; all meetings were open to the public);
- Eleven public forums conducted around the state from October 1999 to April 2000 (The GRAD Committee's initial recommendations were shared in forums specifically organized to take advantage of small group breakout discussions of common questions, and at the end of each evening an opportunity was provided for a large group question and answer session; the notes of every small discussion group from every forum was placed on the State Board of Education web site for public view); and
- Six months of State Board work, including three public opportunities for comment during the rules adoption process.

Student input was particularly important to the GRAD committee and the State Board:

- In early November 1998, the State Board helped sponsor a Student Forum on Graduation Requirements. The forum was the idea of Ms. Emily Carlson, who at the time was a sophomore at Olympic High School in the Central Kitsap School District (Kitsap County).
- The GRAD Committee was presented with the findings of a statewide survey of students on graduation requirements. The survey was the senior project for Ms. Erin Hales. At the time she was a student representative on the State Board of Education and a senior at River Ridge High School in the North Thurston School District (Thurston County).
- In October 1999, the full State Board of Education was presented a graduation requirements survey conducted by students in the Family, Career, and Community Leaders of America (FCCLA) program at Selah High School in the Selah School District (Yakima County).

I will state the obvious: not all policymakers think alike, nor do the citizens they represent. The diversity of views and opinions is the fundamental strength of our representative form of government. It should, and most often does, generate compromise (i.e., balance) in developing policy on complex issues. "Democracy is not designed for you to win over me, or for me to win over you. It's designed for each of us to have a reasonable part of the solution and to feel included and valued for that solution." (Steve Peace, former California State Senator [no date]) The premise used in developing the revised requirements was to develop a framework that would respect and balance both state interests and the need of school districts for flexibility and local control.

The full set of graduation requirements for the graduating Class of 2008 (Washington State Minimum High School Graduation Requirements, Washington State Legislature, 2000) can be found on the SBE web site: www.sbe.wa.gov. The Board also wanted to make changes that would contribute to a more meaningful diploma. Toward these purposes two new requirements and a related policy were adopted:

- The Culminating Project is added as a non-credit bearing graduation requirement (non-credit bearing at the state level; districts/schools may attach local credit at their discretion). Each student shall complete a culminating project for graduation, consisting of demonstrating learning competencies and preparations related to learning goals three and four. It is intended to be a student's authentic demonstration of competencies, show the student's educational progress over time, and be focused on a topic of particular interest to the student. Districts have virtual carte blanche authority to determine how they will implement this new requirement. This requirement was established by the State Board so that Student Learning Goal #4 would be reflected in the set of state minimum graduation requirements. State Board and SPI staff brought together a number of high schools with longstanding experience with culminating projects and developed comprehensive implementation guidelines (not mandates) that are on the SBE web page as resource information.

- The High School+ Education Plan (also referenced as the "Diploma and Beyond Plan") is added as a graduation requirement (non-credit bearing at the state level; districts/schools may attach local credit at their discretion). Students shall have an education plan for their high school experience, including what they expect to do the year following graduation. Again, districts have been granted maximum flexibility in determining how this requirement will be implemented. At its heart, the high school+ education plan is a skills acquisition requirement. It is about the skill of setting a goal, identifying the steps, strategies, and timeline to achieve the goal, and then go for it.

NOTE: The Certificate of Mastery (COM) graduation requirement has also been established by the Washington State Legislature. The State Board has targeted the 2007-08 school year as the date when the COM becomes an official graduation requirement (Class of 2008). This target date will take effect *subject* to a finding by the State Board that the high school Washington Assessments of Student Learning (WASL) are sufficiently valid and reliable for meeting the COM graduation requirement. This decision is targeted for mid-2004.

Beyond the changes to the graduation requirements, the State Board also adopted an important related policy regarding how high school credit is awarded. Currently, a high school credit is awarded for 150 hours of planned instructional activities approved by the school district (i.e., the Carnegie Unit). The Carnegie Unit has not been eliminated and districts may continue to award credit using this option. Now, however, school districts have the option of awarding high school credit based on clearly identified competencies that are locally determined through written district policy and not tied to a specific number of hours of instruction. (Awarding High School Credit, Washington State Legislature, 2000). This new grant of authority, not binding on districts, is intended to push the envelope of performance-based education and help districts create curriculum that is more meaningful, hands-on, and experiential for students. Competency-based credit should facilitate recognition of student effort and learning outside of school, and that students learn at different rates.

Policy: Leadership and Statesmanship

Statesmanship is a special brand of leadership. It is the exercise of wisdom in the management of public affairs that emanates from promoting the public interest and while so doing not worrying about the risk of losing office. In our representative form of government, the easiest trap to fall into is to gain power and then not act boldly for fear of losing it. The statesman and stateswoman operate at a higher level of public service. The person who is not willing to gamble, or is unable to gamble more than they can afford to lose, should not go to a casino. The person who is not willing to boldly use the power of elected office for the public good, or is averse to using the power of their office because they believe they will risk losing it, should not run for office. Leadership characterized by statesmanship is about the willingness to risk the loss of position and title for a higher goal.

Public education policy is stewardship for the future, not management of "the moment." The revised state minimum high school graduation requirements reflect a State Board focus on what students will need to know and be able to do in this century, not the last. The Board rose above the oft-times adult mentality of staying rooted in old ways of doing business, locked into comfort zones linked to life experiences, and instead focused on getting each student to think in terms of "I can succeed." In essence, the State Board's new graduation requirements policy adopted a philosophy expressed on an AIDS T-Shirt: *"Impossible vs. I'm possible."* (AIDS T-Shirt logo, June 4-10, 2000, 7 days—seen while on a bicycle trip from San Francisco to Los Angeles)

Will some of the changes outlined above impact current curriculum programs? Yes. Should some of these Board decisions have been left to local school board discretion? Maybe. The Board exercised its statutory policy responsibility in a way that met its singular challenge: "What do *all* students statewide need to know and be able to do at a minimum in order to graduate from high school?" The focus had to be on students, providing them a foundation of basic skills and knowledge to allow them the best chance of being successful in their first life choices after graduation. The Board acted responsibly and with the character of statesmanship.

Policy: Heading for Home

In 1993, the Legislature's action was a declaration that Washington State could no longer afford a "common" school system for an emerging, extraordinary age. Washington State is realizing significant progress in its effort to transform the state public education system from one that is time-constant with variable learning expectations, to one that is time-variable with constant learning expectations; a public education system that is student-centered, standards-based, and performance-demonstrated.

The writer believes that Washington State is trying to create the learning equivalent of the track and field **decathlon** (see Table 1).

Table 1

DECATHLON Track and Field	DECATHLON Learning
You compete against performance standards—not other students per se.	You compete against performance standards—not other athletes per se.
At every meet,the primary goal is to improve your personal best in each event.	At every assessment opportunity, the primary goal is to improve your personal best in each performance area.
At every meet,your "standing" relative to the other athletes takes care of itself.	At every assessment opportunity,your "standing" relative to the other students takes care of itself.
You control how hard you work and practice in preparation for each meet.	You control how hard you work and study in preparation for each performance assessment opportunity.
You do not control how hard the other athletes work and practice.	You do not control how hard the other students work and study.

Larry Davis – Executive Director – State Board of Education – Updated November 2002

The public education system that is evolving is focused on getting each student to his or her "A" level of performance against the backdrop of common learning standards and higher learning expectations. A young student put it best, "You taught me my best was a lot higher than I thought it was." (A student to Rafe Esquith, 1992 Disney Teacher of the Year.)

The State Board of Education used its policy-making authority to bring together a number of threads to weave a new fabric of graduation requirements (and related policies) that are intended to help support each student in her/his preparation for life beyond high school. The new graduation requirements are aligned with the overall goal of the state's Basic Education Act, which is "...to contribute to their own economic well-being and to that of their families and communities, and to enjoy productive and satisfying lives." This goal can be linked to the 1978, Washington State Supreme Court decision to uphold the landmark Judge Doran (1977) school funding verdict. The Supreme Court opinion states, in part,

> ...the State's constitutional duty goes beyond mere reading, writing and arithmetic. It also embraces broad educational opportunities needed in the contemporary setting to equip our children for their role as citizens and as potential competitors in today's market as well as in the marketplace of ideas. Education plays a critical role in a free society. It must prepare our children to participate intelligently and effectively in our open political system to ensure that system's survival. It must prepare them to exercise their First Amendment freedoms both as sources and receivers of information; and, it must prepare them to be able to inquire, to study, to evaluate and to gain maturity and understanding. The constitutional right to have the State 'make ample provision for the education of all [resident] children' would be hollow indeed if the possessor of the right could not compete adequately in our open political system, in the labor market, or in the marketplace of ideas. (Judge Doran, 1977)

The new graduation requirements and related policies reflect a vision for an unfolding future for our children that is different than what was imagined when we were growing up. The new requirements and policies are aligned with the goal of having a positive impact on student learning, with promoting a curriculum that is relevant to students, with giving students greater responsibility for determining their learning opportunities and goals, supportive of the human nature of learning, and reflective of three lessons from the *Wizard of Oz:*

- Encouraging each student to stretch their **brain** power, so that each becomes a critical, questioning thinker, thereby enhancing the likelihood that his or her potential to realize success is maximized as their future unfolds during and beyond high school.
- Encouraging each student to have a strong **heart**, for compassion and understanding that student diversity - human diversity - is to be celebrated and cherished while recognizing that within diversity there are also common hopes, dreams, and values.
- Encouraging each student to have the **courage** to learn through the journey of exploration and discovery; to have the courage to try, risk; knowing that to do so will lead to growth and first-time success in learning, as well as second-time-around learning resulting from so-called "failure."

In sum, the new graduation requirements policy responds to a simple truth, "The world changes, so must students' preparation to meet it." (Council for Basic Education, *Perspective*, Vol. 4, No. 1, Winter 1991)

Policy: Wrap Up

Washington State's new graduation requirements are an important, significant step forward. Washington students can and will have a more substantive high school experience. There should be no doubt that the combination of Student Learning Goals, EALR-aligned curriculum, instruction, and assessment, the culminating project, and high school+ education plan will produce profoundly stronger high school graduates. The State Board is convinced that the new requirements and policies will make the diploma inherently more meaningful for students. The requirements must be viewed for what they represent — a threshold level of knowledge and skills intended to enable graduating students to move onward with the self-confidence that they will be successful in the continued learning they will experience in life, regardless of their post-graduation plans.

Time to come full circle: Public policy is about an onion, fabric, a Chinese proverb, the *Wizard of Oz*, Bob Dylan, vision, leadership, purpose, a shovel, a balance scale, statesmanship, and the decathlon. The Board's policy work on the revised graduation requirements was thoughtful, inclusive, appropriately visionary, and statesmanlike, all of which support the Board's vision,

"The State Board of Education is a respected leader and trusted partner in developing schools and programs that prepare each student for their future,"

the Board's mission,

*"Providing leadership, support, and advocacy, through policy,
so that each student achieves success in school and life,"*

and the Board's unofficial motto,

"Making decisions to improve the quality of education for kids."

References

AIDS T-Shirt logo (June 4-10, 2000). *Impossible vs. I'm possible.* Seen on a 7-day bicycle trip from San Francisco to Los Angeles.

Authority to Set Graduation Requirements (Fall, 1997). Washington State Legislature, (RCW 28A.230.090). Retrieved from the Washington State Legislature website at: http://222.leg.wa.gov/rcw/index.cfm

Awarding High School Credit (n.d.). Washington Administrative Code, (WAC 180-51-050(1)). Retrieved from the Washington State Legislature website at: http://www.leg.wa.gov/wac/

Basic Education Act (1977). Washington State Legislature,(RCW 28A.150.210). Retrieved from the Washington State Legislature website at: http://www.leg.wa.gov/rew/index.cfm

Competency-based award of high school credit. Washington Administrative Code. (WAC 180-51-050(1)(b)). Retrieved from the Washington State Legislature website: http://www.leg.wa.gov.was/

Council for Basic Education. The world changes...*Perspective*, Vol.4, No.1, Winter 1991.

Dylan, B. (1963). *The times, they are a changing.*[Record]. New York: Columbia.

Doran, R.J. (March 17, 1977). *Respondents v. The State of Washington et al, Appellants.* Thurston County Superior Court. Case No. 53950. Seattle School District No.1, et al.

Education Improvement Act of 1993. Washington State Legislature, (RCW 28A.655) (E2SHB 1209, Chapter 336, Laws of 1993). Retrieved from the Washington State Legislature website at: http://www.leg.wa.gov/rcw/index.cfm

Essential Academic Learning Requirements (EALRs). Retrieved from the Superintendent of Public Instruction (OSPI) website at: http://www.k12.wa.us/curriculuminstruct/ealrs.asp

Four Student Learning Goals. Washington State Legislature, (RCW 28A.150.210). Retrieved from the Washington State Legislature website at: http://www.leg.wa.gov/rcw/index.cfm

LeRoy, M. (Producer), & Fleming, V. (Director). (1939). *The Wizard of Oz* [Motion Picture]. United States: Metro-Goldwyn-Meyer

Merriam-Webster (online) Dictionary. Retrieved July 2, 2002, from http://www.m-w.com/home.htm

New graduation requirements (2000). Washington Administrative Code, (WAC 180-51-061) Retrieved from the Washington State Legislature website at:http://www.leg.wa.gov/wac/

Peace, S. (n.d.) *Democracy is not designed...*Legislative District 40, San Diego County.

Purpose of Graduation Requirements. (2000). Washington Administrative Code (WAC 180-51-003). Retrieved from the Washington State Legislature website at: http://www.leg.wa.gov/wac/

Revised Goal of Basic Education and Student Learning Goals (1993). Washington State Legislature (RCW 28A.150.210) (E2SHB 1209, Chapter 336, Laws of 1993) Retrieved from the Washington State Legislature website at: http://www.leg.wa.gov/rcw/index.cfm

Shreve, D.L., and Liddell, S.A. (May 1992). *The impulse to do something...* The GM School of Reform, State Legislatures.

Washington State Board of Education (SBE) website: www.sbe.wa.gov

Washington State Minimum High School Graduation Requirement. Washington Administrative Code, (WAC 180-51-061). Effective Fall, 2004 for entering ninth graders. Retrieved from the Washington State Legislature website at: http://www.leg.wa.gov/wac/

Washington State Supreme Court (September 28, 1978). *Seattle School District vs. State of Washington.* 2d 476, 585 P.2d 71, Case Number: 44845 Vol. 4, No. 1, (Winter 1991).

Chapter Fourteen

The False Promise of the Diploma: One District's Approach to Improving the System for All Students

Julie Goldsmith

Abstract

In this chapter, the author establishes the importance of rethinking the traditional system for earning a high school diploma and reviews the current trends in education and employment for the United States. Considerable discussion, with the aid of charts, helps to establish the fundamental need for each high school student to attain a set of skills that can be applied in a variety of settings. The author highlights how one district is changing from a time-based to a performance-based system for determining when a student has met graduation requirements. This evolutionary step simply means *that a student must know and be able to do certain things* in order to receive a diploma. That is, only by evolving to a performance-based system of requirements can we ensure the best chance for success by our graduates as they pursue post-high school challenges — whether in further education, vocational education, military service, or in the workforce.

What does the current high school diploma represent for our graduates? Guaranteed entrance into a 2 or 4-year college? An adequate set of skills that will transfer into a vocational training program? Assurance that the young person will not require remedial courses to enter postsecondary training? Guaranteed entrance into the Armed Forces? The answer to these questions is quite troubling. In reality, a high school diploma does not represent much. The confidence in a high school diploma is minimal with the people who receive the graduates at the next level. According to a survey by Public Agenda in 2000, confidence that a diploma represents that students have "learned the basics" tends to diminish with respondents closer to the receiving end of the graduates. Seventy-seven percent of students, seventy-four percent of teachers, and sixty-six percent of parents say the diploma means students have learned the basics. Unfortunately, thirty-nine percent of employers and only thirty-three percent of college professors make this same claim.

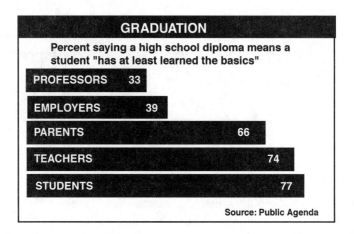

The challenge for educators is to closely examine what is currently being expected of students to learn during high school and then start adding or deleting proficiencies to align with what is being expected after graduation. Schools cannot operate in isolation of the institutions and establishments to which students will be transitioning.

Why shift to new graduation requirements?

To meet the demands of the 21st Century, educators must focus on the traditional basics of reading, writing, and mathematics, but they must also include a focus on higher levels of thinking, communication and technology. Students will need these skills to succeed in this changing world. By any number of criteria, our students will have to meet higher expectations. For example, 80 percent of jobs available to young people after leaving high school will require high-level skills. This is a dramatic shift in the workplace. In the 1950's only 20 percent of the workforce was comprised of skilled (requiring a high school diploma and additional training) or professional (requiring a college or professional degree) workers and 60 percent were unskilled (high school graduates or dropouts). Today, the percentage of professional jobs has remained constant, but the percentage of skilled jobs has more than tripled. The need for unskilled labor has dropped to only 15 percent of the total workforce.

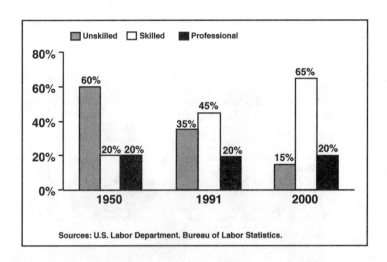

Sources: U.S. Labor Department. Bureau of Labor Statistics.

Until 1960, more than one-third of all the production jobs in the United States were held by high school dropouts. As late as 1973, education and employment were only loosely related. In that era, students with or without high school diplomas, particularly males, could get fairly decent jobs in the manufacturing economy. Widely available blue-collar jobs paid attractive wages and benefits (often with union support), supported families, bought vacation homes, and put the children of working men and women through college. Those jobs are gone. And those days are gone. According to the Bureau of Labor Statistics, education and training are the keys to employment in the future.

The requirements for success in virtually every career path have changed dramatically. New types of occupational fields have emerged, and numerous jobs are obsolete. At the same time, the vast majority of new and existing jobs have become more complex. High performance workplaces stress teamwork and a broader knowledge base for all workers to allow them to adapt to rapidly changing technology and structures.

We also know that education and training pay. The statistics from the United States Census Bureau (2000) demonstrate that the median income goes up with additional training and education. In reverse, the less training or education a person has, the more likely they are to face unemployment. In 1998, full-time workers aged 25 and over, with a professional degree, had a median income of $72,700 and an unemployment rate of 1.3 percent. A person with Bachelor's degree had a median income of $40,100 with an unemployment rate of 1.9 percent. The high school graduate saw an income of $26,000 with an unemployment rate of 4 percent. And finally, a person without a high school degree had a median income of $19,700 and an unemployment rate of 7.1 percent.

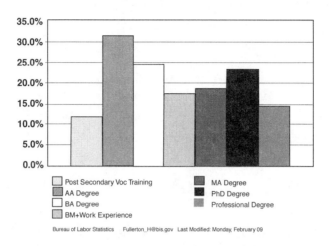

Bureau of Labor Statistics   Fullerton_H@bis.gov   Last Modified: Monday, February 09

A Better Promise: Putting Integrity into the Diploma

The Lake Washington School District in Redmond, Washington is one district that has established graduation standards focused on what students should know and be able to do. Past graduation requirements have focused on the time students spent in the classroom (150 hours per credit). In the Lake Washington School District system, the instruction, assignments, and assessments of student achievement are focused squarely on what and how well students are learning. Teachers, students, and parents have clearer expectations for achievement. These graduation standards are clearly defined expectations against which individual student achievement and progress may be judged. They outline what a student needs to know—and do—in a particular subject.

To graduate, students must demonstrate proficiency in five core areas that are measured by specific district-wide criteria. Students will be given multiple chances and individualized support to show they can meet the standards. Safety nets are currently established, beginning in the primary grades, to support students who are struggling with the established district standards. By clearly defining what students should know and be able to do, teachers have goals to guide them in both curriculum and teaching strategies. There is a fundamental shift from focusing on the specific content of individual courses to how courses prepare and equip students with the skills and knowledge they need to graduate from high school. Extensive teacher and student resource tools accompany the new graduation standards to help every district member shift goals and strategies. All of these materials are available for use by other districts and may be ordered through the district's Curriculum Department, through the website, http://www.lkwash.wednet.edu/lwsd/html/programs/curriculum/level_5.asp

The district will begin replacing Carnegie units with performance-based graduation standards starting with the class of 2005. To ensure connections with higher education, transcripts will provide traditional data as well as student performance on the graduation standards. In addition, the district is working closely with educators in local colleges to ensure that students who have met the standards at high levels of achievement may be placed in upper division college courses without additional placement tests.

To earn a Lake Washington School District diploma, a student would:

1. Pass the Washington State "Certificate of Mastery" (demonstrating competency in mathematics, communication and science) assessed at the end of 10th grade. This will become a requirement as mandated by the State of Washington.
2. Demonstrate basic competency in Social Studies, the Arts, Health/Fitness, School to Career and Life Skills as described by the Lake Washington Curriculum Framework (and measured by district-developed assessments).
3. Demonstrate proficiency, as described by Lake Washington Curriculum Framework and measured by district-developed assessments, in the Advanced Literacies of:
   - Communication,
   - Quantitative and Scientific Reasoning,
   - Citizenship, which includes a Service Learning requirement,
   - Culture, and
   - School to Career and Life Skills, which includes an Education and Career Plan and a Field Experience.
4. Complete a Culminating Project.

Each of the assessments would have three levels of achievement: Proficient, Proficient with Honors and Proficient with High Honors.

Here is an example of what a standard from the Communication learning area looks like:

Writing
A student shall demonstrate the ability to write using grammar, language conventions, and other elements of standard written English for a variety of purposes by writing original compositions that:
   A. describe, narrate, or explain observations of human events or situations,
   B. analyze patterns and relationships of ideas, topics, or themes,
   C. construct support for a position, argument, plan, or idea, and
   D. evaluate an idea, topic, or theme based on expressed criteria.

What does this mean for students?

Students will be involved in relevant hands-on learning activities. Research in many fields shows that activities designed with this approach are an excellent way to learn and remember what has been learned. The new standards acknowledge that knowing and doing must go hand in hand. They stress more math and science than the current requirements. They emphasize technology skills and, for the first time, they include public speaking and career exploration.

The District's new graduation standards set high expectations—and challenges—for all students. They are designed to allow learners to achieve at their own desired level of accomplishment, as long as they meet the proficient standard in each of the five competencies. Most importantly, students will have the ability to design a program of study that will help them to transition to additional education/training or the workforce after graduation.

What are the safeguards for students in special populations?

Currently, special consideration is required in the procedures for granting high school graduation credits for students with special education needs (WAC 180-51-115). With the new graduation standards, special consideration is still provided. Each student's Individual Educational Plan (IEP) will guide the student's requirements for graduation. Most importantly, the IEP should outline what skills the student needs to transition to work or additional training programs after high school.

Developing a Set of Beliefs about High School

Key to this process was the development of a set of beliefs about high school to guide the vision. If community members did not have a common set of beliefs and vocabulary about high school, change would become difficult in the long run. With a common set of beliefs and a vision about high school, the district could avoid the pitfall of many a failed movement for change: indifference and mistrust.

District personnel worked with teachers, students and parents. The yearlong process involved many public meetings, staff meetings, and drafting and revising until a final set of beliefs was agreed upon. An implementation and assessment plan was later developed with the high school principals, who have included the implementation of the beliefs into each high school's academic achievement plan.

The beliefs include:
1. Students require meaningful schoolwork that is actively engaging and demonstrates learning in authentic ways. This work is purposeful, and both teacher and student can articulate why this work is important to a student's progress.
2. Students need to be educated for, and individually guided toward, a successful transition to life after high school.
3. Students learn best from a personalized education that challenges them to achieve their potential.
4. Programs of study should be interconnected and build upon previous learning experiences.
5. Students should build upon their fundamental skills and knowledge beyond the Certificate of Mastery performance levels.
6. Students have a right to excellent schools that deliver a dynamic curriculum and outstanding teaching as measured by student performance according to clear standards.
7. Students have a right to, and a responsibility for, a school environment that honors diversity and promotes good citizenship, mutual respect and strength of character.
8. Parent and community members have a civic obligation to support and enrich and to be actively involved in student learning. Educators have an obligation to encourage parent involvement.

Engaging the Public

Critical to the development of new graduation standards was the involvement of parents and teachers. Through community involvement in an open dialogue about high schools, district educators created the capacity for change; they undertook the task of redesigning high schools to serve as learning communities, where students must demonstrate the academic achievements of a world-class education.

The Result

This change has had a profound impact on the structure and design of Lake Washington School District's high schools. Educators in other school districts can replicate this process by engaging their staffs and communities in a discussion about what the current high school diploma means. District educators need to: ask fundamental questions; provide a safe and comprehensive process to gather ideas and feedback; incorporate the input into the district's plans; find the courage to implement real change; and then support staff members in implementing strategies to reach new achievement levels.

For the Lake Washington School District, the above process resulted in the development of a new set of graduation standards that:
- are performance-based and not based on the Carnegie unit for graduation;
- use the state benchmarks and the Lake Washington School District *Curriculum Framework for Secondary Education (2002)* as a foundation for learning;
- are designed to meet the needs of the future world of work, which is increasingly multicultural and high tech;
- are designed to help students transition smoothly to life after high school: college, military, work, or home;
- are based on current research about learning and brain theory;
- will ensure all students graduate proficient in their fundamental skills by setting clear standards;
- were written with input from all key stakeholders in the process;
- will allow students to distinguish themselves as learners by setting standards for graduating in the five Advanced Literacies at the proficient, proficient with honors and proficient with high honors levels.

Conclusion

High school educators have long been in the business of preparing students for an uncertain future. Educators in the Lake Washington School

District have undertaken the task of redesigning high schools so that they serve as learning communities, where students must demonstrate the academic achievements of a world-class education. By involving the community in an open dialogue about high schools, performance standards and the future world of work, the district has created the capacity for change. Its students must transition to a competitive world marketplace that is increasingly high tech, where the skills of being a life-long learner are crucial. By laying a foundation in the fundamental skills and Advanced Literacies of Communication, Quantitative and Scientific Reasoning, Citizenship, Culture, and School-to-Career and Life Skills, all Lake Washington School District students will be equipped to transition to a new world of possibility. The high school diploma, once again, will have meaning and integrity.

References

Bureau of Labor Statistics, (2001). *Median earnings for year-round, full-time workers age 25 and over, by educational attainment.* Retrieved February 12, 2002 from http://www.dol.gov/dol/topic/wages/educational.htm

Davis, A., & Felknor R. (1994, March). The demise of performance-based graduation in Littleton. *Educational Leadership*, 64-65.

Lake Washington School District, (2002).*Curriculum framework for secondary education.* Redmond, WA: Lake Washington School District Printing Center.

Lake Washington School District, (2003). *New graduation standards for the class of 2005.* Retrieved on January 5, 2003, from http://www.lkwash.wednet.edu/lwsd/html/programs/curriculum/level_5.asp

National Center on Education and the Economy, (1990). *America's choice: High skills or low wages!* Washington, D.C.: Author.

Public Agenda Online, (2000). *Reality check.* Retrieved on March 10, 2002, from http://www.publicagenda.org/specials/rc2000/reality2.htm

United States Census Bureau, (2000). *American fact finder.* Retrieved February 12, 2002, from http://factfinder.census.gov/servlet/BasicFactsServlet?_lang=en

Washington State Legislature, (2002). Washington Administrative Code (WAC) 180-51-115 *Procedures for granting high school graduation credits for students with special educational needs*. Retrieved February 12, 2002, from http://www.leg.wa.gov/wac/

Washington State Workforce Training and Education Coordinating Board (WTECB), (2002). *High skills, high wages – Washington's strategic plan for workforce development*. Olympia, WA: Author.

Chapter Fifteen

Culminating Projects: Providing Real World Relevance and Rigor

Bridgette Belasli

Abstract

College admissions officers are no longer relying on SAT scores and grades alone to determine which students should enter their programs. They are beginning to look at essays, portfolios, service learning, internships, and other performance-based projects. Employers and university staffs alike indicate that students need to be able to bring complex ideas together and to demonstrate time management and goals-setting skills. Thus, many districts are adopting culminating project requirements for all graduating students, which may provide a vehicle for exploring career pathways, developing connections to the community, fostering intrinsic motivation in students, and providing real world relevance and rigor in student work. Twenty models around the country are presented, with permission from the Lake Washington School District (Redmond, Washington). Ideas are shared to help educators with the implementation of culminating projects, along with a checklist of activities to consider. Resources, email addresses of educators, and websites have also been included in the Appendix.

What is a Culminating Project?

A culminating project is an innovative practice, now endorsed not only at the state level (e.g., the Washington State Board of Education), but also at the district level, that may help students to focus on their plans after high school. It is a student-centered project that takes place over a period of time. It requires that students explore their interests to develop a project that applies their learning to a real world setting in a rigorous and relevant manner. In general, a culminating project requires an initial proposal by the student (to do the project), a research component, a final product, sometimes a related internship, and a presentation by the student to a panel. Strong culminating project programs often require students to have a mentor or advisor from the school or community to assist them with their project. State Boards of Education as well as school districts across the United States are now requiring that students complete such a project prior to graduation.

The Power of the Culminating Project

Many university admissions officers no longer rely on SAT scores and grades alone to determine which students enter their programs. These institutions are0 beginning to look at essays, portfolios, service learning, internships and other performances in which students may distinguish themselves. A culminating project represents the culmination of a K-12 education. An in-depth examination of a topic requires that students do extensive research using a wide variety of resources. Such extensive research requires that students understand and organize information from a variety of sources, interpret this information in a meaningful way, and communicate this meaning to others. Culminating projects can serve to provide the student with a portfolio of work to display to a prospective university or to a prospective employer. Students may explore or gain field experience (a job shadow or internship experience) through a culminating project or they may incorporate service learning (a volunteer experience) into a culminating project.

Employers and university admission officers alike indicate that students need to be able to bring complex ideas together in order to be successful. "If students go through school just memorizing names and numbers, they're not learning the skills they need to be successful in the 21st century world. Students need to learn application and thinking skills," according to Will Garner of the Boeing Commercial Aircraft Company. Students also need to demonstrate time management and goal-setting skills as well as researching, problem-solving, and decision-making. These are the same skills that students need for academic and workplace success.

Students who complete a culminating project are prepared for the "culminating projects" that adult life requires. Planning a wedding, remodeling a house, and building a retirement nest egg all require the same skills that a high school culminating project requires: time management, goal-setting, researching, problem-solving and decision-making. The world of work requires the same skills in order to complete goals, be it designing a rocket booster, arguing a court case, or framing a house. Culminating projects often give students their first glimpse of a career path, as students often choose projects related to career interests, such as building a robot, holding an art exhibit, or assisting a physician researching cancer genes. The mission of culminating projects is to give students the skills to successfully navigate adult life, both personal and professional.

Culminating projects provide a vehicle for developing connections to the community. Students develop connections with a mentor, advisor, or other adult. By tailoring projects to a student's strengths, passions and interests, school staffs personalize the learning task so that students can build lifelong, permanent connections to their learning and career interests.

Culminating projects also foster intrinsic motivation in students, and provide real world relevance and rigor to student work. Eastlake teacher Stephanie Monaghan (1997) notes that giving students choices about what they are learning creates many benefits. By looking at the research on intrinsic motivation, Monaghan noted that students are less likely to find a learning experience meaningful when another person has contrived the situation or rationale for learning. "Meaningful learning is more likely to occur when students engage with the subject matter for its own sake, not for that of an extrinsic demand"(Boud, 1990). Monaghan also observed that when students are intrinsically motivated to learn, they spend more time thinking deeply about the topic to be learned and are more motivated to solve problems and issues about the topic. "There is a link between intrinsic motivation and higher order thinking skills" (Guthrie et al., 1996). Monaghan felt this was particularly true for students who have learning disabilities. Her observations are corroborated by Dev (1997) who notes that:

> Academic intrinsic motivation is significantly correlated to achievement for students with learning disabilities. Performance-based assessment with real world emphasis seems to be the best way to develop intrinsic motivation in these learners.

Culminating projects foster intrinsic motivation in students by their very design. That is, they may provide personalized learning experiences with connections to the community on student-centered projects based on real world, relevant and rigorous topics.

Students must do more than simply memorize information and procedural steps in order to be prepared for a successful transition to the adult world. According to Gardner (1993):

> Individuals in the real world are rarely, if ever, asked to diagram sentences, draw a color wheel, complete an isolated analogy, or fill in the pieces of a mathematical formula...instead they are expected to pursue projects over time, collaborate and converse

with others, to take responsibility for their own work, amplify their understandings, and apply them in powerful ways or in new and surprising contexts.

Thus, it is important that educators provide curriculum that has real world relevance and rigor. Students need to understand how what they learn in the classroom applies to events in the real world. Students want to know their school-time learning activities are important to their everyday lives. Their motivation comes from making those connections and understanding that the work they are doing is of importance to their lives. According to Calkins (1990):

> If we asked our students for the highlight of their school careers, most would choose a time when they dedicated themselves to an endeavor of great importance... on projects such as these youngsters will work before school, during lunch, and after school. Our children want to work on endeavors they deem significant.

Such projects also form a rite of passage for students that have valued and powerful results for the student, school, and community. These results might address a genuine problem or need in the school or community. At the same time, learning for the students involved is significant. Once of the most famous examples of the power of culminating projects involved student Hunter Scott in 1998. While doing research for a history project, twelve-year-old Hunter Scott discovered an injustice in American history; he then decided to campaign for rectifying that injustice. Hunter Scott led an initiative to clear the record of a WWII Navy captain who was court-marshaled in a controversial decision after his ship, the USS Indianapolis, was sunk by a Japanese torpedo. The captain later committed suicide. Hunter's project led him to Capitol Hill to have the controversial case reopened (Washington Alliance for Better Schools, 2000). Survivors of the doomed submarine finally received recognition for their bravery and valor in 2001. Students in the Lake Washington School District have developed projects to protect hiking trails from environmental damage, to do volunteer work in senior citizen's homes, to create learning programs for elementary school children, to help the handicapped, and to develop "Students Against Drunk Driving" assemblies for their school. There is no doubt that these experiences have provided benefits for the community far beyond the classroom.

Models

There is no one-size-fits-all model for implementing a culminating project. Each school staff needs to weigh many factors before determining what support structures and resources will work. Each staff will need to explore how much instructional time should be devoted to the project, what the content of the project should contain, how the project will be assessed, how the community will connect with the project, and what support structures are needed to ensure student success.

Table A. Instructional Time

Schools	Instructional Time
Carmichaels Area Senior High School Carmichaels, Pennsylvania	Four-year project. Students meet one period a week with a mentor during a rotating period. No specific number of hours is required.
Cedarcrest High School Duvall, Washington	One semester project during the second semester of senior year. The program is housed in the Social Studies department. The paper is written in Senior English. The students use their advisory teacher (similar to homeroom) as a general mentor to monitor their progress and work with a community mentor in the product portion of the project.
Central Bucks Area High School Doylestown, Pennsylvania	The project takes place over two years. Students are required minimum of 40 hours of work outside the classroom to complete the project.
Council Rock High School Newton, Pennsylvania	One semester junior year course required. Each high school department identifies one course in which a student may complete the project. Students may negotiate the number of hours required to complete the project.
Donegal High School Mount Joy, Pennsylvania	The project is on-going over high school and not tied to one class. Proposal should be presented before the end of the junior year and the project is treated as independent study.

EastlakeHigh School Sammamish, Washington	Students work on the project over a two-semester senior English course known as Senior Connections. A minimum of sixty hours outside of class time is required to complete the project.
Everett School District Everett, Washington	Students take a one-semester Senior Projects course.
Federal Hocking High School Stewart, Ohio	Students take a one semester long Senior Projects class in the spring.
Mountlake Terrace High School Mountlake Terrace, Washington	Students take an independent two-trimester course, not offered in conjunction with another department. Students must complete a project that is 120 hours minimum in time commitment. Students connect with a field expert on their project.
Nogales High School Nogales, Arizona	Students complete the project over a year. Projects are embedded in English and American Government classes.
North and South Medford High SchoolsMedford, Oregon	Basically, this is a year-long course, with a focus on second semester English class.
Northwestern Lehigh High School New Tripoli, Pennsylvania	The student project is a four-year process.
Palo Alto High School Palo Alto, California	Students elect to take a Senior Project class. Students attend weekly seminar meetings.
Palisades High School Kintersville, Pennsylvania	Student takes a one-year Senior Seminar class.
Placer High School Auburn, California	Project is English-based with support from other departments. A coordinated three-year curriculum prepares students for a year-long senior project.
Parkland High School Allentown, Pennsylvania	Students spend two semesters working on the project through a senior homeroom.
Shorecrest High School Seattle, Washington	Students complete the project over their senior year through a Senior Project class.
Sonora High School Sonora, California	Students complete the project over a year. Students must include at least 15 hours outside of class time.

Sumner High School Sumner, Washington	All-staff involvement model. All certified staff, administrators, and counselors shepherd seniors through the year-long process. Students must spend a minimum of 60 hours working on their project.
West Seattle High School Seattle, Wash.	The culminating project takes place during a one semester language arts class for all seniors.

Note: Used with Permission from the Lake Washington School District, Redmond, Washington.

Table B. Project Content

School	Content Requirements
Carmichaels Area Senior HighSchool Carmichaels,Pennsylvania	9th Graders write a preliminary paper. 10th graders write a written proposal. Students must write the research papers between their junior and senior years. Students are required to give an oral presentation.
Cedarcrest High School Duvall, Washington	Second semester seniors create a product and a paper.
Central Bucks Area High School Doylestown, Pennsylvania	A letter of intent, proposal, project inventory, project work record, written component, final product, and oral presentation.
Council Rock High School Newton, Pennsylvania	The project could be in the form of a presentation, demonstration, dialogue, drama, explanation, role play or other. Visual aids are required in the form of technology aids, artwork, demonstrations, or productions. Students must use computer application software and tools of research.
Donegal High School Mount Joy, Pennsylvania	Students are required to write a paper, give a presentation and use visual aids. The student should exhibit the use of technology.
Eastlake High School Sammamish, Washington	Students are required to write a culminating project proposal, a ten-page I-search or Inquiry Paper, and give a presentation using visual aids and technology skills. Students must integrate at least two subject areas.

Everett School District Everett, Washington	Students are required to submit a proposal, write a research paper, give an oral presentation, include their research and an annotated bibliography, and write a reflective paper.
Federal Hocking High School Stewart, Ohio	Students are required to write a proposal, a research paper, a physical product, and letters to their advisors. Students are also required to develop a web page for their project.
Nogales High School Nogales, Arizona	Students are required to write a letter of intent, write a research paper, keep a project portfolio, and present their project. Students also write letters to their judges and self-reflections about their projects.
North and South Medford High Schools Medford, Oregon	Students write a letter of intent, an outline of their project, and a ten-page paper. Their first semester exam is a journal that describes their use of class time during conference weeks. Students complete a private conference and give a presentation.
Mountlake Terrace High School Mountlake Terrace, Wash	Students choose the curriculum through a project proposal. Students choose their own product and are required to present to a panel.
Northwestern Lehigh High School New Tripoli, Penn.	Students write a proposal, write a paper using software, and give an oral presentation. The project may be an individual project or a group project.
Palo AltoHigh School Palo Alto, California	Students write a proposal, write a research paper, develop a product and present to a community panel.
Palisades High School Kintersville, Pennsylvania	Students write a proposal, maintain a log, fill out worksheets, write a research paper and give an oral presentation.
Parkland High School Allentown, Pennsylvania	Students write a proposal, sign contracts, give an oral presentation to a panel of at least three adults, including the project advisor, and include a 4-10 page paper with at least three sources.
Placer High School Auburn, California	First semester (senior year) is centered on mini-research and performance-based projects. In the second semester, students write a letter of intent, a paper, a product, and then present to senior boards.

Shorecrest High School Seattle, Washington	The work consists of writing a proposal, writing a research paper, developing a final product, organizing a portfolio, presenting to a culminating project panel, and writing a reflection paper on the project.
Sonora High School Sonora, California	Students write a letter of intent (project may involve job shadowing or personal growth), write papers, document their progress and present the project.
Sumner High School Sumner, Washington	Students pair up with an advisor in their career advisory. Students write a letter of intent, a research paper, keep learning logs, create a portfolio, and present to a senior board.
West Seattle High School West Seattle, Wash.	Students write a proposal, then a 6-8-page paper with a bibliography, develop a product related to the paper and deliver an 8-12 minute presentation to a panel of judges.

Note: Used with permission from the Lake Washington School District, Redmond, Washington.

Table C. Assessment and Evaluation Practices

School	Assessment and Evaluation
Carmichaels Area Senior High School Carmichaels, Pennsylvania	The project is required to integrate several academic disciplines. There are school-wide rubrics for the presentation and the paper requirements. Mentors keep a Mentor Log of student progress.
Cedarcrest High School Duvall, Washington	Students earn a credit assigned the title "Senior Project." The paper is assessed using the "6+1 Writing Traits' Model." Students are required to self-assess their product with a community mentor. (An "Independent Study" option is created for students who do not pass the project after a second rewrite.) Students are assessed on their presentation to community.
Central Bucks Area High School Doylestown, Penn.	Students are assessed using rubrics for the letter of intent, proposal, project inventory, project work record, written component, final product and oral presentation.

Council Rock High School Newton, Pennsylvania	Each component of the project (written, research, oral, technological, and visual) is required and gives a point value totaling 100. Each component is weighed differently according to each student's unique project. The Project appears on the report card, graded A, B, or C. (The student may redo a below-C project for no higher than a C grade.)
Donegal High School Mount Joy, Pennsylvania	Students complete a self-evaluation and are interviewed. The Evaluation Committee is pre-assigned, interdisciplinary and includes a community member. Projects are evaluated using school-wide rubrics.
EastlakeHigh School, Sammamish, Washington	Proposals, learning logs, papers and self-reflections and a culminating project portfolio are incorporated into the students' English grades. Students are assessed using the "6+1 Writing Traits" and a district-wide presentation rubric. Students must pass the project in order to graduate.
Everett School District Everett Washington	Students are assessed using an oral presentation rubric and research paper rubric.
Federal Hocking High School Stewart, Ohio	Logs, field activity reports, artifacts, self-evaluations, physical project rubrics, and presentation rubrics are required.
Mountlake Terrace High School Mountlake Terrace, Wash	Students choose from a set of rubrics based on their choices in designing their project.
Nogales High School, Nogales, Arizona	Paid evaluators from the local university, who are trained in the "6+1 Writing Traits Model," evaluate student research papers. Presentations are evaluated by community members and teachers in panels. All three components- the research paper, portfolio/project and presentation (speech)- must be completed second semester in English IV and Government classes in order to earn a passing grade on this exhibition. Any student who does not complete all three components will automatically earn an "F" in English IV and an "F" in Government second semester. In order to pass the Senior Exhibition, students must complete all three components of the exhibition and must earn 60% of the total possible points (180/300) for the composite score. The composite score consists of three equal parts: Research paper 100 points; Portfolio/project 100 points; and Presentation 100 points.

North and South Medford High School Medford, Oregon	Students are assessed using specific rubrics for the: project log, self-evaluations, mentor verification, physical evidence, portfolio, written paper and oral presentation.
Northwestern Le-high High School New Tripoli, Penn.	There are checklists for student responsibilities and timelines.
Palo Alto High School Palo Alto, California	Students are assessed using rubrics for the written proposal, research paper, project, and presentation.
Palisades High School Kintersville, Pennsylvania	Students are assessed with a presentation rubric and by log requirements and worksheet requirements.
Parkland High School Allentown, Pennsylvania	Students are assessed using process and product evaluations.
Placer High School Auburn, California	Students are assessed using performance-based evaluations for the paper, product, and presentation.
Shorecrest High School Seattle, Washington	All portions of the culminating project are assessed using performance rubrics. Parents are updated on student progress three times a year. Outstanding projects, chosen by a committee, are recognized during an Awards Night ceremony.
Sonora High School Sonora, California	All work is evaluated using assessment rubrics for the research paper and oral presentation. Community Panels evaluate the presentation.
Sumner High School Sumner, Washington	Work is evaluated through writing rubrics, a performance appraisal, advisor records, and a presentation rubric. Performance appraisal is based on the Secretary's Commission on Achieving Necessary Skills (SCANS).
West Seattle High School Seattle, Washington	All parts of the project are assessed using performance-assessment rubrics and/or checklists.

Note: Used with permission from the Lake Washington School District, Redmond, Washington.

Table D. Community Connections and Support Structures

School	Community Connections and Support Structures
Carmichaels Area Senior High School Carmichaels, Pennsylvania	Project may be completed through business internships, community projects, or entrepreneur projects. All teachers are assigned 9th graders to mentor. Panel is responsible for each student to meet expectations.
Cedarcrest High School Duvall, Washington	Students use advisory teacher (similar to homeroom) as a general mentor to monitor their progress and community mentor in the product portion.
Central Bucks Area High School Doylestown, Pennsylvania	Students are connected to an advisory program.
Council Rock High School Newton, Pennsylvania	Students and parents receive graduation project progress reports.
Donegal High School Mount Joy, Penn.	Each student has a mentor-teacher who monitors the written proposal, study, written work, oral presentation and self-evaluation interview. Each evaluation committee is pre-assigned and includes a community member.
EastlakeHigh School Sammamish, Washington	Each student has a teacher/advisor who monitors student progress and an outside mentor/advisor for their specific project. Students have a pre-assigned review panel of at least three teachers/community members. Since the project is worked on in the Senior Connections class, students also have teacher support from their English teacher. Students have the opportunity to redo the project in order to graduate.
Everett School District Everett, Washington	Each student has a Senior Project teacher and a community panel reviews their work.
Federal Hocking High School Stewart, Ohio	This is a small school. Each student has a senior project teacher to assist him or her. Presentations are open to the community.

Mountlake Terrace High School Mountlake Terrace, Wash	Students connect with a field expert who is qualified to help with the project. (Some students may have more than one field expert.) Students are assisted through a two-trimester Senior Project class.
Nogales High School Nogales, Arizona	Special ESL strategies are in place to support students who speak English as a second language. All students have mentors from the community. English and Government teachers also guide student efforts.
North and South Medford High School Medford, Oregon	Each student has a senior advisor and English teacher to assist him or her.
Northwestern Le-High High School New Tripoli, Pennsylvania	40 staff over 4 years counsel 5 students per year. This provides for 200 students per year to be assigned to staff. Each member will work with a total of 20 students on at least 4 years of the project.
Palo AltoHigh School Palo Alto, California	Students attend weekly seminar meetings and have connections with mentors outside of the school, including business and university mentors from Stanford University.
Palisades High School Kintersville, Penn.	Each student has a Senior Seminar teacher.
Parkland High School Allentown, Pennsylvania	Each student has a senior homeroom teacher. The project advisor may have no more than eight advisees. Project advisors meet at least three times with advisees.
Placer High School Auburn, California	Staff members serve as mentors and board judges. The community also serves as community mentors and board judges. Students complete the project through their English class, required electives, and with support for and support with other departments.
Shorecrest High School Seattle, Washington	Community mentors and panels help connect students to the community and vice versa. Senior Connections teachers teach a required "Senior Project"class to assist students in meeting the standards.

Sonora High School Sonora, California	Students are assisted by their English teachers.
Sumner High School Sumner, Washington	All certified staff, administrators, and counselors assist through advisory. All staff members read letters, research and portfolios while providing students with feedback. Students also work with a community mentor.
West Seattle High School Seattle, Washington	The senior board is made up of community members. The board evaluates presentations; classroom teacher awards a final grade. Students are required to interview at least one person in their research project.

Note: Used with permission from the Lake Washington School District, Redmond, Washington

Resources and Ideas for School Planning

Culminating projects require students to think deeply for an extended period of time about a subject that interests them. In this manner, students become deeply engaged with a topic and explore a variety of career interests and subjects that may, in fact, hold their attention as adults. For example, a high school student may develop a project to assist elementary students in a special education class. As a result, the student may then decide to study special education in college. While some students may discover a passion for a career during the course of a project, others may discover that they are not interested in pursuing that career as a result of their experiences with the culminating project. For example, a student may decide to volunteer in the emergency burn center at a local hospital, thinking that a career in medicine might be interesting. However, after spending time working with severely burned patients, he or she may decide differently. Both experiences, positive and negative, are valuable because they help students direct their interests after high school by allowing them to explore the possibilities.

Table E. Sample Student Projects from Across the Curriculum

Create an art portfolio for art school, including an in-depth study of your favorite style: e.g., surrealism.	Study with a community theatre group and produce your own play.
Translate a famous work from another language into English for publication.	Prepare to run a marathon and then run it, and present your Health and Fitness Plan.
Rebuild a garage as a part of a field experience.	Calibrate a prototype for analytic chemistry equipment.
Design and lead your own school-wide workshop on the dangers of drinking and driving.	Develop a robotics project to participate in a national competition.
Design and patent your own shoe.	Coach a youth soccer team, and then complete a study in youth and motivation.
Work at a local museum as an intern and create a fundraiser for the museum.	Create a book and website of original poetry to publish on-line.
Coordinate and organize a conflict-resolution team at your school.	Research why people commit hate crimes and develop a resource guide for the community.
Create an onstage stand-up comedy routine for a hearing-impaired audience.	Develop a mock or real investment portfolio and investment plan, by researching finance management.
Tutor elementary children in reading and study their progress.	Create an encryption program.

Note: Used with permission from the Lake Washington School District, Redmond, Washington.

Key Questions about Planning the Culminating Project (CP)

These questions, developed by the Lake Washington School District in Redmond, Washington, are meant to spur discussions about various supporting aspects of Culminating Project planning. These are meant to help staff members brainstorm all the issues, so please add or delete questions as necessary.

Numbers:
1) How many students do we have in our school?
2) How many seniors do we have in our school?

3) How many staff members do we have in our school?

Time:
    1) What shall be the length of this project?
       A) One semester
       B) One year
       C) Spread out over two years
       D) Spread out over three years

    2) How much minimum time will students need to successfully complete the project? (40 hours? 60 hours? 120 hours?)
    3) When should students present to a panel? (Once a year, once a semester, etc.)
    4) How shall we schedule panel presentations? (During school day, at night, etc.)
    5) What will other students do during panel presentations?

Staff Support:
    1) Besides the required mentor, how many staff members will be supporting each student?
    2) How many students should each staff member be required to support as a mentor?
    3) Is there a person who would like to volunteer to be the Culminating Project Supervisor?
    4) What would be the role of the Culminating Project Supervisor?
    5) What role could/would homeroom teachers, advisory teachers, or reading period teachers play in the CP?

Auxiliary Support:
    1) What will be the role of administrators in the CP?
    2) What will be the role of school guidance counselors in the CP?
    3) What will be the role of natural helpers, student council, cheerleaders, etc., in the CP?
    4) What will be the role of the PTSA and other parent groups?

Curriculum:
    1) How will student projects be tied to district standards and curriculum frameworks?
    2) Identify classes or a class that already had a lengthy junior/senior project which could be extended or turned into a CP.
    3) Is there a class or are there classes that could serve as the

implementation site for the CP?

4) Could we identify classes across the curriculum, perhaps one in each discipline, where a student could work on the CP?

5) Would we prefer to have the CP be a completely independent project?

6) Could students have the option of completing the CP as an independent project?

7) Could we develop a Senior Project class (one year or semester long) taught by a variety of teachers from across the curriculum?

Skills:

1) What writing processes should be taught previous to the CP and who is going to teach them? When?

2) What research and inquiry skills should be taught previous to the CP and who is going to teach them? When?

3) What presentation skills should be taught previous to the CP and who is going to teach those skills? When?

Communication and the Community:

1) How and when shall we report back student progress?

2) How will we communicate to the community?

3) What will be the role of parents?

4) What will be the role of our local Chamber of Commerce and other business groups?

5) What will be the role of local volunteer organization members ?

Technology and Resources:

1) What will be our policy about technology resources and the CP? (Will seniors have access to computers? When? Why?)

2) How will the library accommodate and support the CP?

3) What information would we like to place on the Internet (school website) about the CP requirements, processes, and products?

Assessment:

1) What process will we put into motion to assess our program after its first year? Fifth year?

2) Who will be involved in the assessing?

3) How often should we assess the school's progress?

Community Involvement

Community members, organizations and businesses may be able to assist students and schools in a variety of ways. There are many options for supporting schools that vary in involvement and level of responsibility.

Table F. A Continuum of Community Involvement in Culminating Project Programs

Role	Responsibilities
Answering Inquiries	Providing time to answer a student phone inquiry, filling out a student survey, answering an e-mail question, or responding to a student letter.
Providing Resources	Providing resources required for culminating projects based on building needs, like the need for cardboard triptychs, markers, paints, borrowed technology (such as a laptop computer, microphone, etc.)
Attending Culminating Exhibitions	Attending Culminating Project presentations and possibly sitting on a panel to judge presentations (once or twice a year). Schools may also need volunteers to greet guests and direct traffic/parking.
Becoming an Advisor	Volunteering time to advise a student on his or her project in a supervised setting an agreed number of times. This is an opportunity to help a student explore career options and learning choices.
Becoming a Mentor	Volunteer to work as a mentor with a student on his or her project over the course of their whole project. This is an opportunity to work closely with a student as he or she explores career options and learning choices.
Providing a Field Experience	Providing a student time to job shadow or observe the organization for a short period of time. Field experiences may lead to jobs and internships.
Providing Internships	Providing a student the opportunity to intern over a period of weeks. Internships may lead to further career opportunities.

Note: Used with permission from the Lake Washington School District, Redmond, Washington.

Conclusion

Adolescence is an age of exploration. High school students need opportunities to explore how their learning in the classroom is connected to real life experiences. They need the opportunity to explore interests and ask questions about topics that are relevant to their life experiences. Students need the opportunity to connect important literacy skills (such as reading, writing, speaking, and researching) to topics that are important to them in their personal lives. College and university admissions officers are seeking to authenticate that their applicants can indeed be successful in working on long-term research projects and in helping to solve problems independently on real-world issues. Employers today are less interested in the student who has memorized a body of knowledge than a student who can analyze, synthesize, and evaluate from that body of knowledge.

By exploring a topic of interest in a culminating project, a student not only has the opportunity to discover a true passion, but also may discover what he or she is *not* interested in pursuing any further. (It is a worthy endeavor in either case.) A student who finds his or her passion in high school will be able to focus the next steps in life with greater ease. A student who discovers that he or she is not interested in pursing a topic any further is able to make the same kind of informed decisions about his or her next steps as the student who does find a genuine interest. Thus, the culminating project is not about forcing students into an early career choice. It is about allowing students the opportunity to explore and discover what possibilities and interests the world may hold for them.

The culminating project experience allows students to demonstrate to the school staff (and to members of local businesses and communities as well as universities and colleges) what advantage they have taken of receiving a K-12 education and how prepared they are for their entrance into the adult world. The workplace may provide culminating projects of every sort—from defending a client in a court case to pouring a new cement driveway. Furthermore, by exploring topics and honing personal strengths, students will develop a better understanding of what options they have after high school. They may learn how to overcome the challenges of long term projects that occur in real life situations, such as on the job—be it designing web pages, developing a community center, landscaping a library, etc.—or in their personal lives—planning weddings, raising their own children, developing family budgets, building houses, pursuing a hobby, or managing retirement. Completion of the culminating project is, in itself, a great achievement and a source of pride for students, regardless of possible long-term benefits. Yet, as has been suggested, the long-term benefits can also be substantial.

Appendix I: Resources for Further Information

Aglio, S. *The graduation project plan*. (Available from the Carmichaels Area School District, 225 North Vine Street, Carmichaels, PA 15320)

Council Rock School District. *Graduation requirement graduation project*. (Council Rock High School)

Donegal School District. *High school graduation project requirements teacher handbook*. (Available from the Donegal School District, PA)

Eastlake High School. (1999). *Culminating project*. (Available from Eastlake High School, 400 228th NE, Redmond, WA 98053)

Federal Hocking High School. (September, 1999). *Senior exhibition program*. (Available online at: http://www.seorf.ohio.edu/~xx008/hide/senproj97/senproj.html)

Gonsalves & Schecter. *Palisades High School senior graduation project*. (Available from Palisades High School, 35 Church Hill Road, Kintersville, PA 18930

Harbison, E., & Mclean, C. (1997). Graduation project student manual. (Available from Central Bucks High School West, 375 W. Court St., Doylestown, PA 18901)

Harm, D. *Pennsbury graduation project*. (Available from Pennsbury School District, 134 Yardley Avenue, PO Box 338, Fallsington, PA 19058-0338)

Henry M. Jackson High School. (September, 1999). *Senior project*. (Available from Henry M. JacksonHigh School, 1508, 136th St. SE, Mill Creek, WA 98012) (Available online at: http://www.everett. wednet.edu/schools/high/hmjackson/curriculum/senproject/html)

Jennelle, A., Laws, N., & Stone, W. (1999). *Central Bucks School District graduation project guide*. (Available from Central Bucks High School West, 375 W. Court St., Doylestown, PA 18901)

Lake Washington School District (2000). *Culminating project teacher support packet.* (Available from Lake Washington School District, PO Box 97039, Redmond, WA 98073-9739).

Lake Washington School District (2000). *Student guide to the culminating project.* (Available from Lake Washington School District, PO Box 97039, Redmond, WA 98073-9739).

Northwestern Lehigh High School. *High school project.* (Available from the Northwestern Lehigh School District, New Tripoli, PA)

Osher, C. & Summers, J. (September, 1999). *Far West EDGE senior projects.* (Available online at: http://www.internetcds.com/Business/WesEDGE/senior.htm).

Palo Alto High School. (1996-1998). *Palo Alto High School senior project exhibitions.* (Available from Palo Alto High School, Palo Alto, CA)

Parkland High School. (1995). *The high school project.* (Available from Parkland High School, 2675 PA Rt. 309, Orefield, PA 18069-9773)

Sonora High School. (1999). *Sonora High School Senior project student handbook.* Available: http://www.sonorahs.k12.ca.us/

Sylvester, R. (1995). *A celebration of neurons: An educator's guide to the human brain.* Alexandria, Virginia: Association for Supervision and Curriculum Development.

Thomson, G (2000). *Nogales Senior High School exhibition.* (Available at: http://www.nusd.k12.az.us/nhs/sp.main.page.html

Wiggins. G. (1993). *Assessing student performance: Exploring the purpose and limits of testing.* U.S.A.: Jossey-Bass Publishing.

Wisely, S. *Medford North and South High Schools senior project.* (Available from Dr. Steven Wisely, Sup't., Medford Public Schools, 500 Monroe Street, Medford, OR 97501)

Appendix II: E-mail Contacts

Duda, Mike. Placer High School. Auburn, California. Senior Project Coordinator. Mike Duda is an experienced high school English teacher who has presented nationally with Far West Edge on Culminating Project programs. mduda@placer.puhsd.k12.ca.us.

Eguchi, Linda. Shorecrest High School. Seattle, Washington. Linda Eguchi is a 30+year veteran family and consumer science teacher. She initiated senior projects at Shorecrest High School in 1992 and serves as the project coordinator. She recently received the 2001 Christa McAuliffe Washington Award for Excellence in Education. linda.eguchi@shorelineschools.org.

Garrison, Perry. Cedarcrest High School. Duvall, Washington. Perry Garrison is a former Social Studies teacher and currently the librarian at Cedarcrest High School. He is the chair of the Culminating Project Committee. garrison@chs.riverview.wednet.edu.

Hill, Fran. Mountlake Terrace High School. Seattle, Washington. Fran Hill is a family and consumer science teacher and the project coordinator for the last five years. HillF@Edmonds.wednet.edu.

Monaghan, Stephanie. Eastlake High School. Sammamish, Washington. Stephanie Monaghan has been the Culminating Project Coordinator at Eastlake High School for the last eight years. She is an English teacher and a teacher on special assignment in the district. Stephanie also serves as a consultant to school districts on integrated thematic curriculum and project-based learning. smonaghan@lkwash.wednet.edu.

Niemann, Dianne. Sumner High School. Sumner, Washington. Dianne has been the senior project coordinator for nine years. For the past five years she has presented nationally with Far West Edge at conferences on many aspects of culminating projects, including: Advanced Placement students and the culminating project; providing strategies for adding sophistication to existing culminating projects; setting up all-staff advisories; and troubling shooting existing systems.
dianne_niemann@sumner.wednet.edu.

References

Boud, D. (1990). Assessment and the promotion of academic values. *Studies in Higher Education*, 15(1), 101-111.

Calkins, L. (1990). *Living between the lines*. USA: Irwin Publishing.

Daniels, H., Hyde, D., & Zemmelman, S. (1993). *Best practices for teaching and learning in America's schools*. U.S.A: Reed Publishing.

Dev, P. (1997). Intrinsic motivation and academic achievement: What does their relationship imply for the classroom teacher? *Remedial and Special Education* 18(1), 12-19.

Gardner. H. (1993). *Frames of mind: The theory of multiple intelligences*. U.S.A.: Basic Books.

Guthrie, J. et al. (1996). The effects of autonomy on motivation and performance in the college classroom. *Contemporary Educational Psychology, 21*, 477-486.

Monaghan, S. (1997). *Intrinsic motivation and performance assessment*. Unpublished review. Seattle, Washington: University of Washington Department of Education.

Washington Alliance for Better Schools (2000). *Engaging the world: The powerful strategies of applied learning*. Bothell, Washington: The Washington Alliance for Better Schools.

LWSD copyrighted material reprinted by permission from Julie Goldsmith, Assistant Superintendent, Lake Washington School District.

Chapter Sixteen

Authentic Assessment—Bridge to the Workplace

Nancy McCorkle Miller

Abstract

Miller develops the theme that "research and experience support what is common sense: skills and knowledge that have obvious application in the adult world are more willingly learned and practiced by students and are more readily carried with them into the community." Authentic assessment is related to real-world activity outside the school's walls and will have an important impact on the next step in students' lives. Miller touches briefly on overcoming difficulties in constructing authentic assessments and then focuses on classroom examples that show how their content connects with real-life after high school. She points out what can be taken from classroom assessment experiences and converted into useful workplace tools. She utilizes many helpful Internet websites for further exploration by the reader.

Authentic Assessment in Context

"Authentic assessment" seems a term designed to rile anyone beyond the education establishment – and many within it as well. The phrase is used so commonly in school reform literature and constructivist writings that it has become trite, while the haze of confusion that it creates has not dissipated. Parents look at the term "assessment" and wonder whether it means testing or grading, and if not either of these, what does it mean? (And why not just call it that?) Teachers growl, "Was the assessment that was going on in past years somehow not authentic?" Like olives that come only in giant, super, and colossal sizes, "authentic assessment" feels like an advertising term.

It would pacify a faculty meeting to acknowledge that assessment –

i.e., testing and grading – has been going on since Socrates and that all of it was authentic – sort of. As generations of students who have been judged based on their grades know, there is something very real about letters and numbers on a transcript. Dig down a few layers below the grades on the transcript and you find the testing instruments and class activities on which the grades are based. But while all of them represent a kind of assessment, not all of it is authentic.

Defining Authentic Assessment

The authenticity of assessment lies not with the instrument or its accuracy, but with the student's activity. And not all assessment is authentic, nor should it be.

Think for a moment of your job. Many of us are required to pass tests in order to get our jobs or in order to earn job advancement. Many of us audition, present work samples, endure a probationary period, gather records of performance, or run a gauntlet of interviews to sell ourselves to an employer. We are judged on what we do and how we do it. Some of us even take sit-down exams that plumb what we know compared to what our employer wants us to know. Assessment? Oh yes. Authentic? Just ask those involved in the process: it is very real and very important to them. Many will have studied manuals and taken practice tests in order to raise their chance of success. Whatever is needed to pass, they will work to push it into their heads and out again when it is called for. The connection between the testing activity and the goal at hand is evident.

One of the criticisms about today's schools is that they are inauthentic. This is raised in the eternal student question, "Why do I have to learn this?" or the more potent assertion, "This has nothing to do with what goes on in real life!" Some students are touching on a fundamental objection to today's educational system, and one so important that it stands in the way of their successful learning. Of what relevance is most school testing to students?

It's not hard to work in an Advanced Placement (AP) classroom in the spring. The kids are focused intensely on a particular day in May when they will have to perform, and they are willing to work hard to do well on that assessment. For them, what they are doing is authentic. It is related to a real-world activity outside their own school's walls and will have an important impact on the next step in their lives. This is not the group of students that asks why they have to do this work; this is the group that is focused on a test that will help lead to a goal that they have adopted – all they want to know is how to do it better. For an AP student, that goal is generally admission to a selective college and to further education that will lead to a profession. And a few love learning for the sake of learning. Most students, however, are not AP students. Not all assessment is for such high stakes and not all is conducted on a national level at a particular day and time, with a numerical grade that will be assigned by strangers.

Other Types of Assessment

Most assessment takes place in a classroom setting, with a variety of goals. Testing and grading can be used to measure the quality of particular student work, decide advancement or failure, sort students into groups, maintain discipline, diagnose strengths and weaknesses, form the basis for planning and later lessons, appraise school quality, quantify instructional competence, compare one student or teacher or school with another, and a host of other purposes. Most of these goals have nothing to do with students and their goals. Many are not even known to the students. But most of the time, testing is used to assign a grade to a student, to label the quality of that student's learning and report that quality to someone else, usually the parent or another school. That assessment is important, but it is not authentic.

Grant Wiggins defines "authentic assessment" as an examination of student performance on worthy intellectual tasks. He contrasts this with what he calls "indirect or proxy" testing which uses "efficient, simplistic substitutes from which we think valid inferences can be made" about the overall quality of a student's learning (Wiggins, 2001).

In other words, proxy assessment is the type of assessment most often encountered in today's classrooms. Proxy assessment is inauthentic. But if we try to listen to Wiggins, what are worthy intellectual tasks? Has not what's been going on in schools for centuries been worthy and intellectual?

Key to Authentic Assessment

The key to authentic assessment is its performance-based nature, its complexity, and its relevance to real life activities in the adult community (Hart, 1994). That's another way of saying what authentic assessment is: an evaluation of students' abilities in 'real-world' contexts (Pearson, 2001). Authentic assessment involves tasks that:
- are similar to those undertaken in the world beyond high school
- require application of skills and knowledge to a novel problem
- are susceptible to a variety of "correct" answers
- involve more than one field or body of knowledge
- entail "doing" rather than "telling about"
- create an experience that will be useful to the student in other

contexts
- are meaningful to an audience beyond the school
- reflect goals and values beyond the immediate classroom.

Authentic assessment is messy, as is life. One question often leads to another. Solving a problem involves planning, reconsidering, connecting, and reflection that no multiple choice test will ever replicate.

Looking at the list above, it becomes clear that authentic assessment will almost always involve a project rather than a single instance of testing. It will almost always involve an elaborate performance, be that an essay or an architectural drawing, rather than a true-false test.

Valuable Activities, Some Authentic and Some Not

No one challenges the usefulness and essential nature of reading and math skills. They are authentic and their authenticity is universally recognized. If a student cannot read, if a student cannot calculate, advancement in almost any field is denied to him/her. At early levels, students learn to read and calculate because the application of these skills to greater tasks that lie ahead is evident. Testing of reading and arithmetic skills is crucial. Repeating the sounds of the letters is not authentic assessment, although learning the sounds is a necessary element of learning to read. Reading aloud a story that one has not encountered before is authentic assessment. It becomes authentic because it applies skills and problem-solving to new materials, in a way that those skills and knowledge are also used in the adult world.

In this, authentic assessment is closely related to the educational approach called constructivism: the student is discovering something new while s/he is being assessed. The knowledge created (or story read or experiment completed or structure built) may not be new to the world, but it is new to the student. The student's activity is authentic and has created something new and of relevance to the larger world, even if he/she is not the first to "construct" that knowledge or product.

Such new knowledge is also much more likely to be retained. Answer quickly: what school lesson do you remember best? It is likely to be the poster you made, a skit you performed, the model you constructed, the presentation to the class that earned applause – something where your emotional involvement and creative investment were high. It probably was not the true-or-false test you took in October of your junior year.

In Today's Classrooms

Looking beyond the acquisition of building block skills, what might a student do to demonstrate his/her learning in an authentic way? The list is probably only as short as a student's imagination or a teacher's ability to point out questions and connections. In vocational arts, home and family classes, art and music programs, physical education classes, there is no trouble visualizing authentic assessment. These classes have always been built around authentic assessment. Students are taught the skills and information needed. They practice and rehearse. Finally, they perform – at the easel, in a kitchen or concert hall, or on the athletic field. Their success is judged based on the product they produce. Their effort is rewarded not only with a grade, but also with a product or performance that they can carry away with them to another coach, school, or employer as a demonstration of skill and a way to gain admission to the next step in the process that they want to pursue.

Internship, practicums, and job shadows are common in these fields. They make the real world connection clear to the students' eyes; they give invaluable exposure to the real nature of the work at hand; they provide the basis for projects, apprenticeships, or shorter practical experiences.

The problem lies in the core disciplines and in the traditional way of approaching teaching and assessment in these areas. The sciences are most easily adaptable to authentic assessment: their mode of advancement is, after all, experimentation. What is experimentation but a problem-solving project? It is the replication in the classroom of the real-life skills and dilemmas practiced by the real-world academic and corporate researchers who practice science for a living.

History (and other social science) teachers have to become comfortable with teaching about how history (or anthropology or psychology) is made, not just dates, definitions, and names. The research skills used by an historian are the same ones used by journalists, investigators, city planners, and family genealogists. The writing skills are the same ones used by narrators, technical writers, columnists, publicists, executives, and secretaries. The thinking skills of comprehension, analysis, synthesis, and evaluation are the same ones used in all productive activities. The information is the same as that applied by any diligent citizen taking active part in a self-governing community.

Mathematics is the natural home of the "story problem." Nothing kills student enthusiasm more quickly than a long page of individual problems or a small paragraph beginning, "A train leaves St. Louis at 9 p.m. traveling 100 miles per hour and another train leaves. . . ." The comment, "I didn't learn my math until I had to use it when I . . . *[fill in adult activity]* . . ." is a cliche. Mathematics can be naturally connected with authentic assessment. It is the language of science and statistics. Its usefulness is in analysis, description and problem-solving. Math presented in this way, as a tool to master real-world problems, is not rote; it is authentic. Learning the basic skill is important, but using the skill is authentic. Rather than presenting pages full of problems and/or story problems unrelated to reality, mathematics can easily be used for meaningful analysis and problem-solving, and when presented that way, is naturally connected with authentic assessment.

Real World Problem-Solving

Sometimes the real world lines adults up in rows and administers written tests: think of the bar exam or of a driver's license test. But more often, the real world gathers teams of people together to accomplish a task: think of a police investigation, designing and testing an aircraft, producing a sales campaign.

Rarely does day-to-day employment culminate in a sit-down examination of the worker. Rather, it ends with a product that must be within production parameters or prototype that will be tested and improved or with a proposal that will be presented to a client and revamped based on his/her reaction. It culminates with a blueprint that will be modified to meet the customer's preferences or with a product that will be marketed and improved and marketed again. The work process is not tidy units punctuated by workers taking exams. It is an ongoing process of presentation, revision, use, and reflection. To do these things well, a worker needs skills in communications, analysis, research, planning and organization, teamwork, compromise, listening, as well as technical and fact-based knowledge. Authentic assessment often replicates this team approach to accomplishment. In doing so, it requires students to practice more than just book learning. They must be able to work with others, to collaborate and cooperate; they must be able to demonstrate promptness, reliability and compromise; they must be able to communicate their goals, ideas, and gathered knowledge and assemble it all into a form that can be presented effectively to others.

The SCANS Report and Authentic Assessment

The necessity for these skills is no secret or new discovery. A decade ago, the Secretary of Labor issued the SCANS (Secretary of Labor's Report on Achieving Necessary Skills, 1990) Report outlining the skills needed for employability. Of the eight SCANS Workplace Competencies and Foundation skills, three (information, technology, basic skills) involve competencies that might be taught and assessed in the traditional way. The other five (using resources, interpersonal skills, understanding systems, thinking skills, and personal qualities) involve complex project- or team-based behaviors that are best taught through project problems and assessed in the way that we have described as authentic.

Life after High School

And how does authentic assessment apply to the student's life after high school? For the business community, the complaints about American education come quickly, whether we are in times of high unemployment or labor shortage. In times of high unemployment, the complaint has been the lack of skilled workers, as we heard in the 1970s and 1980s (National Commission on Excellence in Education, 1983). As unemployment declined and the labor market tightened, the employers' lament changed to the need to retain inadequate or unsatisfactory workers (Konrad, 2000). For the worker, this translates to the inability to get a job, or the lack of advancement and frustration as one is transferred from one dissatisfying setting to another.

Experience with authentic assessment in school could go a long way to alleviate the frustration of both the student and the employer. The business owner would have a more solid foundation upon which to make hiring decisions, and the job applicant would have a clearer knowledge of the work that s/he wanted to do and concrete examples of his/her abilities to show the prospective employer.

How would this work?

Authentic assessment allows – indeed, encourages – students to accumulate portfolios that demonstrate their abilities, knowledge and skills just as artists build portfolios and athletes create highlight tapes. Copies of these portfolios, organized by skill or fields of knowledge or any other principle of importance to the employer, can be presented as part of the job application process. They illustrate the prospective employee's capabilities and ambitions. They distinguish the applicant from the hordes of young people fresh from high school who just "want a job; I can do anything."

Career Pathways and Academies

Some schools are arranged around the idea of the real world as the context for learning. Academies that organize all the coursework around a theme or professional field [e.g., law and justice (Philadelphia), medical skills (Chantilly), business and marketing (Philadelphia), aerospace (Philadelphia), and animation (Rowland)] exist nation-wide. Their students take a curriculum whose hallmark is its attachment to a professional field. The opportunity for authentic assessment through mock trials, lab demonstrations, marketing studies, model construction, or product presentation abound. These products, and the skills that producing them demonstrated, can be taken by the student to the prospective employer as part of a portfolio or resume. Teachers at any school or class can take parts of these programs and use them in their assessment plans.

Some states require that their public schools organize around career pathways (e.g., Washington State), and most provide career counseling for students, either through classroom units or the counseling program. Educators in many school districts (Polk County; Medford) and in some states (Washington State) are requiring a culminating project as part of a student's demonstration of readiness to graduate from high school. These culminating projects provide golden opportunities for every student to have experience with authentic assessment, no matter what their individual course of study or the inclinations of their particular classroom teachers.

Not all authentic assessment would lead to job skills and placements, although the alternative outcome would also be positive. A student with authentic experience (project, internship, job shadow) in the medical field might discover that s/he doesn't have any interest in the field, or may be actively repulsed by its daily work. Far better that this discovery be made early rather than spending years and dollars studying chemistry and anatomy only to hate to get up each day because one is trapped in a field of work that is personally unsatisfying – and where succeeding is that much more difficult due to the dislike for the work.

Real World Grading

When students are involved in authentic assessment, the teaching and grading task will also change. Authentic assessment involves a complex judgment, arrived at using a pre-planned and complex rubric. It must also acknowledge the possibility that the rubric is insufficient to the creative solution, and have the flexibility to look beyond itself. But this sort of assessment has been mastered and respected before: look no further than the Advanced Placement essay grading, juried art shows, or automotive trouble-shooting contests. The technicalities of this complexity are of little interest to students, however. They *can* be graded. And what is important is that students can carry away with them an experience and a product that they can use to gain admittance to the next step of their journey, and that can demonstrate their competence and learning for all to see.

Conclusion

Remember the AP students concentrating on test preparation? Assessment that is authentic maximizes the opportunity for similar eagerness by students in any endeavor. Real-life projects that ask important questions, require student engagement, allow revisions and teamwork, and result in a real product connected to student goals or adult activities in the outside world answer the question "Why do I have to learn this?" for the student. They also give the student a skill or a piece of work to carry away with him/her to a potential workplace and employer to demonstrate readiness to be employed. They are a bridge between the student's school day, where learning is neatly divided into separate disciplines and taught for predetermined periods of time, and the everyday adult world, where one thing leads to another and problem-solving is a complex project that requires social as well as intellectual skills, a variety of knowledge, and where the solution may also present another problem. A student who is capable of dealing with the authenticity of that situation will know what to ask of an employer and will have something to offer to that employer. That student will have a bridge between the classroom and the workplace.

References

Chantilly Academy, Chantilly, Virginia. Retrieved July 18, 2001, from http://www.fcps.k12.va.us/ChantillyAcademy/

Hart, D. (1994). *Authentic assessment: A handbook for educators*. New York: Addison-Wesley.

Konrad, R. *Tight labor market results in fewer firings*. CNET News.com, April 11, 2000. Retrieved July 18, 2001, from http://news.cnet.com/news/0-1005-200-1681542.html?tag=st

National Commission on Excellence in Education, U.S. Department of Education, (April 1983). *A nation at risk*. Retrieved July 18, 2001, from http://www.ed.gov/pubs/NatAtRisk/risk.html

Pearson Education Development Group. Retrieved April 25, 2001, from http://www.teachervision.com/lesson-plans/lesson-4911.html

Philadelphia Academies Incorporated. Retrieved July 18, 2001, from http://www.academiesinc.org/careers.html

Polk County High School, North Carolina. Retrieved July 18, 2001, from http://www.serve.org/UCR/pdfs/UCR7seniorproject.pdf

Rowland High School, Rowland Heights, California. Retrieved July 18, 2001, from http://www.ed.gov/offices/OERI/BlueRibbonSchools/art5.

South Medford High School, Medford, Oregon. Retrieved July 18, 2001, from http://www.creativenet.org.uk/prototypecasestudy.asp?cs_ID=80

U.S. Department of Labor, 1990. SCANS Report. Retrieved July 17, 2001, from http://www.fourhcouncil.edu/ycc/wscans.htm

Washington State Board of Education. Retrieved July 18, 2001, from http://www.k12.wa.us/sbe/

Washington State's Educational Pathways Requirement. Retrieved July 18, 2001, from: http://www.k12.wa.us/reform/edreform.pdf

Wiggins, G. *What is authentic assessment?* Retrieved April 25, 2001, from http://www.ed.gov/databases/ERIC_Digest/ed328611.html

Part IV

Innovative Approaches to Workplace Training

Part IV, *Innovative Approaches to Workplace Training,* has three chapters offering many ideas (such as business-education partnerships and internships) that educators may utilize with students.

(17) *Career Preparation Programs in Secondary Education—A Sampler of Current Trends, Exemplary Programs, Model Practices and the Bottom Line*—Willa Davis, a counselor in a regional occupational program in California, provides a detailed description of a remarkable variety of workplace training programs (with some comments from users) around the country. These training programs include Tech Prep, regional occupational centers, targeted programs such as AYES (the Automotive Youth Educational Systems—partnerships between automotive manufacturers, car dealers, and high schools to encourage students to enter the automotive field), and highly specialized high school programs.

(18) *Working Connections—Business Education Partnerships that Work*—Dopps, an educational consultant in setting up business-education partnerships, discusses the value of business-education partnerships and includes many pointers about setting up these partnerships. She discusses their benefits relative to students and schools, the community, and to employers. She includes examples of business-education partnerships, such as Microsoft's DigiGirlz .

(19) *The Crooked Career Path: Vocational Courses, Work Experiences and Non-Traditional Education need to be part of Career Guidance*—Severson, a counselor in a Seattle area occupational skills center, discusses that the best preparation for young people is both technical and academic, as students really do not know their future paths. Students taking coursework in one path (academic) without the other (technical) are often at-risk of not having proper preparation when they get into the workplace. She encourages students to consider participating in internships and other work experiences to see what the work is really like. She discusses technical training programs with two-year and four-year training certificate options.

Chapter Seventeen—

Career Preparation Programs in Secondary Education—A Sampler of Current Trends, Exemplary Programs, Model Practices, and the Bottom Line

Willa Smith Davis

Abstract

People, data, things and ideas form the foundation of all the work tasks within the world of work, according to the World of Work map (ACT, 2001). From Social Service jobs to occupations in Technical career clusters on the map, all will include one or more of these building blocks. This chapter will focus on what is occurring in career preparation programs at the high school level. *Career and technical education* used to be commonly referred to as *vocational education* or, simply, *voc-ed*. Terms used now are *career and technical education* and *career preparation*; they will be used synonymously in this chapter. Career and technical education programs are more than training to work in occupations that require little prior preparation. In fact, many of these programs now require advanced mathematics and language skills and are often a springboard to careers requiring postsecondary education.

Trends in Career and Technical Education Programs

"Vocational Education: Is the plug being pulled?" was the question Posnick-Goodwin posed in her headline story in the *California Educator* (Posnick-Goodwin, June, 2002a). The story reiterates what research has been indicating for years, that there have been significantly fewer high school students taking vocational education courses, primarily in *trade and industry* and *business* programs according to the National Center for Education Statistics (NCES, 2000).

299

Although this trend seemed to be a reflection of labor market needs between 1982-1998 (NCES, 2001), the current potentially gloomy picture of career preparation programs' status has also been influenced by high schools which are increasingly oriented towards college-bound students. As our society is shifting from a manufacturing-based economy to one that provides primarily services and information, it is important to review what kind of education and training is needed to prepare our nation's workforce in all career fields, not just those requiring a bachelor's degree.

Posnick-Goodwin's (2002a) story cites that ". . . 60 percent of high school vocational programs have disappeared during the last 30 years" (p. 8). Although the needs of the labor market during 1982 - 1998 seemed to warrant it, it must be noted that there are well-paying jobs that are vacant due to a shortage of trained workers in the fields once filled by graduates of secondary training programs (p. 10). The challenge that career preparation programs are facing, and which educators have been responding to, is to make these programs "for all students, integrated with academics - something that can give academics more meaning" (Ainsworth, as cited in Posnick-Goodwin, June 2002a, p. 8).

This is especially true of high school *academies* such as California's Department of Education's Partnership Academy Program which not only prepares students for entry-level high-tech and white collar occupations, but also for college in many cases. Posnick-Goodwin (2002a) writes, "Unlike traditional voc-ed classes, academies are integrated with core curriculum. For example, students in a bio-tech academy may write English papers about DNA research and take science classes that delve into genetics" (p. 11).

As part of school reform overall, what happens to these invaluable practical training programs will have a significant impact on the American workforce, economy and society. And change *is* being made in career and technical education. While it is disconcerting that many traditional programs (such as wood shop, auto shop, and home economics) are being dissolved, there are new programs being established to meet the needs of the new economy. These include computer technology, communications, rocket science and a variety of health care career programs, among many others. As the federally sponsored initiative No Child Left Behind (2001) focuses on ensuring that all students learn and achieve, it will become increasingly critical to focus also on career and technical education so it is not "left behind." The descriptions of the exemplary programs which follow demonstrate what is being done to ensure that America's students have a variety of career options that match their interests and talents, whether they are college-bound or not, all of which contribute to a healthy world of work.

Exemplary High School Programs

School-to-Career

From the Redwood forests to the Gulf Stream waters, from the corn fields of the great plains of Kansas to the snowy mountains in Vermont, School-to-Career (STC) programs have made an indelible mark in school reform. Instigated by the School-to-Work Opportunities Act of 1994, its venture capital funding was to "bring together partnerships of employers, educators and others to build a high quality School-to-Work (STW) system that prepares young people for careers in high-skill, high wage jobs" (School-to-Work Opportunities Act of 1994, HR 2884/S1361, Legislative Fact Sheet, para. 1).

According to National Conference of State Legislators (NCSL) *School -to-Work, a Guide for State Legislators* (p. 1), the goals of School-to-Work were to provide:
 • Better education opportunities,
 • Better employment prospects,
 • Adult role models, and
 • Multiple post-secondary options for *all* students.

The NCSL publication goes on to state that School-to-Work/Career experiences ". . . enable high school students to have more choices after graduation. Whether a four-year college, two-year college, technical training or entry-level position on a career path, School-to-Work opens up options for students where for many, none existed before" (p. 1).

Even though School-to-Career is not a specific technical education program, it does include those programs as a viable option for high school students in making occupational choices. How these programs have been implemented and the success of each is as unique as are the individual states, local school districts and employment communities and educators that have developed them.

The key strategies for building the STW system (School-to-Work Opportunities Act of 1994, HR2884/S1361 Legislative Fact Sheet, p.1) include, among others:
1) flexibility so that programs can address local needs and respond to changes in the local economy and labor market . . . and;
2) allowing the construction of STW systems to build upon existing successful programs such as youth apprenticeships, tech-prep education, cooperative education, and school-to-apprenticeship.

The three mandated basic program components include:
 • *School-based learning* that provides: career exploration and

counseling, instruction in a career major (elected no later than the 11th grade); a program of study that is based on high academic and skill standards as proposed in the Administration's "Goals 2000: Educate America Act" and typically involves at least one year of post-secondary education, and periodic evaluation to identify students' academic strengths and weaknesses.

- *Work-based learning* that provides: a planned program of job training paid work experience, workplace mentoring, and instruction in general workplace competencies and in the broad variety of elements of an industry, and
- *Connecting activities* that coordinate: involvement of employers, schools and students; matching students with work-based learning opportunities; and training teachers, mentors and counselors (School-to-Work Opportunities Act of 1994, HR2884/S1361 Legislative Fact Sheet, para. 3).

As stated previously, each STC program is different. However, typical features include: job shadowing, summer internships, mentoring, community service/service learning, and many other career exploratory opportunities. Additionally, successful completion of a School-to-Work/ Career program will lead to a high school diploma, possibly a certificate or diploma from a postsecondary institution, and an occupational skill certificate. The skill certificate will be a portable, industry-recognized credential that certifies competency and mastery of specific occupational skills (School-to-Work Opportunities Act of 1994, HR2884/S1361 Legislative Fact Sheet, para. 4).

School-to-Career is about success for every student. Now that the sunset provision for this legislation has been exercised, it is up to people in local school districts, business and industry, as well as in each community to continue their support of these programs. This will ensure that every student really will be successful in the world of work and become a productive American citizen.

Tech Prep

Tech Prep is a federal education initiative described and funded by the Carl D. Perkins Vocational and Technical Education Act Amendments of 1998. According to the U.S. Department of Education's Office of Vocational and Adult Education (Carl D. Perkins Vocational and Technical Education Act) (1998a), "legislation restructures and reforms programs previously authorized by the Carl D. Perkins Vocational and Applied Technology Education Act" that was originally authorized in 1990 as a response to technological advances that have changed the workplace in a dramatic way.

No matter what their plans are after high school, all students will need highly technical skills to be competitive in the current labor market.

Tech Prep is the definitive School-to-Work program that prepares students to be successfully employed in mid-level technology careers.

> As defined in the Carl D. Perkins Vocational and Technical Education Act (Perkins), Tech Prep is a sequenced program of study that combines at least two years of secondary and two years of postsecondary education. It is designed to help students gain academic knowledge and technical skills, and often earn college credit for their secondary coursework. Programs are intended to lead to an associate's degree or a certificate in a specific career field, and ultimately, to high wage, high skill employment or advanced postsecondary training (Carl D. Perkins Vocational and Technical Education Act, 1998b).

There are Tech Prep programs in every region in every state in the United States. To try to describe them all would be futile. Yet, to better understand the variety of career options that high school students have, the following have been selected as a sampler of all of the thousands of programs that have been established in communities to prepare their youth for the 21st century world of work and life. They are listed in alphabetical order by state.

- *Shades Valley Technical Academies, The Visual Arts & Communications Academy,* Birmingham, Alabama: As with many Tech Prep programs, students enrolled in this academy begin their career preparation right from the start in 9th grade. According to its pamphlet, *The Road to Completion*, in addition to core general education classes in English, Math, Social Studies and Science, they also take Art I (Drawing) and Photography I (panel 5). Throughout the remainder of high school, they will take six additional art/design electives in conjunction with the specified prerequisites for the *Advanced Academic Diploma*. They will also complete a job shadow during their junior year. And, during their senior year, they have the opportunity to intern at a local company (panel 4).
  Students must maintain a 3.0 G.P.A. in their visual arts courses and a 2.5 G.P.A. in all other subjects to maintain their place in the academy (panel 3). "In order to achieve at the level required for

success in the visual arts field, our standards are high and require a focused effort by our students. We emphasize that every assignment should be treated as a potential portfolio piece of work" (panel 4). All of their efforts will pay off by giving the graduates of this program the competitive edge in both postsecondary education and in the workplace.

- *Pikes Peak Community College, The Area Vocational Program (AVP),* Colorado Springs,
  Colorado: This program serves junior and senior high school students from 25 schools throughout the Pikes Peak region. (See the LHS website at http://academy.d20.co.edu/lhs/dep/business/avp.htm) Students enroll in one of the 16 career education programs offered at the college as part of their daily school schedule and earn high school credits in science, math, English, social studies and technology, depending on the particular program in which they are enrolled.
  As of the 2002/2003 academic year, according to Pikes Peak Community College's online catalog (http://www.ppcc.edu/Academics/HighSchoolPrograms/AreaVocationalProgram.cfm), the occupational programs students may enroll in include: Auto Collision Repair; Automotive Technology; Computer Applications Specialists; Computer Aided Drafting; CISCO; Criminal Justice; Culinary Arts; Diesel Power Mechanics; Early Childhood Professions; Fire Science Technology; Radio, Television, Telecommunications; Visual Communications - Design; and Welding.
  All programs are located at one of the college's campuses as well as in the community where students apply the knowledge and skills learned in the classroom that prepare them for entry-level positions in the workplace. Also, because of the "2 + 2" articulation agreements between some of the participating high schools and AVP, graduates of the program may earn college credit toward a post secondary certificate or degree (Vocational Programs for High School AVP Students, 1993, p. 1).
  Made up of students from various youth organizations, the Student Senate selected the *ant* in 1986 as their mascot. "They wanted a mascot which would represent them as being industrious, intelligent, cooperative and persistent in pursuit of goals" (p. 4). Given this attitude towards work, the employers who hire these "ants" will be fortunate to have them as part of their team.

- *The Allied Health Tech Prep Consortium,* Niagara County, New York: This exciting Tech Prep program is open to both 11ᵗʰ and 12ᵗʰ grade high school students after passing a careful screening process by school counselors. (*Niagara County Tech Prep Consortium* website at http://www.sunyniagara.cc.ny.us/techprep/ bestallied.html). It provides experiential learning opportunities five days a week in local hospitals that start with a job shadow in each student's career area of interest and culminate in a 10-week internship with a health professional mentor. Some of the career areas that students can experience firsthand include nursing, pharmacy, surgery, and speech pathology (para. 3). Industry field trips are also included in the course whose curriculum was developed by both secondary and community college faculty, thus ensuring a smooth transition to postsecondary studies. Field trips to medical institutions in the Western New York area and guest speakers from a variety of allied health fields also provide students with career awareness and exploration experiences that help them decide which health career is a good match for them (para. 4).

- *The Manufacturing Technology Advisory Group,* Washington State: The Manufacturing Technology Advisory Group (MTAG) is a statewide Tech Prep program that is a coalition of industry, labor, education, state government and community service organizations. It is a systemic partnership that was established in 1992 to "address the emerging technological needs of education and the manufacturing/engineering industry." (*Manufacturing Technology Advisory Group* website at http://www.mtag-wa.org/mtag_files/ bio.htm). Its mission is a multi-faceted one to provide leadership, direction and advocacy for industry and education skill standards. As with other Tech Prep programs, students in this educational program begin their training in high school that ultimately leads to a certificate and/or an associate degree at community or technical colleges. The core competencies (p. 2) of the program are:
  - Safety and health
  - Group dynamics and communication
  - Measurement
  - Quality assurance
  - Print interpretation
  - Shop skills
  - Business economics

- Resource management and manufacturing computing
- Product and process control
- Labor in industry

Students start the MTAG program in the 11th grade, and those who seek the *MTAG Certificate of Achievement* must successfully complete a three-part assessment process. The three parts include:
1) a capstone written assessment that demonstrates their knowledge and application of skills in the core competencies;
2) a performance assessment (that can only be started once students have mastered the *safety* core competency) which is a time-pressured project and team-based activity to measure their current manufacturing skill levels; and
3) a portfolio that includes all academic and job application prerequisites, such as: a letter of introduction, a resume, project write-ups, transcripts, letters of recommendation, and certificates of completion/achievement (pp. 3 - 4).

Although it is now a consortium of various societal institutions, the MTAG training program was initially designed by and for the manufacturing industry to support all facets of its operations, and strives to live up to its motto, *"Education: Where Business Begins"* (p. 1).

• *California Association of Regional Occupational Centers and Programs*

Long before School-to-Work and Carl Perkins legislation was enacted, the California Association of Regional Occupational Centers and Programs (ROCPs) started providing "qualified students with the opportunity to attend a career and technical education training program regardless of the geographical location of their residence" (*Operations Handbook for California's Regional Occupational Centers and Programs* [CAROCP], 2000, p.1-1).

The ROCPs are an essential part of the systemic efforts by the California Department of Education to prepare K-12 and adult students to meet the needs of the state's highly skilled, diverse work- force. They have been and continue to be the epitome of career and technical education programs. By participating in these education and industry/business partnerships, graduates from them support the health of their communities in all areas, including cultural, financial, political, and ethical, and become productive citizens of American society.

The *CAROCP Handbook* states that while each ROCP establishes its own philosophy/mission statement based on local geographical needs, the fundamental statement of mission of all ROCPs is:

All students, both high school students and adults, shall have the opportunity to learn marketable skills or upgrade existing skills through courses offered at each ROCP in order to become gainfully employed. . . . [Therefore, ROCPs] serve the state and national interests in providing vocational and technical education to prepare students for an increasingly technological society in which generalized training and skills are insufficient to prepare high school students and graduates, and out-of-school youth and adults for the many employment opportunities which require special or technical training and skills. (p. 2 - 1)

Specifically, ROCPs have three primary goals (p. 1 - 2). They are:
1. To train for career technical occupations;
2. To upgrade existing skills, or retraining in needed skill areas for the local labor market; and
3. To prepare for advanced training.

ROCP courses are designed to provide participant students with basic marketable skills to secure entry-level jobs upon completion of the program. These jobs can be the beginning of a high tech, high wage, higher education career path regardless of the student's eventual career goal. All ROCP courses offer employment options directly from high school, or continued education at the community college or university.

Thus *ROCP training is for all students*, not just those wanting to enter the world of work upon graduating from high school. Not only are ROCP courses designed to be career preparation training programs, they are also "career exploration" programs. They provide students with hands-on opportunities that help them make informed career choices in fields where many years of higher education preparation are required. It saves college and university-bound students much time and money by knowing beforehand if a particular career path is a good match with their own personal interests, personality, values, and aptitudes.

Additionally, ROCP students can earn 5 to 15 high school credits per semester, depending on the choice of training program, with some counting towards the California State University and University of California *Intersegmental General Education Transfer Curriculum* requirements. Also, while enrolled in some ROCP programs, many of the credits earned can count as college credits at local community colleges through the "2+2" articulation agreements. These programs provide for a "career ladder" pathway that allows graduates to exit them after the 12th, 13th or 14th grades with a diploma, certificate or associate's degree relevant to a marketable occupation. And, due to an expanded 2+2+2 joint venture articulation agreement, students can earn a bachelor's degree from the California State University system. (*CAROCP Handbook*, pp. 3 - 19)

Many programs offer community-based training in addition to in-class instruction. These "on-the-job-training" internship opportunities solve the dilemma for most entry-level workers: *"No one will hire me without experience, but how can I get experience if no one will hire me?"* Generally, courses are scheduled five days a week during the school day. For those programs offering community/work-based internships, students go to their work-site four out of the five days after the initial orientation and fundamental skills-building part of each semester, with the fifth day spent back in the classroom for additional knowledge and skill acquisition. When convenient for the work-site sponsor and student, there may be flexibility in the internship schedule for the hours required at the work-site. And, even though the classroom training site might be at another location other than the student's home high school, ROCP instructors strive to establish work-sites close to the student's residence whenever possible.

Also, because they were designed to prepare students for careers, "job getting" skills like resume writing and interviewing skills are part of the curriculum as well. For the most part, students are not "placed" at a work-site; they must be accepted into it by interviewing for it just like one would interview for a job.

ROCP students can be assured of the competency of their instructors to teach them the occupational skills and knowledge required for success in the world of work. Not only have instructors worked for at least five years in their field of expertise, they must meet additional qualifying criteria to earn their appropriate vocational education credential (*CAROCP Handbook*, pp. 5-5 to 5-6).

Additionally, ROCP student support services staff members acquire the appropriate education, credentials and experience to provide quality assistance that supports student career goal achievement. The services that these staff members provide include (*CAROCP Handbook*, p. 6 - 1):

- Establishing an effective student recruitment plan that makes program and service information available through a variety of media;
- Providing students with career guidance and related information;
- Encouragement for the appropriate program placement of students consistent with their abilities and goals;

- Auxiliary activities and referrals which address the needs of ROCP's varied student population; and
- Assistance with acquiring essential employability and job search and job retention skills.

As with other career and technical education programs, ROCPs are supportive of continued professional development. Their leaders and instructors belong to and participate in a variety of professional associations. Some of these include: the California Association of Leaders in Career Preparation (CALCP), the Association for Career and Technical Education (ACTE), formerly the American Vocational Association, and the United States of America/Vocational Industrial Clubs of America (VICA/ SkillsUSA) (*CAROCP Handbook*, p. 1-4). Participation in these organizations, as well as in other professional development opportunities, ensures that ROCP administration, faculty and staff members will continue their own life-long learning so as to provide continuous improvement in their training programs and support services.

Instructional programs are designed and developed with the help and support of their industry and business partners who serve on advisory committees which meet at mutually convenient times throughout the year. According to the CAROCP Handbook, (p. 3-1):

> Subject matter advisory committees are a mandatory component of course development that provides direction in the identification of course goals, objectives and competencies, and in the selection of course content. The course outline will serve as the ROCP teacher's road map for providing learning experiences and opportunities for students to achieve career technical objectives effectively and efficiently, ensuring competency achievement.

All ROCP courses are developed in response to the needs of their particular regional labor market. A thorough job market analysis is conducted with input from industry/business partners, the relevant ROCP, the California Department of Labor's Labor Market Information Division, and the California Occupational Information Coordinating Committee. These same entities also contribute to making revisions to existing ROCP courses as well as making the decision to terminate others when the labor market no longer reflects a need for such training. Additionally, whenever the need presents itself, statewide courses are developed for use by appropriate ROCPs, as was the case in 1999 with *Internetworking, Levels 3 & 4*. This course was developed in conjunction with the California

Department of Education, CAROCP, and the CISCO network company (*CAROCP Handbook*, p. 3-1).

An individualized training plan is developed for each ROCP student, and competencies identified in the plan must directly relate to the course's instructional objective. Additionally, the skills that students acquire must be documented by appropriate evaluation techniques to ensure competencies are achieved at the standard expected by the industry and/or labor market. Upon completion of the training program, each graduate will receive not only a *Certificate of Completion*, but also a *Skills Sheet* that assures a potential employer that the job candidate can do the job with little or no additional training (*CAROCP Handbook*, p. 3-11).

ROCP courses may also offer an invaluable contribution to the *Individual Education Plan* for students in special education programs. "Appropriate placement" is the key for these students to succeed, both academically and vocationally. Working in conjunction with students with special needs, their parents, and their schools, as well as with transition programs such as *WorkAbility I, Transitional Partnership Programs,* and *WorkAbility II,* and possibly other state agencies, such as the Department of Rehabilitation, a ROCP training program can be developed that supports students with special needs toward successful program completion and readiness to enter the workforce (*CAROCP Handbook,*p. 3-11).

Additionally, some ROCPs partner with industry/business apprenticeship programs and serve as its local education agency (LEA), which all such programs are mandated to have. These programs may be union or non-union. The ROCP's role as the LEA often serve as the " . . . related and supplementary classroom instruction (RSI) provider. [The] RSI takes many forms, ranging from examples where the ROCPs provides both instructor and classroom facilities, to the opposite extreme where the ROCPs serve as fiscal agents, with the program sponsor providing both training instructor and facility" (*CAROCP Handbook*, pp. 3-20).

So, whether a person is a typical junior or senior high school student who is exploring and/or preparing to work in a specific occupational field, an adult who is upgrading existing skills or learning new ones to make a career change, a student with special needs requiring vocational preparation, or a participant in a structured apprenticeship program, ROCPs can provide high quality, low-cost job training to meet their individual needs. They epitomize the purpose of California's public education system: "Each child(/adult) is a unique person with unique needs, and the purpose of the educational system of this state is to enable each child(/adult) to develop all of his or her own potential" *CAROCP Handbook* (p. 6-4).

• *Automotive Youth Educational Systems*

"Is it a School-to-Work program? Or, is it a Tech Prep program? Or, is it a ROCP program?" The answer is YES to all of those questions — "AYES", that is. The Automotive Youth Educational Systems (AYES) is an industry-driven national program that is designed for students who like working with their hands, who are natural problem solvers and trouble-shooters, who are intrigued by computers, who are fascinated with high performance cars and trucks, and who want to earn high wages by learning all they can about automotive technology.

For the most part, long gone are the days of "auto mechanics" that conjure up images of Gomer Pyle or unscrupulous businessmen who would take advantage of their customer's ignorance about the workings of the internal combustion engine and related automobile operations. They are now replaced by highly skilled, reputable technicians whose mission it is to fix their patron's vehicles right the first time for their own personal reward and for the highest praise any business could want - "repeat business" of satisfied consumers.

According to its promotional literature, *Focus on the Future* (1997):

> AYES is a dynamic partnership among participating automotive manufacturers, participating local dealers, and selected local high schools/vocational schools. The goal: to encourage bright students with a good mechanical aptitude to pursue careers in the ever-changing field of automotive technology, and to prepare them for entry-level positions or challenging academic options (p. 2).

AYES programs strive to involve everybody in the career preparation of current and future generations of automotive service professionals and managers. This "equation for success" includes students, schools, instructors, and dealerships, with parents/guardians and school counselors as key "career mentors" (*Focus on the Future,* 1997, p. 5). All instructors add their individual ingredients of standards and responsibilities to help create the entry-level technician who has the foundational competencies necessary to "make it" in this type of work. The competencies include:

- Developing a strong knowledge of automotive fundamentals;
- Having a solid grasp of math, reading and writing basics;
- Being a team player;
- Wanting to have the job done right;
- Knowing the operations of a dealership;
- Desiring career growth potential; and
- Striving towards the potential of advanced 2-year and 4-year college degree options (p. 5).

Using the process of the *Professional Development Program* (PDP), developed by the Vocational Industrial Clubs of America (*Focus on the Future*, 1997, p. 10), students are prepared academically as well as experientially by reading service manuals, concisely writing their findings on a work order, and accurately calculating measurements to ensure their work is performed properly, based on the scientific principles that underlie the operation of automotives systems. These real-life situations help to develop the technical skills that prepare them for certification in four of the eight skill areas required to become an Automotive Service Excellence technician. The PDP process also ensures that the student is proficient in another set of skills, too. These are the *employability* skills that help them acquire as well as keep the jobs they are preparing for. These include resume writing and interviewing skills as well as effective self-motivation techniques, and time and stress management skills, among others.

Paid summer and senior year internships reinforce what their mentors have been teaching them throughout the learning process. These industry master craftsmen model what dealerships expect of their young apprentices. By spending quality time with these novice workers, they are a key factor in their success. This creates a "win/win" situation for everyone.

As Robert J. Eaton, former Chairman of DaimlerChrysler Corporation stated, ·

> Automotive YES is a career preparation strategy that actually delivers what it promises: a cadre of young, well-trained men and women who are meeting the demands for qualified technicians at automotive dealers. So both the students and the dealers win.
>
> Customers win too, because Automotive YES is their assurance of receiving quality
> service from skilled technicians. (*Focus on the Future*, 1997, p.3)

So, whether a part of a ROCP or a Tech Prep program, AYES appears to be the quintessential School-to-Career/Work example of what happens when everybody contributes to the common good.

Model and Best Practices

Whether it is part of a School-to-Career, Tech Prep, ROCP, or an industry driven training program such as AYES, "model" or "best practices" can been defined as "activities that support school-based and work-based programs to provide students with the tools and knowledge needed to make career decisions and plan a strategic course of study that leads to a satisfying career pathway for America's youth" (See the *South Central Career Information System* website at http://www.sccis.org/main/careerprov/bestprac/bestexemp.htm).

As has been a frequent refrain in this chapter, these practices are too numerous to mention. A review of the literature yields a multitude of innovative examples. Topics and categories include:

- Applied academics,
- Building productive relationships between business and education, including the design and development of employer databases,
- Capstone projects,
- Career development portfolios,
- Career exploration (including career fairs, job shadowing, field trips, guest speakers)
- Developing career pathways across curriculum,
- Implementing work-ready skills certification,
- Liaison networks,
- Mentoring programs,
- Out-of-school youth projects,
- Personal learning plans,
- Post secondary linkages,
- Professional development opportunities for teachers, student support staff and administrators,
- Work-based learning experiences, and
- Workforce development and training.

Some are self-nominating as model practices; most have had to undergo a rigorous standards-based review and meet the criteria established for designation as a best practice. The following is a sample of what educators, businesses, and students have accomplished.

School-to-Career

A network of liaison people facilitate the "connecting activities," one of the cornerstones of all successful School-to-Career/Work initiatives, between schools and the community. In fact, the title of their position is *Community Learning Coordinators* (CLCs) in the Sierra Regional Career Partnership in Northeastern California, and they "are the heart and soul of the . . . partnership" (*Sierra Regional Career Partnership*, 2002). CLCs "recruit business partners to serve as classroom guest speakers and offer students job shadows, mentorships, and internships. They help prepare students for these activities, and they assist teachers in finding ways to integrate career exploration activities into their curriculum" (p. 23).

These activities are particularly important in working with "at-risk" youth. "For some of the students I work with that are in alternative education programs, the community learning experience is what has kept them going on to their diploma," says CLC Cyndy Bigbee. "Both the sense of connection it builds and the reality that someone believes in them can be a strong motivator" (p. 23).

Since 1997, Vermont has designated four such networks as best practices (*Vermont School-to-Work* website at http://www.state.vt.us/stw/exemplary.html). They include the Central Vermont STW Collaborative, Franklin-Grand Isle Liaison Network, Linking Learning to Life, and Orleans/Northern Essex STW Partnership. As with the Sierra Regional Career Partnership, most have had independent coordinators located on-site at local high schools whereas in other cases, volunteer teachers and guidance staff have served in such positions. This has been especially the case in the past two years as the STW funding sunset provision has been exercised and educators have looked to incorporate ways to retain the essential elements of these programs.

Tech Prep - South Carolina

In addition to apprenticeship and cooperative education programs, internships and academies, students from the career centers and comprehensive high schools in Anderson, Oconee, and Pickens counties in South Carolina have the opportunity to participate in Duke Technical Career Day. Its purpose is to introduce students to specific careers at Duke Energy Corporation (See *Your Child's Career* website at http://www.yourchildscareer.org/textversion/schoolshelp/schoolshelp_bbest.htm).

Each year, teams from this tri-county region are challenged to solve a technical problem. Prizes are awarded by an expert panel of judges for demonstrating excellence in a range of workplace behaviors including technical work, teamwork, communication, and creativity. Exemplary projects that have been produced and recognized include: LEGO robots, a pneumatic soda-can crusher, and an electronic device that automatically waters house plants. Committed to making this best practice an on-going part of career and technical education activities, Duke Energy Corporation funds Duke Technical Career Day with a grant that is coordinated by the Tri-County Technical College's Office of Job Placement and Cooperative Education (*Your Childs' Career*, p. 3).

Regional Occupational Centers and Programs - California

One of the reasons why ROCPs continue to be one of the foremost career preparation programs is due to its *Model Practices Recognition Program*. The program was created by CAROCP and the California Department of Education ". . . to assure the quality of ROCP practices that promote student learning. The committee developed policies and measures to assist ROCPs in the areas of business services, organization structure, personnel services and program accountability" (Model Programs and Practices (2002) website at: http://www.cde.ca.gov/rocp/mpractices/index.html). The criteria established to identify such practices also acts as an assessment for continuous self-improvement.

An example of one of these model practices is Linda Matzek's (2001) *Banking Operations* course at the LA ROP that was awarded model practice designation in 2002. As stated in the application summary (para. 3-5):

> ...The replicable and exemplary qualities are demonstrated by the fact that the course is offered in two different school districts serving two distinct communities. . . .The needs of each of these communities are recognized and met as evidence by the full enrollment, excellent attendance and exceptional placement rate of 90% in both districts. Furthermore, the curriculum for Banking Operations is aligned with industry, state, national, business career path, and model curriculum and career preparation standards... In addition to curricular alignment, the course reflects current trends in the industry. This is accomplished with direct input from the Banking Occupations Advisory Committee. The committee meets annually to review and validate the curriculum including current job titles, job requirements, changing technologies, equipment and supplies review, necessary academic skills, entry level wages, labor market needs and emerging trends. This annual review provides input from all stakeholders to insure students' success.

Automotive Industry - Ford Academy of Manufacturing Sciences (FAMS)

Before the AYES program was formally devised, The Ford Motor Company was a strong supporter of education. In fact, throughout his lifetime, Henry Ford himself "had a deep interest in education, founding more than 70 K-12 schools around the world that linked the academic knowledge that the student learned in the classroom with what he or she might later do in the workplace" (National Employer Leadership Council, 2002, *Best Practices in School-to-Careers, The Automotive Industry*, p. 12). In the booklet, it also describes how in 1990, the Ford Academy of Manufacturing Sciences (FAMS) was started "to build strong partnerships between high schools and the local business community. These partnerships were designed to provide students with three "Core Elements" that they need to understand and succeed in the complex and ever-changing world of their future" (p. 12).

The core elements include: *Academic Knowledge, Interpersonal and Human Performance Skills* and *Consumer-Based Business Concepts.* These core elements teach students rigorous standards-based curriculum and employability skills, and provide hands-on activities via case studies and team projects, internships, and frequent interaction with business partners. Since its inception, more than 10,000 students have participated in FAMS programs in the United States, Canada and South Africa (p. 13), making this best practice international as well as American.

The Bottom Line

Fewer dropouts from high school, higher GPAs, better attendance rates, more advanced course selection, improved postsecondary enrollment, higher employment rates, and greater earnings - what do they all have in common? They are all of the many "outcome variables" that statistically prove that participation in activities and programs related to School-to-Career/Work, Tech Prep, ROCP, and industry-driven programs such as AYES help high school students focus on their plans after high school.

These outcomes are from many research studies from across the nation that conclude high school reform, especially when linked to work-based experiences, is indeed working. Some specific statistics include:

- 86% of the Henry Ford Academy's 2001 graduating class pursued college and university studies and scored almost twice as high as their county peers on the Michigan state achievement test (National Employer Leadership Council, 2002, p. 12).
- School-to-Work students had an 8.1% lower dropout rate than non-School-to-Work students (Philadelphia School-to-Careers programs, Philadelphia School District Study, 1997, as cited in *NCSL,* p. 3).
- Tech Prep graduates in Ohio had significantly higher college-level academic readiness scores. . . . the Tech Prep group scored a mean of 3.96 points higher in the reading assessment, 6.09 points higher in the writing assessment, and 9.08 points higher in the numerical skills/prealgebra assessment (Schaid, 2001, p. 101).
- 68.5% of School-to-Work students maintained a 2.0 or higher GPA compared to 46.9% of non-School-to-Work students (Philadelphia School-to-Careers programs, Philadelphia School District Study, 1997, as cited in the *National Conference for State Legislators*

STW Guide, NCSL, p. 4).
- ROCP students earned about $1.44 an hour more than did non-ROCP students (Mitchell, 2002, power point slide *Wage Rate Comparison: All ROCP Students vs. Control Group*).
- School-to-Work seniors took 13-19% more advanced classes in Algebra, Science and Computer Science – and maintained comparable grades – than non-School-to-Work students (New York School-to-Work Initiative, Westchester Institute for Human Services Research, Inc., 1998 as cited in *NCSL*, p. 3).

While these statistics are impressive, they don't tell of the personal impact that these various programs have had. The following are quotes from students, parents, instructors, and employers that provide *qualitative* information that is as important as the quantitative data listed above. Here is what they have to say:

"BE&K is by far the best program for preparing students for life after high school. They have teachers who have real world experience and really motivate the students. BE&K is the difference between a dead-end, low-wage job and a rewarding career" Mr. Steve Grigsby, father of Michael Grigsby, Electrical Student, (as cited in The BE&K School of Industrial Construction [pamphlet], *Building Your Future*, panel 6).

"Everyone has a chance to feel equal in terms of intellectual ability here. . . Smart kids sometimes rely on kids they didn't consider intellectual. It helps level out the playing field, because being 1the smartest kid doesn't mean you will understand – or do – photography any better. . . He may have trouble with writing, but not with photography" Photography Instructor Anne Battle's comments about a student who was enrolled in special education and whose shot was published in a national magazine ad (Posnick-Goodwin, 6/02 b, p. 15).

"AYES is the premier 'school-to-career' initiative and is the perfect complement to our post-secondary technician development program, T-TEN. Together, they will provide quality service personnel for the high paying jobs and excellent career opportunities our industry can provide" Yale Gieszl, Vice Chairman, Toyota Motor Sales-USA (*Focus on the Future*, 1999, p.3).

While there may be disagreement about which specific practices contribute to these statistics, there is no argument that these initiatives are on the right track in equipping American youth with the skills required for the increasingly complex world of work.

Other Innovative Educational Approaches

The educational initiatives that have been highlighted in this chapter reflect many of the changes that have occurred in career and technical education that are altering the methods and means in preparing American youth for work and life in the 21st century. They do not provide the whole story, however. It's also important to feature other examples that are changing how high schools and, in some cases, whole school systems do business. While all are not exclusive to career and technical education, they are additional samples of what is happening in "schools that work".

Auto-desk Foundation

This section of the chapter would not be complete if it didn't include mention of the Auto-desk Foundation. It helped to define and spread the good news about "project-based learning" to educators throughout the nation from 1992 to its close in 2000. Through its support of many ventures that highlighted "kids who know and do," its work continues through the efforts of Bob Pearlman who led the Foundation in 1996 after its founder, Joe Oakey, retired. Bob maintains his own website dedicated to school reform initiatives as well as a web page entitled, *Great Student Work* (www.bobpearlman.org/BestPractices/StudentWork.htm)(a). He created it to showcase the great work kids do and to encourage teachers and policymakers to support students in putting their best efforts on the web to serve as exemplars to others. (For more information about Bob's efforts to exhibit students' best works, visit www.greatstudentwork.com.)

High Tech High

In San Diego, California, the Gary and Jerri-Ann Jacobs *High Tech High* is a public charter high school of about 400 students, and is one of the project-based learning schools that Bob Pearlman likes (www.bobpearlman.org/BestPractices/SchoolsILike.htm)(b). It is based on three design principles of personalization, academic rigor and real-world immersion. High Tech High has become a "learning community" model for other school districts throughout the state and nation. "Innovative features include performance-based assessment, daily shared planning time for staff, state-of-the-art technical facilities for project-based learning, internships for all students, and close links to the high tech workplace" (*High Tech High* website at: www.hightechhigh.org/about/hth-program.html). Students

318

culminate learning experiences by exhibiting and presenting their projects to industry experts, teachers, peers, and family.

High Schools That Work

Swansea High School in South Carolina is one school that participates in the Southern Regional Education Board's school improvement initiative, *High Schools That Work*. At Swansea, all incoming 9th grade students are required to choose either a tech-prep or college-prep program in one of four career clusters (Wonacott, 2002, p.2). However, most students take both types of courses. "For instance, a tech-prep student in the engineering industry cluster could combine a concentration in automotive technology with applied academic classes like workplace communication; or a college-prep student in the health and human services cluster with a long-term goal of medical school could combine college-prep English with courses from the health occupations concentration" (Wonacott, 2002, p. 2).

The Met
Most often referred to as simply the *Met*, the Metropolitan Regional Career and Technical Center in Providence, Rhode Island, has been described as one of the most innovative public high schools in the nation. (*The Big Picture Company, Inc.* website at www.bigpicture.org/TheMet.htm)(a). Beginning in 1996, the Met was the first of many new high schools that have been designed and supported by the Big Picture Company, an independent non-profit organization, whose primary philosophy is to educate "one student at a time," according to *The Big Picture Company, Inc.* website at www.bigpicture.org/WebSite2002NEW/BigPicturePhilosophy.htm (b).
The Met is a model of what research has concluded as to what works best for student learning. It is small, incorporates personalized learning, and supports real-world learning activities that both bring students to the community as well as the community into the classroom. This leads to authentic student-developed projects and engages students' families as active supporters and mentors. The Big Picture Company's mission is to "encourage, incite and effect change in the education system." (*The Big Picture Company, Inc.* website at http://www.bigpicture.org/WebSite2002NEW/BigPicturePhilosophy.htm)(b). It has been the recipient of more than $20 million from the Bill & Melinda Gates Foundation's *Connecting Schools and Communities* program in Rhode Island to create smaller, personalized environments that help *all* students achieve. (See the Bill & Melinda Gates Foundation website at http://www.gatesfoundation.org/connectedpostings/announce-0211191.htm). The

organization has also received $3,450,000 from the Foundation to open 12 similar schools across the nation over a 5-year time span.

Conclusion

In conclusion, these are a few of the statistics that support the need for various educational programs that prepare new generations of workers who will provide the needed services and products to sustain the American way of life:

- According to some estimates only about 30% of high school graduates possess the aptitude and receive the academic preparation needed for success in college courses (Wonacott, 2000).
- In 1996, only about 20% of America's jobs required a four-year college degree. But many jobs required some education beyond high school, often at the community college level (Carl D. Perkins Vocational and Technical Education Act, 1998c).
- Managerial/Professional jobs are at the top of the salary ladder. One rung down the ladder is Crafts, Precision Metals, and Specialized Repair – all skills that can be acquired without a college degree (Wonacott, 2000).

In addition, the World-of-Work map (ACT, 2001) shows six general career clusters, according to ACT's World-of-Work Map website at www.act.org/wwm/counselor.html. These six clusters are divided into 12 regions where 26 different career areas are positioned in relation to whether they involve working with people, data, things, ideas, or a combination. There is no value assigned to any particular work. There is a need for all types of occupations within the world of work. American society depends on having the right mix of all of them to make its economy a healthy one that supports the operations of all aspects of its citizens' lives. Thus, it is critical to recognize the contribution that all occupations make, and to support career and technical education programs that have a place of importance alongside other postsecondary educational programs.

Because of the contribution to society that is made by the occupations that require career and technical education, it is this writer's view that it is imperative to make an appropriate level of continued funding for these training programs. It is critical to fund other innovative programs and coalitions that simultaneously prepare students for entry into postsecondary education and into the workplace upon graduation from high school. This funding needs to be supported by American government, industry, and its citizenry.

Finally, a statement about School-to-Work from the National Conference of State Legislators' *School-to-Work: A Guide for State Legislators*, emphasizes this point best.

> The School-to-Work learning strategy can provide better education, workforce preparation and the ability to learn throughout a lifetime. We believe that employers, educators and parents must work together to expand School-to-Work opportunities, which serve the best interests of our students, our businesses and our country. (p. 9)

By working together, we can best help our youth to make immediate plans for after high school as well as throughout their entire lives. Career and technical education can provide the foundation for that reality for our young people.

References

ACT world-of-work map: Career clusters and career areas. (2001). Retrieved January 2, 2003, from http://www.act.org/wwm/overview.html

Automotive Youth Educational Systems. (1999). *Focus on the future*. [Brochure] Detroit, MI: Author.

Automotive Youth Educational Systems. (1997). *Focus on the future*. [Brochure] Detroit, MI: Author.

BE&K School of Industrial Construction. (n.d.) *Building your future*. [Pamphlet].

Big Picture Company(a). Retrieved January 19, 2003, from http://www.bigpicture.org/TheMet.htm

Big Picture Company(b). Retrieved January 19, 2003, from http://www.bigpicture.org/WebSite2002NEW/BigPicturePhilosophy.htm

Bill & Melinda Gates Foundation. Retrieved December 29, 2002, from http://www.gatesfoundation.org/connectedpostings/announce-0211191.htm

Bobpearlman(a). Retrieved December 29, 2002, from http://www.bobpearlman.org/BestPractices/StudentWork.htm

Bobpearlman(b).Retrieved December 29, 2002, from http//www.bobpearlman.org/BestPractices/SchoolsILike.htm

Carl D. Perkins Vocational and Technical Education Act of 1998(a). Washington, D.C.: U.S. Department of Education. Retrieved January 22, 2003, from http://www.ed.gov/office/OVAE/CTE/legis.html

Carl D. Perkins Vocational and Technical Education Act of 1998(b). Washington, D.C.: U.S. Department of Education. Retrieved January 22, 2003, from http://www.ed.gov/office/OVAE/CTE/tpreptopic.html

Carl D. Perkins Vocational and Technical Education Act of 1998(c). Washington, D.C.: U.S. Department of Education. Retrieved January 22, 2003, from http://www.ed.gov/office/OVAE/CTE/perkins.html

HighTechHigh - About HTH. Retrieved January 12, 2003, from http://www.hightechhigh.org/about/index.shtml

LHS: Area Vocational Program. Retrieved January 22, 2003, from http://academy.d20.co.edu/lhs/dep/business/avp.htm

Manufacturing Technology Advisory Group. *Education: Where business begins*. Retrieved December 26, 2002, from http://www.mtag-wa.org/mtage_files/bio.htm

Matzek, L. (December, 2001). *Application summary in model practices application: Banking operations*. California Association of Regional Occupational Centers and Programs. Retrieved February 15, 2 0 0 3 , from http://www.cde.ca.gov/rocp/mpractices/index.html

Mitchell, D.E. (2002). Power point slide presentation. *Accountability Study Findings 2002 Technical Report*, [slide] *Wage Rate Comparison: All ROCP Students vs. Control Group*.

Model Programs and Practices - Regional Occupational Centers and Programs (2002). Retrieved November 16, 2002, from http://www.cde.ca.gov/rocp/mpractices/index.html

National Conference of State Legislators. *School-to-work, A guide for state legislators* [Brochure] Denver, CO: Author.

National Center for Education Statistics. (2000). *Changes in high school vocationalcourse taking in a larger perspective.* Washington, D.C.: U. S. Department of Education. Retrieved November 16, 2002, from http://nces.ed.gove/pubsearch/pubsinfo.as?pubid=2001026

National Center for Education Statistics. (2001). *High school facts at a glance.* Washington, D.C.: U. S. Department of Education. Retrieved January 22, 2003, from http://www.ed.gov/offices/OVAE/HS/hsfacs.html

National Employer Leadership Council. (2002). *Best practices in school-to-careers, the automotive industry.* Washington, D.C. Retrieved November 16, 2002, from http://nces.ed.gov/pubsearch/pubsinfo.as?pubid=2001026

Niagara County Tech Prep Consortium, *Best practices: Allied health.* Retrieved January 20, 2003, from http:/www.sunnyniagara.cc.ny.us/techprep/bestallied.html

No Child Left Behind. Retrieved November 21, 2002, from http://www.nclb.gov/index.html

Operations Handbook for California's Regional Occupational Centers and Programs (2000). Retrieved November 16, 2002, from http://www.cde.ca.gov/rocp/handbook.pdf

Pikes Peak Community College. Area Vocational Program. Retrieved January 23, 2003, from http://www.ppcc.edu/Academics/HighSchoolPrograms/AreaVocationalProgram.cfm

Pikes Peak Community College. (1993). *Vocational programs for high school AVP students.* [Brochure]. Colorado Springs: CO. Author.

Posnick-Goodwin, S. June, 2002a. What about the students who are not college-bound? *California Educator, 66*(9), 6-13.

Posnick-Goodwin, S. June, 2002b. Practical skills prove beneficial. *California Educator, 66*(9), 6-13.

School-to-Work Opportunities Act of 1994, HR2284/51361 Legislative Fact Sheet. Retrieved January 4, 2003, from http://www.nhmccd.edu/contracts/toolbox/fact2884.html

Shades Valley Technical Academies. (n.d.). *Visual arts & communications academy. The road to completion*. [Pamphlet]. Author.

Shaid, J.A. (2001). *The systemic impact of Ohio tech prep programs on postsecondary academic readiness rates at two-year institutions - A four consortia study*. Unpublished doctoral dissertation, University of Dayton, Ohio.

Sierra Regional Career Partnership: The community learning coordinator system. School-to-Career Region III. Best Practices Report 2002. p. 21-23.

South Central Career Information Systems. Retrieved January 20, 2003, from http://www.sccis.org/main/careerprov/bestprac/bestexemp.htm

Vermont's School-to-Career. *Liaison networks*. Retrieved December 26, 2002, from http://www.state.vt.us/stw/exemplarybpintro.html

Wonacott, M.E. (2000). *Benefits of vocational education: Myths and realities No. 8*. ERIC/CASS. Retrieved January 20, 2003, from http://ericacve.org/docgen.asp?tbl=mr&ID=96

Wonacott, M.E. (2002). *High schools that work: Best practices for CTE, Practice Application Brief No. 19*. ERIC/CASS. Retrieved January 20, 2003, from http://ericacve.org/docgen.asp?tbl=pab&ID=109

Your Child's Career. *Best practices: What's happening in the schools in Anderson, Oconee, and Pickens Counties?: Duke technical career day*. Retrieved January 20, 2003, from http://www.yourchildscareer.org/textversion/schoolshelp/schoolshelp_bbest.htm

Chapter Eighteen

Working Connections: Business-Education Partnerships That Work

Carola F. S. Dopps

Abstract

Business-education partnerships are a vital component in today's school systems. A successful partnership will ensure that the school curriculum keeps abreast of industry trends, the state of the economy, and the dynamic requirements of the workplace. It further ensures that the emerging students are better prepared to meet the needs and challenges of an ever-changing society. The intent of this chapter is to determine the essential components of a successful partnership, to highlight the value of a successful relationship and, finally, to provide the tools needed in order to develop mutually beneficial working connections. Ultimately, a successful business-education partnership should meet the unique needs of a school and its students as well as the requirements of the business concerned.

Why Are Partnerships Between Business and Education Essential?

Partnerships between schools and businesses help integrate students more productively and effectively into the workplace. Organized activities and exchanges between the two entities further promote the students' understanding not only of business ethics in general but also of their own specific needs and capabilities. Consequently, students should become more focused and be able to choose a more satisfying career. A successful business-education partnership will ensure that the emerging students are more responsible, self-sufficient and better prepared to meet the challenges of an ever-changing workplace. It further helps to ensure that the school curriculum will keep abreast of industry trends, the state of the economy, and the dynamic requirements of the workplace.

Only about half of the students who start college will finish with a degree. According to Susan Quattrociocchi (2000), students are failing to complete college too often for three reasons: lack of financial planning, lack of focus, and lack of academic and technical skills. Therefore, it is becoming increasingly important for students to define their interests and skills at an even earlier age. Middle school and high school students should be provided with the opportunities and tools needed for continuous exploration and self-development. Although more students are expected to graduate with a Bachelor's degree by 2012 (Hussar & Gerald, Pocket Projections, 2002), many graduates may not have a plan for their future. Effective partnerships between schools and businesses will enable students to make appropriate choices and informed decisions throughout their school years, ultimately enabling them to plan more effectively for the years beyond so that they do have a plan for the future.

Reasons for the Business Community to get Involved With Schools

In the past two decades, the business community increased its participation in school programs. This is partly due to the School-to-Work Opportunities Act of 1994. Early studies of school-to-work pilot programs found that employers mentioned their desire to improve their communities as one of the most significant reasons for their participation (Bailey 1995). In 1997, only three years after the Act was passed and before all states had received funding, more than one-quarter of all firms employing 20 or more people were members of partnerships, and membership has grown steadily since (Bailey, Hughes & Mechur, 2001). However, in order for businesses to maintain partnerships with schools and for them to continue to enhance and enrich communities, they need more incentives than just civic-mindedness.

A critical reason for the business community to become involved in school programs is the lack of a skilled workforce. Businesses can help to create a skilled labor force for the region and the broader economy through partnerships with schools. Recently programs such as The Academy of Information Technology (a program of the National Academy Foundation) at Highline School District in Seattle, Washington, and the High Tech Learning Centers (a program of NEVAC—the North East Vocational Area Cooperative in the Puget Sound region of Seattle) were created in schools. These programs were designed to help combat this issue of a lack of skilled workers by delivering state-of-the-art information technology education to high school students. Through these programs, businesses continue to offer various work-based learning opportunities for both students and teachers. Various procedures make it possible for students to obtain industry certification and/or college credits while in high school. As stated by Walt Yeager, former Regional Director for Spacenet and an advocate of business-education partnerships,

> "These technology programs in the high schools are key to the economic future of the Puget Sound area. We must invest in students now to produce a qualified workforce for the future. High tech companies won't come to the area and stay here without qualified employees" (Burton & Dopps, AEA Newsline, 2001).

There is a concern within the IT (information technology) industry regarding the low number of females and minorities who pursue the field of technology. This may be partly due to the stereotypes associated with the technology industry. Therefore, another reason for businesses to partner with schools is to market certain industries to young people with a view to changing their perception and to provide accurate information. Through partnerships with schools, the high tech industry tries to change the perspective of females and minorities about the industry and to encourage them to consider high tech careers. An example of such a partnership is a program called "IGNITE" (Inspiring Girls Now In Technology Evolution) which started in the Seattle School District. The program invites professional women from the high tech industry to share their experience in high tech careers with area high schools girls. The women describe all aspects of their jobs and try to give the girls honest and positive advice. They discuss their likes and dislikes and further highlight their struggles and achievements within their chosen field. Ultimately, they hope to inspire the girls and persuade them to consider a high tech career as an option. The presentations have resulted in an increased number of girls taking technology classes in various high schools. These presentations are very successful because they are an easy way for interested individuals to become involved. Partnerships are an exchange of value. For example, a company will donate time and funds to an organization such as IGNITE in exchange for their work to increase the number of women and minorities to enter the high tech industry, which is valuable to the company.

In order to attract target populations to information technology (IT) industries, it is helpful to know why people from the target groups are currently at work in the IT arena. According to the Information Technology Association of America ("Diversity Survey," U.S. Black Engineer and IT Magazine, April, 2001), what first stimulated the target population in the

IT industry was "early exposure to technology." Of those surveyed, 34% stated this factor as contributing most to their initial interest in IT, followed by 26% of people who quoted contact with a "family member or friend," and only 22% who attributed their interest to "prior work experience." These results show the importance of stimulating and satisfying curiosity in technology at an early age and the significance of mentoring. Career development opportunities, such as internships and mentoring, as well as career awareness, are critical to attracting women and minorities to IT industries.

Finally there are additional benefits to partnerships with schools which may impact a participating business directly, which are discussed in the next section.

What are the Benefits of Business-Education Partnerships?

Traditionally, most business-education partnerships were developed predominantly to benefit education. Businesses often participated out of good will to help public schools in their region. Today, however, partnerships can and should benefit all parties involved. The focus should not only be on education but also on the needs of businesses and the community at large. Mutually benefiting ventures are true partnerships and will offer more effective, and often longer lasting, relationships. The most beneficial partnerships are broad-based, involving multiple organizations, and they require long-term institutional commitment. As mentioned earlier, a major motivation for employers to partner with schools is to help create a skilled workforce that, in turn, helps the local economy. When businesses engage in collaborative partnerships, they look for benefits that affect their operation, productivity, and profit line - elements that enable them to be competitive in a changing society. Benefits such as improved public relations, better prepared entry-level employees, decreased training costs, increased productivity, and heightened potential for local economic development will all affect their "bottom line" (Lankard, 1995).

Partnerships involving students, teachers and employers working together and visiting the work site have countless benefits (see table 1, 2 and 3). During a job shadow at Global Event Services, Inc., Brian and Heath, seniors from Redmond High School in Washington State, recently commented, "What we're seeing and doing here reinforces what we're learning in class. It's a blast!" Owner Terry Escott said, "These are hard working students who come with good skill sets. They get a chance to do some hands-on activities in the high tech workplace, and my employees grow professionally because they're learning mentoring and leadership skills while the students are shadowing them" (Burton & Dopps, AEA Newsline Magazine, Spring 2001).

Partnerships between education and business provide benefits to students, schools, the community and employers. A listing of the benefits in Tables 1, 2 and 3 are taken from the Washington State Guide to Planning, Implementing and Improving Work-based Learning (1997)

Table 1. Partnership Benefits For Students And Schools

Benefits for student:
- Provides opportunities to apply academic proficiencies
- Establishes a clear connection between education and work
- Increases motivation and retention by showing relevance of classroom content
- Provides opportunities to explore possible careers
- Enhances skill development
- Improves post-graduation job prospects
- Develops workplace responsibility
- Provides opportunities to learn about workplace realities
- Provides opportunities for leadership development
- Shows how to participate meaningfully in the community
- Provides opportunity to learn about the non-profit and service sectors
- Provides opportunities to develop relationships with adults outside of education
- Establishes professional contacts for future employment and mentoring
- Provides opportunities for increasing self-determination and self-advocacy skills
- Establishes positive work habits and attitudes
- Encourages staying in school and program completion
- In some cases' paid opportunities can help defray educational costs

Benefits for schools:
- Expands curriculum and learning facilities
- Provides access to latest sophisticated equipment
- Enhances education's ability to meet the needs of diverse student populations

---

Table 1 (cont.)

- Provides opportunities for individualized instruction
- Makes education more relevant and valuable for students
- Increases student retention
- Maximizes enrollment in retraining programs
- Augments interaction between education and the business community
- Promotes faculty interaction with the community
- Contributes to faculty/staff development
- Keeps curricula up-to-date through communication with employers
- Facilitates communication regarding actual proficiencies required by employers/occupations

Table 2. Partnership Benefits The Community

Benefits for the community:
- Ensures cooperation and understanding between education and the community
- Generates opportunities to benefit from the energy and creativity of students
- Provides needed services
- Builds confidence in the educational system
- Encourages respect and tolerance among different groups
- Increases buying power of students
- Enhances awareness of local employment opportunities
- Builds the foundation for a more productive economy

Washington State Guide to Planning, Implementing and Improving Work-based Learning (1997)

Table 3. Partnership Benefits For Employers

Benefits for employers:
- Provides well-prepared entry level employees
- Offers a source of skilled and motivated future employees
- Reduces the costs of recruitment and training
- Improves employee retention
- Provides technical assistance with employee training
- Provides developmental opportunities for the current workforce
- Offers opportunities to provide community service
- Encourages involvement in the curriculum development process

Table 3 (cont.)

- Enables employers to develop new projects with student assistance
- Gives the business a direct return on the tax dollar
- Increases employer visibility in education
- Provides opportunities to communicate required job specific proficiencies to educational personnel.

Washington State Guide to Planning, Implementing and Improving Work-based Learning (1997)

A Systematic Approach to Developing Partnerships

To create partnerships that work, it is essential to know the needs of all parties, have a common vision, and develop shared goals and objectives. School or district personnel may approach organizations to ask for help, but may not seriously consider the needs of the organization or how they may benefit, as discussed earlier. However, the quality of the learning opportunity for students should not diminish when considering the benefits of the employer while recruiting employers. Educators should never sacrifice student outcomes for employer involvement. The next section describes steps that educators can take to develop ongoing partnerships to help teachers be up-to-date with their teachings and students be better prepared for their future.

Steps for Developing Great Partnerships

1) Identify the needs of your students and teachers and create a plan. Without a clear picture and a plan for what your school and your students need, it will be difficult to persuade a business to work with you. Be sure to clarify and outline what students will be able to do and how they will use their newly acquired skills to their benefit as a result of the partnership.
2) Identify potential employers; some firms are better fitting and more likely than others to participate in your program. Some criteria that may help you with your initial recruitment efforts are:
    a) Prior involvement in school-business partnerships
    b) Tradition of leadership in community affairs
    c) Commitment to being a "learning organization"
    d) Industry areas which employ large or increasing numbers of employees; "The likelihood an organization is involved in school-to-work programs increases with the size of the

331

organization" according a report from the School-to-Work Programs Survey (2002). d)

    e) Firms and organizations experiencing labor shortages

    f) Friendly competition with firms in the same industry (or with similar presence in the community)

    g) Familiarity with school programs

    h) Government agencies with many entry-level positions

    i) Organizations with many entry-level positions

3) Approach professional organizations and special interest groups for referrals

    a) Approach parents from your school to recruit their firms

4) Approach the employer with your proposal or request, keeping in mind what motivates the employer.

    a) Highlight specific benefits to the employers

    b) Build a genuine partnership allowing for a sense of ownership and responsibility

    c) Offer various paths of involvement and degree of commitment - be flexible, start with less-demanding participation options to build the relationship and then encourage more involvement after a relationship has been established

    d) Clearly define the expected roles and responsibilities of employers - this can be facilitated in various ways;

        i) Meeting

        ii) Formal orientation event and/or training

        iii) Handbook

        iv) Regular dialogue (various forms of communication are mentioned below)

    e) Use the employer's time and other resources wisely

    f) Anticipate and be prepared to answer employer concerns. Be clear, concise and timely in your answers

    g) Use business leaders to recruit their peers and get referrals

5) Continuous communication is a priority. Ask employers how and when they would like to be informed. Notify employers of any changes; check in on a regular basis and ask for feedback and input. Be considerate of employers' time. Make sure if you call for a meeting that you are prepared and organized; have an agenda to ensure that the meeting will be productive. Have a reason or question ready any time you contact the employer. Other forms of communication may include:

    a) A monthly newsletter to share information about the program.

This is a great way to also highlight a participating business - they will appreciate the PR.

  b) Scheduled phone calls
  c) Unobtrusive e-mail

6) ALWAYS have closure. Any program or activity you start needs to have some form of closure. This may mean a final presentation by a student for a student internship, or a celebration where participants come together and are recognized. Always write a thank you note for the time, effort and talent donated by an employer. Thanking and appreciating employers for their contribution is the most essential component for a dynamic partnership that will last. This should be done not carelessly but thoughtfully. Public announcements of contributions, a handwritten note, or a certificate of appreciation all go a long way. Whenever possible, include pictures of the activities and feedback from students or teachers when thanking employers. For example, one program director showed her appreciation by providing framed student artwork for display at the employer's work site. Be creative when showing your appreciation.

7) Evaluate the effectiveness of the program on an ongoing basis. Make changes accordingly and share your findings with participants.

Business-Education Partnership Activities to Consider

- Job Shadowing - students/teachers observe an employer
- Internships - paid or non-paid entry level jobs and training, associated with school course or program
- Mentoring Programs - industry mentors are role models who help familiarize a student with the workplace, offering information on workplace skills or assisting in school projects
- Student Culminating Projects - similar to a mentoring program, but with a focus on a culminating project
- Mock Interviews - employers interview students for practice and provide feedback on their performance
- Informational Interviews - students interview an employee about their job/career
- Field Trips
- Career Fair - speakers from industry share about their jobs/careers, or set up booths with information.
- Speakers Bureau

- Tutorial Services
- Tours
- Teacher Business Exchange - teacher job shadows an employer and vice versa
- Advisory Board Member
- Technical Services - support a school's technology plan
- Adopt-a-School, Adopt-a-Class, Adopt-a-Subject
- Leadership Training - employer shares sessions with school personnel
- Motivational Speakers
- Corporate News Line - use corporate communication to get your message out
- Employee Recognition - for contribution to business-education partnerships
- Informational Videos - students produce a video highlighting your business and job skills required in the workplace
- Funding Partner

A Working Example: DigiGirlz High Tech Camp at Microsoft Corporation

Consultants for the High Tech Learning Centers in Washington State were given the task to create partnerships with local businesses to provide internships, mentorships, job shadowing, company tours, and related activities for high school students as well as for teachers. One of the participating companies was the Microsoft Corporation. Each year, the Microsoft Corporation receives many more high school student internship application packages than the number of internships they can provide. In addition, Microsoft and the technology industry as a whole are concerned about the lack of women and minorities in technology-related jobs and are spending much time and energy in recruiting efforts. In order to fulfill the needs of students to participate in work-based learning and the need to increase the number of women pursuing technology careers, the Diversity Department at Microsoft Corporation in Spring 2001 (also the department in charge of high school internships) was approached with a proposal to create a high tech summer camp for high school girls at Microsoft's main campus in Redmond, Washington. The proposal was well received and, as a result, a team was formed to develop the activities. The high tech camp for girls was named DigiGirlz (Chen, 2001, Dopps, 2001). The camp was such a success that a second camp took place in the summer of 2002. The camp encouraged and inspired girls to consider a career in the high tech industry, and provided opportunities for high school students to explore various technology careers and to experience the workplace at the software giant. During the camp, students heard from various Microsoft employees, participated in tours and workshops, learned about the various high tech related careers available at Microsoft, and were informed about the latest technologies.

The partnership with Microsoft worked because, in addition to the girls who attended, Microsoft also benefited. The event was great for public relations; it provided Microsoft with the opportunity to gain a better understanding of the Net Generation (technology users) and excited the attendees (potential customers) about Microsoft products (branding). In addition, the camp increased the number of students able to explore technology careers at Microsoft, inspired more (needed) young women to go into the technology field, and excited them about the future of technology, as well as the possibility of working for Microsoft in the future. All participants who made the event possible were thanked in writing. Certificates of appreciation with pictures and student feedback were given to key players. All student evaluations were compiled and analyzed, which formed the basis for the next DigiGirlz high tech camp, which took place in August 2002.

Conclusion

Partnerships between business and education are a vital component of any educational program preparing today's youth for the 21st Century. The most effective partnerships involve multiple organizations, are mutually beneficial, and share common goals and objectives. In order for schools to develop partnerships that work, schools will need to identify their needs first, and select businesses that may make a good match, keeping in mind what works and motivates the potential business partner. After a connection has been made, it is important to continuously evaluate and nurture the relationship to ensure a long-lasting, mutually benefiting partnership.

References

Bailey, T. (1995). *In learning to work: Employer involvement in school-to-work transition programs.* Washington, D.C.: Brookings Institution.

Bailey, T. R., Hughes, K. L., & Mechur, M. J. (2001). School-to-work: *Making a difference in education.* New York: Institute on Education and the Economy, Teachers College, Columbia University.

Bailey, T. R.., & Merritt, D. (1997, May). *School-to-work for the college bound.* Retrieved September, 2002 from http://www.tc.columbia.edu/ ~iee/BRIEFS/Brief15.htm.

Burton, M. P. & Dopps, C. F. S., (Spring 2001) Building the future: Encouraging high-tech talent at an early age. *Newsline-American Electronics Association, 25,* 12-13.

Chen, J. (2001, August 14). *DigiGirlz: High-tech camp for girls promotes careers in information technology.* Retrieved August 14, 2001, from http://www.microsoft.com/presspass/features/2001/aug01/08-14digigirlz.asp.

Diversity Survey—Information Technology Association of America, U.S. *Black Engineer & IT Magazine.* (2001, April). Retrieved October, 2002, from http://www.itaa.org/workforce/studies/diversityreport.pdf.

Dopps, C.F.S. (2001, August). *DigiGirlz high tech camp for girls.* Retrieved August, 2001, from: http://www.hightechlearning.org/overview/ digigirlz.html

Hussar, W.J. & Gerald, D.E. (October 2002). *Pocket projections. Projections of education statistics to 2012.* U.S. Department of Education, National Center for Education Statistics, NCES 2002-2033. Retrieved from http:/ /www.nces.ed.gov/pubsearch/pubsinfo.asp?pubid=2002033

Lankard, B.A. (1995) Business/education partnerships. ERIC Clearinghouse on Adult Career and Vocational Education Columbus OH [ED383856]. Retrieved August 30, 2002, from http://ericacve.org/docs/bed.htm

Quattrociocchi, S. (2000). *Help! A family's guide to high school and beyond.* Bellevue, Washington: Bellevue Community College Printing Services.

School-to-work Programs Survey (2002). Retrieved September, 2002, from http://www.shrm.org/surveys/results/02_SchoolToWork.pdf

Washington State guide to planning, implementing and improving work-based learning: A guide for educators at all levels (1997). Washington State Work-Based Learning Resource Center. Des Moines, Washington: Highline Community College. [ED410421]

Chapter Nineteen

The Crooked Career Path

Laura Jo Severson

Abstract

This chapter is directed primarily to school counselors. The current trends in education reform stress increasing the academic high school graduation requirements, providing more college-preparatory courses, and helping students to develop a career pathway. High school counselors can tell students what courses they need to take to prepare to go to a technical or community college or university, and usually have some suggestions about going directly to work. These actions are based on the premise that the students actually know what they want to do, that their circumstances will not change, and that they will not change their mind. Rather than identifying a pathway leading to a single goal, it is suggested that counselors and educators need to give students a map with alternate routes, planned detours, and permission to go down a crooked path toward a career.

Difficulty in Finding a Career Path

Students who are at risk, unmotivated, or undecided are already having trouble finding any career path, and they especially need tools to keep them going toward a goal. Unfortunately, educational reform stresses an increase in academic requirements based on a decrease in the number of electives, including vocational and technical courses. In school districts in many states, students in high school are faced with standards based on college entrance. Counselors strive to help students identify and follow a career path. What they need to do is examine what they are telling students and align their guidance to how the real career path works.

In many high schools, the staff measures their success by the percent of graduates who go on to a four-year college or a community college. One of the first things that counselors and educators need to do is to stop emphasizing that college is the only goal for their students. While many students will end up going to college for some part of their lives, that choice should not be held up as the right choice for everyone. Students need to be given the information about how to apply, how to pay for, and how to actually attend college, technical or trade school so that they will be able to do so when they are ready.

What Often Happens when Young People Do Attend College

While we have young people who choose a career, go through the appropriate education and enter a lifelong vocation, we also see young people emerging from colleges and universities with limited marketable skills. A college degree is no guarantee of a good job, particularly if its holder lacks experience. People enter college, technical schools, apprenticeships or new jobs at all stages of their lives. The high school student who is not academically oriented may change with maturity and seek higher education, while the academic honor student may decide that he or she prefers a "hands on" career. Counselors need to recognize that the career path is rarely straight; many people make changes in their job, either by choice or as a reaction to situations beyond their control. School Counselors need to review their work in light of the facts reported by Sheryl Gunnels-Perry (1998) in her book, *What in the World is Going On? Understanding, Impacting, and Going Beyond Education Reform*, in which she states that:

1. Research done by the American College Testing Program in 1996 indicated that more than 33% of all college freshmen enrolled in BA/BS programs dropped out after their first year.
2. As many as 25% of employees surveyed a year after completing four-year degrees were not working in the field for which their degrees educated them. Forty six percent of these college graduates surveyed indicated that they were holding jobs that did not require their degree.
3. The average age of students entering two-year colleges in the State of Washington is 29. Twenty-five to forty-two percent of these students already have a baccalaureate degree, but they are returning to technical and community colleges to acquire needed technical skills.

The Value of Internships and Work Experience

While a student is working toward a high school diploma, he or she should be given the opportunity to take vocational/technical courses, pursue internships and work experience, and develop the skills necessary to be gainfully employed. If a student completes a series of technical courses in high school, he or she should have the skills necessary for an entry-level job in that field. Students need to be encouraged to seek employment, either paid or as an intern, in a job related to their career selection. Even working in a low-skills job will give them exposure to the expectations and inner workings of a specific business or industry. An internship is often the best thing that can happen to a young person who is struggling with school and has no plans for the future. Internships give students the opportunity to gain work experience, references, and real training that they can carry back to their regular schools. In the workplace, students are exposed to high expectations in terms of attendance and behavior that often impact their behavior back at school.

Due to increased graduation standards, fitting vocational or technical courses into a schedule is difficult. Counselors need to work with their schools to promote philosophies and scheduling practices which allow students to take more of such courses during their high school career. The *High Schools That Work Consortium* recommends that schools use block scheduling. In block scheduling, students take four long classes per day and complete a full credit of work in one semester. Such scheduling allows a student to complete up to 32 credits in a high school career. This arrangement makes it possible for students to meet college entrance requirements while including vocational and technical training. It also gives students more class time to concentrate on a specific vocational field.

For struggling students, the structure of the high school program makes it difficult for them to take advantage of vocational opportunities that might make school work better for them. Most high school curricula require that students spend their first two years concentrating on required courses. These first two years coincide with the highest incidence of students dropping out of school. Students find themselves with little time for vocational or technical courses which they can see as a link to their future. They are given the traditional Social Studies, English, Math, and Science courses with a heavy emphasis on theory at a time when many students need hands-on and applied instruction. The high school program needs to be restructured so that students have the opportunity to take more vocational classes in their freshman and sophomore years. The academic classes that they take need to be linked more with job requirements and work applications. Students who are struggling or unmotivated in high school usually see the worth of what they are studying if they can link education with success on the job and earning money.

One of the recommendations of education reform is to require more *college preparatory* Social Studies, English, Math and Science classes.

Unfortunately, the greatest frustration for many students is that they do not see any purpose in such classes. The courses that we teach in high school need to have more applications; the term "applied" (when linked with words like physics or math) needs to stop being stigmatized. For many students, courses like English make more sense if taught through actual problems and projects. Vocational/technical teachers seem to be working to raise the academic standards of the classes that they teach. Teachers of the traditional academic subjects need to introduce real-world and work applications into their course materials.

All Students Would Benefit from Vocational Courses, Work-Based Learning and Applied Academics

Most people agree that students who are at-risk benefit from vocational courses, work-based learning, and applied academics, but it is this writer's opinion that *all* students would benefit from the same approach. In order to help prepare a student for the inevitable requirement that he or she work for a living, students should graduate with three things: (a) entry level skills for the job market; (b) work experience; and (c) exposure to people who work in a career field that they find interesting. For a motivated, college-bound student, working on a job related to their career interest would help them graduate with job skills, references, and a greater likelihood of employment. A student who has completed a high school course in carpentry or construction is going to make a much better architect. A student who takes a Medical Careers class and works as a nurse's aid or orderly during college summers will make a better doctor. Sometimes internships and student jobs let a young person know that their career choice is not a good fit, and they have the opportunity to make changes and adjustments.

Already, vocational teachers are working to give education a more seamless process. Tech Prep credits are given from high school courses which meet community college or technical school standards. The opportunity to receive actual college credits is a great motivator for students struggling in school. As a result of the coordination necessary to achieve articulation agreements and to meet college standards, the academic level is being raised.

School Counselors Need to Provide Information About Many Options

School counselors need to provide information for their students on how to move from one type of training to another. Most school counselors accomplish the task of providing each student with the facts about entering the two- or four-year college, technical school, apprenticeship, military or other program upon completion of high school. What they need to do is to remind students that while they have made a choice at this point in time, they may change their minds and go down a different path later. High school students need to graduate with an understanding of how to seek a variety of types of training in case their interests or situations change. There needs to be an emphasis on learning the variety of pathways to careers.

The high school senior who wants further education must face the choice of whether to enter a university or a community or technical college. For many, college will mean spending two years studying general courses in order to prepare them for their major. The student who wants to start on their field of interest often leaves school because they have been expected to spend their time in classes not necessarily related to what they set out to study. Traditionally, many universities steer freshmen into large, difficult required classes to "weed out" the weak and unmotivated. The discouraged student leaves college with little to help him or her on the path to a career. If students start in a technical college program, they may find that many of their courses do not transfer if they choose to continue to a baccalaureate program. Advising students how to deal with this is difficult for the high school counselor. It seems that some colleges are becoming more flexible about this issue, but the process is slow.

Some universities offer what is called an upside down BS/BA program. Students complete a two-year course in a technical field at a community college and then attend a university to complete their general education and professional requirements. While such an arrangement is not practical for all subjects, it does provide an option for the student who finds his academic goals increased by success in a vocational or technical field. Other colleges and universities are increasing the students' opportunities to take courses in their major and to do related internships earlier in their program. Glamorgan University in Wales, UK, begins students in a two-year Technician program. The best students are "creamed off" and remain to become Engineers. The top students from that level remain for graduate school. The obvious advantage is to allow the student to gain marketable skills in their field, even if they do not complete a BS/BA program. A few U.S. colleges have somewhat similar practices, but the traditional approach is hard to change.

Conclusion

School counselors need to provide information for their students as to how to move from one type of training to another. Most school counselors accomplish the task by providing each student with the facts about entering the two- or four-year college, technical school, apprenticeship, military or other program upon completion of high school. What they need to do is to remind students that while they have made a choice now, they may change their minds and go down a different path later. High school students need to graduate with an understanding of how to seek a variety of types of training in case their interests or situations change. There needs to be an emphasis on learning the variety of pathways to careers.

The high school counselor working with students needs to take into consideration the educational opportunities available to their graduates and advise accordingly. For some students, starting out in a technical program may be the better choice, even if it adds some crooks to their career path. These students could learn enough skills to enter a field of work with good pay and a chance at success. They could later pursue further education — armed with experience and exposure to the real world. Counselors seem to work with the purpose of helping the student identify and follow the direct route: enter four-year college, go to technical school, or go to work. Urging students to try a different approach might be a better process.

Counselors' goals are to keep students in school until they graduate, prepare them for life, and send them off to further training and/or work. Instead of assuming that we are sending each one off on a straight and narrow path, we need to prepare them for one that twists and turns. We need to give students the tools to make their own unique paths when the ones that they are on disappear. We need to look upon side trips and planned detours as achievements rather than failures. We need to work with our districts and state programs to promote vocational training, integration of technical and academic courses, and flexibility of scheduling. We need to work with post-secondary institutions to make our graduates' transition from academic training to work flow more smoothly. We need to help our students plan for their future instead of just the year after they finish high school.

References

Bottoms, Gene. (March 2002). State leadership in improving high schools for more students. *Southern Regional Education Board Journal On-Line Journal*, Southern Regional Education Board, 592 10th St. NW, Atlanta, GA 30318.

Gunnels-Perry, Sheryl. (1998). *What in the world is going on? Understanding, impacting, and going beyond education reform.* Redmond, WA: Concept Graphics & Publishing.

The High School That Works Consortium. Web site: http://www.sreb.org/programs/hstw/hstwindex.asp. University of Glamorgan. Web site: http://www.glam.ac.uk

Part V

Involving Parents in their Teen's Career Planning

Part V, Involving Parents in their Teens Career Planning, addresses the influential role that parents play in their student's success in school and in their career planning process. Parents need to understand the importance of their role and what they can do to contribute to their student's education. Parents can learn important information about what is available in school and in the community to help their students with career development issues. Parents also need to be aware of options other than a four-year college. This section contains two chapters:

(20) *The Important Role of Parents in their Teen's Career Development*—Sage details what parents need to know and do regarding their teen's career planning. He discusses that parents need to know: effective parenting skills with teens, knowledge of developmental needs of high school students, knowledge of career management skills, knowledge of the school's curricular and extra-curricular program, knowledge of the school-to-career program, knowledge of postsecondary options, and the steps in career planning. He encourages educators to work closely with parents and see them as partners in working with students.

(21) *The Right Tools—Helping High School Graduates Consider all the Postsecondary Options,* (printed with permission by ASCA, as this article appeared in *The ASCA School Counselor, March/April 2002)*—Hoyt encourages parents and educators to look beyond the traditional four-year college for postsecondary training opportunities in community colleges, public and private technical training institutes, federally sponsored career training programs, and military training programs. Dr. Hoyt discusses the Parent Aspiration Problem, saying that a large majority of parents assume that their children will eventually become college graduates, even though there are not enough jobs requiring a four-year college degree. He estimates that the annual number of college graduates exceeds the number of jobs requiring college degrees by 100,000-300,000 per year. Thus, he exhorts parents to consider other options with their students.

Chapter 20

The Important Role of Parents in Their Teen's Career Development

Howard Sage

Abstract

In the complex society of the early twenty-first century, high school staffs need to develop programs that address the important role of parents in their teen's career development. Comprehensive guidance programs are required that educate parents as to: (a) their critical role in career development, (b) the knowledge they need in order to be helpful to their student, and (c) the facilitative parental skills and attitudes required to enhance teen's career self-assessment, exploration and decision making process.

To accomplish these goals, high school staffs need to articulate and communicate the role parents have in the high school years. Part of the important role of parents should include knowledge of their student and essential career information as well as critical parenting skills and attitudes that facilitate career development. This role needs to be explained and reinforced by the guidance program and information systems of the school and community.

Introduction

"Which occupations should my student explore?" "What do I, as a parent, need to know and understand to help my student in high school?" Before parents get answers to those questions, they need to appreciate the importance of providing for adolescents and the need to understand the developmental and unique personal needs of their children as they grow and change. (Leifer and Lesser, 1976)

Educators know that parents are a significant influence on their teen's career development. Most of us know that caring, involvement and some knowledge are necessary for a parent to help a son or daughter with his or her career development. The literature on parenting for career development is replete with lists, suggestions and knowledge to help parents think about what they should do and how they might go about doing it. A summary of research by Kerka (2002) "indicates that parenting styles, family functioning, and parent-child interaction influence career development" (p.3). Still, in high schools today, parent involvement is very often a minor part of guidance programming.

A variety of experts and journalists during the last quarter century have communicated conflicting, fragmented messages that have served to confuse parents, distance them from school, and have made many feel uncertain about how to approach parenting for career development. Furthermore, for many in the United States, being very involved with your students has been misinterpreted as being "over-controlling." In American culture, individual freedom of choice has trumped parental guidance, resulting in many young adults floundering in their early adult years because of lack of knowledge and guidance. There is also a strong belief among many parents that focusing on career planning in high school may cause students to make a "permanent, premature career choice." And a small number of parents unwittingly try to "live" through their children, placing too much pressure and unrealistic expectations on their student in high school (Middleton, 1992).

On the other hand, education has its own increasing complexities and expanding educational options that many parents do not understand well enough to be effective in helping their teen. Depending on the size of the school and quality of the career and educational programming, access to current, relevant, and accurate career and educational information may be challenging even within the high school program. Also, some high school students experience a tremendous sense of inertia as they face the transition to adulthood; many are overly self-conscious of their weaknesses and are too little confident of their strengths. Some have learning, family, financial or health challenges which engender a sense of frustration that can easily turn to hopelessness. Against this challenging backdrop, educators must develop and implement improved programming to help busy high school parents who want to know how best to help their teen.

Communicating the Critical Parent Role in Career Development

School staffs can be especially helpful by providing information on parent education and adolescents' needs that facilitate communication, growth and development. (Middleton,1992). This information can be provided at "parent nights" and workshops, on school websites, and in parent newsletters and handouts. Parents need to understand the importance of their role clearly. They are critically needed to:

1) provide for the physical, emotional, social and spiritual needs of their teens, which
provides the foundation for an effective parenting relationship with their teen (Cline and Fay, 1990);

2) collaborate with the school staff concerning the education and career concerns of their child (Birk and Blimline, 1984);

3) utilize their knowledge of school and community, to create opportunities toward the educational and career development of their teen;

4) help students set goals and teach the integration of skills most have learned in other contexts (Epstein,1995; Elias, Friedlander, and Chopra, 2002);

5) reinforce performance and practice of work related activities (Knapp & Bedford, 1967);

6) stimulate reflection, processing and decision-making about educational and career information (Knapp & Bedford, 1967);

7) encourage self-assessment and exploration of opportunities;

8) help teens see the relevance and presence of work at home and school (Birk & Blimline, 1984); and

9) remain in a consultant role and develop a pattern of teen choice related to career plans. (A pattern of teen choice refers to an ongoing career decision-making process.)

According to Kerka (2000), high school parents need to understand that an "authoritative parenting style is associated with self-confidence, persistence, social competence, academic success, and psychosocial development. When parents provide a warm family climate, set standards and promote independence, more active career exploration by children results. Family functioning has a greater influence on career development than family structure or parents' educational and occupational status."(p.1).

Parents need to realize that their involvement is critical to the career development of their teen. This realization is important because most parents know the strengths, limitations and interests of their children better than other people. Parents also have great influence on their children even in the college years and early adulthood. Taking a "hands off' approach to educational and career planning denies teens the guidance they need to navigate a challenging transition to adulthood.

Educating Parents – What They Need to Know and Do

1) Effective Parenting Skills with Teens

Many high school parents would benefit greatly by attending a parenting skills course designed for communicating with teens. Parenting skills are very important and all school-based programs involving parents should educate and proclaim the importance of good parenting skills and attitudes. All methods of communication should be used to emphasize it. Counselors and administrators should take advantage of opportunities to reinforce this information in presentations, written communications and in face-to-face contacts with parents.

To effectively function in their role as parents of high school students, the following facilitative parenting skills are helpful:
- Reflective listening and acceptance of your teen's feelings and thoughts about educational and career plans;
- Good questioning and discussion skills to draw out your teen's thoughts and feelings and show understanding;
- Encouraging and inspiring skills;
- Skills in teaching your teen how the skills they have, or are currently learning, fit with chosen career and educational goals (Elias, Tobias, Friedlander, and Chopra, 2000);
- Skill in monitoring the steps of career planning, including decision-making and goal setting (Young, Paseluikho, and Valech, 1992).

2) Parental Attitudes

To effectively function in their role as parents of high school students, the following attitudes are facilitative to a teen's career development:
- Convey an attitude of the importance of your own role in this process (Birk and Blimline, 1984).
- View your student as a valuable person with many wonderful qualities and strengths. Convey an attitude of belief in your child.
- Convey a positive attitude about the importance of education. "Learning is an experience which happens both at school and at home" (Hickman, 1995, p.4).
- Convey high expectations but keep them general enough so that your student does not feel excess pressure to please you.
- Accept it as a challenge to collaborate with your teen in career and educational planning. (Birk and Blimline, 1994)

352

3) Knowledge of Developmental Needs of High School Students
This information is readily available from many sources. Two sources are from the American Academy of Child and Adolescent Psychiatrists (1997) and the American School Counselor Association (2002).
http://www.aacap.org/publications/factsfam/develop.htm
http://www.aacap.org/publications/factsfam/develop2.htm
http://www.schoolcounselor.org/content.cfm?L1=1000&L2=79

4) Knowledge of Career Management Skills Needed by High School Teens
When parents are made aware of the career management skills needed by teens, they are enabled to understand their teen and help them more effectively. They will realize the many changes their teen will experience in the process of career development. While being familiar with the developmental and career development needs of an adolescent is helpful, it is not enough. Parents must also learn what career planning skills teens need to learn during the high school years. This is well outlined in the *National Career Development Guidelines for High School* (National Occupational Information Coordinating Committee (1989)). The three domains addressed are: Self-Knowledge, Educational and Career Exploration, and Career Planning. Students need to learn to understand the importance of work-based learning related to their career interests. They also need assistance in establishing positive career goals and the means of accomplishing them (Perry and Ward, 1997).

5) Knowledge of the School's Curricular and Extra-Curricular Programs
Parents need to understand the opportunities available in the school's curricular and extra-curricular programs, as well as the larger community, and how they relate to career and educational goals. (This information should be presented in easily comprehensible language to parents.) They need to understand academic and career course sequences and pre-requisites. This knowledge is critical for parents to know—to be able to advise and guide their teen.

6) Knowledge of the School's School-to-Career Program
Parents need to understand the details of their school's school-to-career program and how to support and enhance the goals of the program. A school-to-career program should provide self-knowledge related activities, as well as career and educational exploration and job-seeking skill instruction. Examples of self-knowledge activities might include: personal reflection exercises, self-assessment checklists and tests of interests,

aptitudes, work values and aspirations. Educational and career exploration activities might include: job shadowing, internships, field trips, classroom speakers, structured research of career information, summer camps, career fairs with materials, demonstrations, and handouts. Career planning activities might include: instruction in résumé writing, letter of application writing, interviewing, using the telephone, using the Internet and printed resources and simulations. Students might produce portfolios and culminating projects or demonstrate skills to staff, students and community members in classroom or in grade level configurations. If the high school has career pathways or major areas of concentration, parents should understand their function as vehicles to enhance student exploration, learning and planning (Perry and Ward, 1997).

7) Understand Postsecondary Preparation, Environments, and Opportunities

Parents remain a primary source of career information for high school students. Parental knowledge of the preparation required, the nature of the environments and the many options available in a variety of educational and occupational environments is invaluable in consulting with their student to make critical life choices.

8) Understand the Steps to Career Planning

Parents need a basic understanding of the career planning process in order to encourage their student to participate. According to *The Parents' Crash Course in Career Planning*, (Harris and Jones, 1996), those steps are: 1) Self-Assessment; 2) Research & Exploration; 3) Gaining Experience; 4) Developing Marketable Skills & Enhancers; and 5) Learning Job-Seeking Skills.

The High School's Role in Involving Parents

So how do high school staffs articulate and communicate the role parents should play in the high school years? How does a school-to-career program educate, teach and encourage critical parent participation?

First, the school staff needs a vision of their essential well-educated high school graduate. This vision would include a goal related to the transition of the high school student to adulthood. In the context of the development of a comprehensive high school guidance program model described by Gysbers (1994), it would include the kinds of career and educational planning skills a graduate would be able to demonstrate. From that, a school-to-career program is developed using the *National Career*

Development Guidelines (National Occupational Information Coordinating Committee, 1989) and *SCANS Skills* (U.S. Department of Labor, 1991) and many creative ideas from staff members, students and people in the community to accomplish the goals. This process should include: a needs assessment including parents, students and staff; a plan that seeks to implement the program school-wide over a two-or three-year period; and efforts to involve parents and establish support from the entire school community. A sound comprehensive program should involve its stakeholders. Parents should be on guidance program steering committees and governance councils that direct, develop and approve program objectives and activities. Governance councils are usually site-based and have program evaluation and approval functions, while steering committees plan and evaluate a particular program such as a School-to-Career Program or a Guidance Program. The participation of parents should be stated clearly in terms of their relationship to comprehensive guidance program elements, including:

- *Content* (i.e., how parents assist in the development of student competencies);
- *Structural Components* (i.e., parents' role in program rationale and assumptions);
- *Program Components and Sample Activities* (i.e., how parents are encouraged and informed in the guidance curriculum, individual planning, responsive services and system support components); and
- *Resources* (i.e., how parents' resources of time and talents contribute to the program).

High school teens and parents may not come to after-school meetings. There is usually not enough time for all counselors and parents to have individual conferences. Therefore, most materials and information should be developed for use at home between parents and students. School websites are a fast and convenient way for parents to get information. Career fairs, workshops, panels and guest speakers provide important opportunities to attract parents to learn more about school and community resources; they also provide interactive communication opportunities between school staff members and parents.

It is also very important to develop and present most educational and career information for targeted audiences in your school (by grade level or career and educational goals). In the early years of high school, program information should be broader, explaining all programs and options to students. By the spring of the junior year, program efforts should be differentiated into more specific goal areas. For example, military-bound or military academy-bound students and parents should have separate checklists, workshops, and resource information. The use of checklists for parents and students can be very helpful in keeping busy parents and students aware of critical timelines and windows of opportunity.

Conclusion

Career information is of minimal value if teens do not have encouraging relationships with caring adults who provide guidance and consultation as they prepare for the transition to adulthood. High school staffs need to aggressively inform parents as to their critical role in guiding and encouraging their teens toward career planning. Parents need knowledge and skills to parent their high school student. Finally, school staffs need to encourage and guide parents to work as partners with schools to enhance the career and educational transition for their students. Parental involvement is critical to teens' success in career and educational planning, and it is essential to a school staff's efforts to provide a meaningful guidance program for its students.

Appendix

A summary checklist based on key points of this article is provided below to assist school staffs to plan and evaluate parental involvement in school-to-career programs.

Checklist for Educators
To Encourage Parent Involvement and Effectiveness

The critical role of parents with regard to high school students' career and educational development has been communicated in writing, in meetings, and through the school's website. Writing efforts might include: parent newsletters, course description guides, handbooks, handouts at parent meetings and website links to checklists, articles and written reference materials.

This communication should emphasize the importance of the following 8 points:
1) emotional and educational provision for their teen;
2) collaboration with the school;

3) becoming knowledgeable about school programs and resources;
4) goal-setting and skill-building;
5) reinforcing career development behaviors;
6) encouraging (continually) their teen's self-assessment and exploration;
7) identifying relevant connections between educational and career activities; & 8) becoming and remaining an effective consultant to their child.

____ Parent education programs that teach communication skills between parents and teens have been promoted and encouraged by counselors in large and individual meetings with parents, as well as in written handouts and announcements.

____ Helpful parental attitudes have been described to parents in a variety of ways.

____ Resources and descriptions about developmental needs have been provided in writing to all parents.

____ Resources and descriptions of needed high school student career management skills have been provided in writing to all parents.

____ Parents have been updated annually about important high school and postsecondary educational and career related opportunities from a variety of sources.

____ Parents have been provided with a detailed list of how to support the school-to-career program in their student's high school.

____ Parents have been provided with a list of the steps to career planning.

____ School-to-career program goals have been supported by state, district and building vision statements and goals. Parents have been given the opportunity to participate on key groups overseeing career programs.

____ A variety of efforts and venues to communicate with parents have been used including: career and/or college fairs, printed materials, parent workshops, individual appointments, and school website information.

Checklist developed by Howard Sage, Ed.D., September, 2002

References

American Association of Child and Adolescent Psychiatry. (1997). *Facts for families*, Retrieved July 2, 2002, from http://www.aacap.org/publications/factsfam/develop.htm and http://www.aacap.org/publications/facts.fam/develop2.htm

American School Counselor Association. (2002).*Teenagers: Parenting with love, laughter, and limits*. Retrieved July 2, 2002, from http://www.schoolcounselor.org/content.cfm?L1=1000&L2=79

Birk, J. M. & Blimline, C.A. (1984). Parents as career development facilitators: An untapped resource for the counselor. *The School Counselor 31 (4), 310-317.*

Child Development Project. (1994*). At home in our schools, a guide to school wide activities that build community.* Oakland, CA: Developmental Studies Center. Author.

Cline, F. & Fay, J. (1990). *Parenting teens with love and logic: Teaching children responsibility.* Colorado Springs, CO: Pinon Press.

Elias, M., Tobias, S.E., Friedlander, B.S. & Chopra. G. (2000). *Raising emotionally intelligent teenagers, parenting with love, laughter, and limits.* Three Rivers, MI: Three Rivers Press.

Epstein, J.L. (1995). School-family-partnerships: Caring for children we share. *Phi Delta Kappan,* 76 (9), 701-712.

Gysbers, N. C. & Henderson, P. (1994). *Developing and managing your school guidance program.* Alexandria, VA: American Counseling Association.

Harris, M. B. & Jones, S. (1996). *The parents crash course in career planning.* Chicago:VGM Horizons.

Hickman, C.W. (1995, December-1996, January) The future of high school success: The importance of parental involvement programs. Published in *The High School Journal.* Retrieved July 2, 2002, from http://horizon.unc.edu/projects/hsj/Hickman.asp

Kerka, S. (2000). Parenting and career development. *ERIC Digest No. 214, ED440351*.Columbus, OH: ERIC Clearinghouse on Adult, Career, and Vocational Education.

Knapp, D.L. & Bedford, J.H. (1967). The parents' role in career development. Washington, DC:National Vocational Guidance Association.

Leifer, A.D. & Lesser, G.S. (1976). *The development of career awareness in young children* (NIE Papers in Education and Works, No. 1). Washington, DC: National Institute of Education.

Middleton, E. (1992, Fall). My son, the doctor? *American Counselor* 1(4), 15-19.

National Occupational Information Coordinating Committee (1989).*The national career development guidelines, local handbook.* Washington, DC: Author.

Perry, N., & Ward, L. (1997). *Helping students plan careers, A school-to-career guide_for counselors.* Alexandra, VA: American Vocational Association.

U.S. Department of Labor Secretary's Commission on Achieving Necessary Skills (SCANS) (June, 1991). *What work requires of schools.* U.S. Government Printing Office: Author.

Young, R.A., Paseluikho, M.A. & Valech. L (1992, Winter). The role of emotion in the construction of careers in parent and adolescent conversations. *Journal of Counseling and Development,* 76(1).

Chapter Twenty-One

The Right Tools: Helping High School Students Consider Their Postsecondary Options*

Kenneth B. Hoyt

Abstract

An abundance of good research exists that, when put together, produces a number of basic facts that both today's high school students and their parents should consider in deciding what to do after students graduate from high school. These include:

1. Although about 70 percent enter college the next fall after high school graduation, only about 50 percent of them ever graduate from a four-year college.
2. Most high school graduates seeking jobs right out of high school find only low pay, dead-end jobs waiting for them, and plenty of these are available.
3. Most good jobs today require some form of post-secondary education. A high school diploma isn't enough by itself for most of today's youth job seekers.
4. A wide variety of jobs require some kind of post-secondary education but not necessarily a four-year college degree.
5. The most common form of post-secondary sub-baccalaureate institutions are community colleges. Their advantages and disadvantages should both be studied.
6. Increasingly, the advantages and disadvantages of viewing the Armed Forces as a special kind of post-secondary education should also be given consideration.

Kathleen Rakestraw
Director of Communications
American School Counselor Association

High school students used to ask, "Should I go to college, or should I go to work?" For many of today's students, that is the wrong question. Instead, they should ask, "Should I go to a four-year college or to some other kind of post-secondary education?" Helping all high school graduates answer that question calls for several major changes on the part of professional school counselors.

Statistics tell us that between 60 percent and 70 percent of each year's high school graduates enroll in college the next fall intending to get a four-year bachelor's degree. However, about one in four will drop out during the first year in college, and less than 50 percent will eventually obtain a bachelor's degree, but about 90 percent of the parents of these students want them to complete a four-year college degree. We can't continue to simply count these kinds of statistics. Instead, counselors must try to change these statistics.

The Parent Aspiration Problem

It's clear that a large majority of parents assume their children will eventually become four-year college graduates. Of course, if all children did eventually obtain four-year degrees, we would be faced with a huge over-supply of college graduates, many of whom would have to become employed in jobs not requiring a four-year college degree. The prime factors currently preventing this are the large numbers of high school graduates who fail to meet college admissions standards, the high dropout rate at four-year colleges and the growing attractiveness of two-year community colleges and technical institutes. In spite of these factors, many parents continue to count on their children obtaining a four-year college degree and to assume such a degree will pay off later. To many parents, this is an absolute, not a relative, matter.

Most parents are well aware of national statistics showing that, on the average, education pays in terms of job earnings. Four-year college graduates, on the average, earn more than two-year college graduates, and two-year college graduates, on the average, earn more than high school graduates. These figures make it clear that although four-year college graduates, on the average, earn higher wages than do non-college graduates, there are many four-year college graduates who do not. Similarly, many non-four-year college graduates have higher weekly wages than the average four-year college graduate.

Every year, the number of students graduating from a four-year college outnumbers the available jobs requiring such degrees by 100,000-300,000 graduates. Imagine how disappointed both new college graduates and their parents must be when after graduation they fail to find a job requiring a four-year college degree. To some extent, these bad-news statistics are countered by other statistics showing the unemployment rate for four-year college graduates is, on the average, only about half as large as it is for persons without such a degree. For many recent college graduates, however, that is faint hope.

The typical first parental reaction to this information is "But it won't happen to my child." Maybe they're right. However, it would be unfair and unwise of counselors to hide these statistics from parents.

It's usually far better to share these statistics initially with parents in group parent meetings rather than in individual parent/counselor conferences. Parents can then see how some other parents find these figures useful, and they can discuss the statistics with other parents facing the same situation.

In discussing attending a four-year college, it would be a mistake to limit conversations to economic matters. It's also important for students and their parents to recognize and discuss non-economic reasons for obtaining a four-year college degree. In addition to economic benefits, higher education helps produce better and more productive citizens and helps students learn how to enjoy life, appreciate the creative arts, make lifelong friends, learn how to think, develop institutional affiliations and much more.

Career Skills Programs

In the next 10 years, about two in five job openings will require less than three months of on-the-job training. Most of these jobs are low paying, dead end and uninteresting with meager fringe benefits if any. Many are paid at the poverty level and contain no clear opportunity for advancement or tenure. Such jobs are likely to be available both to unemployed adults and to youth with only a high school diploma. The challenge here is to help as many high school graduates as possible avoid these dead-end jobs and, instead, acquire higher level jobs by attending some post-secondary, sub-baccalaureate-level educational institution.

Additionally, only one in three job openings expected to become available in the next 10 years will require a four-year college degree or more. If these are added to the two in five job openings expected to require less than three months preparation, we are left with close to 30 percent of job openings expected to require some more extensive training at the post-secondary sub-baccalaureate level. Helping students consider educational and career choices at this level is one of the major challenges facing school counselors today. Several problems must be overcome if this challenge is to be met.

Opportunities for high-tech skills: Many of the new jobs expected to be created in the next 10-20 years will require, among other things, a high level of expertise in computer usage. Most of today's post-secondary, sub-baccalaureate programs don't have access to some of the sophisticated equipment or the high level of expertise needed to operate true high-tech programs. There are, of course, exceptions, and counselors should take advantage of them where they exist.

Necessity of high-skills programs: If the United States is to compete in the international marketplace, it will be essential that many high-quality, high-skill career programs also be taught at the post-secondary level. The rudimentary career skills taught in many of today's secondary schools will not be enough. It will be impossible to produce high-skill, two-year, post-secondary programs unless high-quality instructors exist for the programs.

Necessity for customer-satisfaction information counselors and students can use in making post-secondary decisions: Too many counselors and too many high school students are largely unaware of what happens to students enrolled in specific post-secondary programs. Today's high school counselors need to learn how to help high school students answer questions about post-secondary opportunities.

Necessity for follow-up information: Almost all post-secondary, career-oriented, sub-baccalaureate educational institutions claim a prime goal is to help their graduates obtain good jobs directly related to the education they have received. Unfortunately, there seem to be few institutions that have collected this kind of follow-up data from former students.

Until and unless these kinds of problems are confronted and solved, it will be extremely difficult for today's school counselors to help students meaningfully consider all of the post-secondary options available to them.

Different Strokes

There is tremendous variation among post-secondary, career-oriented educational institutions. The following is my take on the options.

Community colleges
Unlike most of the other options, community college programs usually combine general education and specific career skill offerings. Their goal is to produce educated, not just trained, graduates. Community college graduates appear to have higher wages, on the average, than graduates of the other kinds of programs. There is also good evidence that, on the average, they have higher wages than do persons who have dropped out of four-year

colleges. Because they exist in specific communities, their costs to students in that community is usually low. Both high-skill and high-tech programs are offered with the majority being high skill. They produce more graduates than any other single type of formal career-oriented sub-baccalaureate institutions operating at the post-secondary level. Most of their programs are two years.

Technical institutes

These programs often concentrate on producing graduates with the know-how to be successful in high-tech occupations. Most of their programs are two years in length and are designed for students with good mastery of basic academic skills such as English, mathematics, communication and decision-making. Because of the expensive equipment, the relatively small numbers of pure high-tech jobs and the special kinds of instructor expertise required to operate such programs, only a limited number of bona fide technical institutes exists in most states.

One of the prime current operational problems existing is that, in some states, some high-skill programs are labeled as high tech. Counselors should be aware of this and be prepared to take it into account when discussing such institutions with students and their parents.

Publicly supported career institutions

In most states, publicly supported post-secondary, career-oriented institutions exist independent from either community colleges or technical institutes. The prime mission of such institutions is typically seen at providing students with high career skills. They differ from community colleges most clearly in their relative lack of emphasis in providing students with general education in addition to specific career skills. This appeals to many persons who, while interested in acquiring specific career skills, have no strong interest in academic education.

Proprietary career-oriented institutions: Some of the best— and some of the worst—career-oriented, post-secondary institutions are owned and operated for profit. Most seem to be offering programs that supplement rather than replace programs offered by community colleges in the state. When these institutions compete with community college programs, they usually do so primarily by using follow-up data from former students. This is, by far, the most expensive kind of post-secondary, career-oriented education available. Where successful graduates are found, they seem to feel these costs are reasonable. Good accreditation information exists for proprietary career-oriented institutions.

Federally sponsored career training programs for youth

Two federal programs contain specific career preparation opportunities for severely economically disadvantaged youth, ages 14-24. These are the Job Corps and the Workforce Investment Act. The most extensive provisions are seen in the Job Corps, where career skills are provided in an atmosphere of residential living. Job Corps enrollees are provided a small stipend along with a residential center that includes both meals and medical expenses. Both provide provisions for career counseling. The Workforce Investment Act provides for acquisition of basic career skills but does not include the residential benefits found in the Job Corps. In my view, the training provided by these two programs is probably at no more than the high school level. For the truly poor youth in need of these skills, however, both of these programs appear to hold much of value. Many professional school counselors are likely to find students who are eligible for and could profit from one of these programs.

Armed Services career-oriented programs

The U.S. Armed Forces is one of the largest suppliers of career skills taught at the post-secondary, sub-baccalaureate level. Literally hundreds of such programs are available after basic training to youth who enlist in the U.S. Army, U.S. Navy, U.S. Air Force or U.S. Marine Corps. Many of these specific career skills have direct counterparts in the civilian society, and almost all are related to civilian occupations in some way. Enlistees are offered an opportunity to choose their training program based on their scores on the Armed Services Vocational Aptitude Battery and the current availability of training programs.

Most of the specific career skill training is provided at a high-skills level along with some at the high-tech level. All of it is considerably higher than that offered in K-12 settings. The overall goal is clearly attainment of excellence. At the conclusion of classroom training, enlistees are assigned jobs for a year that further their skills and draw upon their classroom training. By the time that year is up, most enlistees are able to compete successfully with those who have received their training in some different setting.

Helping almost all high school graduates plan for some form of post-secondary education - be it college or another option - is becoming an increasingly crucial role for professional school counselors. With a little research and first-hand knowledge of a student's needs and abilities, professional school counselors can help point all students down the right path for a successful future.

* This article is being reprinted with special permission from the American School Counselor Association. It appeared in the ASCA School Counselor (March/April 2002), 39, 18-23.

Part VI

Innovative Career Development Activities/Games

Part VI, Innovative Career Development Activities/Games has three chapters, each presenting a unique approach to providing career development concepts to students.

(22) *The Real Game: A Real Hook to Involvement*—Perry explains the Real Game Series, which is composed of six programs, from Grade 3 through adulthood, which offer increasingly challenging concepts and vocabulary related to life and work. Students are involved in real life situations within the safety of the classroom, while seeing the relevance of education and career planning.

(23) *Dependable Strengths—Your Best Plans Should Use Your Best Strengths*—Forster describes the Dependable Strengths Articulation Model, developed by Dr. Bernard Haldane. The rationale for articulating one's strengths is based on the psychological literature describing the advantages of optimism, hope and focus on strengths, according to Forster.

Activities are described to help a student identify significant strengths, based on positive events they have experienced. Although a five-day training session is normally required for users of the Dependable Strengths model, the reader can get a good idea of how this model works just from reading this chapter.

(24) *Designing the Dog—Career Development Activities that Work*—Wishik details two activities for students. In one, Designing the Dog, students learn more about the old (assembly line) and new (quality circle) workplace through a hands-on classroom exercise, included in his *Careers Now Activities Manual* (Wishik, 1991).

The other exercise is called *The 7-minute Job Interview* and gives an entire class the opportunity to practice for a mock job interview in one class period. Students are also given a list of *Fifty Questions Asked by Employers during the Interview*.

Chapter Twenty-Two

The Real Game: A Real Hook to Involvement

Nancy S. Perry

Abstract

Unfocused kids put in seat-time but never become personally involved in school. They graduate with no career goal or skills and often enter into dead-end jobs. This is both an individual and an economic waste. Career guidance programs are meaningless to the student who believes others control his fate. We need a hook to get these students involved in planning for their futures.

The Real Game Series can provide that hook. *The Real Game Series* is composed of six programs, from Grade 3 through adulthood, which offer increasingly challenging concepts and vocabulary related to life and work. In the context of game playing with a serious purpose, students are involved in real life situations within the safety of the classroom. This hooks them into the relevance of education and career planning.

We've all seen them – the students who don't seem to care. They sit in classes day after day, putting in seat time until they are old enough to leave. As a junior high counselor many years ago, I was frustrated by the lack of involvement of those students in their own lives. They have flat scores on interest surveys. The technical manual states that this may be due to lack of exposure to life's experiences. In most cases, I believe, it shows a general indifference to the world – an external locus of control that makes an individual feel powerless, a pawn in life's passage. I tried everything to get them involved. I even went so far with one student as to promise to help him achieve any goal he could set – no matter how trivial or unconventional. He could not, or would not, come up with even one thing he wanted to accomplish. Of course there may be deeper psychological implications, but I still hold to my belief that if we can get these unfocused kids to care enough to become involved in any way, their futures will be brighter.

Why do we care? We care because we can see the future unfold for this boy and so many like him. Since he was bright enough and had the perseverance to sit through high school for lack of anything else to do, he would probably decide to get a diploma and enter the work world – lacking any career goal or the skills to enter the primary labor market. We care because we know that career indecisiveness is an economic drain on our country. Every year, companies spend billions on recruiting and training new workers, only to have them leave because the job did not turn out to be satisfying. Consider the equal amount spent by governments in unemployment insurance and dropouts from government training programs. Add to this the astronomical amount of money in lost productivity because unhappy workers are less productive. It is a staggering and unnecessary waste of human and economic potential.

Good career guidance programs with quality labor market information can certainly help to promote informed career planning but I knew it was not enough. Students had to take control of their lives. Through a government grant, I co-authored a student career portfolio, entitled *Get a Life,* that tried to help students see that they are responsible for their career development and their futures. Others can help with programs and encouragement, but ultimately, each individual must take that responsibility. On the back cover we wrote, "You are the one who is responsible for making the most of your life. Enjoy a wonderful journey of exploration as you discover who you are and what you want for your future." Most students with whom we worked became enthusiastically involved in that journey. The portfolio became the cornerstone for parent/student/teacher conferences in which students discussed their thoughts about the future and how they might achieve their goals. We now had the map for guiding students through their career planning, but the "hook" to get the uninvolved student excited still eluded me.

At this time, I was "loaned" to the National Occupational Information Coordinating Committee (NOICC), a government interagency focused on career information and development, to manage the *Get a Life* project. While there, a Canadian colleague, Phillip Jarvis, contacted NOICC about a program he had "discovered" in Newfoundland. It seems that Bill Barry, a writer and actor, had been disturbed by his 12-year-old daughter's lack of interest in school. She had come home with the usual complaints about irrelevant subjects. Most of us would have given the "you'll understand when you grow up" lecture, but Bill took it to heart and said, "What if we could give young people a practice run at being an adult while they're still in school – something that feels like the real world they'll soon be part of?" Bill set out to develop an engaging tool that would make learning about careers and work fun and interesting. This became the genesis of *The Real Game*. Jarvis had observed the magic of excited students in the pilot program in St. John's, Newfoundland. He knew this would be something big. Could this be the hook I had been searching for?

In the space of six years, *The Real Game* evolved into a series of six internationally-recognized career education programs serving over 3 million young people in ten countries (at any given time). NOICC became a partner in the project by piloting the Canadian version in several U.S. states. The response was so overwhelming that NOICC invested in adapting the program for U.S. schools and in the development of training programs. To date, teachers in over 50,000 classrooms in North America are using the program series. The hook had been found.

The Real Game Series consists of six separate programs, each of which is tailored to a specific range of age and grade levels. The basic aim of the series is to introduce realities of the adult world of work in a meaningful way and to help participants master the life/career building competencies stated in the Canadian Blueprint for Life/Work Designs, adapted from the NOICC National Career Development Guidelines. All of the activities of *The Real Game Series* have been keyed to competencies in the three areas of: personal management, learning and work exploration, and career building.

THE REAL GAME SERIES

PROGRAM	GRADES	AGES
The Play Real Game	3 to 4	8 to 10
The Make It Real Game	5 to 6	10 to 12
The Real Game	7 and 8	12 to 14
The Be Real Game	9 and 10	14 to 16
The Get Real Game	11 and 12	16 to 18
Real Times, Real Life	Post-secondary	Adults

The programs are packaged in three-ring binders that include all facilitator and student materials (including overhead transparencies, posters, and reproducible masters) needed to implement the programs for as many participants as desired, year after year. The series is extremely flexible with the ability to customize the lessons to fit almost any institutional framework. Currently the series is being used in K-12 schools, colleges, universities, one-stop career resource centers and employment service sites, vocational rehabilitation and workers' compensation settings, human resource offices, correctional institutions, military settings and community volunteer agencies across Canada, the United States and internationally. The series incorporates increasingly challenging concepts and vocabulary which students learn by taking on real life and work roles in the safety of the classroom. Through playing the games, students and teachers get dramatic new insights into the relevance of the curriculum to future life and work opportunities. They see connections not obvious to them before, such as why math, science and English lessons are important to their lives.

Below is a synopsis of the six programs:

The Play Real Game: Grades 3 & 4

The Play Real Game introduces grade 3 and 4 students to basic life/work concepts and vocabulary as they play the roles of adults who create neighborhoods, find jobs for themselves and others, and work together as town citizens to accomplish a worthy goal. While having fun with maps and role-playing, the students learn the value of community, the joys and responsibilities of teamwork, the importance of essential employability skills and how education can relate to occupational choices.

The Make It Real Game: Grades 5 & 6

The Make It Real Game takes grade 5 and 6 students on a simulated journey into the global economy while reinforcing the importance of teamwork and cooperation. Role-playing as adults, each with a unique personal history, students form companies that research and develop creative projects, which are presented to an audience at the conclusion of the program. Language arts and social studies abilities are developed as students discover for themselves that there are many different ways to achieve an occupational goal and that everybody's work is important.

The Real Game: Grades 7 & 8

The Real Game gives grade 7 and 8 students the opportunity to explore adult realities such as taxes, living expenses, workplace environments, and unexpected emergencies. Students role-play adults in randomly assigned occupational roles and see how schoolwork relates to occupational choices and, therefore, to lifestyle and income. Delving deeper into their roles, students learn how to budget time and money and see the value of a balanced lifestyle, community involvement and lifelong learning. By the end of the game, students realize that satisfaction in work is a priority issue in life and

374

that it is an outcome that they can achieve by making the choices that are right for them.

The Be Real Game: Grades 9 & 10

The Be Real Game shows grade 9 and 10 students how a person's career is built with everyday choices and decisions, starting in childhood and encompassing every area of life including family, friends, education, recreational activities and lifestyle choices, community involvement and dealing with labor market conditions. As they role-play a high school student through to an experienced adult worker in a variety of employment, unemployment and family situations, students explore in-depth the importance of transferable skills, self-knowledge, lifelong learning and career planning. They are exposed to dozens of occupational possibilities and encouraged to actively pursue their dreams.

The Get Real Game: Grades 11 & 12

The Get Real Game presents students in grade 11 and 12 with a wide array of occupational possibilities and lets them simulate a 5-year school to work transition as they try to achieve the occupational goal they have chosen. In-depth factual information is supplied for each option so that students can realistically explore different possible gateways to their goals, including postsecondary education, various forms of on-the-job-training, workplace experience, internship or apprenticeship, military service, volunteer and community work, entrepreneurship and self- employment. As they pursue their occupational goals, students learn how to budget their time, research their options, define their goals, plan a course of action and present themselves well in an interview.

Real Times, Real Life: *Adults*

Real Times, Real Life helps adult learners to put their lives in perspective, relieving the negative self-image that often comes with unemployment so that they can begin to plan their careers with confidence. Role-playing as workers from 1900 to the present day, participants get a short course in modern history, learn to appreciate that change is constant and inevitable, develop an understanding of the modern labor market and see how skills acquired in one area of life are transferable to another. Working in teams, participants learn how to assess their situations and create realistic action plans, and where to go for help when they need it.

Example of a Real Game

Let me illustrate how these "games" involve students in real life situations within the safety of the classroom. *The Real Game* for the middle school level begins by letting the students dream about the lifestyle they want to have as adults. They choose housing, transportation, luxury items – whatever they want for their future. Each choice has a price tag attached but the students are told to ignore those. Then each student is randomly assigned an occupation from a set of occupational profiles – which are arranged in an order to assure a diverse working population from untrained to professional workers. It is made clear to the students (and their parents) that the assignment has nothing to do with the child; it is simply a way of dividing the occupations. Therefore, each child must become an actor and role-play for the rest of the game. Each profile contains basic information about the occupation – gross monthly income, usual vacation allowance, education/experience requirements, licenses or certifications needed, transferable skills, and a short job description. This information is followed by an essay on "A day in the life of a (occupation)" which also serves as a language arts lesson, introducing the vocabulary related to that occupation. Each student is told that he/she is now the expert on that occupation and must help others to learn about it. This is accomplished by a gathering, maybe a tenth high school reunion, where students meet old classmates and answer the usual question, "What are you doing now?" Each student must then tell about his/her occupation. Other activities follow that help students to see the range of requirements and financial rewards of different occupations. Then students are told that they must prepare a budget (math skills) based on the role assigned. One of the first "real life" lessons is that a certain percentage comes right off the top for taxes, retirement plans, insurance, etc.

> *What!* cried the seventh grader. *You mean I don't get to bring home what I make? It's not fair.*

Then, of course, there are those lifestyle plans. What are the payments on the house you chose? The car? The boat? Every adult knows that monthly payments are only the beginning – all require upkeep or maintenance. Of course, we also have to eat and wear clean clothes and maybe have a little fun along the way.

> *I thought my parents didn't like me because they kept saying no to the Reeboks. Now that I'm playing The Real Game, I can't*

understand how they have been able to say yes so often.
—7th grade student

Budgetary adjustments are made as students face reality – maybe keep the house but get a less expensive car and forget the boat. These are individual decisions, based on individual values. The only requirement is that the budget must be balanced. Then students must face the task of time management, "So much to do and only 168 hours in a week to do it all!" They learn that time, like money, must be budgeted. Work, commuting, sleep, meals, shopping, cleaning, etc., are necessities but there should also be some leisure time. How will that be spent and what will be the cost (budget implications)? The class, which has been divided into neighborhood groups, is ready to plan a vacation. Each neighborhood is to travel together and must not only agree on the destination but also on the cost and length of the vacation. Another reality strikes home – those that have the money may not have the time and those that have the time may not have the money. Innovative problem solving is encouraged – as long as it is legal. (No, Mr. Postal Worker, you cannot steal social security checks.) Bartering is rampant and the credit card shows its dangerous face (budget implications). Amazingly, decisions are made and everyone has learned a bit about the give and take of teamwork. No occupational road is completely smooth. Changing technology, economic recession, environmental catastrophe, resource depletion – these are some of the causes of layoffs and cutbacks. A worker in each neighborhood receives a pink slip. Their services are no longer needed. After the initial shock, the neighbors rally. It is not the end of the world. Various solutions are considered – networking, retraining within the industry or in a new occupation, relocating, self-employment and entrepreneurial pathway are explored. Résumés are prepared and, using their transferable skills, students apply for new work.

The Real Game offers many more activities than outlined here but this should give you an idea of why *The Real Game* is enthusiastically received by students, teachers, administrators and parents.

An extensive piloting program has been a key factor in the success of the Real Game programs. In Canada and the U.S., at least 100 pilot sites from coast-to-coast have participated in the testing of each program. These involved over 5,000 individuals (students, teachers, parents, and community members) and over 125,000 hours of focus testing over a period of two to three months. The volumes of feedback are used to improve the programs to meet the real needs of students and teachers.

Program Evaluations

Extensive evaluations have been done in Australia and the United Kingdom. In Australia, over 100 schools participating in the pilot program have been involved. Students, parents, teachers and administrators were given written evaluation forms for both individual activities and the program as a whole. Teachers, or facilitators, also participated in focus groups. Students were given the opportunity to complete pre- and post-program World of Work Surveys and a supplementary questionnaire to self-report the impact of *The Real Game* in the understanding of 20-core career issues. The overall reaction to *The Real Game* from teachers, parents and students was overwhelmingly positive. As one teacher said:

From this resource came a realization that secondary school studies have a direct impact on their future lifestyle, an aspect that can only have a positive impact on school retention rates.

Students, too, echoed the lessons learned. As one student said:

I liked TRG because it made me realize that being grown up is harder than it looks.

Even parents were enthused about the program. Here are samples of two parent responses:

At last school subjects can be seen to relate to real life and provide a reason for learning. She has learned that to gain most of her dreams, she has to work hard along the way.

On a more formal note, the following areas of student competency were identified as having improved through the delivery of *The Real Game*: (Evaluation of The Real Game 12-14: Final Report, 2001)

- Understanding about the world of work
- Increased vocabulary relating to the world of work and other aspects of adult life
- Literacy/numeracy (mathematics) skills
- The importance of budgeting and managing money
- Working in groups
- Prioritizing what is important in life
- Researching and exploring issues
- Problem-solving and negotiating skills

- Communication skills
- Using technology
- General knowledge
- Interpersonal skills
- Awareness of different ways of earning income
- Knowledge about a variety of jobs
- Awareness of relative earning capacities

Conclusion

The Real Game Series is unique in that it provides a personal career-building context that participants and facilitators at all levels find enjoyable and stimulating. Using the Blueprint for Life/Works Designs (www.blueprint4life.ca) competency and performance indicator template, each game in the series incorporates increasingly challenging ideas and vocabulary. The games focus on teamwork and community interactions, involving parents throughout the process. Why is it so successful? Because it demonstrates that learning can be fun. It is also successful because of thorough research, extensive development involving educators, parents, students, and labor market specialists, and good management strategies – developed and administered by the National Life/Work Centre. An innovative approach to partnerships has produced a winning formula for implementing *The Real Game Series*. Partnerships begin with government contacts and finding effective networks across the countries that wish to implement the program. A "TRG Series Partnership Framework" outlines the roles and responsibilities of all partners involved in the development and implementation of these programs. Agreed upon phases include program conception and definition, prototype development, piloting, evaluation/revisions, and implementation. International partners have agreed that the series needs to be financially self-sustaining, on a not-for-profit basis, with cost-recovery pricing well below commercial equivalents. The dream can become a reality when *The Real Game Series* is used to provide that "hook" of involvement.

As one teacher said:

I had several students who would be classified as at risk of leaving early. For this group it was definitely of value as they realized that having aspirations/dreams is necessary and that education is needed to help achieve these.

NOTE: The National Life/Work Center and Real Game Inc. partner with America's Career Resource Network Association (formerly NOICC/SOICC) for on-going development and implementation of The Real Game Series throughout the United States. For further information visit www.realgame.org or www.acrna.net, or contact:

National Life/Work Center
1410 King Street, 4th Floor
Alexandria, VA 22314
Toll-free Tel: 1-888-700-8940
Toll-free Fax: 1-877-929-3343
Email: info@lifeworkinc.us
Web: www.realgame.org (U.S) www.realgame.com (International)

References

Barry, B. (1996, revised 2000). *The real game facilitator's guide.* St. John's, Newfoundland (Canada): Real Game Inc.

Edwards, A., Barnes, A., Killeen, J., & Watts, A.G. (1999). *The Real Game: Evaluation of the UK national pilot.* NICEC Project Report. Cambridge: CRAC.

Evaluation of the real game 12-14: Final report. (2001). Commonwealth of Australia: Training and Youth Affairs, Department of Education.

Jarvis, P. (2003). *Career management paradigm shift: Prosperity for citizens, windfall for governments.* Memramcook, New Brunswick, Canada: National Life/Work Centre.

Jarvis, P. (December 2, 1988). *A nation at risk: The economic consequences of neglecting career development.* Paper presented at the Annual Conference of the Association of Computer-Based Systems for Career Information (ACSCI). St. Louis, MO.

Jarvis, P. (2000). *The Real Game Series: Bringing real life to the classroom.* Memramcook, New Brunswick, Canada: National Life/Work Centre.

Perry, N. & Van Zandt, C.E. (1993). *Get a life career portfolio.* Alexandria, VA: American School Counselor Association.

The Real Game Series Brochure. (2000). Memramcook, New Brunswick, Canada: National Life/Work Centre. Author.

Chapter Twenty-Three

Your Best Plans Should Use Your Best Strengths

Jerald R. Forster

Abstract

High school students are encouraged to articulate their strengths and use those strengths when making their most important plans. The rationale for articulating strengths is based on the psychological literature describing the well-documented advantages of optimism, hope and focus on strengths. Haldane's process of Dependable Strengths Articulation (DSA) is recommended. Activities that can help a student identify significant strengths are suggested for those who cannot gain access to the recommended DSA process right away. Those activities encourage a participant to describe a few events which are very positive. Using those events to look for strengths, participants are encouraged to find three or more peers to help in the identification of strengths. Identified strengths are then prioritized, reviewed for reliability, and seriously considered when making plans.

High school students are rapidly approaching the most crucial crossroad in their young lives. For many of these students, high school graduation will mark the beginning of the most momentous transition period they will face. Many will not have thought a great deal about what comes next, and many others will be anxious about their uncharted future. For many, this marks the first time in their lives when their daily decisions will not be influenced or determined by the structure of their school's schedules and rules laid down by their parents and the other significant adults in their lives. After graduation they will probably be more responsible for the plans they make. As these students increase their personal decision-making and make more of their own plans, they will require somewhat different guidelines than they have been using. These new guidelines will be coming more from their personal experiences than from their parents, their teachers and the authority figures in their lives. More than ever before, they will be using themes and patterns from their personal experiences to inform their ideas of personal identity and choice. More than any time before in their lives, their self-identities will influence what they choose and what they do. Decision-making will be confusing because they will have many changing identities. As they become aware of changing identities, they may be unsure as to which identities should receive their primary focus. They will have choices as to which aspects of themselves will get the most attention and focus. They may not recognize that they are taking a bigger role in choosing who they are and what they will do, but it will be happening.

The primary idea of this chapter is that high school students approaching graduation can be more successful and make better plans if they focus on their strengths. This recommendation is based on the premise that if a student's self-identity is more firmly grounded on his or her strengths, that student will be more optimistic and hopeful. Better plans will be made if those plans are based on awareness of personal strengths.

One purpose of this chapter is to build the case for articulating and using strengths when building self-identities, making plans and implementing those plans. Another purpose is to provide suggestions as to how strengths can be articulated and then used to make plans.

Strengths, Optimism and Hope Are Related to Personal Success

The psychological literature on optimism and pessimism (Chang, 2001) demonstrates the "optimistic advantage." Scheier, Carver and Bridges (2001) tell us:

> ...this 'optimistic advantage' is due to differences in the manner in which optimists and pessimists cope with the difficulties they confront. That is, optimists seem intent on facing problems head-on, taking active and constructive steps to solve their problems; pessimists are more likely to abandon their effort to attain their goals. (p. 210)

In his book, The Optimistic Child, Seligman (1995) makes a strong case for optimism, when he writes:

> I have studied pessimism for the last twenty years, and in more than one thousand studies, involving more than half a million children and adults, pessimistic people do worse than optimistic people in three ways: First, they get depressed much more often.

Second, they achieve less at school, on the job, and on the playing field than their talents augur. Third, their physical health is worse than that of optimists. So holding a pessimistic theory of the world may be the mark of sophistication, but it is a costly one. It is particularly damaging for a child, and if your child has already acquired pessimism, he is at risk for doing less well in school. He is at risk of greater problems of depression and anxiety. He may be at risk for worse physical health than he would have if he were an optimist. And worse, pessimism in a child can become a lifelong, self-fulfilling template for looking at setbacks and losses. The good news is that he can, with your help, learn optimism. (pp. 51-52)

In his book, *Authentic Happiness*, Seligman (2002) expands on his case for using the new positive psychology to realize your potential for lasting fulfillment.

Another branch of the psychological literature focuses on the quality of hope. Snyder, Sympson, Michael & Cheavens (2001) write "...furthermore, individuals with higher levels of hope would be expected to have an enhanced sense of self-esteem both because of past successes and because of their beliefs that workable routes to future goal pursuits are likely." In his Handbook of Hope, Snyder (2000) demonstrates how hope is correlated with psychological adjustment, achievement, problem solving, and coping with health-related concerns.

Optimism and hope are marked by the extent that people focus on positive experiences and expectations. As Carver & Scheier (1990) write: "Optimists, by definition, are people with favorable expectations about the future. Such expectations should make success on a given problem seem more likely and should thereby promote continued problem-solving efforts, resulting in better outcomes." Scheier et al., (2001), when describing one of their research findings, write "Optimists, as compared to pessimists, also tended to report being less focused on negative aspects of their experience - their distress emotions and physical symptoms." (p. 202)

Optimists more often focus on their positive experiences, which are experiences wherein they are using their strengths. People who can articulate their strengths and focus on their most positive experiences have more hope about their futures. The research evidence is quite clear. People who focus on their strengths cope better than those who are more pessimistic and depressed. In light of that evidence, it is somewhat puzzling why educators and parents make few attempts to focus on the strengths of young people. Why do those who are responsible for the optimal development of youngsters ignore the psychological literature that describes the "optimistic advantage?" Maybe it is because we still lack well-developed methods that encourage people to articulate their strengths. Maybe most people think that optimism and pessimism are like temperaments that are programmed by genetic codes. Whatever the reasons, young people are not usually encouraged to focus on their best experiences and their strengths. In the remainder of this chapter, I will suggest activities that will encourage high school students to articulate their best strengths and then use those strengths to help them plan their futures.

Identifying and Using Strengths

How Can Dependable Strengths Be Articulated
The most effective approach to identifying strengths has been developed by Bernard Haldane (1996). This approach, called Dependable Strengths Articulation (DSA), evolved from Haldane's pioneering work when helping World War II returnees identify their motivated skills (Haldane, 1960; Haldane, et al., 1982). During the 1980's and 1990's, Dr. Haldane spearheaded a research and development program at the University of Washington, wherein an eighteen-hour workshop was devised to help people identify their strengths and increase their employability. This carefully developed process emphasizes the oral description of Good Experiences and the identification of strengths in small groups. The small groups usually have four members and are called quads. Professionals are trained to implement this basic 18-hour workshop by taking a full-week course that includes the basic DSA process in the first half of the week, and training in how to implement the basic course during the second half.

Curriculum materials have been developed to carry out the DSA process. Boivin-Brown (2001) wrote a comprehensive manual for use in the 18-hour basic DSA program for adults. Boivin-Brown(1990) also wrote the curriculum guide for using the DSA process in high schools. The curriculum guides developed by Boivin-Brown were written in a way that potential users are expected to take a training session before they use the written materials. Usually, potential trainers are encouraged to take the one-week course mentioned above.

There is also DSA curriculum for helping students in grades two through six identify their strengths. Huggins (1994) wrote a curriculum guide that can be used by teachers and counselors in elementary schools. Fortunately, these curriculum materials are written in a way that the users do not need special training. Even though such special training would certainly benefit the person who plans to use the written materials, such training is not required of people who want to use the materials authored by Huggins.

There is also software available to help high school students go through the DSA process on a computer. This software is available from the Washington Occupational Information System (WOIS, 1997). While this computer program is useful, it does not include the aspect of the DSA process that is generally considered most important, that being the small group (usually a quad) wherein participants take turns describing their good experiences to each other. During the workshop-format, other quad members listen to these stories of good experiences and then suggest the names of possible strengths that were demonstrated in the stories. The WOIS software enables a person to go through the strengths-articulation process working alone on a computer.

Results of DSA Workshops

Participants who have been trained in the one-week courses at the University of Washington have offered hundreds of DSA workshops to others. In evaluations of the one-week courses, as well as the workshops offered by graduates of the one-week courses, participants report very positive results. More often than not these participants used the very much description to rate statements like "I have learned new things about myself" and "I can articulate my strengths more clearly."

In addition to standard evaluation results, Forster (1991) collected evidence that most DSA participants changed their self-descriptions after participating in a workshop. He administered the Adjective Check List (ACL) prior to and after three workshops. Post-workshop measures indicated that participants described themselves with adjectives that were more favorable than the adjectives used prior to the workshop. Scales measuring Self-Confidence and Achievement increased so much that such a difference could have been found only 1 out of 1000 times by accident.

Limited Opportunities for DSA Training

Since the evaluations of the DSA process have been so positive, I urge school practitioners to get the training and to use the DSA curriculum materials. Unfortunately, I make this recommendation with the knowledge that most of the curriculum materials for high school students were written with the intention that curriculum users would be trained in workshops or courses requiring approximately 35 hours of participation. The only exception is the set of computerized materials available through WOIS, and evaluation results using this approach are limited.

At the time this chapter is being written, accessibility to DSA training and related materials is somewhat limited. It is likely that there will be more opportunities in the future to obtain the training suggested for using DSA methods. For information about future workshops designed to prepare you to use DSA methods, write to:

Center for Dependable Strengths
c/o Highline Community College
MS-Omni/PO Box 98000, Des Moines, WA 98198-9800.
For more information, contact (phone/toll free) 866-398-9474
(fax) 206-870-5915 or Internet address:
http://www.dependablestrengths.org/

Given the immediate need for guidelines to help high school students articulate their strengths, and the limited access to training and DSA curriculum materials at this time, some suggestions are offered for identifying strengths in this chapter. As a temporary measure, I will describe activities that might be used until you have access to appropriate DSA materials and training.

The activities described in the next section are not the same as are included in the DSA process, but they do use general principles articulated by the DSA process. These activities should help motivated participants articulate and use their most significant strengths. Participating in these activities will not be nearly as effective as programs offered by professionals who have been trained to help others participate in the Dependable Strengths Articulation (DSA) process. I offer these suggestions because I believe that even limited efforts to articulate strengths will be better than no efforts. Hopefully, well-developed materials and methods, such as the DSA process, will be readily available in the future.

How Can High School Students Identify Their Strengths
Described below is a six-step process designed to help high school students identify and then use their most significant strengths. It is recommended that school personnel who have special interests in the articulation of strengths provide guidance to high school students who are participating in the six-step process. Before school personnel attempt to help students go through this process, they should themselves go through the process.

Step 1. Identify 15 positive events. The first important activity of students who are trying to identify their strengths is the systematic review of events recalled from their past. The events that should be reviewed are those that are remembered by the student as being very positive. The remembered events should be ones where the student took an active role in making the event happen. The events should be remembered with very positive feelings, including feelings of accomplishment. After a systematic review of at least the last ten years of his or her life, the student should identify about 15 remembered events and label each event. After prioritizing the events, the student should write a brief description or a short story about seven of his or her most highly prioritized events.

Step 2. Look for strengths demonstrated during positive events. Strengths are positive qualities characterizing a person. Strengths can be thought of as skills, personality variables, resources, attitudes, temperaments, talents, or other positive qualities. Participants in this activity should be encouraged to come up with their own definitions of strengths, in that strengths are often in the eye of the beholder. There is no final authority that determines if a quality is a strength. Generally, a person's definition of a strength will be similar to what is held by the general population.

During Step 2 the student studies each of his or her seven stories describing the most positive events and then attempts to name personal qualities or skills that might be called strengths. The student then writes a name for each potential strength on a sheet of paper entitled: Strengths I have demonstrated. Hopefully, the student will list several strengths that were demonstrated in each of the seven positive events, resulting in a list of at least 20 to 30 strengths.

Step 3. Get help for identifying possible strengths. Students need to find other people who will help them identify possible strengths that were demonstrated in each of the seven positive events they have written about. This step is very important because strengths become more real to the person when there is consensual support for identifying the strengths. While it is possible for students to find people who will listen to them talk about their seven positive events, most high school students find it difficult to ask people to do this. I recommend that a particular staff member in the school take responsibility for organizing small groups of students who will participate in the process of listening to other students talk about their positive events. The process works best when three to five students agree to take turns sharing their most positive events. While one person tells each story of a positive event, the other group members write down names for the strengths being demonstrated in the story. After all of the stories have been told, the lists of strengths are given to the storyteller. When everyone gets a turn, the whole process becomes satisfying and beneficial for all of the participants. The person responsible for organizing these small groups should prepare everyone for the experience by explaining the process and exploring the enthusiasm of all participants. Those students who are not enthusiastic might be told to wait until they talk to other students who have already participated in the process. In other words, students should be screened before they are included in small groups.

It is also possible to arrange for small groups that include adults. It is even possible for family members to participate in the process of listening to descriptions of positive events. Whenever small groups are organized to do this, it should be agreed that all group members will have a turn to talk about positive events from their lives.

Step 4. Name those strengths that are most significant. After a participant has identified many strengths that were used during each of the seven positive events, those strengths should be carefully named and prioritized. The strengths that are listed should include those identified by the student, plus those that were named by others in the small groups who listened to descriptions of the most positive events. The student should take a lot of time considering all of the possible strength names. After considerable study and analysis, the student should write the names or short descriptions of at least eight most significant strengths. These eight strengths become the ones that the student agrees to claim as his or her most significant strengths.

Step 5. Verify the reliability and validity of each significant strength. The student should carefully consider each significant strength to ensure that the strength does in fact show up in two or more of the seven most positive events. Only strengths that were clearly evident in two or more positive events should be considered sufficiently reliable to qualify as significant strengths. If a strength only shows up in one of the seven positive events, it should be put aside and only considered after several other strengths have been examined for highest significance. Hopefully, the eight significant strengths that are finally listed will be sufficiently different from each other, so that they don't all seem like the same quality with slightly different names.

Step 6. Use identified strengths as foundations for plans. When high school students are making plans, they should start with a review of their eight significant strengths. This does not mean that their plans are totally based on their significant strengths. But it does mean that all plans should be screened through the filter of the individual's most significant strengths. If significant strengths are not being used, the plan should be re-evaluated and modified so that significant strengths will be used. If a plan does not allow the student to use at least one significant strength, the plan does not suit the student very well.

A cautionary warning on Step 6. In Step 6, students were advised to make sure that their significant strengths are being used in any plan they devise. This advice works well except in the case of students who have not done a very good job of identifying eight significant strengths that represent a somewhat broad spectrum of possibilities. In other words, if the strengths are very similar to each other, it will be difficult to devise complex plans that are not too narrow and restricted. If a student is not able to come up with a somewhat diverse listing of significant strengths, that student may not be able to devise realistic plans that also use strengths. The sixth step of devising plans which always allow the student to use one or more strengths requires that the person was able to articulate strengths that have some variety or diversity.

Despite the qualification on Step 6, I repeat the basic idea that all plans should be grounded on one's significant strengths. If the significant strengths are different from each other and if they are developed with care, they should be seriously considered when devising any plans for the future.

An Example of Articulating Strengths in a High School

Jennifer was a junior in high school when she heard about the opportunity to identify and clarify her strengths. Her school counselor, with the help of Career Center staff, had put a notice in the school paper describing a process in which interested students could get together in small groups to articulate their strengths. Jennifer signed up and was assigned to meet with three other students who had volunteered for the same process. The four students met with the school counselor who laid out several steps in the process. The first step was to identify fifteen positive events that had occurred during the past ten years. She worked on this assignment at home. After writing down the names of 15 events, she studied and prioritized the list. She then selected seven of the events that seemed particularly meaningful. After this she described the seven events by writing a short story about each event. Later in the week she met with the other three classmates who had also written about seven of their most positive events. When it was her turn, she read four of her short stories and her classmates wrote down the names of strengths that they thought were demonstrated by Jennifer during her most positive events. Jennifer had described one event where she had organized all of her notes and handout materials for three of her classes. She described with pride her new system for keeping track of things, and her classmates all mentioned her strengths of being organized and systematic in how she kept track of things in her life. In her second story, she described her work in the school's library, where she helped the librarian implement a new system of keeping track of pamphlets and brochures. In her third story, she described how she had helped other members of the debate team collect and store information on their debate topics. Although she was not one of the top debaters, she was proud of her role in helping all members of the debate team assemble their case materials and to think of ways to retrieve ideas. Her fourth story was about how she had prepared for a five-week summer trip to Costa Rica with a small group of students.

After telling her stories, Jennifer received lists of possible strengths from the other three listeners. These lists included descriptors such as being organized, a good planner, and able to devise systems for keeping track of things. Later in the day, she studied the lists of strength words she had received from the others and compared their feedback with ideas she had about her own strengths. She eventually came up with eight short descriptions of her strengths. They were: (1) being organized, (2) being a superior planner, (3) being able to see patterns in masses of data, (4) being able to devise systems that allow people to find what they need when they need it, (5) being able to see the big picture after getting a lot of detailed information, (6) being intelligent, (7) getting along with people, and (8) being a good researcher.

During her senior year, when she was making her post-high school plans, Jennifer considered several options. Since she had been a good student who did well in science classes, she thought about being a pre-medicine major at a school known to have strong science programs. Jennifer also considered teacher preparation at the local branch of the State University. Jennifer's mother (who had been a teacher before she had her own children) recommended that she consider this option.

After considering the science and teaching options, Jennifer decided to develop a plan that would fit more closely with the strengths she had articulated during her junior year. She decided that she would apply at universities having strong programs in Information Sciences and Library Sciences. She considered her special strengths to be organizing and managing information or data. By using the Internet, she found a university that was known for its programs in Information Sciences and she applied to that university. As she is making her plans, she remembers that her strengths might be especially well suited to being a librarian or a specialist in some related field. She plans to start college in a general liberal arts program that will eventually help her get into a more specialized program of information sciences or library sciences.

Conclusion

In this chapter, I have urged that students be encouraged to be optimistic, to have hope, and to focus on their strengths. I have identified the Dependable Strengths Articulation (DSA) process as the best approach I know about to help high school students identify and use their strengths. I have also offered a series of activities described as steps by which students can identify and use their strengths. These steps are suggested if training for the DSA methods is not accessible to staff members in a given school at the present time. While the DSA methods are clearly superior, the activities described in this chapter will be useful until DSA methods can be offered.

References

Boivin-Brown, A. (1990). *Dependable strengths: Curriculum unit, grades 9-12*. Seattle, WA: University of Washington Dependable Strengths Project.

Boivin-Brown, A. (2001). *Facilitator's manual for the Dependable Strengths Articulation process*. Seattle, WA: Dependable Strengths Institute.

Carver, C. S., & Scheier, M. F. (1990). Principles of self-regulation: Action and emotion. In E. T. Higgins & R. M. Sorrentino (Eds.), *Handbook of motivation and cognition* (Vol. 2, pp. 3-52. New York: Guilford Press.

Chang, E. C. (2001). *Optimism and pessimism: Implications for theory, research, and practice*. Washington D.C.: American Psychological Association.

Forster, J. R. (1991). Facilitating positive changes in self-constructions. *International Journal of Personal Construct Psychology, 4*, 281-292.

Haldane, B. (1960). *How to make a habit of success.* Englewood Cliffs, NJ: Prentice-Hall, Inc.

Haldane, B. (1996). *Career satisfaction and success: A guide to job and personal freedom.* Indianapolis, IN: JIST Works, Inc.

Haldane, B., Haldane, J., & Martin, L. (1982). *Job power: The young people's job-finding guide.* Washington, DC: Acropolis.

Huggins, P. (1994). *Helping kids find their strengths.* Longmont, CO: Sopris West Publishing.

Scheier, M. F., Carver, C. S., & Bridges, M. W. (2001). Optimism, pessimism, and psychological well-being. In E. C. Chang (Ed.), *Optimism and pessimism: Implications for theory, research, and practice.* (pp. 189-216). Washington D.C.: American Psychological Association.

Seligman, M. E. (1995). *The optimistic child.* New York: Houghton Mifflin.

Seligman, M. E. (2002). *Authentic happiness: Using the new positive psychology to realize your potential for lasting fulfillment.* New York: The Free Press.

Snyder, C. R. (Ed.). (2000). *Handbook of hope: Theory, measures, & applications.* San Diego, CA: Academic.

Snyder, C. R., Sympson, S. C., Michael, S. T., & Cheavens, J. (2001). Optimism and hope constructs: Variants on a positive expectancy theme. In E. C. Chang (Ed.), *Optimism and pessimism: Implications for theory, research, and practice.* (pp. 101-126). Washington DC: American Psychological Association.

Washington Occupational Information System, (1997). *Dependable Strengths software.* Olympia, WA: WOIS (1-800-700-WOIS)

Chapter Twenty-Four

Designing the Dog:
Career Development Activities
that Work

Anton Wishik

Abstract

This chapter describes two of many career development activities developed by the author. These two activities are included in the *Careers Now Activities Manual* edited by the author in 1991 and now available through WOIS/The Career Information System at www.wois.org. Both activities are tied to the Washington State Essential Learning Requirements, the Washington State Learning Goals, the Washington State Guidelines for Comprehensive Counseling and Career Guidance Programs, the American School Counselor Association National Standards for School Counseling Programs, the National Career Development Guidelines, and the SCANS Report. The activities are: *Designing the Dog*, a game that depicts the changing workplace; and *The 7-minute Job Interview*, an activity in which an entire class practices job interviewing skills in one period. (Both activities are copyrighted by Anton Wishik.)

Designing the Dog

The middle school principal is strolling down the hall when he hears noise coming from the home economics room. He knows there's a guest speaker - the new career specialist from the high school. He doesn't really like his students getting riled up, especially about the high school, and particularly his seventh-graders. He hurries to the door and listens; it sounds as if there's no teacher in the room. He gently eases the door open and peers through the doorway.

395

Usually when he arrives, heads turn and behavior instantly improves. What he sees and hears before him seems to be chaos - a chaos so engaging that he, the principal, is being totally ignored. The class is in five groups, each gathered around a table. Nobody is seated (one of his pet peeves); some are standing and others kneeling on their chairs. They're all hunched over their tables, arguing, pointing, some drawing on scraps of paper. From the five loud debates, he catches snippets of conversation: "We've got to work as a TEAM.... Hurry up!.. Look at this prototype... Who's an expert at drawing a dog?"

On the long blackboards around the room shine five colored chalk drawings of the strangest-looking dogs the principal has ever seen. Kindergarten work, it looks like, and far afield from Home Economics. His teacher wanders about the room, serenely reviewing the dogs; the Career Specialist is listening to one of the five arguments. The principal is just about to say something when the Career Specialist, the guy down from the high school, rings a bell and calls "Time."

Silence reigns, equal to the usual response to the principal's arrival. Instantly each group has stopped working and turned to face the front of the room. Some glance at the principal, then back at the Career Specialist. "I am the Company President," says the Career Specialist. "Are there any questions?"

Several students ask questions but the answer is always the same: "All the rules from the assembly line method are off; you as a team may decide how best to Design a Dog." The principal finds this vaguely disconcerting; he doesn't much care to hear the phrase "all rules are off" at his school.

And then the Career Specialist rings a kitchen timer and chaos rules again. Some of the teams rush to the blackboard. Others send one or two representatives, with the rest cheering and kibitzing from their seats. Each team draws a dog, exactly below the kindergarten dog they apparently had drawn previously, except these new dogs are not so strange. Within a minute the principal recognizes Snoopy and a couple of drawings that could have been in a children's book of dog breeds. The principal smiles his small smile and slips out of the room. It was pretty loud in there, and he has no idea what drawing a dog has to do with Home Economics or careers or the high school. But clearly he has seen significant improvement from the first round of drawings to the second. And if there's one thing the principal favors (and is willing to be flexible to achieve), it's improvement...

Designing the Dog is a game developed more than a decade ago to provide a graphic representation of the changing workplace, from assembly line to quality circle - and the new skills needed in that workplace (SCANS

Report, 1991). It has been used with groups from kindergarten through adult, and is one of the most popular activities in the *Careers Now Activities Manual* (Wishik, 1991).

In the game, a class or group is divided into at least four "assembly lines" (five on a line are preferred). Have them count off so each Worker has a number (Worker 1 can also be Worker 5 if a line only has four students). Give each line five different colors of chalk, with a color designated for Worker 1, Worker 2, etc. (This may also be done with markers and butcher paper, with the advantage of saving the work.) Tell them they are part of a toy company which is designing a new product, a dog. Each assembly line will work on a section of the chalkboard, starting with worker No. 1. When a bell rings, Worker 1 goes to the board and begins designing a dog; after a short time the bell rings again, Worker 1 sits down and Worker 2 hurries to the board and works on that assembly line's design. This continues until all five workers in each line have worked on the design.

The rules are that Workers may only use the tool (piece of chalk) they have been given, and may only add to another worker's efforts (but not subtract by erasing). They also may not communicate with co-workers, as per the assembly lines of old. They work in the top half of their section of the blackboard. There is a time limit but do not tell them how much time they have.

Ring the bell: Worker No. 1 on each line rushes to the board. Time for twenty seconds and ring the bell; Worker 2 rushes to the board. Give each worker 20 seconds - for a total of one minute, forty seconds for five workers. At the end, have them sit back down and laugh at their work. Discuss assembly line rules: *Work alone; do your task only; use designated tool only; and do not communicate.*

Tell them they are going to get another chance, except this time instead of an assembly line, they will be a team of workers. They will work on the bottom half of their section of the board, and may not disturb the top-half creations. Before they go the chalkboard, they will have one minute to meet and determine "How Best to Design a Dog." All the rules from the assembly line method are off (but give no suggestions); they as a team may decide "How Best to Design a Dog." In their one-minute team meeting, they also must select a team leader who can discuss their design afterwards. Solicit questions. When you get questions such as "Do we all have to work on the drawing?" or "Can we share chalk?" answer with the mysterious response, "You as a team may decide how best to design a dog."

Ring the bell for the one-minute meeting. Listen to some of the ensuing debate so you can comment later. Then proceed as described above as seen through the eyes of the Middle School Principal.

In the second round, the teams get exactly the same amount of "production time" (1:40). Again they will laugh and remark for several seconds.

Now evaluate the designs. First the entire group compares the assembly line designs across the top with the teamwork designs across the bottom. The bottom set will always be superior. Why? Let them share the advantages of the teamwork method *(planning, sharing ideas, working together, utilizing the most skilled members of a group)*. Remind them they had no additional time at the chalkboard - only the additional time for planning and communication.

Now consider individual group designs - assembly line against teamwork. Ask the team leader to stand by the work of the group and explain what happened in their group's one-minute meeting and how the design was accomplished.

Your discussion now can lead in many directions. You can discuss the history and development of the assembly line and the change to teamwork systems of production (Washington State Essential Learnings 1-3 in History, and Essential Academic Learning in Economics). Leave your designs up for a while if possible. They are great conversation pieces and a graphic demonstration of the need for communication, imagination and teamwork in the workplace of today!

Designing the Dog addresses these learning standards:

Washington State Learning Goals (Education Reform Act of 1993)

Goal 1 "...Communicate effectively and responsibly in a variety of ways and settings."

Goal 3 "Think analytically, logically and creatively, and to integrate experience and knowledge to form reasoned judgements and solve problems."

Goal 4 "Understand the importance of work and how performance, effort and decisions directly affect career and educational opportunities."

Washington State Essential Learning Requirements:

Communication
1. The student uses listening and observation skills to gain understanding.
2. The student communicates ideas clearly and effectively.
3. The student uses communication strategies and skills to work

effectively with others.
4. The student analyzes and evaluates the effectiveness of formal and informal communication.

Economics
2. Students understand the essential characteristics of past and present economic systems.

History
2. The student understands the origin and impact of ideas and technological development on history.

Arts
2. The student demonstrates thinking skills using artistic processes.
3. The student communicates through the arts.

American School Counselor Association National Standards

II. Career Development:
2. Develop Employment Readiness (work as a team, time skills, motivation)

III. Personal/Social
2. Acquire Interpersonal Skills

Washington State Counseling and Career Guidance
Components and Benchmarks

Educational Development Competencies:
1.5 Demonstrate decision-making skills

Personal/Social Development Competencies:
2.5 Get along with others
2.6 Have effective conversation and listening skills
2.7 Work cooperatively with others in a variety of group situations
2.8 Utilize appropriate conflict resolution strategies

National Career Development Guidelines

Competency II: Skills to Interact Positively with Others
Competency IX: Skills to Make Decisions

SCANS Report

Basic Skills:
D. Listening
E. Speaking

Personal Qualities:
A. Responsibility
C. Sociability

Thinking Skills;
A. Creative thinking
B. Decision making

C. Problem solving

D. Seeing things in the mind's eye
E. Knowing how to learn
F. Reasoning

Workplace Competencies:
Interpersonal - Works with others
Systems - Understands complex
inter-relationships
Technology - Applies technology
to task

The 7-Minute Job Interview: How an Entire Class Practices in One Period

Career Specialists often are asked by teachers and parents to help prepare students for job interviews. But the students themselves often are extremely hesitant to practice. They tend to be willing to talk about the job interview, but not actually try a mock interview.

Counselors know that when a client balks it means some less-threatening intervention must occur first. While practicing anything is usually less threatening in private than in public, in this case it seemed advisable to get students to practice as a group - with numerous classmates all doing the same. Thus was the 7-minute job interview born.

In this activity, the class is divided into fours. All students know that each will get a chance to practice job interviewing, and a volunteer from each group is solicited to go first.

Chairs or desks in the classroom are arranged in groups of four so that one chair faces three. The "applicants" who have volunteered to go first are directed to the front of the room. Each panel of three is seated with copies of the Handout "Fifty Questions Asked by Employers during the Interview." The panel also has a copy of the "Assertive Interview Score Sheet."

When the facilitator starts time, the applicant approaches the panel, makes an introduction and states the job being applied for. The student may choose any job, but must answer all questions truthfully (and not make up experience or education). If the class has previously done resumes, they could be presented to the panel.

The three panel members take turns asking questions from the handout. After seven minutes, the facilitator calls time and the applicant immediately returns to the front of the room. The panelists now have two minutes to score the applicant on the Assertive Interview Score Sheet.

After two minutes, the facilitator calls time and one panel member delivers the score sheet to the applicant. The panel member stays in front of the room and becomes the next applicant. The applicant takes the score sheet and joins the panel. This exchange takes about a minute. Thus the total time for each interview is ten minutes (seven-minute interview, two minutes to score, one minute to trade places).

Four interviews take a total of 40 minutes, leaving some measure of time for a class discussion about the experience and about job interview skills.

Fifty Questions Asked by Employers During the Interview

1. What are your long-range and short-range goals and objectives, when and why did you establish these goals, and how are you preparing yourself to achieve them?
2. What specific goals, other than those related to your occupation, have you established for yourself for the next ten years?
3. What do you see yourself doing five years from now?
4. What do you really want to do in life?
5. What are your long-range career objectives?
6. How do you plan to achieve your career goals?
7. What are the most important rewards you expect in your career?
8. What do you expect to be earning in five years?
9. Why did you choose the career for which you are preparing?
10. Which is more important to you, the money or the type of job?
11. What do you consider to be your greatest strengths and weaknesses?
12. How would you describe yourself?
13. How do you think a friend or instructor who knows you well would describe you?
14. What motivates you to put forth your greatest effort?
15. How have your experiences prepared you for working here?
16. Why should I hire you?
17. What qualifications do you have that make you think that you will be successful in this field?
18. How do you determine or evaluate success?
19. What do you think it takes to be successful in a company like ours?
20. In what ways do you think you can make a contribution to our

company?

21. What qualities should a successful applicant possess?
22. Describe the relationship that should exist between a supervisor and those reporting to that supervisor.
23. What two or three accomplishments have given you the most satisfaction?
24. Describe your most rewarding experience in school.
25. If you were hiring someone for this position, what qualities would you look for?
26. Why did you select this occupation?
27. Why did you select the training program you did?
28. What school subjects did you like best? Why?
29. What school subjects did you like the least? Why?
30. If you could do so, how would you plan your education and training differently?
31. What changes would you make in your high school? Why?
32. Do you have plans to continue your education in some way? What are they?
33. Do you think that your grades are a good indication of your capabilities?
34. What have you learned from your hobbies, interests and outside activities?
35. In what kind of a work environment are you most comfortable?
36. How do you work under pressure?
37. Which of your past jobs have you found most interesting? Why?
38. How would you describe the ideal job for you right now?
39. How did you decide to seek a position with this company?
40. What do you know about our company?
41. What two or three things are most important to you in your job?
42. Do you prefer a company of a certain size? Why?
43. What criteria are you using to evaluate the company for which you hope to work?
44. Do you have a geographical preference? Why?
45. Will you relocate? Does relocation bother you?
46. Are you willing to travel?
47. Are you willing to spend at least six months as a trainee?
48. What questions would you like to ask?
49. What major problem have you encountered and how did you deal with it?
50. What have you learned from your mistakes?

Assertive Interview Score Sheet

Did the person

1. Know about the type of work they were
   applying for? (0-10)   _____

2. Know about the specific employer and
   the job opening? (0-10)   _____

3. Show that they are really interested in
   the job? (0-10)   _____

4. Give complete and interesting answers to
   questions — more than yes or no? (0-10)   _____

5. Volunteer lots of information about themselves —
   background, work history, education, goals, etc.? (0-20) _____

6. Ask good questions of the interviewers about
   the employer and the job? (0-10)   _____

7.
   A. Make eye contact? (0-5)   _____

   B. Have good posture? (0-5)   _____

   C. Speak clearly? (0-5)   _____

   D. Smile and use facial expressions? (0-5)   _____

   E. Answer quickly and easily? (0-5)   _____

   F. Say something especially interesting? (0-5)   _____

TOTAL (0-100)

The 7-minute Job Interview addresses these standards:

Washington State Learning Goals (Education Reform Act)

Goal 1   "...Communicate effectively and responsibly in a variety of ways and settings."

Goal 3   "Think analytically, logically and creatively, and to integrate experience and knowledge to form reasoned judgements and solve problems."

Goal 4   "Understand the importance of work and how performance, effort and decisions directly affect career and educational opportunities."

Washington State Essential Learning Requirements:

Communication
2 The student communicates ideas clearly and effectively.
4. The student analyzes and evaluates the effectiveness of formal and informal communication.

American School Counselor Association National Standards

I. Academic Development
A. Students will acquire the attitudes, knowledge and skills that contribute to effective learning in school and across the life span.
1. Improve academic self-concept (competence and confidence)
2. Acquire skills for improving learning
3. Achieve school success (responsible, independent and group work)

II. Career Development
A. Students will acquire the skills to investigate the world of work in relation to knowledge of self and to make informed career decisions
1: Develop career awareness
2. Develop employment readiness
B. Students will employ strategies to achieve future career goals with success and satisfaction
2. Identify career goals

III. Personal/Social
A. Students will acquire the knowledge, attitudes and interpersonal

skills to help them understand and respect self and others.
1. Acquire self-knowledge
2. Acquire interpersonal skills
B. Students will make decisions, set goals and take necessary action to achieve goals.
1. Self-knowledge application.

Washington State Counseling and Career Guidance Components and Benchmarks

Educational Development Competencies:
  1.1 Develop an education plan
  1.5 Demonstrate decision-making skills
  1.6 Demonstrate goal-setting skills

Personal/Social Development Competencies:
  2.1 Acquire and demonstrate self-awareness and self-acceptance.
  2.2 Identify and handle feelings appropriately
  2.3 Acquire and demonstrate self-management and responsibility for behavior
  2.5 Get along with others
  2.6 Have effective conversation and listening skills
  2.7 Work cooperatively with others in a variety of group situations

Career Exploration and Planning Competencies
  3.1 Understand interests, strengths, preferences and skills as they relate to career development
  3.3 Identify and use career and educational information and opportunities
  3.4 Demonstrate the skills necessary to obtain, maintain, change and create new employment opportunities
  3.5 Demonstrate career planning and career management skills

National Career Development Guidelines

Competency I: Understanding the influence of a positive self-concept
Competency II: Skills to interact positively with others
Competency VII: Skills to prepare to seek, obtain, maintain and change jobs
Competency IX: Skills to make decisions
Competency XII: Skills in career planning

SCANS Report

Basic Skills:
D. Listening
E. Speaking

Personal Qualities:
A. Responsibility
B. Self-esteem
C. Sociability
D. Self-management
E. Integrity/honesty

Thinking Skills:
A. Creative thinking
B. Decision making
C. Problem solving
E. Knowing how to learn
F. Reasoning

Workplace Competencies:
Interpersonal - works with others
Systems - Understands complex
inter-relationships

References

Coats, R., Dorsey, C.J.H., & McDonald, K. (1997). *Washington State guidelines for comprehensive counseling and career guidance programs from kindergarten through community college.* (Packet 1-C) Olympia, WA: Office of the Superintendent of Public Instruction.

Dahir, C.A. & Campbell, C.A. (1997). *Sharing the vision: The national standards for school counseling programs.* Alexandria, VA: American School Counseling Association.

National Occupational Information Coordinating Committee. (1986). *The National career development guidelines.* Des Moines, WA: National Training Support Center of the Center for Learning Connections.

Essential academic learning requirements technical manual. (2002). Olympia, WA: Office of the Superintendent of Public Instruction.

Secretary's Commission on Achieving Necessary Skills (SCANS Report). (1991). *What work requires of schools.* (NTIS Order Number: PB92-146711INZ). Springfield, VA: National Technical Information Service, Technology Administration, U.S. Department of Commerce.

Washington State Legislature, *Education Improvement Act of 1993.* (RCW 28A.655) E2SHB 1209. (Chapter 336, Laws of 1993). Olympia, WA: Washington State Legislature.

Wishik, A. L (1991). (Ed.) *Careers Now activities manual.* Olympia, WA: WOIS/The Career Information System.

WOIS/The Career Information System. Website: http://www.wois.org

Innovative Career Development Practices for Special Populations

Part VII, Innovative Career Development Practices for Special Populations includes issues regarding rural students, students of color, at-risk students, and special education students.

(25) *Career Guidance in Rural Schools: Special Needs, Concerns, and Strategies*—Carlson and Yohon focus on the issues of isolation, limited resources and role models, and family pressures influencing the career development of rural students. Strategies include free/inexpensive curriculum, technology, advisory committees, and school-based enterprises.

(26) *Career Development from a Multicultural Perspective*—Coy, Simpson and Armstrong consider a number of factors that influence the career development of Asian American, Latino, and African American students, including the importance of family and mentors as well as some cultural values and concerns.

(27) *The Dream Board—A Visual Approach for Career Planning with At-Risk 8th and 9th Grade Students*—Jim Allen offers a hands-on approach for educators to help at-risk students better understand the connection between "Education + Skills=Job + Money=Your Future Dreams," using a "dream board" so that students can graphically see the connection between what they want, the training/education they need, and how to obtain it to reach their goals.

(28) *Career Education for Special Education Students*— Jackie Allen discusses the changes in the IDEA 97 (Individuals with Disabilities Education Act), requiring transition services for special education students (an ITP—Individual Transition Plan, as well as the IEP—Individual Education Plan). She suggests that counselors and others need to collaborate in providing counseling for career planning and transition for special needs students.

(29) *Successful Transitions for High School Special Education Students from School to the Workplace*—Fabish discusses the Individual Transition Plan and how educators and community resource people may work together to bring to fruition a special education student's transition to adulthood. Specific programs include Career Ladders and Service Learning Projects.

Chapter Twenty-five

Career Guidance in Rural Schools: Special Needs, Concerns, and Strategies

Laurie A. Carlson and Teresa I. Yohon

Abstract

This chapter focuses on the special needs and concerns of rural students in the delivery of career guidance services. The purposes of this chapter are to increase an awareness of social and cultural factors in rural schools that impact the career planning and decision-making of students and to introduce strategies for schools and communities to meet the unique career needs of rural students. Demographic, social, and economic factors such as limited role models, social norming, family pressure, and financial resources of rural schools are all explored as possibly impacting the career development of students. The authors complete the chapter by introducing strategies that can be employed to meet the unique needs of rural students. These strategies include free/inexpensive curriculum, technology, community advisory committees, and school-based enterprises.

Career Guidance in Rural Schools: Special Needs, Concerns, and Strategies

"Rural schools" can have very different meanings for individuals. Some may envision a small idyllic center of the community where inter-age learning takes place, while others may glimpse a poor, run-down facility demonstrative of isolation and lack of opportunity. Regardless of the perception, rural communities and schools do present unique characteristics that must be understood and addressed when helping students plan for their future (Jeffery, Haché, & Lehr, 1995). The focus of this chapter is on those small communities whose primary income comes from occupations associated with farming, mining, or other natural resources, and whose population experiences some degree of isolation and economic challenge.

The purpose of this chapter is two-fold. The first intention of the authors is to increase the reader's awareness of the social, economic, and geographic issues endemic to rural schools that impact the career planning and decision-making of students. The second purpose of this chapter is to introduce strategies that schools and communities can employ to meet the unique career needs of rural students. Both of these purposes meet the mission of this book: to identify and present "innovative practices to help students focus on their plans after high school."

Special Needs and Concerns

Although little past research on the career decision-making process considers specifically the influence of rural context (Vermeulen & Minor, 1998), many factors appear to impact the experiences of rural school students, particularly in relationship to career planning and decision-making. When students see limited opportunity and perceive insurmountable obstacles to careers that will provide them with financial security and meaning, they can become discouraged and disengaged from the career planning process and all of the learning experiences connected to that process. This is why it is so important for educators and those working with rural youth to not only be aware of such factors, but to also consider strategies for re-engaging those youth. The factors that influence career development of rural youth are best understood by considering them within three possible contexts: geographic, social, and economic.

Geographic Factors

Students in rural areas may experience limited exposure to a variety of career choices (Herr, 1995). Although in recent years we have seen a concerted effort by rural communities to attract industry and there are some rural communities that are not based primarily in agriculture (Sutton & Pearson, 2002), the fact remains that the economy of many rural communities is primarily driven by agricultural, service, and small business ventures. Almost every person that a student knows is a farmer or rancher, serves farmers or ranchers, educates, provides limited health care, or owns a small business. This issue may be compounded by the fact that the rural workforce is aging at an alarming rate. As young people migrate from rural areas to urban areas that have greater career promise, the rural workforce is not only dwindling, but also becoming increasingly older (Herr, 1995). These factors leave rural students with an impression that career options are very limited if they desire to remain in their community.

A second limitation that emerges due to geographical isolation is access to training and education. Certainly, the community college system, technical schools and the Technical Preparation (Tech Prep) program (Kucker, 2000) have served to ease this limitation, but training opportunities may still be limited for some professions such as upper end medical careers, business, engineering, education, and human services. In addition to formal training programs, informal training opportunities such as assistantships and apprenticeships are often difficult to find in rural areas. This is partly due to issues identified in the previous paragraph, but also may be impacted by the tendency for such opportunities to be passed down from one generation to the next in particular families. This "passing of the torch" may not only impact those who would like an opportunity to enter a particular profession, but may also impact the career decision-making process for the young inheritors.

Social Factors

Rural work values and orientations are grounded in the socialization process and are largely affected by social factors (Scharzweller, 1959). These factors include family pressures that are often intergenerational and can be important players in the rural student's career development and decision-making. This is particularly important for farming families where if there is a break in the link of intergenerational ownership, reclaiming or restarting the business can be close to impossible for individuals in subsequent generations. In a 1998 study by Vermeulen and Minor, rural women indicated that parents and families of origin strongly influenced their career decision-making process. Further, Lee (1984) found that career choice attitudes were affected more by parental influence in rural Black and Native American youth than in White students. It is important for educators and those working with such youth to listen seriously to these concerns and engage the youth in an open discussion about what those pressures mean to them. Perhaps situations such as this call for creative solutions involving consultation with other professionals such as lawyers, bankers, and financial planners. The key is to help the student get in touch with resources that can engage him/her in creative problem solving.

Community identity and survival is very important to rural populations. Rural populations are typically less transient than urban populations and family roots become very tied to the community (Sutton & Pearson, 2002). There is great pressure on the young people of a small community to keep the community alive. Indeed, pictures of boarded up storefronts and dusty empty streets tug at the heart of every person who at one time or another has felt deeply connected to a small, rural community. When young people move from the community for education, training, or employment, the community deeply feels the loss, and the expression of the loss is open and honest.

Familiarity and safety are incredibly strong human motivators. Attachment to the rural way of life and the feelings of safety that it instills can inhibit students from considering certain careers if they perceive that those careers require training or education in an unfamiliar, urban environment (Sutton & Pearson, 2002). Even exposure to a large campus community can be extremely threatening to students who have experienced only small learning environments and may serve to further limit educational and training opportunities.

Economic Factors

Several economic factors impact the career development and decision-making of rural school students. Limited financial resources in the schools themselves present three particular challenges. School counselors are typically the school-based professionals who assume responsibility for the educational and career planning of students. Many rural schools, however, lack the financial resources to employ specialists and full-time, licensed school counselors (Herr, 1995). Furthermore, even if a school counselor is on staff, many rural schools cannot afford to purchase much of the curriculum that has been produced to address K-12 career development. The third issue for rural schools with limited financial resources is the inability to purchase equipment that can provide students with job skills and training in the public school. Computer technology is becoming as integral to automotive and manufacturing trades as it is to business and office trades. Much of this equipment easily exceeds the limited budgets of public schools and may jeopardize a vocational education program.

Limited employment opportunity after high school forces many young people to look to larger urban areas for economic security. It is increasingly difficult for American families to experience economic security based on one income, and the vast majority of two parent households are two working parent households. This makes it doubly difficult for families with two adults to find satisfying employment in rural areas where job availability is limited.

Suggestions and Strategies for Educators

The school is key to opening doors of possibility for rural students and re-engaging them in their educational process and career development journey. Nationally, pessimism exists concerning the public school staff's ability to adequately serve students' career development needs (Starr, 1996). Because of the unique challenges discussed in the paragraphs above, educators in rural schools must be proactive, creative and relentless in their search for materials and services for rural youth. Following are ideas and suggestions for interventions that are school-based, community-based, and connecting.

Within School Walls

The demographic and social factors identified above emerge early in a student's experience, and therefore, are appropriately addressed early and consistently throughout a student's educational experience (Cole, 1982; Miller, 1989). Kindergarten is the appropriate time to begin exposing children to core life skills such as self-esteem (Miller, 1989), self-understanding, responsibility, cooperation, and intrinsic rewards. Further, many kindergarten and primary grade classrooms possess unlimited opportunity to expose children to the world of work through play. At http://www.usoe.k12.ut.us/stc/ccc/home.htm, elementary lesson plans based on various career fields are available to teach standards in math, social science, and other content areas. Some classrooms incorporate activity centers that are modeled after such places of employment as medical offices, stores, and hair salons. The challenge in using such centers is to ensure inclusion of non-traditional careers and expose children to experiences that combat traditional gender and race role stereotyping (Miller, 1989).

Utilization of free or inexpensive K-12 curriculum through such federal programs as School-to-Work and Perkins can introduce students formally to the world of work and the career development process (Kucker, 2000). Both of these programs are federally instituted and funded. The school-to-work program was initially established in 1994 with the purpose of providing education and materials "to stimulate the creation of systems that foster young people's transition from being primarily students to being productive workers" (Hamilton & Hamilton, 1999, p. 3). The School-to-Work legislation officially sunset in October of 2001 (U.S. Department of Education & U.S. Department of Labor, n.d.), but many valuable materials remain available. "Under the Perkins Act, federal funds are made available to help provide vocational-technical education programs and services to youth and adults" (U.S. Department of Education, 2002, par. 1). Careful review of such curriculum can uncover material that addresses specific challenges such as geographic isolation and social norming, and can be used to combat demographic and social barriers early in a student's education. Resourcefulness is the key to locating such curriculum. Professional associations such as the American School Counselor

Association (ASCA) and the National Career Development Association (NCDA) often provide free or inexpensive curriculum material to schools.

The Internet is perhaps the best way to find career development resources from a number of organizations and associations. The Occupational Outlook Handbook, a tool used by counselors everywhere, is online at http://www.bls.gov/oco/. An example of an online career unit (interest inventories, job search tools, resume writing, etc.) is available at http://www.angelfire.com/ks/tonyaskinner/interview.html. Other online resources are presented in the following table:

Online Location	Information Provided
http://www.careers.org/	Gateway to a wide assortment of career tools and information.
http://www.careermag.com/	Interviewing tips, virtual company tours, and job postings.
http://www.careergames.com/	Online games that focus on career skills such as self-assessment, interviewing, and targeting a job.
http://careers.lycos.com/tools.asp	Occupational profiles, résumé writers, and job seeking advice.
http://careers.yahoo.com/	Résumé builder, salary comparisons, and special articles on various career development topics.
http://www.udallas.edu/career/Primary%20Pages/Careerexploration.htm	List of Internet links about careers
http://www.acinet.org/acinet/library.htm?category=1.2	Online career videos. Use Real Player plug-in to view.

Keep in mind that one does not need formal career curriculum to expose children to the world of work. Classroom teachers can seamlessly integrate world of work information and career skills into the regular curriculum (Cole, 1982). When classroom teachers make a conscious effort to include such material, learning becomes more relevant for their students, children become engaged in the entire educational process, and there is shared responsibility for career education in the school (Kucker, 2000). This is especially important in those schools and districts that cannot financially support a full-time, licensed school counselor. Following are two examples of such integration. A junior high mathematics teacher exposes students to elementary algebraic concepts by giving them an assignment involving the surveying of their yard. In a high school physics class, the teacher educates students about pollutant chemicals by volunteering the entire class to serve the Department of Natural Resources through the River Watch Program.

School-Based Enterprise

Student organizations that can provide resources and structure to innovative learning opportunities include Future Business Leaders of America (FBLA), Distributive Education Clubs of America (DECA), Future Farmers of America (FFA), Family Career and Community Leaders of America (FCCLA), and extension services. In particular, these organizations provide detailed information and support for school-based enterprises.

A school-based enterprise (SBE) is a school-sponsored activity that involves a group of students in producing goods or services for sale to or use by people other than the students involved (Blank, n.d.). SBE's can provide many of the same work-preparation advantages as employer-based apprenticeships along with important academic benefits. In a house-building project, for example, students can acquire construction skills and also work out the mathematics of structural design components. Students in a school restaurant can make salads and also analyze their nutritional value.

School based enterprises range in scope from school stores and construction companies (Kucker, 2000) to website development businesses (Advance Com, n.d.). Students can build or rehabilitate houses, staff childcare centers, publish books or magazines, run restaurants, complete office administration tasks, raise crops or livestock, repair automobiles, operate retail outlets and provide other services as part of their school programs. More school-based enterprise examples can be found online at:
http://www.schoolbasedenterprises.org/sbearticleopen.htm
http://www.utc.edu/~careered/bestprac/category/schoolbased.html
http://www.state.ia.us/educate/ecese/stw/sbe.html.

When working in an enterprise, students are engaged and involved emotionally, psychologically, intellectually and often physically. School-based enterprises can be designed to prepare students for both college and work. Some of the proven benefits of using school-based enterprises are (Stern et al., 1994):
• Real world application of academic skills and concepts

- Integration of academic and vocational education
- Learning about multiple aspects of an industry
- Problem-solving skill development
- Social support for one another's learning
- Time management skill development
- Teamwork and leadership skill development

DECA provides a start-up guide for school-based enterprises at http:/ /www.schoolbasedenterprises.org/starting.html.

Securing and Utilizing Technology

The Internet and the World Wide Web hold the greatest potential in transforming teaching and learning. The most significant reason for this is the massive set of information resources that is now accessible for the classroom and the virtual experiences that students can have via a web environment. No matter how isolated a community, a student with an Internet connection, a modem, and a fairly inexpensive computer can interact with people and information.

To search through the endless supply of information on the Internet, use search tools such as search engines and subject directories. In general, a search engine is a powerful computer program that searches the World Wide Web for sites that contain the information that you want. In a subject directory, websites are hand-selected and usually evaluated carefully by human experts. Each search tool will find different resources. The University of California at Berkeley has a five-step search strategy for searching the Internet (http://www.lib.berkeley.edu/TeachingLib/Guides/Internet/ Strategies.html).

Good search engines are dwindling in number. Currently www.google.com provides the best search protocols available. Using Google you can also search for web directories (summary of resources on a specific topic) or databases. Add terms like "web directory," "guides," or "database" to your search terms to find these special information groupings. To find career development information, use search terms such as "career counseling resources" and "online career guidance." If you receive too many matches or hits, you may want to be more specific. Many search engines offer advanced search tools that allow you to narrow your search by defining a phrase (words placed within quotation marks) or linking multiple words or phrases by the word "and."

Using online resources means that computers and online access must be present. New federal education legislation known as "No Child Left Behind" consolidates federal technology grant programs and E-rate funds (monies for Internet access). States will receive a block of money by formula for technology programs. These funds can be used for software purchases and development, wiring and technology infrastructure, and teacher training in the use of technology. Rural schools can apply for these monies via their state's grant proposal process.

Diverse organizations provide foundation and grant monies for technology improvements and support for lower income schools. To see what monies are available, go to one of the following grant databases: http://www.techlearning.com/grants.html, http://www.schoolgrants.org/grant_opps.htm, and http://www.eschoolnews.com/resources/funding/. These sites also offer tips for writing grants. Federal grant announcements are located at: http://www.ed.gov/legislation/FedRegister/announcements/index.html.

Utilizing Community and Outside Resources

Community organizations that can provide partnerships and local resources include the local chamber of commerce, National Federation of Independent Business, Jaycee's, Rotary International, the American Legion/Auxiliary, Service Corps of Retired Executives (SCORE), the Small Business Development Centers, 4-H, Boy Scouts, Girl Scouts, and the Boys and Girls Clubs of America. These organizations often offer materials and learning experiences that can increase student knowledge and career skills outside of the school setting. Examples include providing guest speakers concerning non-traditional careers, sponsoring students for participation in such experiences as Boy's/Girl's State, or work and student exchange programs through the National 4-H Federation. Organizations such as this are relatively easy to find in small, rural communities.

Through the federal Carl D. Perkins Vocational and Technical Education Act of 1998 (also known as Perkins III), monies are accessible to rural areas in general and for career resources and vocational training specifically. Basic information about the Carl Perkins Act can be found at http://www.ed.gov/offices/OVAE/CTE/perkins.html, with specific information about career and guidance counseling at http://www.ed.gov/offices/OVAE/CTE/cgcp.html. Perkins III funds can be used to support career guidance and academic counseling, improve accessibility to career-related information, develop career-related educational resources, and improve coordination and communication among administrators and planners of programs that deal with career information and employment. States receive Perkins funds based on a formula and then school districts access Perkins monies through a statewide competitive process. State staffs can also allocate additional monies to rural areas. A minimum of $15,000 must be requested so rural school districts often form consortiums to share resources and to reach the minimum limit. It is important to note that each state allocates Perkins funds differently. Before valuable time is spent writing a proposal, determine whether funds are available for the program you envision. You can do this by contacting your state (or district) Perkins Coordinator. For help in writing a Perkins grant, go to http://www.academicinnovations.com/cptoc.html .

Although apprenticeships and internships may be difficult to find in rural areas, an organized and concerted effort by the school can help to increase the potential. Students are often willing to engage in such apprenticeships for graduation credit in lieu of pay, and this may open up possibilities with rural businesses that are often under financial stress. Such arrangements require forward thinking by the school administration and common commitment among school staff to embrace non-traditional forms of education to meet the unique needs of individual students. Sometimes smaller scale policies can be employed if a school staff is not willing to buy into full-scale apprenticeship opportunities. One example of this is a rural high school that allows juniors and seniors two full school days each year as excused absence to job shadow career interests.

Connecting School and Outside Resources

Stronger programs result from positive partnerships between schools and communities. Schools have recently been adopting ideas and strategies employed by businesses and organizations. The next section of the chapter addresses the issue of strong school/community partnerships.

School-Community Advisory Committees
Rural schools indeed are often the center of rural communities (Cole, 1990; Sutton & Pearson, 2002). It makes sense then that a strong partnership between school and community is essential to provide optimum opportunity for rural youth to learn about and explore career options. Schools that form an advisory committee with representation from the business community lay a strong foundation for a working partnership. It is essential that the school advisory committee be sanctioned and appointed by the school board so that it is not susceptible to changes in school administration and staff. Further, a formal document outlining the roles, responsibilities, and decision-making power of the advisory committee should be drafted and formally adopted by the board. Such a formal and stable committee, with representation from all the district stakeholders, can help to ensure that

every stakeholder group is heard in decisions regarding educational programming. This also provides an avenue for the school to connect with community business leaders so career education and opportunities are enhanced for students.

Public Relations

Closely related is the need for schools to invest time and money in public relations. This is particularly critical for any special services or programming provided to students. When the public is aware of the rationale and need for career development curriculum and resources, support from the community is much easier to secure. Strong community support provides volunteers and chaperones for related activities such as career fairs at local universities or field trips to regional places of industry. Needs may be advertised through local newspapers, radio, television, flyers, or school newsletters.

Conclusion

Geographic, social and economic factors do influence the career development and career decision-making process of rural youth. These factors have been outlined in this chapter and strategies including curriculum and program development are discussed. Further, the chapter provides the reader with a comprehensive list of Internet-based resources. Identifying and utilizing a wide range of resources provides the foundation for best practice when it comes to addressing the career development needs of these students. As partnerships develop between the school and community organizations, access to resources such as curriculum, technology, work-place knowledge, volunteerism, and program leadership emerges.

References

Advance Com (n.d.). Retrieved April 15, 2002, from http:// fertilebeltrami.k12.mn.us/advancecom/ Advance%20Com.htm

Blank, W. (n.d.). School-Based enterprises. Retrieved April 15, 2002, from http://sparky.occ.cccd.edu/wbl/School-Based/SB_Connections/ School_Enterprises-Pg1/school_enterprises-pg1.html

Cole, C. G. (1982). Career guidance for middle - junior high school students. *The Vocational Guidance Quarterly, 30*, 308-314.

Cole, R. (1990). Ghosts in small town schools. *International Journal of the W. K. Kellogg Foundation, 1,* 44-48.

Hamilton, S. F., & Hamilton, M. A. (1999). *Building strong school-to-work systems.* Ithaca, NY: Media and Technology Services at Cornell University.

Herr, E. L. (1995). *Counseling employment bound youth.* Greensboro, NC: ERIC Counseling and Student Services Clearinghouse. (ED: 382899)

Jeffery, G., Haché, G., & Lehr, R. (1995). A group-based Delphi application: Defining rural career counseling needs. *Measurement and Evaluation in Counseling and Development, 28,* 45-60.

Kucker, M. (2000). South Dakota's model for career and life planning. *Journal of Career Development, 27,* 133-148.

Lee, C. C. (1984). Work values of rural Black, White, and Native American adolescents: Implications for contemporary rural school counselors. *Counseling and Values, 28,* 63-71.

Miller, M. J. (1989). Career counseling for the elementary school child: Grades K-5. *Journal of Employment Counseling, 26,* 169-177.

Schwarzweller, H. L. (1959). Value orientations and educational and occupational choices. *Rural Sociology, 24,* 246-256.

Starr, M. F. (1996). Comprehensive guidance and systematic educational and career planning: Why a K-12 approach? *Journal of Career Development, 23,* 9-22.

Stern, D., Stone, J., Hopkins, C., McMillion, M. & Crain, R. (1994). *School-Based enterprise: Productive learning in American high schools.* San Francisco: Josey Bass.

Sutton, J. M. & Pearson, R. (2002). The practice of school counseling in rural and small town schools. *Professional School Counseling, 5,* 266-276.

U.S. Department of Education. (January, 2002). State basic grants and tech-prep grants. Retrieved May 8, 2002, from http://www.ed.gov/offices/OVAE/CTE/vye.html

U.S. Department of Education & U.S. Department of Labor. (n.d.). Retrieved May 8, 2002, from http://www.stw.ed.gov/

Vermeulen, M. E. & Minor, C. W. (1998). Context of career decisions: Women reared in a rural community. *Career Development Quarterly, 46*, 230-245.

Chapter Twenty-Six

Career Development from a Multicultural Perspective

Doris Rhea Coy, Christopher Simpson, and Steve Armstrong

Abstract

As schools across the nation have culturally and ethnically broadened, the educational and career concerns of students have expanded as well. In fact, school administrators, teachers, and counselors are required to face a variety of issues that must also be considered when assisting a student in their educational and career choices. Students are now faced with issues such as dropping out of school, school violence, and teen pregnancy. In addition to understanding the individual needs of students, school counselors must have a comprehension of the students' culture and ethnic concerns and values (Lara & Pande, 2001; Trueba, 1999). This chapter will focus on current issues that face Asian American, Latino and African American students, the importance of family and mentors in career development, some cultural values and concerns of Asian Americans, Latinos and African Americans and counselor considerations when working with these students.

The National Career Development Association (NCDA) commissioned four nationwide surveys that were carried out by the Gallup Organization. These surveys indicated that approximately 1 in 10 adults are involved in selecting, changing, or acquiring a new job each year and that they need assistance. The need for career development services is not equally distributed across populations. Members of ethnic minority groups (African Americans–79%, Hispanics Americans–75%, and Asian Americans–71%) reported that they would seek more information about jobs than did white European Americans (65%). (Brown & Minor, 1989, 1992; Hoyt & Lester, 1995; NCDA, 1999). If this is a concern of adults, then perhaps educators of students in grades K-12 need to address career issues before students either leave or graduate from high school. While this is an area that should be addressed by all educators, the school counselor is in a unique position through his/her work in counseling (individual and group) and through classroom guidance to provide career decision making information to students and to assist them as they make career decisions.

Asian Americans

Population Profile

According to the 2000 census, 75% of the population of the United States reported being only white; 12% of the total population reported being only black or African American; approximately .9% of the total population reported being only American Indian and Alaska native; 3.6% of the total population reported being Asian; and .1% of the total population reported being only native Hawaiian and other Pacific Islander. Approximately 12.5%, or more than 35 million respondents, reported being only Latino (U.S. Bureau of Census, 2001a). Between 1980 and 1990, the Asian American/Pacific Islander population grew by 107%. Since 1990, the Asian American/Pacific Islander population has grown about 4.5% every year (Bennett & Martin, 1995). For much of this growth, about 86% is accounted for by immigration. By the year 2000, this population is projected to reach 12.1 million people, or about 4% of the total U.S. population (U.S. Bureau of the Census, 2000).

Asian Americans

Asian Americans in this chapter include: Chinese, Japanese, Filipinos, Koreans, Asian Indians, Southeast Asians, Vietnamese Laotians, Cambodians, Hmongs, Pacific Islanders, Hawaiians, Guamanians, and Samoans. This group has been growing rapidly and has shown a large increase because of the change in immigration laws that occurred in 1965 and the entry of over 1.5 million Southeast Asian refugees since 1975 (Peterson & Gonzalez, 2000). The immigration pattern changed the characteristics of the Asian American population. In fact, with the exception of Japanese Americans, Asian American populations are now principally composed of foreign-born individuals.

The Chinese and Japanese were the first Asians to settle in the United States in large numbers. Like other minority groups, they arrived with the hope of improving their economic conditions, lifestyles, and social and political life (Zunker, 2002). Today Asian Americans are dispersed throughout the United States. A large percentage is located in urban areas of the west and east coast. Although some Asian American groups have been portrayed as "model minorities" in terms of significant educational and economic success, large percentages of these groups live in poverty and suffer high levels of psychological stress (Sue & Sue, 1999). Between-group differences within the American population may be quite great, as the population is composed of at least 40 distinct subgroups that differ in language, religion, and values. The tremendous heterogeneity both between and within various Asian American groups defies categorization and stereotypic description. This group has been subjected to continuing societal oppression, discrimination, and misunderstanding.

Asian Americans have many values that are different from those of European Americans. Unlike other ethnic groups, their time orientation is more likely to be past future (cyclical and eternal), although other time orientations can be found among members of this diverse group. Some members place the desires of the group ahead of individual concerns. They also hold what is termed a "lineal social value," which means parents or elders make career decisions for them. This issue is often addressed in the counselor's office where the individual social value of the client is in conflict with the lineal social values of the parents (Isaacson & Brown, 2000). According to Landrum-Brown (1994), Asian Americans value the following: family focus, humility, emotional restraint, tradition, transcendence, parental obedience and obligation, conformity, interdependence, role rigidity, indirect expression, formality, harmony with the universe, and a reverence for ancestors and elders. Given the importance of cultural identity and the acculturation process of minorities, it is important that we not use general information about Asian Americans (or others) in a stereotypical fashion. What may be true of one individual may not be true of another (Sue, Ivey, Pedersen, 1996).

Educational Attainment

While education is highly valued in Asian and Asian American cultures, it is not universal, as "Access to education is mediated by immigrant status and class background" (Leong & Gim-Chung, 1995). Even though education may be valued, some families and individuals may not be able to invest in education nor afford to wait for delayed income. Awareness of these divergent levels of educational attainment within the Asian American/Pacific Islander population smashes the "model Minority stereotype" (Suzuki, 1989, p. 209).

Much media attention has been given to the "model minority stereotype." Several articles include data that indicates that the educational pace for the rest of America is being set by young Asian Americans, largely those with Chinese, Korean and Indo-Chinese background. Many young

Asian Americans are finishing well above the mean on the math section of the Scholastic Aptitude Test and, according to one comprehensive study of San Diego-area students, outscoring their peers of other races in high school grade-point averages. They spend more time on their homework, a researcher at the U.S. Department of Education found, take more advanced high school courses and graduate with more credits than other American students. A higher percentage of these young people complete high school and finish college than do white American students. (Sue & Okazaki, 1990). It is the belief of Harvard psychology professor Jerome Kagan that the simple answer for these students being super achievers is because they work harder. Laurence Steinberg (1996) also confirms this in his book.

As a whole, Asian Americans/Pacific Islanders have high educational attainment. In 1993 nearly 9 out of 10 males and 8 out of 10 females (age twenty-five and over) had at least a high school diploma. But among Asian American /Pacific Islander ethnic groups, high school graduation rates vary widely. Data from 1990 shows a graduation rate of 31% for Hmongs, and 88% for Japanese. The Hmongs are among the most recent group of Asian American immigrants (Tapp, 1993), while most Japanese have been in this country for several generations. Among the population 25 years old and older, 85% of Asian and Pacific Islanders had completed high school compared to 88% of Whites. However, 42% of Asians and Pacific Islanders in this age group held at least a bachelor's degree, compared to 28% of Whites.

Poverty

Child poverty rates were higher than the total poverty rate for each of the following groups: 11% for Whites, 18% for Asians, 34% for Latinos, and 37% for blacks. The share of families in poverty was about 23% for both Black and Latino families. The 1993 poverty rate for Asian American/ Pacific Islander families at 14%, was higher than the 8% of White families (Bennett & Martin, 1995).

The 1993 median income of Asian American/Pacific Islander families ($44,460) resembled that of white families ($41,110).

Securing Information about Work Ethic

School counselors can gain information about the work ethic of their students by asking the following questions:
1. Can the student tell a story about the exact origins of his/her work ways? Of his/her time ways?
2. Who taught them about work ways? About time ways?
3. What explicit messages has the student received about work ways? About time ways?

4. In what context (e.g., time and place) were these messages imparted to him/her?
5. Are these messages useful for the student now?
6. Does he/she wish to retain such practices as part of his/her behavior?
7. What kinds of coworker conduct does the student deplore, seek to avoid/admire and seek to emulate?
8. How would the student prefer to use his/her spare time? What, if anything, prevents him/her from using his/her "spare time" as he/she would like?
9. Does the student's family take vacations? If so, how regularly? If not, why not?
10. What is the student's opinion about charity? About welfare?
11. Has he/she ever received charity? Been on welfare?
12. Under what circumstances would he/she accept charity? Welfare? (Peterson & Gonzales, 2000).

Personal, Social & Emotional Information

Sue & Sue (1990) made the following observation about Chinese Americans that would be helpful to the school counselor: Chinese American students inhibit emotional expression and do not actively participate in the counseling process. They are discouraged from revealing emotional problems by their cultural conditioning and react more favorably to well-structured counseling models. Sue & Sue (1990) note that counselors must have an understanding of cultural influences when counseling Chinese Americans. Behavioral approaches are the preferred counseling methods to use when working with Southeast Asian students according to Fernandez (1988). In her eyes it is inappropriate to use counseling techniques that require clients to verbalize excessively. The use of bi-lingual materials and role models in workshops directed toward parents of Chinese and Korean children that exposed them to methods of accessing a variety of occupations was used successfully by Evanoski and Tse (1989).

Kaneshige (1979) and Sue (1992) offer the following suggestions for counselors when addressing the special needs and problems associated with Asian Americans. Especially in group encounters, Asian Americans are very sensitive about verbalizing psychological problems. When asked to discuss personal achievements and limitations, Asian Americans tend to be impressive. The role of counseling in general and the benefits that may be derived from it tend to be misinterpreted by Asian Americans. With authority figures, Asian Americans can be perceived as very passive and nonassertive but in reality they are reacting to cultural inhibitions that discourage them from being perceived as aggressive. Suggestions to modify behavior that is unassuming and nonassertive may be strongly resisted by Asian Americans.

According to Sue (1994), offering what is considered to be desirable help includes giving advice and suggestions but avoiding confrontation and direct interpretation of motives and actions. It is most important when discussing personal issues to be indirect and the counselor should do most of the initial verbalization with a rather formal interactive approach.

Employment Limitations for Asian Americans

There are many limitations for employment for first-generation Asian Americans. The following problems and difficulties may confront the individual:

1. The need to learn English.
2. The need to address transferable skills.
3. The need to consider past work history as relevant.
4. The need to understand the concept of career ladders.
5. The need to locate information about unemployment; and
6. The need to recognize the importance of résumé preparation and interview skills training.

The lowest rate of unemployment as a group belongs to Asian Americans (Smith, 1983). Asian Americans are viewed as very industrious workers, seem to value education, and have taken advantage of higher education to enhance their career development. They do well in business administration, engineering and sciences. Because they are seen as being capable in sciences but lacking in verbal skills, this could limit their access to careers that require communication skills. While many Asian Americans are employed in service occupations, they can also be found as workers in the professions, in office and clerical jobs, and as service workers (Zunker, 2002).

Latinos

Current Issues

The Latino people are comprised of a broad racial, social, and economic diversity (Trueba, 1999). This population encompasses many individuals from a wide variety of countries and regions. Within the U.S., individuals of Mexican descent make up the largest subgroups of Latinos (60%), followed by those from South and Central America (23%), Puerto Rico (12%), and Cuba (5%) (Gloria & Rodriguez, 2000). While many Latinos have been residents of the United States for generations, statistics suggest that a significant number are 1st or 2nd generation residents.

Statistics also point to the increased population and influence of

Latinos. The U.S. Census Bureau (2000) reports that between 1990 and 2000, this population increased by 58%. It has been estimated that by 2010, Latinos will make up the largest minority group within the U.S. (Miranda & Umhoefer, 1998). To a large extent, this population increase has been experienced in the schools. In 1970, California public schools were comprised of 30% ethnic and racial minority students. In 1990, that number increased to 50% (Trueba, 1999).

Unfortunately, some current disturbing trends also exist within the Latino population. In 1998, 30% of Latino children dropped-out of high school (Lara & Pande, 2001). Latinos are underrepresented among students enrolling in high school mathematics courses that prepare them for college and math-based careers (Lopez, 2001). Furthermore, evidence suggests a continuing trend that Latino students are generally being guided more toward vocational rather than college-based educational tracks (Arbona, 1990). With demographic trends pointing toward an increase in Latinos within the U.S., the time has come to ensure that these children receive encouragement to attain higher education. As these students are better prepared to face career and life challenges, the welfare of a multicultural society and economy will be assured. School and career counselors will likely share in this responsibility. For this to occur, it is imperative that counselors have an understanding of the unique factors that comprise the Latino student.

Influence of Family and Mentors

In working with Latino students, mental health professionals must be conscious of the influence and value of the family. Generally, the family is central within the Latino community. Students will often view the family and community as an integral part of religious, economic, and social life. Consequently, these students generally do not value individuation as much as Anglo-American students or students from other cultures (Gloria & Rodriguez, 2000; Trueba, 1999). In fact, students from Latino backgrounds may find leaving home for college to be especially stressful (Stern, 1999).

The transition from home to school can have a significant affect on the students' academic and personal success. Difficulty for the student can be further exacerbated by the fact that many parents may not have experienced college life and cannot relate to the college experience. This can make the home to school transition difficult for the family, as well as the student. Counselors may assist Latino students in providing means for parents and families to be actively involved in the students' academic life. Parents visiting the students' school, dormitory, and even classrooms can be an enlightening and relieving experience for students and family alike.

Many Latino parents, particularly immigrants, having low levels of education, may provide more emotional support than instrumental guidance to their children's educational and professional development (Lopez, 2001). The counselor who understands this variable may assist the student in seeking a mentor. The role of a mentor can be significant in the student's life. Research has identified that Latinos who have an interested and invested mentor are more likely to succeed (Gloria & Rodriguez, 2000). The cultural and ethnic diversity of staff and faculty in a school setting can be useful in assisting the student in finding an appropriate role model (Alicea, 1998). In the absence of role models, peers may take over the role as mentor. In any case, the guidance and understanding provided by a mentoring relationship with a student may prove to be essential in the comfort and success of the Latino student (Gloria & Rodriguez 2000).

Considerations for School and Career Counselors

Several factors are important for the counselor working with Latino students. The following factors should be considered when working with this population of individuals.

Attending Skills

In hurried and busy school settings and career centers, it is natural for counselors to feel the need to be directive and concise. While these are often facilitative qualities, counselors would be well served to concentrate on basic attending skills with Latino students. The qualities of unconditional positive regard, empathy, and congruence have been found to be facilitative with a variety of individuals. With many Latino students reporting experiences characterized by intolerance and discrimination, these qualities integrated with excellent listening skills can be particularly useful to the career/school counselor in developing a relationship with the student (Gloria & Rodriguez, 2000; Jackson, 1998; Rogers, 1961).

Often focusing on career and academic concerns of these students will serve as a means for establishing rapport and trust. However, it is important to note that the students' goals and concerns must be acknowledged before a trusting relationship can be reached (Jackson, 1998). Integral in this process is the message to the student that he or she "can do it" (Stern, 1999). It may be useful to point out examples of individuals from similar cultural backgrounds who have been successful (Gloria & Rodriguez, 2000).

Acknowledging Culture and Language

As previously mentioned, the Latino culture encompasses a broad range of countries, regions, and characteristics. Counselors need to be aware of the differences and similarities among the various Latino subgroups. Although Latinos share some common heritage, no generalizations can be made that apply to all members of this multi-ethnic group (Arbona, 1990). Consequently, counselors should understand how the student perceives his or her culture.

Culture/ethnic identity is centered on language. A large number of emotions and ideas have appropriate translations that convey the intensity of the individual. Latinos in the U.S., especially children and adolescents, struggle to define who they are in an environment that negates and deprecates their language and culture (Alicea, 1998).

Counselors working with Latino students must refrain from referring to a student's primary language as a deficit. Similar to persons of any cultural or ethnic background, Latino students will likely respond to their positive qualities being acknowledged, as well as their weaknesses. Students naturally feel a greater sense of acceptance when qualities as significant as language and culture are celebrated and acknowledged as important to the student (Trueba, 1999).Counselors can assist in ensuring acceptance and acknowledgement by encouraging teachers to use strategies that reinforce the importance of students' strengths and cultural background. Cooperative learning, language experience, reciprocal teaching, and whole language activities are potentially useful in creating effective and comfortable learning environments. Techniques like these allow the student to be "the expert" by capitalizing on that student's existing knowledge (Lara & Pande, 2001; Trueba, 1999).

Understanding Bicultural Factors

Latino students often feel the need to adopt a bicultural stance in society. In a society that is not understanding, or perhaps intolerant, of Latino culture, students may find themselves emotionally exhausted. A great deal of energy may be expended functioning in a predominantly Anglo-American culture that values the use of English as a primary language and other cultural norms. Many Latinos will act in a culturally consistent fashion when at home but feel the need to deny that identity and embrace the more appropriate " North American" personality (Alicea, 1998).

Counselors may need to help the student balance the amount of energy that is required to fulfill these perceived roles. Helping a student become acquainted with the Latino community may help. Latino student groups and sororities/fraternities can be helpful in the student bridging the gaps that are left when leaving home. As previously mentioned, the family must be included in this process. Visiting the campus, professors, and those individuals that the student surrounds himself or herself with can help the student, in addition to providing the family with an opportunity to understand his or her new environment (Gloria & Rodriguez, 2000).

In conclusion, counselors must be prepared to communicate with Latinos effectively and to understand the critical role of Latinos in our future (Trueba, 1999). Schools are beginning to realize the importance of personal relations with students and their families. Campuses are beginning to address the diversity of students through celebrations and special events (Alicea, 1998). However, research shows that more work exists for counselors and educators.

African Americans

According to Brown (1995), the career development of African Americans needs urgent attention. African Americans are the third largest ethnic group in the United States behind Whites and Hispanics. They represent over 12% of the country's population. Unfortunately, however, the poverty rate for African Americans is approximately 32%, which is more than twice the national rate. Unemployment is much higher for African Americans as well. Unemployment for African Americans is about 2.5 times the rate for Whites; among teens, the rate is more than twice that of Whites.

Historically, African Americans have been disadvantaged in the workplace due to discrimination and fewer educational opportunities. Isaacson and Brown (2000) noted that discrimination and lack of educational opportunity have resulted in lower earnings, lower employment rates, and increased family instability. In fact, African American families frequently encounter poverty and live in extremely disadvantaged communities (Sampson & Wilson, 1995; Wilson, 1996). Poverty not only causes difficulty in the family itself, but it also creates problems in the neighborhood. High-poverty neighborhoods are more likely to offer adult models of non-work and lower levels of community support and organization (Sampson & Groves, 1989; Wilson, 1987, 1996).

Swinton (1992) noted that African Americans are disadvantaged occupationally as well. According to Swinton, only 36.9% of African American men were employed in "good" jobs such as executives, managers, and sales occupations. By contrast, 61.8% of Whites were employed in these jobs. Swinton stated that similar patterns among women were also observed. Many African Americans have grown up believing that only certain careers were open to them because they were black (Bowman, 1995). These trends and issues underscore the importance of the career development of African Americans.

Education

Many people believe that education is the means by which occupational patterns such as these can be impacted. According to Brown (1995), African Americans have historically held this view. However, even though data has shown that African Americans have made some gains in college participation since 1985, the margin of difference between Whites and Blacks has not been significantly reduced. Also, the proportion of men in African American college enrollment has declined over the past decade.

Concerns about educational issues among African Americans also focus on school-age children. McBay (1992) noted that many African American children are not prepared to enter school. Others have expressed concerns that the educational opportunities for African Americans in schools are limited and that educational placements often are inappropriate. According to Patton (1998), many African American students are inappropriately placed and, as a result, fail to receive a quality education because they miss essential academic and social curricula. The U.S. Department of Education (1997) found that African Americans accounted for 16% of the total student population, yet African Americans represented 32% of the students in programs for students with mild mental retardation and 29% of the students in programs for students with moderate mental retardation.

Family Issues

Another cultural issue that is important for career development specialists to understand about African American children is that many of them grow up in families that face tremendous difficulties. For instance, many grow up with a single parent who may have difficulty providing the financial security that children need. Only about 25% of African American children live with both of their biological parents (Teachman, Tedrow, & Crowder, 2000).

In fact, many African American children do not live with either biological parent. Far more African American children live with grandparents or other relatives than do Hispanic or European American children. Census data indicate that 4.1 percent of white children, 6.5 percent of Hispanic children, and 13.5 percent of African American children live with their grandparents or other relatives (Casper & Bryson, 1998).

Religion

Another part of culture that many African Americans consider important is religion and spirituality. For many African Americans, organized religion is an important source of support. The church is considered to be a refuge from many of the above-mentioned difficulties that African American children encounter. Studies within the last 10 years have reported that a majority of African Americans are affiliated with a religious denomination (Gallup & Castelli, 1991). In addition, African Americans are more religiously involved than the general population in the United States (Chatters, Taylor, & Lincoln, 1999).

In fact, in many African American communities, the church is viewed as central to the functioning of these communities (Boyd-Franklin, 1989; Lincoln & Mamiya, 1990). Many African Americans today view the church as much more than a place to worship. The church is a means of coping with adversity and preserving family values. The church also encourages involvement in social issues such as discrimination, and poverty (Brashears & Roberts, 1996).

Research

Research findings have indicated that many African Americans prefer low-level occupations that are social. African Americans tend to be more group centered and less individualistic than Whites. There is some research to indicate that African American women tend to avoid occupations in which discrimination is evident (Brown, 1995; Swinton, 1992). Further, there is research support that indicates that African Americans expect less out of an occupation than Whites.

Regarding vocational choice, research indicates that mothers influence the career development of their children (Brown, 1995). Parental influence on children's career interests has been found to be greater among African Americans than Whites. In a national survey, African Americans indicated that they were more likely than Whites to need help in finding information about jobs (Brown, Minor, & Jepsen, 1991).

Career Intervention and Assessment

This need for help can be a starting point for career counselors. As several of the authors above have stated, African Americans have a critical need for assistance in their career development, and apparently, many of them recognize that need. However, they also have many obstacles to overcome in their career development. It is important for career development specialists to understand the magnitude of the economic, occupational, and social disadvantages that African Americans face.

In addition, career counselors have to contend with the belief that only certain jobs are available to African Americans. Apparently, many African Americans may not even consider certain "good" jobs because they believe that these jobs are only open to Whites. The goal of career interventions is to help clients identify careers that are the best fit for them.

Many African Americans, however, are not ready to consider which careers might fit them because they may not believe that they even have a chance to acquire a position in a field of interest. Obviously, these perceptions and beliefs must be addressed in order to find the "best fit."

One implication for career specialists working with African Americans is to help them broaden their perceptions of what is available to them. Obviously, the issue of financial aid for college is even more critical for African Americans than for Whites. Also, if other family members have not attended college and work in labor-intensive jobs, work needs to be done to help high school students consider all of the options that are available.

Another important resource for career counselors is information about racial identity development. Many White counselors have a limited understanding of their own racial identity and the racial identity of clients. According to Bowman (1995), White career counselors tend to have a naive understanding of the cultural differences between Whites and African Americans. White career counselors may downplay the importance of race in the early stages of working with African Americans. Bowman suggests that it is helpful for Whites to have an understanding of their own racial identity as well as the racial identity of African Americans. If White career counselors develop a deeper understanding of a racial identity model, they may be able to understand and accept some of the real differences between African American clients and themselves.

According to Bowman (1995), little is know about the career aspirations of African Americans. Researchers have questioned whether career inventories are valid with African Americans. Bowman cited a few studies that used the Strong Interest Inventory (SII) with African Americans. One such study yielded moderate predictive validity among African American male and female college students. However, Bowman noted that career specialists should not assume that inventories that are appropriate and helpful for Whites also are helpful for African Americans.

In summary, the more that White career counselors understand about the differences between African Americans and Whites, the more effective they may be able to be with career interventions. Hopefully, the above-mentioned issues give career development specialists a glimpse into the unique experiences of the African American culture. The worldview, history, and values of African Americans have a significant impact on their career choice-making process. Career development specialists need to understand the current economic barriers that exist for many African American students (Isaacson & Brown, 2000). According to Brown (1995), facilitating the career development of African Americans may be a key to their economic emancipation. Culturally sensitive career development specialists also should be aware that there is as much variation in the African American culture as there is in any culture.

References

Alicea, I. (1998). New realities/ new imperatives: Four perspectives on Latino students. *The Hispanic Outlook in Higher Education, 8*(13).

Arbona, C. (1990). Career counseling research and Hispanics: A review of the literature. *The Counseling Psychologist, 18*(2).

Bennett, C. E. & Martin, B. (1995). The Asian & Pacific Islander population. In U.S.Bureau of Census, current population reports, Series P23-189, *Population Profile of the United States: 1995*(pp.48-49). Washington, D.C. U.S. Government Printing Office.

Boyd-Franklin, N. (1989). *Black families in therapy: A multisystems approach*. New York: Guilford Press.

Bowman, S. L. (1995). Career interventions strategies and assessment issues for African Americans. In F. T. Leong (Ed.), *Career development and vocational behavior of racial and ethnic minorities* (pp. 7-36). Mahwah, NJ: Lawrence Erlbaum Associates.

Brashears, F., & Roberts. M. (1996). The Black church as a resource for change. In S. L. Logan (Ed.), *The Black family: Strengths, self-help, and positive change* (pp. 181-191). Boulder, CO: Westview.

Brown, M.T. (1995). The career development of African Americans: Theoretical and empirical issues. In F. T. Leong (Ed.), *Career development and vocational behavior of racial and ethnic minorities* (pp. 7-36). Mahwah, NJ: Lawrence Erlbaum Associates.

Brown, D. J. & Minor, C. W. (1989). *Working in America: A status report on planning and problems*. Alexandria, VA: National Career Development Association.

Brown, D. J. & Minor, C. W. (1992). *Career needs in a diverse workplace: A status report on planning and problems*. Alexandria, VA: National Career Development Association.

Brown, D. J., Minor, C. W., & Jepsen, D. A. (1991). The opinions of minorities about preparing for work: Report on the second NCDA national survey. *Career Development Quarterly, 40*, 5-19.

Casper, L., & Bryson, K. (1998, March). Co-resident grandparents and their grandchildren: Grandparent maintained families. (*Population Division, Working Paper, No. 26, U.S. Bureau of the Census*). Washington, DC: U.S. Government Printing Office.

Chatters, L. M., Taylor, R. J., & Lincoln, K. D. (1999). African American religious participation: A multi-sample comparison. *Journal for the Scientific Study of Religion, 38*, 132-145.

Evanoski, P. O. & Tse, F. W. (1989) Career awareness programs for Chinese and Korean American Parents. *Journal of Counseling and Development, 67*, 472-474.

Fernandiz, M. S. (1988). Issues in counseling southeast Asian students. *Journal of Multicultural Counseling & Development, 16*, 157-166.

Gallup, G., Jr., & Castelli, J. (1991). *Religious activity of Blacks is up*. Kansas City Star, E-11.

Gloria, A.M. & Rodriguez, E.R. (2000). Counseling Latino university students: Psychosociocultural issues for consideration. *Journal of Counseling & Development*, 78 (2).

Hoyt, K. & Lester, J. (1995). *Learning to work: The NCDA Gallop survey*. Alexandria,VA: National Career Development Association.

Isaacson, L. E., & Brown, D. (2000). *Career information, career counseling, and career development*. Needham Heights, MA: Allyn & Bacon.

Jackson, M. (2000). Racism in counseling: Reflections from within. *The Hispanic Outlook in Higher Education, 10*(8).

Kaneshige, E. (1979). Cultural factors in group counseling and interaction. In G. Henderson (Ed.), *Understanding and counseling ethnic minorities* (pp. 457-467). Springfield, IL: Charles C. Thomas.

Landrum-Brown, J. (1994). *Impacts of culture on teaching and learning.* Workshop given at University of California, Santa Barbara.

Lara, J. & Pande, G. (2001). Latino students and secondary school education. *Gaining Ground Newsletter,* May/June 2001.

Leong, F. T. L. & Serafica, F. C. (1995). Career development of Asian Americans: A research area in need of a good theory. In F. T. L. Leong (Ed.). *Career development & vocational behavior of racial and ethnic minorities* (78-99). Mahwoh, NH: Erlbaum.

Leong, F. T. L. & Gim-Chung (1995). Career assessment and intervention with Asian Americans. In F. T. L. Leong (Ed.). *Career development and vocational behavior of racial and ethnic minorities* (193-226). Mahwoh, NH: Erlbaum.

Lincoln, C. E., & Mamiya, L. H. (1990). The religious dimension: Toward a sociology of Black churches. In C. E. Lincoln & L. H. Mamiya (Eds.), *The Black church in the African American experience* (1-19). Durham, NC: Duke University Press.

Lopez, E.M. (2001). Guidance of Latino high school students in mathematics and career identity development. *Hispanic Journal of Behavioral Sciences, 23*(2).

McBay, S. M. (1992). The condition of African American education: Changes and challenges. In B. J. Tidwell (Ed.), *The state of Black America 1992* (141-156). New York: National Urban League.

Miranda, A.O. & Umhoefer, D.L. (1998). Acculturation, language use, and demographic variables as predictors of the career self-efficacy of Latino career counseling clients. *Journal of Multicultural Counseling & Development 26*(1).

NCDA. (1999). *Career counseling in a changing context: A summary of the key findings in the 1999 national survey of workers in America.* Tulsa, OK: Author.

Patton, J. M. (1998). The disproportionate representation of African Americans in special education: Looking behind the curtain for understanding and possible solutions. *The Journal of Special Education, 32,* 25–31.

Peterson, N. & Gonzales, R. C. (2000). *The role of work in peoples lives.* Belmont, CA: Wadsworth/Thomson Learning.

Rogers, C.R. (1961). *On becoming a person.* Boston: Houghton Mifflin.

Sampson, R., & Groves, W. B. (1989). Community structure and crime: Testing social-disorganization theory. *American Journal of Sociology, 94,* 774-802.

Sampson, R. J., & Wilson, W. J. (1995). Toward a theory of race, crime, and urban inequality. In J. Hagan & R. Peterson (Eds.), *Crime and inequality* (pp. 37-56). Stanford, CT: Stanford University Press.

Smith, E. J. (1983). Issues in racial minorities' career behavior. In W. B. Walsh & J. H. Osipow (Eds.), *Handbook of vocational psychology*: Vol. I (161-222). Hillsdale, NJ: Erlbaum.

Stern, G.M. (1999). Recruitment: Ten colleges aggressively recruit Hispanics. The *Hispanic Outlook in Higher Education,* (5).

Sue, D. W. (1992). The challenge of multiculturalism: The road less traveled. *American Counselor, 1,* 7-14.

Sue, D. W. (1994). Asian American mental health and help seeking behaviors: Comments on Solberg, et al.(1994), Tota & Leong (1994), and Lin (1994). *Journal of Counseling Psychology, 41,* 292-295.

Sue, D. W., Ivey, A. E., & Pedersen, P. B.(1996). *A theory of multicultural counseling &* therapy. Pacific Grove, CA: Brooks/Cole.

Sue, S. & Okazaki, S. (1990). Asian American educational achievement: A phenomenon in search of an explanation. *American Psychologist, 45* (8), 913-920.

Sue, D. W. & Sue, S. (1990). *Counseling the culturally different: Theory and practice* (2nd ed.). New York: John Wiley & Sons.

Sue, D. W. & Sue, S. (1999). *Counseling the culturally different: Theory and practice* (3rd ed.). New York: John Wiley and Sons.

Suzuki, H. (1989, Nov./Dec.) Asian Americans as the model minority: Outdoing whites or media hype? *Change*, 13-19.

Steinberg, L. (1996). *Beyond the classroom: Why school reform has failed and what parents need to do.* NY: Touchstone.

Swinton, D.H. (1992). The economic status of African Americans: Limited ownership and persistent inequality. In B. J. Tidwell (Ed.), *The state of Black America 1992* (pp. 61-117). New York: National Urban League.

Tapp, N. (1993). Hmong. In P. Hockings (Ed.), *The encyclopedia of world cultures* (Vol. 5, 92-95). New York: G. K. Hall and Co.

Teachman, J. D., Tedrow, L. M., & Crowder, K. D. (2000). The changing demography of American families. *Journal of Marriage and the Family, 62*, 1234-1246.

Trueba, E.T. (1999). *Latinos unidos: From cultural diversity to the politics of solidarity.* Lanham, MD: Rowman & Littlefield.

U.S. Census Bureau (2000). *Difference in population by race and Hispanic or Latino origin, for the United States: 1990 to 2000.* Retrieved November 2, 2002, from http://www.census.gov/population/www/cen2000/phc-t1.html

U.S. Department of Education. (1997). *Nineteenth annual report to Congress on the implementation of the Individuals with Disabilities Education Act.* Washington, DC: Author.

Wilson, W. J. (1987). *The truly disadvantaged.* Chicago: University of Chicago Press.

Wilson. W. J. (1996). *When work disappears: The world of the new urban poor.* New York: Alfred Knopf.

Zunker, V. (2002). *Career counseling applied concepts of life planning* (6th ed.). Pacific Cole, CA; Brooks/Cole.

Chapter Twenty-Seven

The Dream Board — A Visual Approach for Career Planning with At-Risk 8th and 9th Grade Students

James W. Allen and Jackie M. Allen

Abstract

James Allen was hired with special funding in his district to work out a program to identify and help retain highly at-risk students who were in imminent danger of dropping out. This 30-year educator created a "Dream Board" to graphically show 8th and 9th grade students what the consequences of their academic and work decisions would be. He experienced great success in keeping students in school who would have otherwise made destructive personal choices. Once at-risk students are identified, this chapter shows how an experienced educator with effective tools, such as a Dream Board and Postsecondary Educational Pathways chart, can make a great difference with kids. Allen's fundamental formula that the kids understood so well was:
EDUCATION + SKILLS = JOB + MONEY=YOUR FUTURE DREAMS
This concrete approach with highly at-risk students will be of great interest to school counselors. Jim Allen has recently developed a website showing educational pathways for students in the state of California,†which may be accessed at http://www.edpathways.com

The predominant learning modality in contemporary society is visual; nearly one half of the student population prefers the visual modality for learning (Sousa, 1997; Swanson, 1995). At-risk students, even more than other students, need a specialized approach to career planning. This chapter explains how an at-risk transition counselor uses a unique approach to work with 8th and 9th grade students in academic, personal/social and career counseling domains. Emphasis is on a visual approach to career planning in school and on preparation for the world of work through the use of Postsecondary Educational Pathways and a Dream Board.

The Need for A New Approach

The at-risk transition counselor concept in the Fremont Unified School District was born out of the desire for more school counseling and a specific counseling program designed to meet the needs of 8th and 9th grade students in their transition from junior high to high school. In 1992-1993, budget cutbacks took place in the school district and despite extensive negotiations, the entire counseling program was disbanded and all counselors were returned to the classroom for four years. During those four years, the Board of Education directors grew increasingly concerned as they watched the dropout rate grow and the number of students prepared for a four-year college decrease. Therefore, after four years without counselors in the Fremont Unified School District (FUSD), a basic counseling program was reinstated with approximately two counselors in each high school. The counselors were back, and students, parents, teachers, and administrators were happy to see them return. However, the specific concerns of junior high to high school transition had not been addressed, and the dropout rate continued to be a problem.

In response to the crucial need for more specialized counseling, a transition counselor program for at-risk 8th and 9th grade students was authorized in 1998 by the FUSD Board of Education and funded through equalization funds. An at-risk counselor was assigned to each of the five attendance areas, spending half time at the junior high school and half time at the corresponding high school each week. The specific schedule and division of the time was left up to the two principals and each counselor to schedule. Some schools split the counselor time evenly with two and a half days of time at each school; others divided the school day in half, with half time at each school every day; and some schools were assigned three days a week of counselor time for one quarter at one school and then rotated to two days a week of counselor time for the next quarter.

Characteristics of At-risk Students

The FUSD specialized counseling program was designed to help at-risk youth have an opportunity for success in school with access to the academic curriculum in 9th grade with the end goal of preparation for high

446

school graduation. Minga (1988) defined at-risk youths as:

> ...children who are not likely to finish high school or who are apt to graduate considerably below potential. At-risk factors include chemical dependency, teenage pregnancy, poverty, disaffection with school and society, high-mobility families, emotional and physical abuse, physical and emotional disabilities, and learning disabilities that do not qualify students for special education but nevertheless impede their progress. (p. 14)

According to Capuzzi and Gross (1989, p. 12), students who are at-risk of making adequate academic progress may exhibit many of the following factors:

a. Tardiness;
b. Absenteeism;
c. Acting out behaviors;
d. Lack of motivation;
e. Poor grades;
f. Truancy;
g. Low math and reading scores;
h. Failing one or more grades;
i. Lack of identification with school (connectedness);
j. Failure to see the relevance of education to life experiences;
k. Boredom with school;
l. Rebellious attitude toward authority;
m. Verbal and language deficiency;
n. Inability to tolerate structured activations; and
o. Being two or more graduation credits behind one's age group.

Asset theory (Search Institute,1997; WestEd, 2002) tells us that connectedness (that is, the identification with significant adults) in the school reduces at-risk behavior in students. This program provides a significant adult in the school system to address the needs and develop a support system for the at-risk student. The transition counseling program was designed to have the school counselor be that significant adult.

Demographics of School District

The Fremont Unified School District 1999-2000 enrollment (PreK-12) was 31,900 students. In the suburban school district, there are 29 elementary schools, one charter school, 5 junior high schools, and 5 comprehensive high schools and one continuation school. Built in 1859, Centerville Junior High School had 438 seventh graders and 477 eighth graders, for a total of 915 students during the 1999-2000 school year. The racial/ethnic composition of the students at Centerville was: 5% African American, 1% American Indian, 18% Asian, 5% Filipino, 15% Hispanic, .44% Pacific Islander, 55% White, and 1% other. The students speak sixteen foreign languages, with Spanish being the dominant foreign language. Special education students made up approximately 8 % of the student population. The 8th grade students transition each year to the adjacent high school that basically has the same demographics.

School Counselor Role in New Program

Academic counseling at Centerville Junior High School is available to all 7th and 8th graders. The 1999-2000 academic counseling program consisted of: one full-time counselor who helped students maintain proper placement in classes; a half-time transition counselor who helped each student focus on the classes that they were in danger of failing; an Outreach Counselor, in partnership with the City of Fremont, who assisted the on-campus, full-time counselor; a counseling intern who took care of attendance problems one day per week; and an adult mentor, funded by state grants and business partners, whose focus was to provide career connections and job shadowing for students.

According to Centerville's California School 2001 Recognition Program Distinguished Middle School Application (12/2000), the function of the transition counselor included the following:
1) Counsels with students on strategies that will help them improve their grades;
2) Follows up with students throughout the year to monitor the use of strategies;
3) Transitions 8th grade students to high school;
4) Monitors, advises, counsels and supports all 9th grade demoted and identified at-risk students;
5) Helps students identify their educational pathways and career goals; and
6) Develops intervention plans for making up failed classes and/or remediation of deficient academic skills as evidenced by 4-year plans, intervention forms, and letters.

The Transition Counseling Program

The first step in the transition counseling program is the identification of the at-risk students. At the beginning of the year, students are identified for the program by their failing grades on their previous year's report card. In addition to these students, other at-risk students who are referred by counselors, administrators, parents, and psychologists are included in the identified group. As the year progresses, students who are passing their classes are dropped from the group and new candidates who are identified by failing grades on their quarter report card are added to the program. Students who are passing and dropped from the program are monitored quarterly to make sure that they continue to succeed.

After academically at-risk students are identified, a priority list of students is developed, initially based on academic grades. Students are prioritized according to the number of failing grades they receive on their current report cards. For example, students with six Fs on their report card receive counseling before students with one or two Fs. Identifying students in this way usually provides a group of most of the school's academically at-risk students. Any other students with serious high-risk behaviors (such as suicidal ideation, violent behaviors, etc.) are given immediate attention with the development of an intervention plan, including in-school support and referral to community agencies if appropriate.

After identification of the at-risk students, each student is given a personal interview. The counselor initially establishes rapport with the student and provides the student with positive unconditional regard as he seeks to draw out the student's personal perception of the situation. Questions are asked to help the student identify the problem, what is going on in his or her mind, how he or she perceives the problem, and how he or she feels about his or her progress (i.e., in effect, a reality check). The counselor develops a personal profile of the student: awareness of the school situation, attitudes, self-image, home-family situation, academic goals and abilities.

The counselor's goals and desired student outcomes of the counseling process are: (a) growth and progress in academic, career, and personal/social domains (*ASCA National Standards*, 1998); (b) success in school, as evidenced by learning and academic achievement; and (c) high school graduation. Each student needs to be prepared with the knowledge, skills, and attitudes to succeed in postsecondary education, work, and life. In order to accomplish these goals, the counselor proceeds with the counselee through the counseling process. First, the counselor attempts to discover the student's basic personal and social needs, addressing apparent barriers to learning that inhibit the student from focusing on academic concerns.

Transition from junior high to high school is a challenge for most students. Students encounter increased teacher expectations, increased demands in quantity and quality of academic work, often a more impersonal atmosphere due to increased student teacher ratios and the number of students on a high school campus, and less support from parents and community members. All these factors contribute to the alienation felt by 9th grade students as they try to deal with the challenges of peer group relationships and academic demands.

Next, the counselor works with the student to identify academic strengths and weaknesses in successful and difficult classes, using school records, transcripts, test scores, and student self-reports. The counselor asks if the student is aware of current personal academic problems, the number of "F's," and the reasons for the failing grades. The counselor explores for external or internal problems and checks the student's attitude, ascertaining whether the student accepts responsibility for academic progress or blames it on someone else, such as a teacher. A discussion of possible solutions follows with suggestions of a study buddy, homework club, family help, and/or tutoring after school. The last part of the counseling process focuses on career exploration through using the Dream Board and Postsecondary Educational Pathways chart. The student's hopes, dreams, wishes, and images of the future are explored. The student is asked if he/she wants to participate in the American way of life by working hard to achieve the desired dreams.

On the wall or bulletin board, the counselor has placed a collage of pictures of possible items that a high school student might desire; this collage is called a Dream Board. At-risk students can create their own personal Dream Board by cutting out pictures from magazines and placing them to make an interesting collage. The collage can show anything the student desires now or in the future, such as the student's favorite dream car or truck (e.g., a red Mustang convertible), clothes, house, vacation, hobbies, or other desired items. Using the Dream Board, the counselor works with the student exploring the student's personal dreams, wishes, and desires. Then there is a discussion about the money needed to fulfill the student's dreams, followed by a discussion about the job or career that will provide the money, the relevant skills, knowledge and experience required to qualify for the job or career. Finally, there is a discussion about the educational program that will provide the needed training.

The student's current classes are related to SCANS foundational skills for competent workers: (a) basic skills in reading, writing, math, speaking, and listening; (b) thinking skills–ability to learn, reason, think creatively,

450

and make decisions; and (c) personal qualities of responsibility, self-esteem, self-management, sociability, integrity, and honesty. The questioning process utilizes the skills of the counselor to draw out each student's wishes and dreams and relate those to the concrete reality of completing the classes and subjects required to graduate from high school.

The dialogue between student and counselor uses the Socratic questioning method. The counselor invites the student to think about his or her future through a series of questions, using the Dream Board and summarized in the following steps:

a. What is your dream car, dream home, family, clothes, image, or vacation? (Focus the student on the Dream Board or on his or her personal collage.)
b. How much money do you think your dream items will cost? (Clarify choices and costs.)
c. Where will your money come from? (List sources.)
d. What kind of jobs/career do you want? (List jobs/careers using the Job-O or other information.)
e. What kind of special skills do you need for your job/career? (Use career books and handouts—stressing experience and skills needed)
f. Where will you get these skills?
g. What Postsecondary Educational Pathway do you plan to travel? (Use the Postsecondary Educational Pathways Chart – Figure 2)
h. Do you have a clear job or career choice?
i. What Postsecondary Educational Pathway leads to your job or career? (If none, what Postsecondary Educational Pathway are you considering?)
j. What are the entry requirements for your Postsecondary Educational Pathway? (grade point average, classes, high school diploma)
k. Do you have the current classes and grade point average to prepare you to enter the desired pathway in the future? If not, what is required? (Reality Check)
l. Do you have a 4-Year High School Plan to accomplish the career pathway?
m. If not, what changes can be made in your 4-Year Plan to prepare you for the desired pathway? (Or, is there another pathway you can enter to achieve your goal?)

Educational Pathways	
EDUCATIONAL CONTINUUM	**POSTSECONDARY PATHWAYS**
K 1 2 3 4 5 6 7 8 9 10 11 12 Elementary Middle High School School	Private Colleges & Universities University of California System California State University Community College System
Secondary Programs and 4-Year Plan for High School Graduation Career Pathways	Apprenticeship Programs Business and Vocational Schools Military Services Regional Occupational Programs Adult School Programs On-the-Job Training Work/Service Experience

Every student has dreams, wishes, and desires that cost money and take time and effort. It is important to link the student's desired items to today's reality, by discussing the amount of money needed to purchase each item. The local newspaper can be used to determine the prices for cars, houses, apartment rent, and other items. When students are asked where they plan to get the money needed to buy the desired items, most students respond by saying that they will get a job. The newspaper or Job-O list of occupations shows the amount of money each occupation pays. At this point, taking time to give examples, such as the cost of a new car (e.g., $25,000) that equals a full year's salary (or takes five or more years to pay off a loan) makes the experience real for the student. The counselor works with the student to determine if the monthly salary will adequately cover apartment rent, food, car payment, entertainment, and other desired items. Very quickly the student begins to see the relationship between job income and real life expenses.

The Job-O list of occupations shows the amount of money each occupation pays and the amount of education required for the job. It does not take long for students to understand that the more education and training experience a person has, the more money they make in their desired job or career. The relationship between better pay and more education is obvious. A U.S. Department of Labor Bureau Statistics chart can be used to demonstrate income and education. For most students, this is a real eye-opener that motivates them to complete their education.

If a student does not know which particular career or job he/she wants to pursue right now, he or she is asked what educational pathway he/she would like to investigate. Many students do not know enough about jobs, but they do know what educational pathway they are willing to investigate based on: (a) their educational experiences; (b) a transcript of their grades; and (c) their family expectations. The development of SCANS skills in current classes and actual job skills required in their chosen job are discussed. Then those skills are related to the 4-year educational plan and the Post Secondary Educational Pathway the student plans to pursue in the future. The entrance requirements for a particular job or career training are linked to the proper academic preparation in junior high and high school. The door for further training will only open if the student is willing to prepare, by completing the right entrance requirements. The key to academic achievement and career success is the relationship between the desired job and essential skills and the completion of the appropriate entrance requirements to train in that career. Finally, the areas of personal motivation, health, and time needed to reach the student's dream are discussed.

Through the Dream Board process, using the student's personal interests and dreams, connecting those dreams to a realistic Postsecondary Educational Pathway, and making a 4-Year High School Plan, the student makes the important connection between education, effort, and motivation and the desired rewards in life. The Dream Formula is the key to the student's success in life and the fulfillment of the student's dreams.

EDUCATION + SKILLS = JOB + MONEY=YOUR FUTURE DREAMS

Conclusion

Most parents work hard today—working from early morning to late afternoon or evening to provide for their families. Most teachers work extremely hard, with limited time, resources, and support to educate all students including those with special cognitive, social, and emotional needs. Most students want to be successful in school and in life, but they may have many problems in the academic, career, and personal/social domains that interfere with the realization of their full potential. Individual student problems will be addressed when significant, caring adults (such as school counselors) intervene. Many problems could be avoided or eliminated if preventive measures were taken ahead of time. The Dream Formula makes sense to most at-risk students and has been shown to be an effective tool.

In the words of Eleanor Roosevelt:

The future belongs to those who believe in the beauty of their DREAMS

References

American School Counselor Association (1997). *ASCA national standards.* Alexandria, VA: Author.

Centerville California School 2001 Recognition Program Distinguished Middle School application. (12/2000). Unpublished document.

Capuzzi, D. & Gross, D.R. (1989). *Youth at risk: A resource for counselors, teachers and parents.* Alexandria, VA: American Association for Counseling and Development.

Minga, T. (1988). States and the "at-risk" issues: Said aware but still "failing" *Education Week, 8*(3), 1-16.

Search Institute (1997). *The asset approach: Giving kids what they need to succeed.* Minneapolis, MN: Author.

Sousa, D.A. (1997). Sensory preferences of New Jersey students, grades 3 to 12. Unpublished data collected by graduate students at Seton Hall University, 1994-1997.

Swanson, L.J. (1995, July). *Learning styles: A review of the literature.* ERIC Document (ED: 387067).

U.S. Department of Labor. (1991). *What work requires of schools.* A SCANS Report for America 2000. (Secretary's Commission on Achieving Necessary Skills) Washington, D.C.:U.S. Government Printing Office.

WestEd. (2002). Resilience & youth development module. California Healthy Kids *Survey.* CA: Author.

Chapter Twenty-Eight

Career Education for Special Education Students

Jackie M. Allen

Abstract

Dr. Allen discusses the importance of the integration of services and the coordination of career guidance and counseling programs for Special Education students. "One professional cannot provide all the services a special needs student requires to prepare for post-secondary education; therefore, only a collaboration of personnel and careful coordination of services will provide that compromise." She details the role of school counselors and other support professionals in providing counseling for career planning and transition, and discusses both the Individual Education Plan (I.E.P.) and Individual Transition Plan (I.T.P.), required by law for each Special Education student. She also discusses how specialized collaborative school programs and specialized parental approaches will facilitate the connection from school to career for special needs students.

Introduction

With the increased emphasis on standards-based education, academic achievement, high stakes testing, and accountability in California schools, the areas of career development and personal/social development have been neglected for many students. Helping students meet graduation standards and post-secondary planning has been focused primarily on two-year and four-year college programs. Unfortunately, "one size does not fit all," and perhaps the most important area for a student's real future is career life planning (planning for the future including possible careers). Equally important for special education students, the area of career education must be emphasized in order to transition students appropriately into the world

455

of work and into successful and productive citizenship.

The Individuals with Disabilities Education Act (IDEA), formerly Public Law 94-142, established the entitlement of millions of children who annually receive special education and related services to a free appropriate public education, known as FAPE. In 1997, after much discussion the previous year, a House of Representatives bill (HR 5) was resubmitted to the 104th Congress and through a bipartisan process of addressing and resolving all issues, IDEA was amended, passed by both houses of Congress, and signed by President Clinton. IDEA 97 made some major changes in special education law. Among those changes was an addition of a transition requirement stating that certain transition services begin at 14 years of age. Transition services provide preparation for the special education student to transition from school to employment or assisted adult living. According to IDEA, transition services must include instruction, community services, employment, and other adult-living objectives. Therefore, in each Individualized Education Program (IEP), a link between a student's course of study and the proposed transition services was to be established for students by the age of 16. Other significant changes relating to IEPs and delivery of services were: (a) an emphasis on accurately measuring and reporting a student's progress toward annual goals that included short-term objectives; (b) reporting progress of those goals to special education parents as frequently as parents of a non-disabled child; and (c) the participation of students with disabilities in district or state assessments, with specification of modifications and accommodations or alternative assessment in the IEP. (Telzrow & Tankersley, 2000)

IDEA 97 has emphasized the importance of Individual Transition Plans (ITPs) for special education students. Although ITPs are mandated, they often focus on academics, not on career counseling or living skills. Also, they lack coordination among secondary, postsecondary, and community agencies, and are developed too late in the educational process to facilitate proper planning (Cummings et al., 2000). The purposes of this chapter are: (a) to examine the Individual Transition Plan process; (b) explore how that process can be included in a comprehensive counseling and guidance program based on the *American School Counselor Association National Standards*; and (c) delineate the important roles school counselors and other student support personnel have in assisting special education students to realize a smooth transition from secondary education to post-secondary education options.

Beginning the Individual Transition Plan Process

Initially a case manager is designated to work with the student and his or her family to develop an Individual Transition Plan (ITP). The role of the case manager is to set up the Individual Education Plan meeting, notify all the participants, make sure all proper forms are present, consult with the student and sometimes the family prior to the meeting, and facilitate the meeting. The case manager helps determine which individuals and agencies will be present at the meeting to assist the student and his or her family in developing an appropriate IEP/ITP team. Required members of the IEP team are the student's classroom teacher(s), a regular education teacher, the parent, the administrator, the student when appropriate, and others presenting assessment results. Usually the special education student's classroom teacher (the resource teacher or the special day class teacher) is the case manager. The special education teacher is well acquainted with the curriculum but often lacks training and experience in career development. The school counselor who has been trained in career development is a valuable asset as a consultant and student advocate for career development and the Individual Transition Plan.

By law, the ITP must include a statement of needed services beginning at age 14 for all special education students. In order to prepare to participate in the ITP meeting, the student and his/her family must answer pertinent questions about the student's future. Some schools use a special brochure, which is sent home to the families before the meeting; the Fremont Unified School District (FUSD) in California uses a brochure entitled *Life After High School* (FUSD, 1996) and asks the student to think about the following questions:

> What kind of job or career do I want?
> Do I want to go to college or vocational training?
> Do I want to continue to live with my family or to live on my own?
> What kind of recreation and leisure activities do I want to join in?

In addition, the brochure includes a list of post-secondary choices and community resources for students with references, phone numbers, and addresses of community colleges, vocational training programs, job opportunities, work study programs, regional training center programs, and residential placements for the more severely handicapped. Another helpful publication for students seeking a college or university education after high school is *Charting Your Future*, published by the San Mateo County Office of Education (2001) in California.

School Counselor Role

Before the official ITP, the intervention of the school counselor is very important. The school counselor is responsible for providing services and a comprehensive counseling and guidance program to all students in a secondary school, and that includes special education students (Allen & LaTorre, 1998). The *ASCA National Standards for School Counseling Programs* (Dahir, Sheldon, & Valiga, 1998) provide the framework for the comprehensive counseling and guidance program and include the three major domains of academic, personal/social, and career. The standards infused into all "...counseling programs help ensure equal opportunity for all students to participate fully in the educational process." (Campbell & Dahir, 1997) The National Occupational Information Coordinating Committee Guidelines (NOICC, 1989), delineate the specific career development skills and competencies by grade level and area appropriate for all students.

Distinct counselor roles have been established (Allen, 2001) in the provision of a standards-based comprehensive counseling and guidance program for both regular education and special education students. Expanding upon the general school counselor role, the school counselor can specifically fulfill the following functions in the career development domain of the comprehensive counseling and guidance program:

Program Area	Role	Function
Integrated Services	Member	Identify career development needs
Team	Case Manager	Consult on career programs/opportunities Observe student strengths & needs Develop plans for career exploration Refer students to Career Center
Comprehensive Counseling & Guidance Program	Coordinator Counselor Instructor Evaluator	Infuse ASCA Standards & NOICC Guidelines Counsel- individual, group, family Provide career guidance in classroom Evaluate career program

School System	Staff member	Assist Career Day Committee
	In-Service provider	Provide professional development workshops- connect career guidance with academic curriculum
	Advocate	Champion special needs student rights for career development program
	Consultant	Guide the IEP/ITP process
	Coordinator	Coordinate career program
	Leader	Act as change agent- change school environment for students to learn SCANS skills, choose career pathways, and prepare for post secondary opportunities
Community	Coordinator	Coordinate linkage to community agencies for volunteer services, job shadowing, work experience, and jobs
Community	Collaborator	Work with community programs to develop mentorships, job matching, shelters, and Career Day speakers Refer to local employers, armed forces, training programs, and community-based organizations

The American School Counselor Association, in a *1999 Position Statement* entitled "The Professional School Counselor and the Special Needs Student," recommended the following school counselor roles in working with special needs students:

Multidisciplinary team member
Collaborator with other pupil personnel specialists
Instructor of social skills training
Coordinator of group guidance activities to improve self-esteem
Counselor- individual, group, and family
Advocate for students in both school and community
Observer and facilitator of behavior modification plans
Coordinator of career planning and transition

    Facilitator - in the understanding of special needs students
    Referral agent to other specialists in the school system and
    community

Each of the above roles is unique and contributes to the overall preparation of each special education student in the transition process to post-secondary goals. The pupil support services team (school psychologist, school social worker, and school counselor) may collaborate with special education teachers, paraprofessionals and community agency professionals to provide the wide range of career development services necessary to prepare special education students for post-secondary success. The school counselor should be a member of the IEP/ITP team and serve as a consultant and advocate for the student. In collaboration with other pupil personnel specialists, the school counselor assists the student to prepare for short- and long-range goals that will be addressed on the ITP. The school counselor or school psychologist may invite the student to participate in social skills training and may lead a series of specialized social skills training sessions for a special day class (a self-contained special education class with low teacher to pupil ratio). Depending upon the cognitive level of the students, the counselor might collaborate with the classroom teacher or psychologist to develop training in community living skills and development of social/ emotional areas. Community living skills would include money management, use of public transportation, community access, health needs management, and family life education. Developing satisfactory relationships with peers and adults, a sense of independence, relationships with employers, and developing maintenance of good mental health are social/emotional skill areas.

Coordination of guidance lessons in the special day class, as in regular education classes, may be seen as an important aspect of the school counselor's role. The new ASCA comprehensive counseling and guidance program model emphasizes service to all students, including special education students, which meets the intent and spirit of IDEA 1977. Collaborative efforts with the school nurse, the school social worker, the school psychologist, the adaptive physical education instructor, the speech and language therapist, and other school and community support staff will provide a rich environment for the career development of all students. Guidance activities may include: self-esteem building exercises, physical exercises, health and nutrition lessons, socialization skills, conflict resolution, and career education.

The school counselor and school psychologist are indispensable in their ability to offer individual, small group, and family counseling as appropriate to the special needs student. With older students, primary concerns are: developing peer relationships, independence, sexuality, mental and physical health issues, employability, and participation in community activities. Although many families are beginning to accept the special needs of their student, the challenges of adolescence and post-secondary options sometimes become overwhelming. Working with families on these issues is both rewarding to the counselor and to the student's family. In the ITP process, both at school and in the larger community, the counselor functions as an advocate for student rights and the opportunity for the learning and growth of each individual special education student. Using a team approach, the counselor may work with other student support services specialists and special education teachers to find appropriate community experiences and programs for each student.

Behavior and discipline often become crucial issues in transition plans. Emotionally and socially immature students do not always act their chronological and mental age. Behavior modification plans may need to be developed to improve on- campus behavior as well as classroom behavior. Although the school psychologist may work more directly with the classroom teacher in the assessment and development of a behavior modification plan, the school counselor can provide valuable observations and feedback from classroom visits, campus observations, and individual and small group sessions with the student and his/her family. During the ITP process the counselor may advocate for the student and make sure that the behavior goals are developmentally appropriate and individually specific. The counselor or school psychologist may need to communicate the behavior goals and behavior plan to all teachers and staff members, which includes secretaries, noon supervisors, custodians, teacher aides, and outside agency staff such as law enforcement officers, outreach specialists, and other community service providers who frequently come on campus. Working together with a common plan and consistent monitoring and reinforcement, the entire school staff can work with the teacher to shape the behavior of the special needs student.

Career Guidance And Counseling

All these other interventions set the stage for career planning and transition. The counselor or career counselor responsible for the career guidance and career counseling of all students needs to pay special attention to the unique needs of the special education student. " In each phase of career development the special needs student requires not only special encouragement but specialized information" (Allen & LaTorre, 1998).

Career planning encompasses several phases or stages as delineated by the National Occupational Information Coordinating Council Guidelines (NOICC, 1996). First, self-knowledge provides students with the initial understanding of self and how they relate to others and how they can grow and learn. Next, educational and occupational exploration provides a student with the opportunity to explore many fields of interest and perhaps narrow those fields to one or more career pathways of intense interest. Career planning is the phase in which students match skills and interests with career areas and begin specific planning for appropriate preparation and training to enter the area of choice after high school or after further education. And finally, career experience is the developmental milestone in which the student actually participates in service learning (volunteering) or work experience.

Often students in special day classes are not included in career guidance programs and may not receive appropriate assessment, career exploration, and the opportunity to do career planning and have career experiences. Part of the purpose of the ITP is to provide career planning for all special education students. Many special education teachers and school psychologists do not have any specialized training in career development, assessment and planning and may only have general training in the ITP process. In fact, the school counselor is the only staff member that is required to have training in career development in order to receive state certification. Therefore, it is very important that the school counselor include special education students in the school's career guidance and counseling activities, as part of the career domain of the counseling and guidance program, to fulfill IDEA 1997 requirements to ensure student access to the general curriculum.

In the first phase of career development–career awareness–the classroom career guidance experience is very important. It may be difficult, but certainly worthwhile, to make sure that special education students understand the connection between school and preparation for the world of work. Elements of career awareness that make career planning relevant to all students are discussing: (a) what parents do to make a living; (b) where their parents go during the day to work; (c) how the money they earn provides the home, food, car, and leisure time activities that the whole family enjoys; and (d) what might happen if a parent loses his or her job.

Special education students need to be exposed to a variety of career areas through speakers, field trips, videos, career games, and activities that will give them a foundation for making career decisions in the future. Through a planned educational and occupational exploration program starting no later than middle school and continuing through the initial years of high school, students learn about jobs that interest them and may lead to future careers. *Pathways to Satisfaction* (Grayson et al., 1997) is a comprehensive, age-appropriate career development transition program for 7th-12th graders.

Starting at age 14, when the official Individualized Transition Plan process begins, is an appropriate time to begin career planning. In this phase of career development, students begin to focus their interests through career assessment, skill identification, interest surveys, and personal experiences. Special attention to the reading level of special education students will provide the counselor and the career center technician valuable information that will help them in choosing an appropriate career interest survey, such as the Job-O or Chronicle Career Quest (that have appropriate reading levels). Aptitude, learning style, and skill levels may be measured on specialized tests appropriate for special education students. Considerable time and effort need to be taken in this important career phase for each special education student to identify a realistic area of interest, a possible career pathway, and the motivation to complete career planning.

SCANS skills (basic employability skills, such as honesty, promptness, decision-making, etc.) may act as benchmarks for effective career planning. Special needs students must develop their optimum level of competency in the basic skills of reading, writing, math, speaking and listening that are foundational skills for job success. Cognitive skills in reasoning, decision-making, and the ability to learn must also be optimized. Life skills, such as individual responsibility, self-esteem, self-management, sociability, integrity, and honesty are emphasized in life skills guidance lessons across settings at home, in school, and in the community.

Work experience is the final area in the career development continuum. Most high school students want to have a part-time job that provides them with extra money of their own and a sense of independence. It is very important to arrange appropriate placement for special education students taking into consideration their social skills, emotional maturity, reading and math levels, and any other handicapping conditions that may cause them difficulty in the work place. The success of work experience or in-service learning placements depends upon the match between the employer and the student. The employer must understand the strengths and weaknesses of the special education student and possibly be willing to make modifications in the job assignment. The student, on the other hand, needs to understand exactly what is required on the job or service and have immediate support from a caring adult to succeed with difficult job requirements.

The ITP Meeting

Once the student is ready to participate in the ITP meeting, the purpose of the ITP meeting is to review relevant data, summarize current functioning and goals achieved (if there was a previous ITP), develop transition goals and objectives based on identified needs and student preferences and interests, and decide appropriate interagency linkages (Fremont United School District, 1995). The case manager, who may be the special education teacher or program specialist, conducts the meeting, making introductions and setting the stage for the meeting. A specific time frame for the meeting may be set, and it is important to emphasize initially that this meeting is for the benefit of the special education student and his or her family focusing on the values and goals for the student. All ITP team members must be aware of the options for educational programs and additional services that exist in the community and provide information and feedback at the meeting, always advocating for the student and the family.

The next steps in the ITP process are moderated by the case manager: handing out and reviewing the Parent and Student Rights form and summarizing relevant information and current level of functioning. Each member of the ITP/IEP team is asked to present a summary of the evaluation of the student's current skills as related to the individualized transition plan. Next, the ITP form, if not previously presented, needs to be introduced. The purpose of the ITP is to develop long-range goals as the student moves from school to the adult world of work and also to plan activities that need to be accomplished in order to meet these goals.

Student strengths and weaknesses are determined and student needs are defined. First, what the student needs to accomplish to progress to the next level in order to meet long-range goals is initially determined. The graduation or transition date is established and, thus, the calendar for the number of years before leaving the school system is set in place. In some school districts, a separate optional transition plan is available for K-8th grades and emphasizes: self-awareness, educational awareness, career awareness and exploration, attitude development, and career preparation.

The ITP goal development process is divided into several major areas. On the Fremont Unified School District (1999) forms the following areas were listed:
1. Employment
2. Community Living Skills
3. Training/Education
4. Living Arrangements
5. Community Recreation Leisure

6. Social/Emotional
7. Financial/Economic

The IEP/ITP team works with the student and family to describe their preferences in all areas. If the student requires interagency linkages, those are indicated in a separate area on the ITP form. A student may not need assistance in any of the areas, and that will also be listed with an explanation on the ITP form. A third option is writing "undecided" in any of the areas.

When long-range goals have been determined, then annual short-term objectives and activities are determined on the following pages of the ITP. Special education services and interagency linkages that are required to attain the objectives are also listed. At this point, team members can provide valuable information about school and community resources that will support the short-term objectives and long-term goals. It is very important to match the needs, goals and objectives with program service options. Transition goals should reflect "family/cultural values, student capabilities, instruction and community experiences, and post school agency linkages as appropriate" (Fremont Unified School District, 1995). Timelines and who will provide support services must also be determined and recorded on the ITP form. A checklist for high school students 16 years or older is provided to ensure that all areas have been documented.

In summary, the case manager needs to review the decisions that have been reached and make sure that both parents and students agree with the goals. Then all parties sign the ITP, and it will be reviewed in a year or sooner by special request. Ongoing quarterly or trimester updates of the progress of goals and objectives are provided to parents at the same time that report cards are distributed.

Conclusion

In all aspects of the ITP process, the school counselor and other pupil personnel specialists have an important role to play in supporting the student and his or her family. A successful ITP process provides the special education student with a plan for the present and the future with short-term and long-term goals, designed especially for his/her individual skills and interests. The completion of the plan prepares the student for a smooth transition into community living and the world of work. The school counselor is an important player in the formation of the ITP plan, the ITP meeting, and the days following the meeting in which the plan must be implemented into the school program and into the life of the community. It takes all the players, all the members of the ITP team, and all student support staff members to implement a successful ITP plan.

References

Allen, J.M. (2001). Counseling special needs students. In D. Sandhu (Ed.), *Elementary school counseling in the new millennium* (pp.173-181). Alexandria, VA: American Counseling Association.

Allen, J.M. & LaTorre, E. (1998). What a school administrator needs to know about the school counselor's role with special education. In C. Dykeman (Ed.), *Maximizing school guidance program effectiveness: A guide for school administrators and program directors* (pp. 117-122). Greensboro, NC: ERIC/CASS Publications.

American School Counselor Association (2000-2001). The professional school counselor and the special needs student (Position Statement adopted in 1999). In *ASCA Membership Directory and Resource Guide: 2001-2002* (pp. 59-60). Gainesville, FL: Naylor Publications, Inc.

Campbell, S., & Dahir, C.A. (1997). *The national standards.* Alexandria, VA: American School Counselor Association.

Cummings, R. Maddux, C.D., & Casey, J. (2000). Individualized transition planning for students with learning disabilities. *Career Development Quarterly 49*(1), 60-72.

Dahir, C.A., Sheldon, C.B., & Valiga, M.J. (1998). *Vision into action: Implementing the national standards for school counseling programs.* Alexandria, VA: American School Counselor Association.

Fremont Unified School District (1995-96). *What are the steps?* Unpublished document.

Fremont Unified School District (1996). *Life after high school.* Unpublished brochure.

Fremont Unified School District (1999). *Individualized transition plan.* Unpublished document.

Grayson, T.E., Wermuth, T.R., Holub, T.M., & Anderson, M.L. (1997). Effective practices of transition from school to work for people with learning disabilities. In P.J. Gerber & D. S. Brown (Eds.), *Learning disabilities and employment*, (pp. 77-99). Austin, TX: PRO-ED, Inc.

National Occupational Information Coordinating Committee (NOICC) (1996). Competencies and indicators for elementary school level, middle/junior high school level, high school level, adult level. *The national career development guidelines*. Stillwater, OK: NOICC Training Center.

San Mateo County Office of Education (2000-2001). Student guide for career and *college planning 2000-2001*. San Mateo, CA: Author.

San Mateo County Office of Education (2001). *Charting your future: A guide to high school and beyond for middle school students and their families*. San Mateo, CA: Author.

Telzrow, C.F. & Tankersley, M. (2000). IDEA amendments of 1997: Practice guidelines *for school-based teams*. Bethesda, MD: National Association of School Psychologists.

Chapter Twenty-Nine

Successful Transitions for High School Special Education Students from School to the Workplace (Emphasis on Learning Disabled, Attention Deficit and Behavior Disordered Youth)

Diane Fabish

Abstract

This chapter details aspects of the Special Education Program, particularly at Lake Washington High School, in the Lake Washington School District of Redmond/Kirkland, Washington. The ITP (Individual Transition Plan), which is part of the IEP (Individual Education Plan), is described, and the process is explained as to how school staff, parents and community resource people may work together to bring to fruition a special education student's positive transition to adulthood. Specific programs, such as "Career Ladders," NEVAC (a vocational cooperative, Northeast Vocational Area Cooperative), paid internships for teachers, the Post-ITT program, and Senior Service Learning Projects are described. The importance of teaching strong work ethics to special education students is also discussed.

The Individual Transition Plan (ITP) is required by federal law for each special education student. It is an integral part of a special education student's Individual Education Plan (IEP). The United States Federal Government mandates that critical areas must be addressed for special education students beginning at the age of 14. These areas include: postsecondary education (which may include college programs, vocational training, and job internships); employment (which may be on a continuum from supported to competitive); and community living (which may be independent or supported). In addition, adult living or self-help skills may be identified. By the time the student leaves high school, the Individual Transition Plan has driven goals and objectives in vocational skills, educational self-help skills, and advocacy categories from approximately the eighth grade. Special education students, parents, and teachers work together toward a transition beyond high school that is productive and meaningful for the student with special needs. Flexibility, tenacity, and patience are components for successful transition plans.

How do school staff, parents and community resource people work together to bring to fruition a special education student's positive transition to adulthood? There are programs, procedures, and partnerships in Lake Washington School District and the surrounding community that foster and support special education students' school-to-career transition. Further, the author will draw from 15 years of special education experience to describe those traits that parents and educators must identify, encourage, and develop to help special education students meet the demands and pace of post secondary work.

The Value of Work-Experience Credit for Special Education Students

In Special Education, a definition of terms is helpful in understanding disability categories. For example, the term "specific learning disability" means a disorder in one or more of the basic psychological processes involved in understanding or using spoken or written language that may manifest itself in an imperfect ability to listen, think, speak, read, write, spell, or do math calculations. This category includes such conditions as: perceptual disabilities, brain injury, minimal brain dysfunction, dyslexia, and developmental aphasia. The term "emotionally/behaviorally disabled" indicates students who exhibit, over a long period of time and to a marked degree, one or more of the following characteristics which adversely affect their educational performance and require specially designed instruction: inability to build or maintain satisfactory interpersonal relationships with peers and teachers, inappropriate types of behavior or feelings under normal circumstances; a general pervasive mood of unhappiness or depression, or a tendency to develop physical symptoms or fears associated with personal or school problems. (Bergeson, Wise, & Gill, OSPI Publication, 2000)

Many of the LD (learning-disabled—a category in Special Education), ADD (attention deficit disordered—students with a medical diagnosis that, in part, indicates a shortened attention span which adversely affects one's ability to learn) and BD (behavior disordered) students in high school have part-time jobs in the community at local businesses such as Pizza Hut, Taco Bell, Safeway, Costco, and the Rose Hill Car Wash. Historically, educators at Lake Washington High School (a three-year high school in Kirkland, Washington) have given work experience credits for students with part-time jobs. These credits are normally granted under the "elective" or occupational education categories for graduation purposes. Unlike traditional work experience credit (which ties credit to a specific number of hours earned per semester), this credit is based on achievement and progress toward goals and objectives tied to the IEP Monthly, the employer is requested by a special education teacher, via phone conversation or in a written format, to respond to questions relative to those goals and objectives for the student who is the employee. Or, if the objective "appropriate interaction with peers and adults" is part of the IEP, then that is what the employer evaluates.

By crediting part-time jobs, the IEP becomes a bridge between the schoolhouse and the workplace. Skill building, role-playing, and discussion can be provided by the school special education team in those areas employers indicate need more improvement. For example, recently a sophomore boy who was on work-experience credit worked at Dairy Queen. Although he was punctual and pleasant on the job, when the business was busy with customers, he would place his arms on the counter and rest. His teachers also had commented on his "resting" classroom behavior. This information was then privately discussed with the student. Role-playing and other strategies were devised in order to correct this behavior in both work and school settings. By the next month's employment progress check, the behavior had been extinguished and replaced with more acceptable behaviors on the job as well as in the classroom.

The Career Ladders Program

Career Ladders is a job-training program which students may take for credit (toward graduation) in the Lake Washington School District. This district-wide program (began some years ago in San Francisco, California) attracts students from the five district high schools. Students in the Career Ladders program attend their elective, required and special education classes at their home school for part of the school day and then go to work in an actual work setting for the remainder of the day. This is a strong community-based program with partnerships with corporations (such as Costco), area hospitals, building supply companies, and golf courses. The students are visited and coached on the job by district-provided teachers, who help in job training, job acquisition, and problem-solving. The teachers conduct weekly support classes for students in the program. Students learn specific job skills such as: personal presentation, resume and application writing, interview techniques, proper grooming, and role-playing job-related situations. Over the years, the Career ladders program has been valuable in keeping marginal learners engaged in education. Students on an IEP may earn Occupational Education, math, science, English, and elective credits toward graduation, depending on the scope and nature of their job.

According to the *Lake Washington School District Student Profile* (2002), Career Ladders is a successful school-to-careers program that "serves students who want or need to make their transition directly from school to a job. Students participate in a work internship and a community classroom that replicates the competitive marketplace. Support and supervision are designed to teach student interns how to survive and thrive in the real work world" (p. 201).

NEVAC

The Lake Washington School District is one of nine member districts in the Northeast Vocational Area Cooperative (NEVAC), which provides courses for students from 30 neighboring high schools in the Eastside area of Seattle, Washington. Students do not have to pay tuition but must provide their own transportation to and from their NEVAC class. Instructors in the NEVAC program operate approximately 80 different high school professional and technical classes in five "Educational Paths": Business and Marketing; Technology, Engineering, and Science; Social Services and Education; Arts and Communications; and Health and Recreation. These classes are generally year-long and provide credit in Occupational Education, elective education, and/or equivalency credit in areas such as math and science. Many classes offer advanced placement options at area community colleges and technical schools through the Tech Prep program, in which students must earn a "B" grade or better to qualify for college credit. There are thirty-four courses in such diverse areas as: auto body, small engine repair, radio broadcasting, fire service, criminal justice, hotel management, culinary arts, computer networking, sports medicine, graphics design, and carpentry, to name a few. Typically a NEVAC student is in his or her junior or senior year and takes three classes at his or her home high school and then a two-hour NEVAC class at another high school. Students in the Lake Washington School District are given Metro bus passes, form car pools, or drive themselves to the NEVAC sites. Some surrounding districts bus their students to the appropriate NEVAC sites. Many special education students have had a successful transition from school to the workplace as a direct result of their NEVAC experience.

NEVAC Success Stories

The NEVAC success stories for special education are as diverse as the students themselves. One ADHD boy, a challenge to parents and teachers alike, progressed from a NEVAC culinary arts class to the West Coast School Culinary Institute in Portland, Oregon, and then to a career with one of Seattle's top catering firms. Another ADHD student in NEVAC culinary arts went on to the Lake Washington Vocational Technical College and is now a chef with a local restaurant chain. Many young men on IEP who have gone through the NEVAC auto body class are now gainfully employed by Honda, Toyota, Dodge, and Volvo dealerships throughout the Puget Sound region. A recent graduate of The Seattle Art Institute was an LD student at Lake Washington High School; while a senior, he took a NEVAC class in graphic design. Today he is employed by the Microsoft Corporation where he is a computer animator. Several young LD/ADD women have taken beauty college classes through NEVAC. They now work at one of Washington's premier hair salon chains. Yet another LD student took a NEVAC hotel careers class as a senior in high school. (The Hyatt Regency Hotel in Bellevue, Washington is one of the NEVAC training sites.) She then went on to earn her hotel certificate through the Lake Washington Technical College. Recently, she has been promoted to a supervisory position within the Hyatt Corporation and was offered a job at the Hyatt Hotel in Palm Springs.

The NEVAC teachers work in tandem with special education school staff to incorporate the I.E.P goals and accommodations into meaningful components of employment preparation. Students who have struggled all their lives in the traditional classroom setting are now working as chefs, police officers, carpenters, welders, computer repairmen, licensed practical nurses, and auto technicians as a direct result of their NEVAC training.

Paid Internships for Teachers

The Lake Washington School District offers paid internships for teachers in business and industry. During the internships, the teachers participate in a variety of job shadow experiences within their chosen field. The goal is for teachers to see the job opportunities, requirements, and expectations, and to take that knowledge back to the classroom to help direct students in their respective career choices. The philosophy of this program is that if teachers get out of the schoolhouse and into the business and trade sectors of our economy, they are better equipped to guide students into job paths in which the students can succeed. For example, some teachers complete summer internships in the construction field. Such experiences greatly expand the knowledge base available to educators concerning the spectrum of jobs available in the trade, as well as in the office and safety aspects of construction. Teachers are then able to share this information and provide contacts to special education students who have an interest in the construction industry.

Post-ITT—a Web-based Resource for Students with Disabilities

Post-ITT (Postsecondary Innovative Transition Technology Project) is a collaborative career preparatory project between the Lake Washington School District and the Washington Research Institute. (See the website: www.wri-edu.org/postitt) It is a free, web-based resource designed to help students with disabilities make the transition from high school to college, including two-year, four-year, vocational, and technical colleges. It has comprehensive information about disability providers and services for colleges and universities throughout Washington State. The Post-ITT project includes a multitude of activities that students, teachers, and parents may select online. These activities are designed to be part of a "work in progress" during grades nine through twelve. For example, the activities in the workbook and online suggested for ninth grade include assessments of the student's likes, strengths, and disabilities. There are activities that teach the student to advocate for his or her needs. The tenth grade activities include a planning inventory, college selection research tools, and topics to discuss with the school career or guidance counselor. The eleventh grade activities focus on pre-college testing, scheduling and accommodations for that testing. (Initial contact with disability support staff at colleges is facilitated by information and documentation of disabilities obtained through Post-ITT.) The twelfth grade activities include follow-up contact with colleges, research of colleges, and determination of how supportive technology can help students once they arrive in the college setting. According to an information sheet provided by Post-ITT,

> With the support of the U.S. Department of Education, Washington Research Institute (WRI) has developed a curriculum, supporting resources, and teacher training to assist students with disabilities in transition to college. Known by the acronym Post-ITT, these free resources have proven to be effective through pilot trials with the Lake Washington School

District. WRI has developed invaluable partnerships with the Washington Association of Postsecondary Education and Disability (the professional association of disability services coordinators), the DO-IT program, the Center for Change in Transition at the University of Washington, and other national and regional disability advocacy associations. (Post-ITT website: www.postitt.org)

Senior Service-Learning Projects

Many schools have begun to implement senior service learning projects. Seniors at Lake Washington High School are released from classes in the spring during a four-day period when the sophomores and juniors are engaged in mandated state and national testing. Seniors have an opportunity to participate in a job shadow and have "hands-on" work experiences in areas in which they have an interest. They may work alongside a veterinarian or other professional in the community for several days to see firsthand what that job experience actually entails. They are required to write a short report of what they've seen and accomplished, as well as a letter of thanks to the employer. Special education students fulfill this requirement and receive support from their IEP providers in the writing tasks. These experiences are positive and valuable. They serve as bridges from school to the workplace.

Developing Strong Work Ethics in Special Education Students

Parents, teachers, counselors, and administrators can help develop strong work ethics in our special education students. Psychologist Bruce Baldwin (1996) has written specific directions for parents who want to raise healthy, achieving children. He says children need to have regular work responsibilities at home beginning at the age of two. Consistent chores at home and in the classroom foster a work ethic. Teens in special education classes may be held responsible for taking out and properly shelving all books, clearing the desks and floors of papers, and cleaning the whiteboards. Baldwin also strongly believes that parents and teachers should insist on good manners from our teens. This trait is very important for our special needs youngsters. Good manners are expected in the workplace. Adults must model proper manners and insist that manners matter in the classroom. Many school districts are setting civility standards for students, parents, and teachers. Expectations must be kept high to let our teens know that swearing, ethnic/gender jokes, slovenly behavior and sexually provocative attire are not permissible, just as these behaviors are not tolerated in the workplace. Adults should set clear limits on television viewing because much of the television programming presents a distorted view of work. Many prime-time sitcoms do not project a positive, nor even a realistic, workplace.

Parents and teachers can help special education teens learn sound money management practices. Classes in Lake Washington High School, such as marketing (DECA—Distributive Education Clubs of America), accounting, and senior math are mainstream classes that are available to special education students. These classes present a practical, "real world" approach to work, earnings, and independent living. Parents are encouraged to support the curriculum by providing follow-through on skills development—such as grocery shopping, budget building, and money management.

Finally, punctuality and on-time performance must be developed and expected at home and in school to strengthen the likelihood of job success. The most successful special education teens are the ones who are responsible enough to show up on time. They are the ones with good attendance and few "tardies". This behavior needs to be rewarded randomly by parents and teachers. Some teachers and schools give certificates, candy, and accolades to those students with good attendance and good attendance improvement. Several high schools in the Lake Washington School District offer yearly "Turnaround Award" receptions in which one-hundred or so students (in special education and in mainstream classes) who have made significant improvement in academics, behaviors, or attitude are honored before their families and friends. Many special needs students are nominated by their general and special education teachers as an acknowledgement of their progress toward positive adult traits. Over the years there have been many students who have struggled academically, but who have demonstrated good attendance at work and at school. One young man worked at a restaurant in a nearby city while in school. His employer commented on how much he valued the employee because "we can always count on him to be here." Another example is a former student with ADD who began work in a NEVAC auto technology program and went on to an internship and then a full-time job at a car dealership. He prided himself on being one of the first to work each day at 7:00 a.m. and often volunteered to work on Saturdays. Today, after three years, he makes $60,000 per year. He just kept showing up on time and proving he could be counted on!

Conclusion

Collaboration, creative thinking and high standards for behaviors are essential components of a successful Individual Transition Plan for special education students. Parents, teachers, counselors and administrators play critical roles in blending community opportunities with school curriculum. The transition portion of the IEP can be the vehicle to empower special needs students to their full potential and help them transition successfully to the workplace.

References

Baldwin, Bruce. (1996). *The cornucopia kids*. Reston, VA: National Association of Secondary School Principals. Website: http://www.nassp.org.

Bergeson, T., Wise, B.J. & Gill, D.H. (April 2000). *State of Washington rules for the provision of special education to special education students*, (Washington Administrative Code: Chapter 392-172 WAC.) Olympia, WA: Office of the Superintendent of Public Instruction.*ake Washington High School Course Catalogue, 2002-2003* Program Offerings (NEVAC*)*, Redmond, WA: Lake Washington School District Printing Center. Author.

Lake Washington School District Student Profile: Curriculum Framework for Secondary Education. (2002). Career Ladders. Redmond, WA: Author.

Post-ITT Project. *Information sheet.* Seattle: Washington Research Institute. (Lee Bassett, Project Director, e-mail: postitt@postitt.org) Website: http://www.wri-edu.org/postitt or www.postitt.org

Part VIII

Internet Delivery Systems in Career Guidance

Part VIII, Internet Delivery Systems in Career Guidance, includes two chapters about recently developed Internet-based career development systems. Students who do not use electronic resources for their career development will be missing many opportunities to communicate and to present themselves to others. Educators may assist students in learning how to utilize these online resources.

(30) *The Electronic Portfolio*—Palmer discusses why school staffs might want their students to use the WOIS/The Career Information System *electronic portfolio* program. Advantages include ease of updating portfolio information as well as ease of storage. The WOIS Electronic Portfolio's components are described. A guest password may be obtained from www.wois.org so that readers may explore this Washington state online portfolio program.

(31) *O*NET In Action—Expanding Youth Career Horizons*—Schmelter-Davis's chapter, with a number of captured screens showing various online programs, helps readers to understand the potential power of using this Internet career exploration resource, O*NET OnLine and the companion O*NET Career Exploration Tools. These programs may be used to help young people to develop career focus. The O*NET, which has been developed by the U.S. Department of Labor, offers a comprehensive occupational information and exploration system. A Web-based viewer called O*NET OnLine provides easy public access to information in the database. It also has links to labor market, education and career information in America's Career OneStop on the Internet. Readers may access the O*NET at http://online.onetcenter.org

Chapter Thirty

Electronic Portfolios: Convenient Storage for Career and Educational Planning Records

Tami Palmer

Abstract

This chapter discusses why school staffs might want their students to use an electronic portfolio for storage of career and educational planning. The WOIS Electronic Portfolio is described, including the process used to create it and the components included within the Portfolio. Details are also provided about the integrated management tool for counselors and teachers. To request a guest password to view the WOIS Electronic Portfolio, send e-mail to tami@wois.org or call 1-800-700-WOIS. If you send e-mail, please include your full name and the name of your school or agency. Website: http://www.wois.org

Why Electronic Portfolios?

Online portfolios are an innovative practice to help students keep track of their own information. Portfolios have become an important tool for storing records of student classes and grades, test scores, coursework samples, career and educational research and planning, and more. Many portfolios are in hard-copy format, filling file drawers and requiring time and effort from students, teachers and/or counselors to ensure that the appropriate paperwork makes it into those files. (If a student transfers to another school, the portfolio may or may not follow him or her to the new school.)

More and more, educators in schools have been moving to electronic storage of some of the portfolio components. Educators in some schools have used prepackaged programs, and others have developed their own computer-based storage for portfolio components. These electronic portfolios may free up file cabinet space, and be easier to update from any computer in the school that has access to the portfolio program, but computer storage issues may arise as students add items over the years.

Over the last two years, WOIS/The Career Information System (the Washington State Career Information Delivery System) has worked with an advisory group of teachers, counselors and career specialists to develop the WOIS Electronic Portfolio. The WOIS portfolio is unique from other electronic portfolios in that it is a web-based program, accessed via the WOIS web site from any computer that has Internet access. This means students, with the appropriate password, can edit and update their portfolios not only from school, but from home, from the public library, or anywhere else they can access a computer and the Internet. In addition, storage and file management are no longer issues for the schools, because all of the portfolios are stored on the WOIS web server. Students have more flexibility for when and where to update their portfolios, and it's easy for them to share the information in their portfolios with their parents or potential employers.

What Should Be Included in an Electronic Portfolio?

As the WOIS staff worked with the Electronic Portfolio advisory group, the following were developed as the items to be included in the Portfolio as storage options:
1. Educational Planner
2. Work/Community Experience
3. Career Research
4. Assessment Results
5. Postsecondary Training Research
6. College Essays
7. Scholarships/Awards/Honors
8. Best Works and Accomplishments
9. Resumes
10. Cover Letters
11. Informational Interviews
12. Hobbies/Extracurricular Activities
13. Journal
14. To Do List

For each item listed above, the student is given a form to enter information about the item. For example, the form for Work/Community

Experience asks for the following information:

- Position held
- Name of organization
- Type of Experience (with a drop down box from which they can choose Paid, Volunteer, Internship, Job Shadow, Culminating Project, Work-Based Learning, Service Learning, and Other)
- Supervisor's name
- Supervisor's e-mail
- Address of organization
- Start and end date
- Number of hours worked per week
- Total number of hours worked
- Wage
- Credit earned
- Description of organization
- Duties performed
- Comments

By providing a format for the student to enter information, the portfolio solicits information that the student may not have thought about including.

In addition to the forms for each component in the portfolio, a student using the WOIS Career Information can import assessment results from the WOIS system directly into his or her portfolio. The student may also add any of the WOIS Career Information descriptions directly to his or her portfolio. This makes it easy for students to go back and work with the research again and again, without having to find the "paper folder" in which the information is stored in the counselor's office.

An additional interactive portion of the portfolio is the résumé writing component. As a student creates a résumé, he or she has an opportunity to import the work or community experience, already entered into his or her portfolio, directly into the work experience section of the résumé. This can still be edited once it is imported, because the student may decide he or she does not want a particular work experience to be included in his or her résumé. The ability to import the information saves the student from having to re-type the work and community experience information again and again.

A Management Tool for Counselors, Career Specialists and Teachers

The final, but very important, feature of the WOIS Electronic Portfolio is the ability for counselors, career specialists and teachers to view each individual student's portfolio. When the staff person logs on to the WOIS

Portfolio, using the school's unique counselor password, he or she will see a list of all the students who have created a portfolio, along with the student's career path, user name and password (in case the student forgets) and e-mail address. The staff person can access an individual portfolio to see what a student has entered, but does not have the ability to change any of the information.

Future plans for this tool include the ability to sort students by a variety of criteria, including grade and career path. Also proposed is a message center, which would allow the staff person to correspond via e-mail to all the students with a portfolio (for example: "remember, you need to have at least one functional résumé completed in your portfolio by October 31") or to select students (such as an e-mail message to all the students in the science career path about the aquatic biologist who will be speaking in the gymnasium at lunch time).

A Work in Progress

The WOIS Electronic Portfolio was launched in February 2002 in a format that was scaled down from its original scope. (It was launched prior to completion because the WOIS customers were anxious to have a portfolio in place.) The portfolio is an important tool because it specifically addresses one of the new graduation requirements in Washington State for the graduating class of 2008: that all students will complete a *culminating project* and will have a *high school + education plan* before leaving high school. The portfolio is a good place for the students to record their *high school + education plan* and also information about their *culminating project*. Students in those schools that choose to use the electronic portfolio system will have access to this convenient storage tool.

The Portfolio Advisory Committee directed the WOIS staff to release the Portfolio with the following components: Educational Planner, Career Research, Assessment Results and Work/Community Experience. Since the initial release, the résumé and cover letter writing component have been added, as well as School Research and Best Works, and the ability to import the results from all three of the WOIS assessment tools and career descriptions. (All of the additional items listed previously in this article will be added over the next year or so, with each being released as it is completed.)

Conclusion

To date over 6,000 students have created portfolios electronically through WOIS. The WOIS staff have talked with school personnel around the state of Washington who have said they are making the WOIS Electronic Portfolio an integral part of their school programs for the 2003-2004 year. The flexibility afforded by making the portfolio accessible through the Internet, as well as the elimination of the storage issue for schools, make this web-based portfolio a convenient tool for maintaining career and educational planning records.

References

WOIS/The Career Information System. (2002). *WOIS electronic portfolio*. Olympia, WA: Author.

Address: WOIS/The Career Information System,
1415 Harrison Ave NW, Suite 201
Olympia WA 98502.
Phone: 1-800-700-WOIS or 360/754-8222
E-mail: info@wois.org
Website address: http://www.wois.org

Chapter Thirty-One

O*NET in Action-Expanding Youth Career Horizons

Harvey Schmelter-Davis

Abstract

This chapter helps the reader understand the potential power of using an Internet career resource, O*NET® OnLine and the companion O*NET Career Exploration Tools ™, to help youth gain career focus. Developed by the U.S. Department of Labor, the O*NET database offers a dynamic framework and comprehensive information for exploring occupations. A Web-based viewer called O*NET OnLine provides easy public access to information in the database. It also has links to labor market, education and career information in America's Career OneStop on the Internet. Public and private developers are using the O*NET database to develop supportive products such as career interest and work value assessment instruments. Many are available on the Web. This chapter presents examples of how O*NET OnLine and the Career Exploration Tools are being used to help youth have career focus.

Introduction

The Occupational Information Network - O*NET® - an advanced technology database, has taken the place of the Dictionary of Occupational Titles (DOT) as the nation's primary source of occupational information. The core of O*NET is a database, available on the Internet, from which many products and services have been - and can be - developed by private and public developers. The U.S. Department of Labor's Employment and Training Administration sponsors and administers the O*NET system. The author is indebted to Donna Dye and Marilyn Silver, whose work on the origins of the O*NET System (1999) provided the basis for this summary of O*NET beginnings.

An Occupational Information Network for a Net-Working World: Its History and Development

In the mid-1990s, the U.S. Department of Labor introduced a new concept of collecting, organizing, and presenting information about work in the U.S. economy and the workers who do it. The concept provided the framework for a new system, equipped to respond to the transformations occurring in the U.S. workplace. It would provide comprehensive information and a common language for use in job training and placement, school curriculum development, and in meeting employer needs for workers with particular skills. Designed to improve the country's labor exchange process, the new system is called the Occupational Information Network, or O*NET ®.

Need for a New Tool

By the late 1980s, the American workplace was feeling the impact of global competition, demographic shifts in the workforce, and rapid changes in technology. Jobs in manufacturing, once the heart of the U.S. economy, were disappearing, thanks to intensive international competition, new technology, and cheaper labor overseas. Displaced workers often lacked the skills needed for employment in new fields. Gaps appeared between the skills business needed and the qualifications of entry-level workers.

Employers, educators and human resource specialists needed more efficient tools for identifying the connections between occupations and the transferable skills of workers. Their primary resource on occupations was the Labor Department's venerable Dictionary of Occupational Titles - the DOT. But the DOT, originally designed to meet the needs of the industrial economy of the 1930s and 1940s, had become outmoded. Determined that the American workforce be prepared to meet the challenges of a new and changing economy, the Labor Department introduced a Workforce Quality Agenda. Its mission included improving labor market efficiency by updating the tools used to identify workplace skills and place workers in jobs.

Initially the Labor Department considered revising its well-established and respected DOT. The decision to replace it came only after several years of expert review, research, consultation with users, public hearings, needs assessments, and analyses of the findings. The conclusion was that updating the DOT would not suffice. The DOT was, in fact as well as in name, a "dictionary." It defined discrete occupations, based largely on what they produced. Its emphasis was on products, not information — on tasks that were mostly manual rather than mental.

Describing the labor market of the "information age" required not a dictionary but a comprehensive and flexible electronic database. It needed a common language to describe what workers do, the skills and abilities they use, as well as the requirements and demands of the work itself. Its focus would be on the connections between occupations and the transferability of skills common to groups or families of occupations. The Labor Department wanted a tool that employers, educators, and workforce development personnel could use to respond to a dynamic and rapidly changing workplace.

Creating the O*NET System

Using the findings of its research, the Labor Department went to work on developing a new system. With help from technical contractors and market research specialists, it produced a beta version of an electronic database and released it to vendors who were ready to develop their own "value added" products. Pilot projects tested the new database in several states. To ensure broad participation and appropriate expertise in the development, the Department funded a state-based consortium headed by the North Carolina Employment Security Commission, to support O*NET data collection and the development of technical assistance guides and career exploration tools.

In 1998, the O*NET 98 Database and Viewer software were released to the public in CD-ROM format. The Consortium developed training for users and outreach materials, including three technical assistance guides designed for the workforce investment system, business, and the public. In 2000, the Labor Department released the O*NET 3.0 database, which was compatible with the new (1998/2000) Standard Occupational Classification (SOC). A web-based viewer, called O*NET OnLine, provided public access to the database via the Internet. In 2002, an enhanced and streamlined O*NET OnLine went on the Web.

In 2002, the first two of three O*NET Career Exploration Tools™ were completed and published. They are the *O*NET Interest Profiler* and the *O*NET Work Importance Locator*. The *O*NET Ability Profiler* will be released in 2003. The O*NET database is being translated into Spanish. In a major collaboration with businesses and industry associations, the Consortium is surveying current workers to update and enhance the database. (O*NET Team, 2001)

Overview of Basic O*NET Components

The O*NET database is available in a flexible electronic format to enable private and public developers to incorporate parts or all of it into their own "value-added" products. It includes information about occupational requirements and characteristics, as well as the skills, abilities, knowledge, and experience of workers in the occupation. It is comprehensive, covering 950+ occupations across the U.S. economy.

The O*NET Content Model determines the kind of information collected for the database. As reported by the O*NET Consortium (2002):

> Questionnaires are being used to collect data [from incumbent workers] for four Content Model Domains: Skills, Generalized Work Activities, Work Context and Knowledge. A 5th (fifth) Content Domain, Abilities, will be updated through a new analyst rating project. The data collection project calls for gathering data on 200-300 occupations per year, with the goal of replenishing the database every 5 years.

Currently the O*NET-SOC classification titles in the database are broad enough to cover most job titles in the United States. These titles may be expanded or contracted based on the ongoing research. Crosswalks have been developed to relate O*NET titles and codes to the many occupational classifications and lay job titles used in the workplace. The database can be downloaded from the O*NET Resource Center at: http://www.onetcenter.org

Three O*NET Career Exploration Tools™ are available. They are the *O*NET Interest Profiler*, a career interest assessment inventory; the *O*NET Work Importance Locator*, a work values inventory; and the *O*NET Ability Profiler*, an ability assessment.

O*NET OnLine (http://online.onetcenter.org) is a Web-based viewer that provides easy public access to O*NET information from any Web browser. O*NET OnLine offers a dynamic framework for exploring occupations because information is drawn directly from the O*NET database online. This Web tool also provides connections to labor market, education, and career information in America's Career OneStop on the Internet.

Finding O*NET Resources

To use O*NET information online . . .
> Go to: O*NET OnLine at: http://online.onetcenter.org
> Available 24/7, this website gives easy access to information in the O*NET database. Use it to find and explore occupations of interest or to identify occupations that use selected skills.

To locate or learn more about O*NET resources . . .

Start at: O*NET Resource Center: http://www.onetcenter.org
The O*NET Consortium's portal page is the hub for information about the O*NET Project and products. It links to other official O*NET websites and the Labor Department's O*NET homepage.

To find out how people are using O*NET products and information
See O*NET in Action on the Labor Department's O*NET website. To get there directly, go to: http://www.doleta.gov/programs/onet/oina.cfm Or you can jump:

From O*NET OnLine (http://online.onetcenter.org)
Click "Related Links" at the top of the O*NET OnLine welcome screen.
Scroll down the list of links under O*NET and click O*Net in Action.
Scroll down the page to Table of Contents.
In the list of titles that follows, click any title to jump to the story.

From the O*NET Resource Center portal page:
Scroll down the left-hand menu to Using O*NET.
Click on the first link to jump to O*NET in Action.
Scroll down the page to Table of Contents.
In the list of titles that follows, click any title to jump to the story.

Using O*NET OnLine

The O*NET OnLine homepage provides the following major features:
   a. Occupational Search - obtain information about an occupation using a key word or code search.
   b. Skills Search - select skills from a list of those commonly used in the U.S. workplace to identify occupations that use the specific skills selected.
   c. Crosswalk - match titles or codes in other classifications (such as the Military Occupational Classification) with related O*NET-SOC occupations.
   d. Job Accommodations - obtain job accommodation information for specific disabilities through links to the Job Accommodation Network's website.

e. Code Connector - match O*NET occupational titles with specific job titles used by U.S. companies and vice versa.

O*NET OnLine's homepage has connections to two major online career resources: the O*NET Resource Center, which provides users with various O*NET products, services and updates; and America's Career OneStop, which provides extensive job search assistance, labor market and career information, and OneStop system links.

O*NET Online Homepage

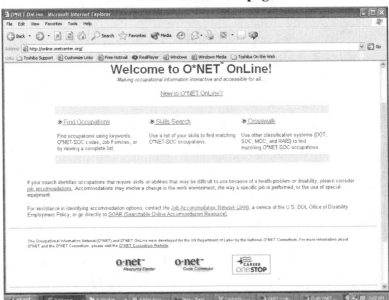

Occupational Search

This feature allows one to search for an occupational description in the O*NET database using "key words" or an O*NET-SOC code. One can also identify occupations by browsing through a list of O*NET "Job Families." Summary and detailed reports are available for occupations of interest. They provide the following information about each occupation: Tasks, Knowledge, Skills, Abilities, Work Activities, Work Context, Job Zone, Interests, Work Values, Related Occupations, Wages and Employment Outlook. (The definitions for these topics are found when an occupation is displayed by clicking the Online Help icon at the top of the page.)

Reports also provide a link to a list of Related Occupations, thus expanding the universe of career or training possibilities. The Wages and Employment Outlook Information link was added in 2002 so one could easily access state and national data for the selected occupation from America's Career OneStop. This upgrade is an example how O*NET is continually being evaluated and improved.

Skills Search

This feature allows one to select relevant skills from a list of skills in six categories. The search then returns a list of occupations in which the selected skills are commonly used and their importance to the occupation. One can obtain summary or detailed information about occupations on the list. The following is an example of occupations identified in a skills search.

Sample Skills Search Results

The skills selected are listed at the top under "Skills Search Results for:" The Summary report will provide the additional skills that are needed and their importance for that occupation.

Crosswalk

The Crosswalk allows one to see how an occupation in one of the classifications listed (Dictionary of Occupational Titles-DOT, Military Occupations Classification-MOC, Registered Apprenticeship Information System-RAIS, and Standard Occupational Classification-SOC) are cross-referenced to O*NET occupational titles.

Job Accommodation -
Searchable Accommodation Resource (SOAR)

O*NET OnLine links directly to the Job Accommodation Network's SOAR program. It enables one to search for information on job accommodation for persons with specific disabilities. The page shown below provides an example of the beginning of the listing of disabilities included in this resource.

Sample of Disabilities to Access SOAR Job Accommodation Recommendations

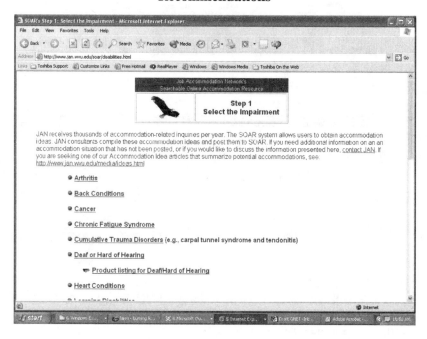

O*NET Code Connector

This feature allows one to input a job or occupational title and obtain possible related O*NET codes and/or "lay titles." The example below is a screen captured when a search was conducted for related titles for an accountant.

O*NET Code Connector

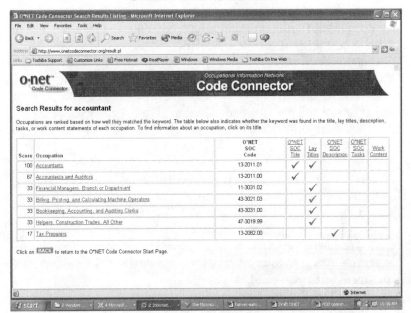

O*NET Career Exploration Tools

The Labor Department's O*NET Team, in the Office of Policy, Development, Evaluation, and Research, has overseen the development of the O*NET Career Exploration Tools[tm], a set of career counseling instruments. The tools are designed to assist a wide variety of users with identifying information about themselves. They can use this self-knowledge to guide their exploration of occupations included in O*NET OnLine. The tools stress self-directed, whole-person assessment. Users are able to take a variety of valid and reliable assessments, each providing important information that can help them explore career options and the world of work.

To download O*NET Career Exploration Tools free of charge, go to the O*NET Resource Center Web page, www.onetcenter.org and under **Products** select the **Career Exploration Tools** link on the left hand side of the page. Paper-and-pencil versions may be purchased from the U.S. Government Printing Office.

Private developers have incorporated two of these tools - the *O*NET Interest Profiler* and the *O*NET Work Importance Locator* - into career information delivery systems (CIDS) and other computerized resources available on CD-ROM or on the Internet.

The **O*NET Interest Profiler** (IP) can be self-administered, with no outside assistance. It enables individuals to receive a profile of their vocational interests that:

- provides valuable self-knowledge about their vocational personality types;
- fosters career awareness of matching occupations; and
- directly links the client to the entire world of work via the 950+ occupations within O*NET OnLine.

The *Interest Profiler* is based on Interest Areas compatible with Holland's (1985) R-I-A-S-E-C constructs: Realistic, Investigative, Artistic, Social, Enterprising, and Conventional. The Holland typology was used because it is grounded in a rich and extensive research history, is widely accepted and used by counselors, and is well received by clients when used in either automated, Internet or paper-and-pencil delivery format (U.S. Department of Labor — USDOL 2000a).

The *O*NET Work Importance Locator* (WIL) is a work values assessment instrument. It focuses on the aspects or conditions of work that are important to people in a job or career. The WIL helps clients identify their highest work values and use this information to:

- gain a valuable piece of self-knowledge and career awareness, and
- directly link to the entire world of work via the 950+ occupations within O*NET OnLine.

The *Work Importance Locator* is based on a previously developed measure of work values, the Minnesota Importance Questionnaire (MIQ) (Rounds, Henly, Dawis, Lofquist, & Weiss, 1981). Clients use a simple card-sorting format to rank the importance of 20 cards, each describing an aspect of work that satisfies one of six broad work values. The six values are updated versions of the work values defined in Dawis and Lofquist's (1984) Theory of Work Adjustment: Achievement, Independence,

Recognition, Relationships, Support, and Working Conditions (U.S. Department of Labor, 2000b).

Uses of O*NET in Providing Career Assistance to Youth

Public and private developers are using the O*NET database to produce or enhance career exploration programs and resources directed at helping youth explore career opportunities and make plans for future work. Many state career information delivery systems (CIDS), widely used in secondary schools and career centers, now use O*NET occupational information. Some have built in either the *Interest Profiler* or the *Work Importance Locator*. Other career resource developers now offer Web-based products that use O*NET information.

To help public and private vendors use the O*NET system, the Labor Department posts examples of how others are using these resources. The following examples are drawn from the O*NET in Action Web page (http://www.doleta.gov/programs/onet/oina.asp).

Building Stronger Communities by Building Better Careers
Community Preservation and Development Corporation (CPDC), Washington, DC

The CPDC is a non-profit organization operating in northeast Washington, DC. Its primary mission is to create affordable housing for low- and moderate-income residents. CPDC has built partnerships with residents to address important economic, education, health, and social needs through a range of community services, including programs for youth. For example, the CPDC has created a Career and College Resource Center for teens, complete with a CyberCafe. It also offers an extensive career and skills enhancement program for residents and neighbors in the nearby community, many of whom are out-of-school youth or young adults seeking better employment opportunities. O*NET information is used in one component of the career development program.

The program helps applicants assess their academic skills, interests, values, temperaments, and learning styles. Participants use O*NET OnLine to do research on occupational characteristics and requirements and to compare their skills with those required in a particular field. As they learn more about the career possibilities on their lists, they begin to eliminate some and to focus their investigation on two or three top choices. Information from O*NET, as well as job-specific information from local employers, helps them in their analysis and decision-making.

Participants leave the program with a long-term career plan fashioned as a résumé-builder. Some go on to specialized training programs in information technology. Others seek employment or further education in other fields. But all have an action plan, with next steps toward a better future. The career enhancement program is a vital part of a much broader and long-term effort "to revitalize an inner city neighborhood plagued with economic and physical deterioration and crime" (O*NET in Action, 2001b).

The CPDC's evening activities offer working adults access to facilities and assistance in improving job and career skills. Daytime programs provide unemployed youth and adults with assessment and career development, GED and External Diploma preparation, basic computer skills, and advanced training for jobs in information technology.

A key ingredient in CPDC's career development approach is making sure participants leave with a long-range but attainable goal, with a concrete plan and specific steps toward achieving it. The plan must include specific resources, for example, who to call for information or assistance. It must have realistic timelines for interim steps that help a client move ahead. Participants also have access to e-mail for six months after leaving a program to help them keep in touch with classmates and instructors. Staff follow-up focuses on steps taken and next steps needed. This is not just a get-a-job approach; it's establishing a long-term goal and an action plan.

One can obtain more information by contacting Career and Skill Enhancement Programs, Community Preservation and Development Corporation, 601 Edgewood St., NE, Suite 25, Washington, DC 20017. Telephone: 202-832-0500, x3135

Boys & Girls Clubs of America: Connecting Teens to the Future

Boys & Girls Clubs of America (B&GCA) is "the nation's fastest-growing youth development organization," (O*NET in Action, 2001a) with a primary focus on young people from disadvantaged backgrounds. The Clubs offer a broad range of age-appropriate activities, focused on helping members develop aspirations and acquire the skills they need to succeed as responsible and productive adults.

The Clubs developed CareerLaunch™ as part of their career preparation program to give Club members a Web-based career exploration resource. Drawing on the New York CareerZone O*NET project and other tools using O*NET, the Clubs designed a user-friendly interface to connect Clubs to O*NET and other occupational data. Teens can access job descriptions, skills, interests, educational requirements, and work activities for hundreds of O*NET occupations.

CareerLaunch includes the *O*NET Interest Profiler*. The results of the assessment bring up a list of possible careers drawn from the O*NET database. A link to the U.S. Department of Education's colleges/technical schools helps members determine further academic or training requirements for a particular career. Additional links to America's Job Bank and other employment sites provide current job opening information for teens searching for jobs in their area of interest. Teens can identify careers, set personal goals, identify potential barriers to employment, and search for jobs. CareerLaunch Version 1 was released to Clubs in May 1999 and has been updated and enhanced subsequently.

In its pilot phase, CareerLaunch was used as a support to the career preparation program, available in more than 600 Clubs. Staff reported the Clubs had recruited and trained more than 5,000 teens and placed more than 4,000 in summer jobs. These participants used CareerLaunch as a tool to explore areas of interest, make career decisions, set realistic goals based upon sound data, and find jobs.

To find out about CareerLaunch and/or the location of Clubs using it, check the B&GCA homepage at: http://www.bgca.org.

NYCareerZone www.nycareerzone.org

New York CareerZone was first developed as a pilot program using the O*NET database. In 1996, the New York State Department of Labor (NYSDOL) was one of five sites that received a federal grant to develop an application using the new database. The project team at NYSDOL decided to focus on the career development needs of students, and the system now called CareerZone was born.

The CareerZone system utilizes the *O*NET Interest Profiler* to help students identify occupations to explore. The system integrates New York-specific education and labor market information with O*NET data to give students a comprehensive occupational view. CareerZone continues to be expanded and enhanced and is an integral part of the career development system in New York. Counselors, teachers, and career center staff use this system to involve students in the career development process.

The NYCareerZone homepage allows one to access occupational information, complete an informal assessment, create personal portfolio information, and access resources for counselors, teachers and students.

NYCareerZone Homepage

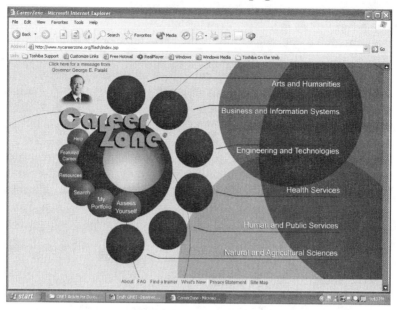

A portfolio module was added to the CareerZone system to help students begin career planning for the future. More than 90,000 users have registered to create their personal portfolio. This module is tied into the New York State Education Department Career Plan initiative and is being implemented all over the State. Interactive activities walk students through the process of identifying interests, abilities and, most importantly, skills. Students can use the skill checklist to highlight the job-specific skills they currently have or need to acquire for specific occupations. They can also complete a soft skill activity to link skills they have learned to specific academic and community activities. This system is usually introduced directly in a school's computer lab by a team of teachers and counselors. Because CareerZone is Internet-based, students can share information with parents at home and access the system from any Web browser. The CareerZone Portfolio system expands the way career information is disseminated and used as one prepares for the future.

NYCareerZone Portfolio Topics

After entering their individual portfolio, students can take the *O*NET Interest Profiler* online by opening the **My Interests** option. The student's portfolio is automatically summarized and updated when new information is added in the student's career plan under **View My CareerPlan**. The career plan is designed to follow the National Career Development Guidelines template and can be printed out as a PDF file. Below is a sample career plan form.

As a result of this project, many new and exciting developments are occurring including:

    a. introduction of an adult version of NYCareerZone,

    b. creation by the developers of the CareerZone website (IRADIX at: www.iradix.com) of a system to help teachers and counselors create lesson plans that are connected to the National Career Development Guidelines and state accountability standards, and

    c. involvement of OneStop Career Centers in the use of NYCareerZone.

NEW YORK STATE EDUCATION DEPARTMENT
Career Plan
Commencement Level

1. Personal Data

Name: student sample_____

Student ID Number:_____

School Name:_____

2. Review of Student Career Plan

Grade Level:	Date of Review:	Student:	Parent/ Guardian:	Teacher:	Guidance	Other:

3. Knowledge

   A. Self-knowledge: *'What am I?'*

   1. Interests: *List your top three choices for each of the following areas of interest:*

Grade Level	1a.Personal:*Out-of-school activities that you enjoy the most*	1b.Academic:*Classes or subjects you enjoy the*	1c. Work Preferences: *Working with people, ideas, and things*
9			
10			
11			
12			

   2. Abilities: *List personal skills and talents that will be helpful in a career choice:*

Grade Level	"My Personal Abilities..."	"Career areas where my abilities will be useful...:"
9		
10		
11		
12		

   3. Personal and academic areas I need to strengthen:

Grade Level	"I need to strengthen...:"	"Steps I will take to strengthen areas...:"

   B. Career Exploration: *'Where am I going?'*

   1. School and/or Community Experiences: *I have participated in the following school and/or community experiences:*

Grade Level	School and/or Community Experiences:	Skill Acquired through Experience:

   2.Work Experiences: *I have participated in the following work experiences:*

Grade Level	Work Experiences:	Skills Acquired through Work Experience:

3. Careers of Interest and Characterizes: *I am interested in the following careers and have discovered the following information about these careers:*

Grade Level	Careers of Interest:	Education Requirements	Skills I need to Acquire	Work Environment:	Job Outlook:

C. Future Goals and Decision Making: *'How do I get there?'*
1. Career Goals and Action Steps:

Grade Level	Goals:*(resulting from exploration activities)*	Education Plan:*(courses that relate to my career Interests)*	Action Steps:*(what I need to do to acomplish my goals)*	Check off completed steps

4. Skills "What I need to know?" "What skills are important to me?" "What am I learning?" "Why am I learning it?" "How can I use it?"

Directions: *The following skills are needed to succeed in life, work, and education beyond high school. Using the scale provided, identify for each skill the level of achievement you believe you possess at the beginning of the commencement level and the level you believe you achieved by the end of your senior year. Briefly describe a classroom experience or an activity that helped you develop each skill and identify how each skill can be used in your life and future work experiences.*

Skills	Beginning Skill Level I Possess	Experiences/Activities/Application	Final Skill Level I have Achieved
Basic Skills – Basic skills include the ability to read,write, listen, and speak as well as perform with meticaland mathematical functions.	o o o o o highly ⟷ least developed developed		o o o o o highly ⟷ least developed developed
Thinking Skills- thinking skills lead to problem solving experimenting and focused observation and allow the application of knowledge to a new and unfamiliar situation.	o o o o o highly ⟷ least developed developed		o o o o o highly ⟷ least developed developed

505

Skills	Beginning Skill Level	Experiences/Activities Application	Final Skill Level I Have Achieved
Personal Qualities- Personal qualities generally include competence in self management and the ability to plan, organize, and take independent action.	o o o o o highly ⟷ least developed developed		o o o o o highly ⟷ least developed developed
Interpersonal Skills- Positive interpersonal qualities lead to teamwork and cooperation in large and small groups in family, social, and work situations.	o o o o o highly ⟷ least developed developed		o o o o o highly ⟷ least developed developed
Technology- Technology is the process and products of human skill and ingenuity in designing and creating things from available resources to satisfy personal and societal needs and wants.	o o o o o highly ⟷ least developed developed		o o o o o highly ⟷ least developed developed
Managing Information - Information management focuses on the ability to access and use information obtained from other people, community resources, and computer network.	o o o o o highly ⟷ least developed developed		o o o o o highly ⟷ least developed developed
Managing Resources – Using resources includes the application of financial and human factors, and the elements of time and materials to successfully carry out a planned activity.	o o o o o highly ⟷ least developed developed		o o o o o highly ⟷ least developed developed
Systems – Systems skills include the understanding of and ability to work within natural and constructed systems.	o o o o o highly ⟷ least developed developed		o o o o o highly ⟷ least developed developed

5. Culuminating Activity

  Directions:
  Describe the activity that you completed to show your career development accomplishments at this level:

Activity:	Self Knowledge/Future Plans:

Texas Career Development Resources' Winning OSCAR

The Occupation and Skill Computer-Assisted Researcher (OSCAR) was developed by the Texas Workforce Commission/Career Development Resources (CDR) under a grant from the U.S. Employment and Training Administration. The current version was expanded in scope and audience to include high school students, welfare-to-work clients, and other persons with limited work experience. It used O*NET version 3.0, which allowed for an expansion of occupational profiles. Two O*NET assessment tools, the *Work Importance Locator* and *Interest Profiler*, were incorporated. Links to hundreds of websites for workforce, education, and emerging occupations were included. First available on CD-ROM, the system was used as the model for a similar resource called ORCA (Occupational Researcher's Computer Assistant), developed for Washington State by its Employment Security Department (ESD) and State Occupational Information Coordinating Committee (O*NET in Action, 2000).

More recently, the Arkansas Employment Security Department contracted with the Texas CDR staff to produce an Internet version of OSCAR now referred to as iOSCAR. The Arkansas system includes all the same features of the previous versions of OSCAR, including an online version of the O*NET Interest Profiler and Work Importance Locator. Arkansas users can take these assessments online, and iOSCAR scores them and produces a list of occupations with Arkansas-specific labor market information that match their preferences. Users can go to www.iOSCAR.org to access the Arkansas, Louisiana, and Texas versions of the iOSCAR system.

The Texas CDR reports as of February, 2003, that it has sold 3,000 copies of CD-ROM OSCAR. The Internet version has had 16,449 hits to date in Arkansas and Texas (Texas 2003). Further information can be obtained from the Texas CDR staff by going to their website at: http://www.cdr.state.tx.us/

Conclusion: Implications for Educators and Career Services Providers

The opening chapter of this book (Wakefield, 2003) offers insight into the behavior of disengaged "unfocused kids" and their issues, including their apparent unwillingness or inability to focus on school. Their lack of focus has many causes, including peer influence, working long hours, or being overly involved in activities. Also, disengaged parents tend to produce disengaged teens.

For many teens, college is just the next step after high school. But "going to college" does not necessarily mean that they will be successful. Many continue to flounder on campus and leave without completing a degree (Lester 1995). As Wakefield notes, "It is important for educators (and parents) to provide needed support and guidance to help teens make sound educational decisions instead of choosing 'the path of least resistance'."

Comprehensive career guidance programs can help students learn how to understand their own strengths, abilities and interests; explore career opportunities; and choose paths that engage their attention, talent, and energies. As other authors in this volume have pointed out, career development programs can help "unfocused kids" learn to set goals and make informed decisions about their future.

However, if teens are to make informed decisions, they - as well as their parents, teachers, and counselors - need to know more about the enormous number of occupational possibilities in the workplace. As reported in an article, "The Skills Gap and the American Workforce," that appeared on Monster.com, some "57 percent of companies with 100 or more employees have had difficulty hiring workers with the required skills, according to a Heldrich Work Trends study, published by Rutgers University in February 2002. This was despite the fact that there is an economic recession with a supply of workers waiting in the wings" (Van Horn, 2002). Teens need to know what skills companies are seeking to make informed career choices.

Providing comprehensive occupational information can strengthen career development programs. Such information is readily available, either through O*NET OnLine or some of the career resources that use the O*NET database and the O*NET Career Exploration Tools. In the past, career information has been the sole responsibility of school guidance counselors (or career specialists). The realities of pressing concerns in education today make it nearly impossible for counselors to shoulder this responsibility alone. Others in education must help, with the counselor as the facilitator of programs and activities involving parents, teachers, and teens. The availability of occupational and career information on the Internet makes this a feasible goal (Gray, Cernansky & Schmelter-Davis, 2002).

Students also need access to recently developed Internet career guidance resources using O*NET information to help them with their career exploration and planning. Among these are career information delivery systems using the O*NET database and career exploration tools available through www.acsci.org. The Labor Department offers the widely used career information and job search assistance website called Career OneStop at http://www.careeronestop.org/ and O*NET OnLine at http:// online.onetcenter.org.

Public access to the Internet has spread - in schools, colleges, libraries, and other public facilities. The challenge in the future will be how and when to deliver this information to students, enabling them to obtain it on their own or through career development or education programs. Introducing easily accessible career and labor market information to youth, and especially to "unfocused kids," is not only important but imperative in helping them set realistic career goals and action plans.

The Internet is home to thousands of career and labor market information websites, many of them now using the O*NET database. O*NET OnLine is an easily accessible resource that can meet the information needs of students and educators who want to learn more about the labor market. Once utilized, it can serve as a life-long resource as one moves from one job, occupation and/or career to the next. The examples in this chapter have given the reader a taste of the potential of this powerful resource. Articles about these and other O*NET applications are continually posted on the Department of Labor's Employment and Training page entitled "O*NET in Action" at: http://www.doleta.gov/programs/onet/oina.asp

As Lester noted (1995), "Today far too many of our children are adrift. Many live in impoverished homes or come to school with impoverished spirits . . . We can do something to help them by broadening their horizons, helping them discover their strengths and talents, and teaching them how to make responsible decisions about their own lives." In an "information age," occupational information is vital to expanding the horizons of our youth.

References

Dawis, R.V. & Lofquist, L.H. (1984). *A psychological theory of work adjustment*. Minneapolis, MN: University of Minnesota Press.

Dye, D. & Silver, M. (1999). The origins of O*NET. In N. G. Peterson, M. D. Mumford, W.C. Borman, P. R. Jeanneret, and E.A. Fleishman, (Eds.). *An occupational informationsystem for the 21st Century: The development of O*NET* (pp. 9-19). Washington, DC: A m e r i c a n Psychological Association.

Gray, V., Cernansky, J. & Schmelter-Davis, H. (2002). *Recruitment, O*NET: How to define human resources occupations.* (Vol. 11, pp. 12-13). Beijing, China: Scientific Talents People Communication Development Center, Science and Technology Department of the Peoples Republic of China Publishers.

Holland, J.L. (1985). *Making vocational choices: A theory of vocational personalities and work environments.* (2nd ed.). Englewood Cliff, NJ: Prentice-Hall.

Lester. J. (1995). The necessary art of making connections. In K. Hoyt & J. Lester, (Eds.).*Learning to work: The NCDA Gallup Survey.* (pp. 15-30). Alexandria, VA: National Career Development Association.

O*NET in Action (2000). ORCA - The Occupational Researcher's Computer Assistant. Washington Employment Security Department and the Washington State Occupational Information Coordinating Committee. [Online] Available: http://www.doleta.gov/programs/onet/oina.asp

O*NET in Action (2001a). Boys & Girls Clubs of America: Connecting teens to the future. [Online] Available: http://www.doleta.gov/programs/onet/oina.asp

O*NET in Action (2001b). Building stronger communities by building better careers.Community Preservation and Development Corporation (CPDC), Washington, DC. [Online] Available: http://www.doleta.gov/programs/onet/oina.asp

O*NET Team, U.S. Department of Labor (2001-03). Internal documentation on O*NET development. Washington, DC. The author wishes to thank the O*NET Team and Roberta Kaplan for their assistance in assembling this information.

O*NET Consortium (2002). Addendum Appendix D - The Development of the Occupational I n f o r m a t i o n (O * N E T (t m)) A n a l y s t Database. Raleigh, NC: Author. p.25. [Online] Available:http:/www.onetcenter.org/dl_files/appendix_d.pdf

Rounds, J.B., Henly, G.A., Dawis, R.V., Lofquist, L.H., & Weiss, D.J. (1981). *Manual for the Minnesota Importance Questionnaire: A measure of needs and values.* Minneapolis: University of Minnesota, Department of Psychology.

Texas Workforce Commission/Career Development Resources (2003). E-mail note and project fact sheet from R. Froeschle, Director, February 19, 2003.

U.S. Department of Labor, Employment and Training Administration (2000a). *O*NET Interest Profiler user's guide, Version 3.* pp 4 & 17. [Online] Available: http://www.onetcenter.org/dl_files/IP_zips/IP-desk/IP-UG-deskp.pdf

U.S. Department of Labor, Employment and Training Administration (2000b). *O*NET Work Importance Locator user's guide, Version 3.*pp 4 & 19. [Online] Available: http://www.onetcenter.org/dl_files/WIL_zips/WIL-desk/WIL-UG-deskp.pdf

Van Horn, D. (2002, February). *Standing on shaky ground* . Work Trends survey published by the Heldrich Center for Workforce Development at Rutgers, New Brunswick, NJ, and the Center for Survey Research and Analysis, University of Connecticut, Storrs, CT.

Wakefield, S. M. (2003). *"Unfocused kids" tend to choose the path of least resistance.* Abstract of unpublished draft manuscript.

Conclusion-Summing Up

Suzy Mygatt Wakefield and Howard Sage

How Do We Put All of this Together? What Needs to be Done?

In a book with eight sections and 32 chapters, it is difficult, if not daunting, to decide which are the essential issues. In our effort to put all of this together and to consider what needs to be done, several issues do appear to stand out.

1. The lack of integrated career guidance services

Due to large counselor caseloads, it appears that often school counselors are unable to help develop and implement comprehensive career guidance programs. One suggestion to remedy this problem is to help educators understand the difference between the terms *school counseling* and *school guidance*. School counseling services are provided one-on-one or in small groups by a credentialed school counselor trained to help students with academic, personal/social and career development issues and barriers to school achievement. On the other hand, all appropriate educators (and even community members) may participate in school guidance programs and activities to provide needed information about many items and issues, such as: college applications, financial aid, postsecondary education opportunities, in-school career seminars, guest speakers, the dangers of substance abuse, AIDS education, and so forth.

Recommendation: When career guidance is seen as a broad responsibility, then it is appropriate for teachers, school counselors, career specialists, and community members to participate, so that no single professional position bears the brunt of this responsibility.

2. Important changes in the workplace

To be successful in today's workplace, students must become technically competent, flexible in the workplace, willing to take on broad responsibilities, and resilient. Students need to see the connection between

513

what they are learning in school with what they will need to know both in the workplace and in their postsecondary education and training programs. Students with an overall career plan tend to see this connection; when school is relevant to goals, students tend to be more motivated.

Recommendation: Students need to develop both technical skills (to function successfully in today's workplace) as well as employability skills, such as getting along with others, being a team member, communicating clearly, understanding and following instructions, and solving problems.

3. Climbing high school dropout rate-the need to teach career planning tools early

Although no official national high school dropout rate is available, several researchers now speculate that it may be one student in three (if not one in four) who does not graduate with his or her class. This means that we must help students while they are still in school to learn important career planning skills and tools. These can be incorporated in three fundamental projects: an education and career plan, a career portfolio, and a culminating project, all of which help students express goals, develop timelines, and figure out the steps they need to achieve their goals. These projects may incorporate skills for the workplace (such as developing one's re_sume_ and cover letter, learning effective interviewing techniques, and learning Internet and other job search skills).

Recommendation: We need to begin teaching these skills and tools, through career projects, early. The education and career plan may be taught in the 8th grade (in middle school or junior high school), the career portfolio may be begun in the 9th grade, and the culminating project may be implemented in grades 11 or 12. Students will be able to take these skills and tools with them into the workplace.

How do we put all of this together? What needs to be done? Analysis of the Book's Eight Sections

We have also decided to use a second approach in analyzing the information presented in this book, which is to capture the essence of each section, suggesting recommendations for each.

Part I-Societal Trends and Workplace Issues

"Unfocused kids" tend to choose the path of least resistance, unless responsible adults can intervene and help young, unfocused teens make more responsible decisions. Otherwise, these students tend to make poor choices and not go on for further education or technical training, to their detriment, as they may lock themselves into a low-wage earning cycle indefinitely.

Recommendation: We recommend that educators and others develop programs to show youth the great variety of educational opportunities and explain the realities of today's workplace, which values workers who are flexible, resilient, technically competent, interested in lifelong learning, and who understand the importance of employability skills.

Part II-Comprehensive School Counseling Programs

The great value of comprehensive guidance and counseling programs is that all students are served. As the Introduction in the *ASCA National Model: A Framework for School Counseling Programs* (ASCA, 2003) states:

> The model provides the mechanism with which school counselors and school counseling teams will design, coordinate, implement, manage, and evaluate their programs for students' success. It provides a framework for the program components, the school counselor's role in implementation and the underlying philosophies of leadership, advocacy and systemic change. School counselors switch their emphasis from service-centered for some of the students to program-centered for every student. (p. 9)

Recommendation: We recommend that educators from around the country choose to incorporate the ASCA National Standards and National Model into their local school counseling programs, as students will benefit by receiving the targeted services and programs that are implemented, based on identified student needs. Hopefully, career guidance programs (which support student growth in all three domains of academic, career, and personal/social development-as all domains are involved in career development and planning) will be prioritized, if that is consistent with local needs assessment results.

Part III-Project-Based Career Guidance Models

Project-based efforts to provide effective career guidance to all students have real relevancy and value to high school students of the 21st century. They serve to stimulate all students to develop the necessary career development competencies in self-knowledge, education and career exploration and career planning. *Portfolios* and *culminating projects* allow creative demonstration of students' plans and achievements. They are produced in relevant, engaging and creative ways that help to motivate students to discover knowledge and learn skills that will help them reach meaningful education and career goals. Authentic learning helps students better understand worker and citizen roles, responsibilities and skills. Students also learn lifelong career management skills (in the process of doing these projects) that can be replicated at later stages of their lives. Developing and having a vision of one's future is a critical skill.

Recommendation: We recommend that these project-based activities be supported at the local and state levels. The sanctioning of these creative, authentic and personalized activities by state policies communicates the importance of project-based learning to parents, employers, educators, students, and community members. State support lends legitimacy and credibility that is needed for implementation and maintenance of career guidance programs at the local level.

Part IV-Innovative Approaches to Workplace Training

Many career preparation programs (models and best practices) from around the country are explained in this section, including school-to-work programs, tech prep, specialized high schools, and so forth. Further, specific suggestions regarding business/education partnerships (how to set them up, how to work with business people, and who would benefit from these partnerships) are included. It is also suggested that students understand that they need both academic and technical preparation while still in high school, as their career paths may go differently than they anticipate.

Recommendation: We encourage school staffs to set up business/ education partnerships, learn more about models and best practices regarding career preparation programs, and advise (implore!) students to become academically and technically proficient while still in high school.

Part V-Involving Parents in their Teen's Career Planning

While students are the major focus in career development, parents, nevertheless, play a highly influential role in their student's career planning process.

Recommendations: Educators need to encourage parent involvement in many aspects of their teen's career planning. Parents need to clearly understand the importance of their role, learn important knowledge about what is available in the school and community to assist their student, and demonstrate helpful attitudes and communication skills. Furthermore, parents should be knowledgeable about multiple pathways available to obtain meaningful employment, as a four-year college is not the best option for every student. There are many educational options and pathways that lead to good jobs, including two-year colleges, private technical training institutes, apprenticeships and military service.

Part VI-Innovative Career Development Activities/Games

It was felt that readers would find specific activities and games, or at least resources where they could get more information, very useful. These games include The *Real Game Series*™ as well as the *Dependable Strengths Articulation Model*, and some classroom models, called *Designing the Dog*, and the *7-minute Job Interview* (with 50 Questions asked by Employers during the Interview), providing mock job interview practice in the classroom.

Recommendation: Although the purpose of this book is not to market any one approach, these career guidance activities have been presented so that the reader knows that they exist. The reader is encouraged to look into any appropriate career guidance games and activities, as these approaches can be fun, worthwhile, and instructive, and can make a difference in what teens learn about the workplace and adulthood responsibilities.

Part VII-Innovative Career Development Practices for Special Populations

To effectively reach and serve some students, school staffs need special knowledge and strategies to be effective in promoting career development. The creative use of free or low-cost resources, preventative personalized interventions, collaborative and coordinated efforts involving families, and specialized knowledge in crafting interventions are some critically important strategies to enhance our work with these populations (Bowman, 1990). These special populations are in greater need of advocacy with school staff members and other adults who support career development, as additional support is critical to their success (Hotchkiss & Borow, 1990).

Recommendations:

- *Rural students need strategies that promote business, education and community partnerships to enhance the available experiences locally.*
- *Special Education students need careful planning in education and work placement with specific goals and objectives.*
- *Ethnic minority students have special needs and concerns that require consideration and awareness when designing and implementing career guidance programs.*

Part VIII-Internet Delivery Systems in Career Guidance

Students who are not aware of and do not use electronic resources for their career development will be missing many opportunities to communicate and present themselves to others. The WOIS Electronic Portfolio is an example of a tool that supports and enhances career development competencies in students. Guests may log on at www.wois.org and get a password to explore this system in Washington State.

Recommendation: We recommend that students be made aware of Internet delivery systems in career guidance, such as their own state career information delivery system (CIDS) as well as the national O*NET. The O*NET is a lifelong resource that our students should understand and be able to use to gather current occupational information and job accommodations at no cost. Students can learn which abilities, knowledge, work activities, and interests are inter-related, with over 1000 occupations. Because this information is updated frequently and has links to more detailed information, it is a valuable tool for students and adults. Additional low-cost tools, like interest and work value profilers, can be used at any age to assess or re-assess critical self-knowledge. Several states have integrated the O*NET into their state career information systems to assist students in career and educational planning. Users may log on at http:// online.onetcenter.org

Summing Up:

The editors of this project hope that it will serve as an important hands-on resource book for educators, as they work with young people to help them with their plans after high school. We want students to feel prepared as they enter the new millennium. The 21st century workplace awaits them and we wish them well.

Suzy Mygatt Wakefield
Howard Sage

References

American School Counselor Association. (2003). *The ASCA national model: A framework for school counseling programs.* Alexandria, VA: Author.

Bowman, S. (1993). Career intervention strategies for ethnic minorities. *Career Development Quarterly, 42,*14-25.

Hotchkiss, L., & Borow, H. (1990). Sociological perspectives on work and career development. In D. Brown, L. Brooks, & Asso. (Eds.),*Career choice and development* (pp. 262-307). San Francisco, CA: Jossey-Bass.